CONTEMPORARY CHICANA POETRY

CONTEMPORARY CHICANA POETRY

A Critical Approach to an Emerging Literature

MARTA ESTER SÁNCHEZ

UNIVERSITY OF CALIFORNIA PRESS
Berkeley   Los Angeles   London

University of California Press
Berkeley and Los Angeles, California

University of California Press, Ltd.
London, England

Library of Congress Cataloging in Publication Data

Sánchez, Marta Ester.
    Contemporary Chicana poetry.
    Includes index.
    1. American poetry—Mexican American authors—History and
criticism.   2. American poetry—Women authors—History and
criticism.   3. American poetry—20th century—History and criticism.
4. Mexican American women in literature.   I. Title.
PS153.M4S26   1985   811'.54'0986872073   84–8816
ISBN 0–520–05262–5

Printed in the United States of America

1 2 3 4 5 6 7 8 9

Para Paul, mi mamá, y Marisa Verónica

CONTENTS

PREFACE

This book has grown out of my desire, as a Chicana and a scholar, to contribute to an emerging body of literature that traditionally has had no voice in dominant academic discourse. In some sense, it also expresses my interest in working toward an understanding of the ambiguities suggested in the identities of "Chicano scholar" and "Chicana feminist." It is important to note that fifteen years ago the roles of Chicano scholar and Chicana feminist did not exist as self-conscious identities. Today, though these terms are recognized by some and embraced by others, Chicanos and Chicanas remain underrepresented in the various disciplines of the academic community. Chicano women are underrepresented in professional sectors where Anglo women have made important advances. Inequalities based on ethnicity and gender help explain why the identities of Chicano scholar and Chicana feminist continue to seem ambiguous and contradictory. My book is an attempt to understand the divided allegiances implied by these two terms. Just as the Chicana poets studied in this book articulate ideas and sentiments that are responses to the conflicting relationships between dominant and ethnic communities, so I, too, form part of a group of Chicano scholars and professionals who are in the process of examining their relationship to these two traditions at the level of academic critical discourse.

The dilemmas resulting from the intersection of the identities of "Chicana" and "feminist" and of "Chicana" and "poet" are the subject of my book. The four Chicanas I present in this book confront, through their poetic language, the dilemmas of their dual relationship to American and Mexican societies and of their dual identity as Chicanas and as women writing in a contemporary setting. I have chosen to concentrate on Alma Villanueva, Lorna Dee Cervantes, Lucha Corpi, and Bernice Zamora because their work dramatically demonstrates the range of sociocultural positionings that make up the label "Chicano." These Chicano women writers come from a variety of literary and cultural backgrounds, and their reputations among Chicano and other scholars alike are steadily growing. I view their poetic texts as strategies for articulating a sense of self arising from their conflicting social situation as women and as minority writers.

I do not claim in this book to present a full-fledged theory of Chicano literature or poetry. I believe that no such enterprise is possible at present. Instead, I have attempted to lay the preliminary groundwork that will facilitate the reading and interpretation of Chicana poetry.

Chicano authors, men as well as women, have so far received little attention in the Anglo-American literary world. Their poetic expression, their literary affiliations, and the importance of their writings have remained, for the most part, unknown or misunderstood. In this book I suggest that broadening the traditional definition and scope of American literature to include the writings of ethnic groups in the United States will help American communities to understand the richness and diversity of modern American culture. I also suggest that it is possible, and indeed necessary, to study ethnic literatures as intertextual dialogues with mainstream sources without having to desecrate the cultural and political aspirations of minority literatures. My book, then, is an effort to encourage scholars of mainstream and ethnic American literatures to enter into dialogue and to rethink the conventional assumptions about culture and literature which have so far served to keep them apart.

All the essays in this volume are published here for the first time. Because Alma Villanueva's poetry is more difficult than that of the other three poets, I have included some of her poems in the Appendixes. Chapter 5 is a revised and enlarged version of a preliminary study of Bernice Zamora's poetry which appeared in *MELUS* in 1980. The remaining chapters were developed from presentations I have given at various symposia, including the

Modern Language Association and the National Association of Chicano Studies.

I wish to acknowledge the support given me by the Academic Senate of the University of California, San Diego, and by the Affirmative Action Office for one quarter's leave. The National Chicano Council for Higher Education generously provided a grant that freed me to conduct preliminary interviews with the poets and to collect their poetry, and the Rockefeller Foundation's Grant for Minority-Group Scholars supported me during the writing of the book.

I am grateful to Alma Villanueva, Lorna Dee Cervantes, Lucha Corpi, Bernice Zamora, and Catherine Rodríguez-Nieto, the translator of Corpi's poems, for permissions to reprint their material. I would also like to express my gratitude to Sandy Dijkstra for her help in the publication of this book. I also wish to thank my colleagues in the Department of Literature at the University of California, San Diego, for their thoughtful suggestions and advice on the manuscript. Among these are Jaime Concha, Margit Frenk, Michael Davidson, Stephanie Jed, and especially Susan Kirkpatrick, whose searching criticisms of my chapters at various stages of writing were most helpful. I also wish to express my gratitude to Don Matson and to Cecilia Ubilla-Arenas for their helpful discussions. I am also grateful to my lifetime friend, Mary Prose, for her many hours of discussion and her unfailing support.

One of my greatest debts is to Saul Steier who stimulated much of the initial thinking for this study. He was a demanding and astute critic from the very first drafts to the time the manuscript was submitted to the University of California Press. I have benefited from both his vast knowledge of critical theory and his sensitivity to ethnic culture.

My other outstanding debt is to my husband, Paul Espinosa, who did more than understand and encourage me throughout my research and writing. He read every word of the manuscript in its many versions, urged me to rethink crucial concepts, cautioned me against making vague and obscure statements, and offered good humor that made a light and healthy exercise out of what seemed at times an impossible enterprise. He has been an unfaltering source of strength.

I
SETTING THE CONTEXT

Gender, Ethnicity, and Silence in Contemporary Chicana Poetry

The decade of the 1970s was a critical period for ethnic minorities and women in the United States. The intellectual and political atmosphere of this period made these groups more introspective, leading them to examine critically their own history and culture. The result was an outpouring of writing, both creative and analytical, which offered a new way of seeing what had always been there. For the first time in the history of people of Mexican descent in the United States, a significant body of written literature emerged. To be sure, Spanish-speaking people in the United States had written and published before the mid-1960s.[1] In the contemporary period, however, a literary expression has emerged from working-class Mexican-Chicano communities. Since the 1960s such writings have been designated as Chicano literature, including works by a modern generation of Chicano authors in various classifications: poetry, novel, dramatic play, essay, and short story.[2] Although continuous with the literary expression, usually transmitted orally, which previously existed in Mexican-Chicano communities, these contemporary writings have had a different perspective: the modern generation of Chicano[3] authors has exhibited a political, social, and cultural self-consciousness.

Despite the flourishing of a literature representative of the most rapidly growing ethnic group in the United States—a growth explained both by demographic increase as well as by constant arrivals of new immigrants—this literature continues to receive little attention. Critical essays have appeared in scattered fashion

1

in university journals. A few studies devoted to the critical evaluation of Chicano literature have introduced seminal authors to university communities. Most important among them is *Modern Chicano Writers*,[4] a collection of essays by Chicano and Chicana critics on the various genres, edited by Joseph Sommers; Juan Bruce-Novoa, *Chicano Poetry: A Response to Chaos*, is the only book to date on male Chicano poets.[5] *A Decade of Chicano Literature*,[6] edited by Francisco Lomelí, devotes one chapter to each genre of poetry, novel, short story, theater, and essay. Jorge Huerta, in *Chicano Theater: Themes and Forms*,[7] presents the historical development of Chicano theater in analyzing different dramatic works in a literary and cultural context.

Although Chicano literature as a whole continues to receive scant critical attention, the paucity of scholarship on Chicana literature is even more dramatic. Isolated articles on Chicana writings have appeared,[8] but no book examining Chicana literature in detail and in a critical, systematic manner has yet appeared. In this book I introduce to the English- and Spanish-speaking scholarly communities of the United States a representative group of Chicanas who reexamine and reevaluate their gender and their cultural identity through poetic language. My fundamental concern is to define and clarify the relationships between gender and cultural identity in poetry written by Chicanas. To this end I describe and analyze the themes, images, patterns, and forms that characterize the poetry of four outstanding contemporary Chicanas—Alma Villanueva, Lorna Dee Cervantes, Lucha Corpi, and Bernice Zamora. Through a systematic presentation and analysis of their poetic texts, I propose a literary paradigm for reading and evaluating Chicana poetry. Thus this volume, besides contributing to an emerging Chicano literary criticism, addresses the absence of an academic and literary discourse on writings by Chicanas.

THE HISTORICAL CONTEXT

Writings by Chicanas during the 1970s form part of an emerging literature by and about Chicanos which helped to characterize that decade as the period in which what we have come to know as the Chicano movement began. For several reasons, however, I suggest that this movement began in 1965. First, the Civil Rights Act was passed and signed in 1964. Second, in 1965, César Chávez launched the modern union of farm workers. The first strike of the National Farm Workers Association took place in McFarland, California, on May 3, 1965. The Teatro Campesino, a theatrical group serving as an adjunct to the farm workers' struggle, was formed by Luis Valdez in Delano, California, in 1965.[9] Although poetry and songs were read and sung at political and community events during the early years of the Chicano movement, it was not until 1971 that the first literary expression by a single author, Alurista's *Floricanto en Aztlán*, appeared. The first Chicano press established during this period was Quinto Sol, in Berkeley, California. In 1967 Quinto Sol launched *El Grito*, a critically oriented journal that provided a genuinely independent forum for Chicano writers and critics in the humanities and social sciences.[10] Two years later Quinto Sol published the first full-scale anthology of short stories and poetry by Chicanos, *El Espejo / The Mirror*, all of whose contributors were men. In 1973 Quinto Sol devoted an entire issue of *El Grito* to the creative expression of Chicanas. *Chicanas en la literatura y el arte / Chicanas in Literature and Art*, edited by Estela Portillo, includes a three-act musical comedy, short prose pieces, and poems.[11]

The social and artistic exigencies to which both male and female Chicano authors responded concerned the dynamics of a culture in the process of defining itself with respect to two larger societies: the United States and Mexico. The struggle for civil rights and educational opportunities, the opposition to the war in Vietnam, and the development of ethnic pride in Chicano communities were among the most pressing objectives of this cultural group during the late 1960s and early 1970s. A generation of Chicanos was beginning to realize that its history and culture had been conditioned by social oppression. The Chicano movement set out to confront this oppression directly and to expose its effect on Mexican-Chicano communities in the United States. The struggle was reflected in the literary writings of the period.

Chicano writers of this generation saw at least two possible strategies for articulating a response to social oppression. They could reject the history and culture of the dominant society and thus refuse to reenact "white" history in their literary expression. By so doing they would create their own history and culture. Or they could acknowledge that United States history did in fact contain the history of the Chicano's oppression. The latter choice would lead them into a dialogue with and participation in that history in order to show their audiences how it had oppressed them.

By far, most Chicano authors of the early period (1965–1975) embraced the first alternative.[12] Although their choice resulted in forms of cultural nationalism which often prevented them from analyzing their relationship to other oppressed groups in the United States, it did lead to the development of bilingual-bicultural art forms rooted in popular culture. Two examples are Alurista's early poetry, which he read and sang at numerous political and cultural gatherings in schools and communities, and the dramatic forms of *mito* ("myth") and *acto*[13] ("one-act skit") performed by the playwright Luis Valdez and his Teatro Campesino.

Chicanas who began to publish a few years after their Chicano brothers wanted to tell their literary counterparts and the larger society what Chicanos had not articulated, or perhaps could not articulate. At the time Chicanas found themselves at the juncture of two parallel, and for them seemingly contradictory, movements in the United States. The first movement, which comprised both men and women, centered on the struggle of the Chicano ethnic group for cultural determination. The second was the women's movement, which was primarily white and middle class. Sharing common needs and objectives with Chicanos, Chicanas desired to affirm their commitment to the struggle against racism and to the political goals of La Raza. Their Mexican-Chicano communities, however, imposed upon them as women certain cultural constraints. Their participation in student and community-based activities of the Chicano movement brought home to Chicana activists and writers the fact that they were being denied positions of authority within their own culture. As women they held a subordinate status in both cultures. Male-dominated organizations excluded them from voting and holding office. Their realization of the sexual biases and the chauvinism of Chicano males, together with the impact of the women's movement, motivated them to express their feminine identity and to challenge the prerogatives accorded to men by Mexican-Chicano culture.

As women who participated in the larger society, Chicanas, like women of other Third World groups in the United States, shared with Anglo women the need to define their position in a society built on a male system of values. Certain social imperatives—the elimination of rape, the need for day-care centers, the lack of employment opportunities, and, to some extent, the abortion issue—put them squarely into the struggle of Anglo women. As Chicanas, however, they faced alienation in the larger society. Through participation in white women's groups, Chicanas learned that certain items on their agenda (such as the struggle against racism and the crusade for bilingual and bicultural education) were not among the priorities of white women. Chicanas also found racism, tokenism, and ignorance in white women's groups. Chicana intellectuals became conscious that social and cultural disparities existed not only between them and white women but also between Chicano men and white men, and some of them refused to embrace white feminism precisely because of such inequalities. The commitment to struggle against racism united some Chicanas with Chicanos in opposition to white society. Other Chicanas, desiring to express their feminine identity yet unable to support Chicano males unilaterally because of social inequalities based on gender, formed their own autonomous women's groups even at the risk of being judged, by Chicanos and other Chicanas who disagreed with them, as divisive and disloyal to La Causa.[14] The affirmation of a feminine identity thus seemed incompatible in many ways with the struggle for racial and social justice.

The Chicanas of this particular generation, then, faced a double set of social restrictions.[15] Primarily related to ethnicity and gender, these restrictions operated inside and outside their Chicano communities. Like Chicanos, Chicanas experienced racial discrimination in the larger society; like white women, they also experienced sexual discrimination. Chicanas thus had reason to identify with both communities. They drew strength from both cultural environments, profiting from their participation in a racial struggle that united them with Chicanos as well as from the visibility of the Anglo women's movement which focused attention on women's issues. Significantly, this double identification was characterized by a double ambivalence. As Chicanas, they supported Chicanos in a struggle for racial equality, but Chicanos were also their sexual oppressors. As women, their ethnic position as Chicanas precluded a smooth interaction with white women's groups.[16]

Besides their desire to contest racism, Chicanas had another reason for wanting to affirm their Mexican-Chicano culture. Although the women's movement inspired them to search for new definitions of feminine identity, an awareness of their own cultural heritage encouraged them to affirm the traditions bequeathed to them by their female predecessors, active in both private and public realms. Mexican women have had a history of community and political involvement.[17] Chicanas turned to their mothers, grandmothers, and great-grandmothers, who alone or with husbands, within or outside the home, had struggled daily, often in low-paying and demeaning employment, to ensure their families' survival. Though oppressed as women in traditional Mexican culture, Chicanas, ironically, had often been the mainstay of their culture. These women had persevered in the face of racist, classist, and sexist obstacles. They had educated and nurtured children. Some Chicana writers therefore chose to celebrate the history of Chicana women in their families, either by showing what their maternal ancestors had contributed to their personal formation or by documenting these ancestors' experiences as memorable in their own right.

The contradictory position of modern Chicanas—apart from, yet necessarily within, each of their social milieus—informed their prose writings and critical essays as well as their poetry.[18] As women and as Chicanas at the confluence of social and aesthetic currents proceeding from the two distinct environments, the poets treated in this book may be expected to hold conflicting allegiances to the two main historical and literary traditions that shape and influence their work—an English-speaking, Anglo-American tradition and a Spanish-speaking, Mexican-Chicano tradition. Writing within and against these two traditions, the Chicana poets of this generation created a cultural discourse responding primarily to issues of ethnicity and gender.

THE LITERARY PARADIGM

In ensuing chapters I propose a literary paradigm for reading the poetry of a generation of Chicana writers. I view Chicana poetry as a poetry of conflict and struggle. Since the term "Chicana" designates at once both a gender and an ethnic identification, two

6

central determinants of my paradigm are gender and ethnicity. One option available to these writers was to see themselves as members of a community of women, or a community based on gender. A second option was to see themselves as members of a racial minority, a community based on ethnicity. "Woman" and "Chicana" thus represent the two main social identities that shape and determine these poets' responses to their dilemma. The third important identity, the one that makes this paradigm a literary one, is that of "poet," for these writers may also view themselves as members of a poetic community. The hypothesis I set out to test, describe, and modify in the following chapters is that tension and play exist among the three identities that form the basic coordinates of the paradigm. I visualize this paradigm as a triad. The four Chicana poets I present are always Chicanas, women, and poets. Because of their varied social reality, however, each writer's relationship to these identities is unique. Their individual responses produce different forms of struggle and conflict. The identities of "woman" and "Chicana" imply the counterpart identities of "male" and "Chicano." The identity of "poet" implies the contexts of English-American and Mexican-Chicano traditions.

I concentrate on four Chicana writers whose poetry offers diverse and representative responses to the tensions inherent in the relationships among the three identities. Alma Villanueva, Lorna Dee Cervantes, Lucha Corpi, and Bernice Zamora, who rank among the outstanding Chicana poets writing in the contemporary period,[19] have each produced a substantial body of work. Villanueva has published three collections: *Bloodroot, Poems,* and *Mother, May I?* The other poets have produced one collection each: Cervantes is the author of *Emplumada / In Plumage*; Corpi has written *Palabras de Mediodía / Noon Words*; Zamora's publication is *Restless Serpents.* Together their poetry is of sufficient quantity to enable me to analyze the predominant themes, the recurring patterns of imagery, and the rhetorical strategies they employ to articulate their social and aesthetic identities. Their poetry reflects the major aesthetic, social, and cultural positions that a Chicana poet can adopt with respect to the three identities and to the two traditions that inform and constrain Chicana poetry.

The tensions among the three identities in the poetry of the four Chicanas are localized between different points of the triad:

between "woman" and "Chicana"; between "woman" and "male"; between "Chicana" and "Chicano"; between "Chicana poet" and "English-American poet"; between "woman poet" and "English-American poet"; between "woman poet" and "Mexican poet"; between "Chicana poet" and "Chicano poet." In subsequent chapters I attempt to determine which of the three identities is primary for each writer. It is the relationship of the primary identity to the other two which conditions the nature of the poetic discourse.

The triad of identities is not an ironclad structure by which to read and evaluate Chicana poetry, but rather a heuristic device allowing me to determine the nature of a Chicana poetic discourse within a given historical moment. My triad is a continuum intended to trace the moving and changing relationships among the three identities. By demonstrating how variants unfold in poems by each author, I work toward the construction of a paradigm that is the sum of the different combinations of the relationships in Chicana poetics.

In presenting the responses of these Chicana poets, I have relied on a descriptive rather than a prescriptive approach. That is, rather than beginning with strict political or aesthetic criteria by which to evaluate a Chicana poet, I try to empathize with each author's unique social and poetic concerns and experiences, without implying that their responses should be other than what they are. In describing what their poetic language says and does, my intention is to help my readers to understand why these poets make the choices they do with respect to their double dilemma as well as to make them aware of the consequences and implications of their choices.

Let me present in advance a summary of the positions adopted by these writers with respect to the three identities. Alma Villanueva responds primarily as a woman to the dominant masculine society in the United States. The relationship between her identities as woman and as poet is one of harmony and integration. In contrast, a Chicana identity plays but a minor role in her poetic sensibility, and the relationship between her Chicana identity and her other two identities is one of juxtaposition rather than fusion. Lorna Dee Cervantes, however, offers a different combination. Whereas Villanueva juxtaposes her identities as woman and as Chicana, Cervantes' identity as woman is inextricably bound to her Chicana self. The central tension in her poetic voice is between her identity as Chicana and her role as poet. For Lucha Corpi, the identity as woman is stronger than the identity as Chicana, but in contrast with Villanueva, who defines her identity as woman in relation to United States society, Corpi defines her identity primarily in relationship to traditional Mexican society. Bernice Zamora is particularly problematic, for she best exemplifies my hypothesis that Chicana poetry is a poetry of conflict and tension. Zamora's female consciousness enters into sharp conflict with her Chicana ethnic self. As the most conscious of these poets of the conflicting relationships implied by the two identities of woman and Chicana, Zamora reflects a shifting poetic consciousness: she responds either as woman or as Chicana but seldom as both. Because I argue that Chicana poetry is grounded in conflict, and because these poets as Chicanas are different from women poets of other cultural groups in the United States, I structure my presentation as a sequence moving from the poet whose work evidences the least conflict between her woman and Chicana identities (Villanueva) to the poet whose work reflects the most conflict between them (Zamora).

Because these Chicana writers mediated the tension of their social situations and literary traditions in poetic language, my method is to present close readings of several key poems by each author. Some of the poems are based on the experiences that prompted the authors to examine the contradictions of their lives as women and as Chicanas. Their poems, therefore, convey significant emotional force and impact. My analyses probe beneath the surface structure in order to reveal the different ways that issues of gender and culture are embedded in language. My readings show that these linguistically rich and complex texts are dramatic enactments of different responses to the double dilemma.

The thematic oppositions characterizing the relationships among the three central identities generate different kinds of poetic modes. I use the term "mode" to identify and describe the different strategies of address used by these Chicana poets to communicate with their audiences. These strategies fall into two main categories: narrative, discursive modes and lyrical, imagistic modes. These modes are not mutually exclusive. In some poems they interrelate and interact with each other. In "Beneath the Shadow of the Freeway," by Cervantes, and in "Gata Poem" /"Cat Poem," by Zamora, for example, the two modes are mingled.

In *Mother, May I?* Villanueva's most interesting and most dynamic work, the poet relates the private and intimate details of her life. By doing so she suggests that her own private world is as meaningful and as important as any public one.[20] Villanueva's personal confession, inspired by Sylvia Plath and Anne Sexton, reveals her use of variants of the two main modes mentioned earlier: a documentary, narrative mode and a mythic, cosmic mode. She relies on the first mode to express her social, concrete reality and on the second mode to express the universal vision she longs to obtain. These two modes of address are directed to different audiences.

The tensions in Cervantes' dual vision of herself as Chicana and as poet generate her two basic poetic strategies: the narrative, discursive, "hard" mode to communicate the real, divisive world she knows as a Chicana; the lyrical, imagistic, "soft" mode to evoke contemplative and meditative moods. The poems written in the latter mode speak to an audience that is not aware of the social context of her ethnic group. They suggest that Cervantes, the Chicana, is now Cervantes, the poet, on vacation as it were, from her concerns as a Chicana with a strong commitment to La Raza. Thus poems in this second mode are spoken by disembodied lyric speakers, whereas poems in the first mode are spoken by someone who is clearly identifiable as a Chicana, in both an ethnic and a gender sense.

The predominant mode of Corpi's poetry is lyrical and imagistic. Of these four poets, Corpi is the most indirect in style, suggesting rather than stating, evoking rather than specifying. Her arguments unfold by way of images rather than by logical connections. The understanding of her arguments depends on her readers' ability to relate the meaning of one image with that of another more than on their ability to capture the rhetorical force of her statements and counterstatements, as is true of Cervantes' discursive poems.

From an analysis of Zamora's "Gata Poem," the central text in her creative universe, I derive her two main poetic modes or strategies: narrative and dialogue. Probably because Zamora is the most conflictual among these poets, her modes reveal a multiplicity of gradations, ranging from the meditative, erotic, mythic, lyrical, and impassioned to the discursive, ironic, comic, satiric, and analytical. Some of these gradations may be the dominant modes of address in the work of the other poets, but in Zamora's poetic discourse, they are all present, in varying degrees of intensity and duration.

Zamora's poems in the dialogue mode presuppose specific male interlocutors to whom Zamora's fictional female speakers respond. At times, these poems imply Chicano males; at other times, they imply males of no specific ethnic group. They are spoken by a female speaker who attempts to persuade males to alter their beliefs and their behavior. In contrast, Zamora's poems in the narrative mode are spoken by someone who wants to express an identity with two cultural and literary traditions. Nonetheless, her poetic voice, whether in dialogue or narrative, slips in and out of her two cultural and literary contexts.

These four poets, then, offer us an opportunity to experience the different modes and audiences of Chicana poetry. In the chapters that follow I describe these modes and their variants to show how they interrelate to create a rich and varied output.

ORAL VERSUS WRITTEN TRADITIONS

These poets operate in the discursive areas of both Mexican and Anglo-American literature. They also respond, albeit in different ways, to a culture that is neither exclusively Anglo nor exclusively Mexican but is composed of elements from both. The United States and Mexico are characterized by established traditions of belles lettres. In contrast, Chicano communities do not have a long history of expressing themselves through middle-class forms of writing, such as the novel, the play, the short story, or poetry of the kind written by T. S. Eliot or Octavio Paz. It is important to recall that forty years ago most Chicanos and Chicanas could not read or write, because historically they have lacked access to education at secondary and postsecondary levels in the United States. Mexican-Chicano communities were, by and large, rurally based until the twentieth century. In fact, it was not until World War II that Chicanos and Chicanas were incorporated into the urban work force of American society.

Having limited access to the written word and to its forms of distribution, Chicano communities primarily expressed themselves through forms of oral and popular culture. For a number of generations, Mexican-Chicano communities conserved, stored, and orally communicated their history in Spanish, and in some instances they continue to do so even today. In the past, certainly, important events were passed on from generation to generation in oral forms such as narratives, anecdotes, *corridos* ("ballads"), tales, legends, and songs. In contrast with other cultural communities in the United States, such as Jewish-American groups who were able to read great books, Chicano communities developed a philosophy of life based primarily on direct and tangible experiences. When segments of Chicano society did transmit their cultural expression in print, they did so mainly in local newspapers and personal letters. Poets like the four I am considering, either male or female, therefore had to search oral and popular traditions when they began to write in the contemporary period. That was the only way they could learn about the experiences of their great-grandparents and grandparents, and sometimes even of their fathers and mothers.

Even so, one feature distinguishing this generation of Chicanos and Chicanas from earlier generations is their level of formal education. Although my chosen poets, with the exception of Corpi, had working-class origins, they all obtained some higher education in the United States. Villanueva has a Master of Fine Arts in writing from the Goddard Program, Vermont College. Cervantes has her college degree from San Jose State University and is currently at the University of California, Santa Cruz pursuing a doctorate in the History of Consciousness program. Corpi obtained a bachelor of arts degree from the University of California, Berkeley, and a master's in comparative literature from San Francisco State University. Zamora is finishing her doctorate at Stanford University in English and American literature. Chicano males writing in this period have also benefited from exposure to higher levels of education. Although these writers are the sons and daughters of the Chicano working class that mushroomed during the forties and fifties, they represent an emerging professional sector within Mexican-Chicano communities that even today are marked by comparatively low levels of educational achievement.

Their educational experiences exposed these Chicana poets

to the written forms of the two dominant literary traditions, Mexican and Anglo-American. Each poet reveals influences from one or the other of these traditions, and sometimes from the works of specific writers (male and/or female). For example, as I explain in chapter 2, Villanueva's poems are inspired by Walt Whitman (via Pablo Neruda), Sylvia Plath, and Anne Sexton. Although no specific writers seem to have influenced Cervantes' work, her poetic persona both accepts and rejects an Anglo literary tradition that assumes that a poet is expressing an inner world free of social tension, so that the self enjoys a harmonious relationship with the natural landscape. Zamora's poems, in contrast, sometimes presuppose an erudite relationship with texts by specific (usually male) authors, such as Shakespeare, Herman Hesse, Edward Dahlberg, and Robinson Jeffers, her most important poetic precursor. Villanueva, Cervantes, and Zamora were born and educated in the United States; Corpi emigrated from Mexico at age nineteen. Having been born and socialized in Mexico, Corpi has a different relationship to United States society and culture from that of the other Chicana poets. Corpi's closer ties to Mexican society make the influence of Mexican literary traditions stronger in her work than in that of the other poets. Corpi's poems allude to the codes and conventions of a lyrical and romantic tradition; they reveal traces of influence from Pablo Neruda, Gabriel García-Márquez, and Federico García-Lorca. Because she also writes against a background of life in the United States, however, she treats Mexican culture and tradition from a perspective of acquired experience in her adoptive country.

In addition to the barrio culture of song and music and the white Anglo tradition, these poets also had recourse to writers of the Hispanic world who were becoming known and admired in the larger culture. Chicanos and Chicanas read and came to know such authors as García-Lorca, Neruda, García-Márquez, and Octavio Paz.[21] Some Chicanos read these exemplary writers in the original language, as Tino Villanueva read García-Lorca; others read them in translation, as Alma Villanueva read Pablo Neruda. Some of the Latin-American poets had been translated by contemporary Anglo poets. For example, Robert Bly in *Leaping Poetry*[22] presents translations of poems by César Vallejo, Neruda, and García-Lorca, and W. S. Merwin translated Neruda's *Veinte poemas de amor y una canción desesperada / Twenty Love Poems and a Song of Despair*.[23] The desire of Chicano poets to express their Latino heritage was thus given cultural support by the accessibility of writers who came from Spanish and Latin-American cultures.

Because of the oral and popular traditions of Mexican-Chicano culture, the incidents narrated and the strategies employed by these poets derive from oral as well as written systems of thought, experience, and expression. In their own ways and in varying degrees of intensity, these poets capture the oral experience of their specific cultural environments. For example, Alma Villanueva expresses states of consciousness coming from the oral and Spanish-speaking world of a Mexican grandmother who raised her in the absence of a mother. Having lost her original Spanish language, Villanueva uses English to relate events that occurred in the Spanish-speaking bygone world of her grandmother.

Cervantes, on the other hand, sees herself as a mediator between the Chicano community and the larger English-speaking audience. In "Beneath the Shadow of the Freeway," her richest and most complex poem, she alludes to herself as "Scribe," as a translator and interpreter of letters, to indicate her position in a family composed of three women. The other two women are also described in terms of medieval images: her grandmother is a "Queen"; her mother is a "Knight." The image of scribe is appropriate for Cervantes, a poet who sees her Chicano culture as being closer to the oral than to the written word: its "gesture is an utterance more pure than word," she writes in "Visions of Mexico." In contrast, she unambiguously characterizes the larger society as a print culture. Cervantes, in her role as scribe, is translating the experiences of an oral culture to a society that relates primarily to the printed word.

Corpi's poetry presupposes knowledge of the Mexican popular legends and expressions, including some of pre-Columbian origin, which have survived to the present day in the folk traditions of Mexico and the Southwest. Foremost among these is the tale of la llorona ("the weeping woman"). Originally an Aztec goddess, la llorona sacrificed babies and then disappeared shrieking into the night near lakes or rivers.[24] The legend has undergone various transformations in Mexico and in areas of the United States with Mexican and Chicano populations.

Zamora's poems presuppose a knowledge of the oral lexicon of a Spanish-speaking Chicano culture. Words and their connotations from an oral, popular Spanish language intersect, some-times within a single poem, with the meanings of words derived from the literary lexicon of the English-speaking culture, which Zamora sometimes translates into Spanish. For this purpose she employs the rhetorical strategies of the English sonnet, as in "Sonnet, Freely Adapted"; in "Notes from a Chicana 'COED'" and in "When We Are Able" she uses such devices as refrains which connect these poems to an oral rather than to a written literature.

Chicano literature, then, emerges from the background of two cultures (Mexican and Anglo-American) with established traditions of middle-class literary forms. It has survived within a United States society that now enjoys not only a tradition of a long-established print culture but also a tradition that is highly postliterary and technologically advanced. Walter Ong has termed this phenomenon of communication "secondary orality," mean-ing an oral form of communication established by radio and tele-vision and "by no means independent of writing and print but totally dependent on them."[25] Chicano culture thus has roots in an oral tradition that is slowly becoming more and more literate but still lacks the access to forms of writing which characterize the dominant society.

Given this Mexican-Chicano culture that has its roots in oral tradition yet has begun to connect itself increasingly with forms of print, I propose that the poetic texts discussed in the following chapters are complex networks of traversing and interlocking codes and conventions deriving from the two sociocultural and literary traditions that have conditioned their authors. These texts echo other texts (written and oral) in the vast expressive systems of these two traditions. They are hybrid constructions, tissues of voices that result from the relationship and interaction of written and oral utterances.[26] Within these codes and conven-tions, these poets mediate the pressures inherent in their di-lemma as Chicanas and as women living in United States society.

DISTRIBUTION AND ACCESS

Because Mexican-Chicano communities historically have lacked access to the kinds of opportunities—educational, cultural, and otherwise—which foster and promote authors of written literature, Chicanos and Chicanas have had no experience in approaching large-scale publishing houses. Compounding the lack of representation of Chicano and Chicana literature among large presses is the bilingual character of the Mexican-Chicano population. Significantly, when literary expression did emerge, a substantial portion of it was written in Spanish or in a mixture of Spanish and English. Not surprisingly, Chicano works were accepted by small publishing houses and by university and community journals, most of them begun by Chicanos and Chicanas. Among the publishing houses at the time were Quinto Sol and Justa Publications in Berkeley, Pajarito Publications in Albuquerque, Maize in San Diego, and Bilingual Review Press in Ypsilanti, Michigan. Journals sprang up at major universities where Chicanos and Chicanas were faculty members and students: *El Grito* at the University of California, Berkeley; *Metamorphosis* at the University of Washington; *Mizquitli* at Stanford University; *Revista Chicano-Riqueña* at the University of Texas, Houston; and *Aztlán* at the University of California, Los Angeles. Since 1976 Chicano faculty members at the University of California, Irvine, have sponsored creative writing contests in short story and poetry and have published the winning entries. A third vehicle for literary expression was community journals, such as *Encuentro Femenil* in Austin, *Caracol* in San Antonio, *Tecolote* in San Francisco, and *Mango* in San Jose. In fact, *Mango* was edited, printed, and distributed by Lorna Cervantes (see chap. 3).

A smaller number of poems have appeared in anthologies published by major presses, though as yet no complete anthology of Chicano or Chicana poetry has been published. Dexter Fisher's *The Third Woman: Minority Women Writers*[27] includes the poetry of women in different groupings: native American, black-American, Asian-American, and Chicana. *Chicanos*, an anthology published by a major press in Mexico and compiled by the poet Tino Villanueva, introduces Chicano and Chicana poets who write in Spanish to Mexican audiences.[28] A more recent anthology, *Fiesta in Aztlán*, presents thirty-three poems, mainly by men, in categories of the family, the barrio, and the universe.[29] Two poets, Lorna Cervantes and Gary Soto, who write poetry for English-speaking audiences, have been published by the University of Pittsburgh Press.

As most of the poetry of the late 1960s and the 1970s was

presented in limited editions by small publishing houses or in community journals, poems by Chicanas are now not easily available to the larger mainstream audience. I therefore include all the poems I analyze in their entirety. Because Zamora's writing includes Spanish, I provide translations of entire poems when necessary. For other poets I translate certain words or phrases so as to eliminate any possible difficulty for non-Spanish readers.

POETRY: THE CHOSEN FORM OF EXPRESSION

Like their male counterparts, Chicanas, with few exceptions, have chosen poetry and short prose as their primary media of expression. More prolific in poetry than in short prose, Chicanas chose to write poetry in the 1970s for the same reasons that Alurista, José Montoya, Tino Villanueva, and Raul Salinas wrote poetry in the late 1960s. During the 1960s and 1970s poetry was better able to meet the needs of the Mexican-Chicano community, which urgently wanted to redefine its relationship to American society and concomitantly to explore its own cultural roots. Of prime importance were three factors: communication of the message, time, and money. In the early phase of the Chicano movement, poetry may be regarded as having functioned in the same way the *corrido* functioned in earlier decades in the Mexican Southwest. The *corrido*, an oral ballad with a strict stanzaic structure and rhyme scheme, usually composed on a guitar, imparted information about a historical event or a figure of central importance to the community's welfare. Composed on the spot with the primary intention of communicating a message and circulated by way of recitation or song, it was passed on orally. Only later was it transcribed into print by those who recognized its value. Some *corridos* were sung on Spanish-language radio stations[30] or eventually appeared in Spanish-language newspapers. The poetry of the early phase of the movement exemplified characteristics of the *corrido* form. It was communal more than personal, written for the ear more than for the eye, and concerned with the communicative more than with the expressive aspects of language.

Conventionally shorter than other generic variants, poetry provided Chicanas and Chicanos during the 1960s and 1970s with a vehicle not only for the rapid communication of a message but also for a quicker audience response to social and personal concerns. Because poems did not require the logistics and support required by novels and plays they were easier to write and took less time. A poem—especially a contemporary one—required only the author's time and dedication. It could be written, sent off to a journal, and published. Or it could be circulated in manuscript form and even mimeographed for quick presentation to audiences. In contrast, the production of a play required a director, actors, props, and a building to serve as a theater. It was a far more costly undertaking. A novel had to be researched; writing it demanded the handling of more levels of history, thereby necessitating a longer period of gestation. More objectivity was needed to depict characters and events in a novel, whereas a poem was simply the expression of the writer's personal attitudes and feelings. For these reasons the poem was a more flexible and less intimidating form for Chicanos and Chicanas.

Furthermore, the currents of modern Anglo poetics helped to broaden the base of poetry as a form of communication at a time when minority cultures were making themselves heard. The period after World War II marked the beginning of a post-Modern tradition favorable to oral readings of poetry. Before Donald Allen introduced their work in *The New American Poetry*,[31] a young generation of Anglo poets (among them Charles Olson, Robert Duncan, Denise Levertov, Robert Creeley, Lawrence Ferlinghetti, Allen Ginsberg, Gregory Corso, and Frank O'Hara) had already published their poems in small magazines, pamphlets, and broadsides. It was these younger poets who developed poetry readings as a means of creating their own public. In this way poetry readings helped to focus attention on the poem as a form of communication, to create an atmosphere congenial to the oral and popular tradition of a Chicano culture, and to give poets an opportunity to express their personalities in a public setting.

Also significant to modern poetics was the publication in 1950 of Charles Olson's essay "Projective Verse," in *Poetry New York*. Serving as a manifesto for Olson himself and for the Black Mountain poets, "Projective Verse," antirationalist and anti-academic, was a landmark piece for Anglo poets who were excluded from the mainstream of American poetry because their work did not appeal to the tastes of established literary journals.[32] Olson called for a new definition of the poem. Instead of being a "closed," "tight," and "well-made" artifact, scored for the page and created for silent reading (as in the tradition of T. S. Eliot, for example), it should be "open," and "discovered," a "field of composition" scored for the ear and written for oral performance. This new definition by the early post-Modern poets, such as Olson and Ginsberg, was aimed at capturing as much as possible of the actual poet on stage in front of an audience. By focusing attention on poetry that was regarded as unorthodox and unacademic, these poets helped to transform the poem into a less elitist form of discourse.

Other groups of poets emerged, such as the beat poets, the poets of San Francisco renaissance, and the New York poets. Although characterized by divergent poetics, these post-Modernists have in common their reaction against the impersonality of T. S. Eliot, Wallace Stevens, Ezra Pound, and the New Critics. Some of the post-Modern poets, active in the development of an oral and popular poetry, were especially important for emerging Chicano and Chicana writers. For example, the readings with jazz bands and the recordings of the beat poet Lawrence Ferlinghetti helped to recreate a popular oral poetry.[33] Displeased with modern American materialism, the beat and other poets turned, in part, to the cultures of Oriental peoples for inspiration. Sometimes they looked, as Ginsberg did in *Kaddish,* to the roots of their own Western culture to discover and memorialize its oral and nontraditional elements. This fascination with ideas outside the traditional European culture proved congenial to a poet like Alurista, who derived his images and symbols from pre-Columbian mythologies.[34] In fact, this trend proved useful to all who were not well versed in Western literary traditions, for now a poet did not have to know the established mythologies of Western culture to write a poem. Poets freed from such restrictions could even begin to create their own personal mythologies. As a consequence, the historical shift in the style of writing poetry after World War II—from an aesthetic of impersonality and abstract meditation to one of personal vision and insight, from established mythologies to personal mythologies, from classical Western, Judeo-Christian models to Oriental and native American sources, and from print to oral poetry—helped to create a cultural and literary milieu in which Chicanas and Chicanos, as well as other cultural minorities, could function. The open form of poetry, as an alternative to the closed form, was far more congenial and sympathetic to the abilities and objectives of cultural minorities than the dense linguistic structures and typologies of the academic style of Eliot, Pound, and Stevens.[35]

THE IMPLIED AUDIENCE

Few scholars have taken Chicano and Chicana poetry seriously enough to study it in terms of the literary structures used to analyze mainstream poetry. Although I discuss the oral reverberations of words and phrases in these poems, I also treat the poems as aesthetically pleasing groupings of words. I am concerned not only with formal features, such as themes, recurrent patterns of imagery, and rhetorical strategies, but also with the analysis of these poems as social acts, that is, these poems are not purely individual creative acts. In the following chapters I seek to identify the implied audiences of Chicana poetry. Briefly, the phrase "implied audiences" means that these poems hold a status within a determinate context. Rather than seeing Chicana poems as self-sufficient or autonomous artifacts, I see them as the output of individuals who entertain specific values and ideas about the world. I believe that an author's values, assumptions, and attitudes presuppose, directly or indirectly, specific reading communities to whom they convey their message and that these readers or audiences are implied in the text, that is, are embedded in the language employed by the authors.[36]

One significant adjustment in this definition of the implied audience is necessary when considering Chicana and Chicano poetry. In the attempt to identify the audiences, a major factor is language choice. These poets may have the option of writing in Spanish, in English, or in a combination of the two languages, the choice usually depending upon such factors as family background, area of origin, and educational opportunities. They may have had to learn English, Spanish, or even both languages. To some Chicana and Chicano authors only one option may be available; to others, perhaps all three.

Nevertheless, these languages, whose mixing is a central stylistic feature of this poetry, are combined in at least two ways. First, Chicano authors may write bilingually, using Spanish for one poem and English for another. Tino Villanueva, Bernice Zamora, and Carmen Tafolla all fall into this group. Second, Chicano writers may also intermix the two languages within the same poem, as Alurista, Tafolla, Zamora, Xelina, and José Montoya have done in varying degrees. The cultural and literary phenomenon of using two languages interlinearly has been referred to as "interlingualism,"[37] a term coined to distinguish the mixture of language within one poem from "bilingualism," the use of English and Spanish in different poems. Both interlingualism and bilingualism require the reader to move from one language to another. The difference lies in how the movement takes place. In a bilingual experience, the reader must mentally juxtapose poems in English with poems in Spanish; in an interlingual experience, the tensions in syntax, the connotations, the ironies, and the reverberations of words and images interlock, pulling in two directions at once. Poems written interlingually engage rival sets of reader expectations and desires. They graphically enact on the surface of the page the conflicts and tensions between the two main audiences of Chicana-Chicano poetry, the English-speaking audience and the Spanish-speaking audience.

In *Palabras de Mediodía*, Lucha Corpi offers her own form of bilingual poetry. By working closely with her translator, Catherine Rodríguez-Nieto, Corpi places the original poem in Spanish on one page and its English translation on the facing page. This strategy permits her to address Spanish, English, and bilingual readers individually and collectively, though only the latter can really understand the tensions between the two cultures. In contrast, Bernice Zamora's *Restless Serpents* contains poems in which the two languages are mixed. Thus she offers readers who are capable of reading both languages the possibility of directly experiencing the conflicts between the two cultures. Poets who use this linguistic medium are enacting their own experience of living between two cultures.

Chicano authors who choose to write in the same language they speak may use that vehicle of expression with different intentions and for different purposes. For example, Alma Villanueva and Lorna Cervantes come from similar personal backgrounds. Both were raised in father-absent families, lived in urban, working-class environments, and had two generations of women—grandmother and mother—play a central role in their lives, and both chose to write in the English language. Villanueva's primary intent is to express to other women an intimate record of her existence as a woman. Bonds of gender rather than of race or class characterize her implied audience. For example, *Mother, May I?* contains relatively few markers of ethnicity and none of social class. This silence about ethnicity in a poem that makes numerous references to gender suggests that Villanueva wants to reach an audience that shares values similar to her own about a womanhood unbounded by race or class. Cervantes' primary intent, on the other hand, is to record and translate to a larger audience the experience of a communal group. The problem, as she conceives it, lies not in expressing her personal poetic "I" but in expressing the experience of a historical, collective community. Her discursive, narrative poems contain specific linguistic signs of ethnicity and gender. Nevertheless, both Villanueva and Cervantes seek to address a broad English-speaking community, Chicano as well as Anglo, though they have different reasons for doing so.

In addition to choice of language, I also look at the compositional qualities of the language, the rhetorical force of the poem's arguments, and the literary codes and conventions derived from English-American, Mexican, and Chicano cultural contexts. By the word "code" I mean the cultural associations of words based on their specific functions in a given, determinate context. For example, Villanueva primarily employs an oral, colloquial language, as if she were attempting to remove the barriers between herself and the reader or listener. In contrast, Zamora's Spanish, and at times her English, are derived from literate, formal usages. These different codes—oral and colloquial versus literate and learned, for example—imply different readers. Although Villanueva uses the mainstream language, her poems do not assume educated, intellectual readers, whereas Zamora's poetry does, even when written in the minority language.

I judge the implied audience in Corpi's poetry from a different perspective. The poems of Villanueva, Cervantes, and Zamora use specific compositional elements to indicate female speakers and therefore a female audience. Villanueva, for example, makes explicit references to the female human anatomy, celebrating woman's ability to menstruate, lactate, and give birth. Although they employ different rhetorical strategies, Cervantes and Zamora make references to conflicts that are distinctly rooted in male-female sexual relationships. Corpi's poetry, in contrast, depends less on overt textual markers. Her poetic voice is more impersonal, making no explicit references to a female audience. Instead, she expresses her main concern—the representation of a woman's consciousness—by strategically setting up her modes of address to interrogate her own female persona as well as her fictional women's states of mind and heart. Corpi probes her own emotional states and those of her characters by means of images rather than direct statements. The tragedies her characters face are often caused by the male's insensitivity to the woman's person and wishes. Corpi's female voice attempts to inject a woman's passion and emotion into a male literary tradition.

In choosing to respond as women, as Chicanas, or as both, these poets articulate what has hitherto been unsaid in their written traditions, Mexican-Chicano as well as Anglo. They express in writing what women have not said to men and what men have not permitted women to say, as well as what men simply have not said. It is important to stress that this silence characterizes a written, not an oral, form of expression. In responding to the silences in mainstream and minority traditions concerning Chicanas, as women and as members of an ethnic group, these poets help to bring various notions to consciousness. Paradoxically, the contradictions and complexities of their situation leads them to create other silences. In other words, these Chicana poets make choices that displace other possibilities,[38] which in turn become the muted discourses of a Chicana poetics.[39]

In subsequent chapters I show how each poet's relationship to the three identities of the triad creates a muted discourse. As one particular poet's relationship to questions of gender, race, and social position is not necessarily another's, these poets teach different lessons about what it means to be a Chicana and a woman writing poetry in a cultural sphere defined by the relationship between Mexico and the United States. Together, they help to clarify the broader issue with which this book is concerned: the conflicts between gender and culture in contemporary Chicana poetry.

II
THE BIRTHING OF THE POETIC "I" IN ALMA VILLANUEVA'S MOTHER, MAY I?

The Search for a
Female Identity

1

As a poet Alma Villanueva is consciously preoccupied with a search for a universal female community. The influence of the women's movement in the United States seems to have reached her without significant interference from the Chicano social movement of the 1960s and 1970s. Like the other poets discussed in this book, Villanueva is the product of a process of socialization; yet, unlike the rest, she has an overriding objective: to transform her concrete experience into a vision of a personalized myth. She achieves this objective in *Mother, May I?* her most interesting and dynamic work.[1]

In 1977, a year before *Mother, May I?* appeared, Villanueva published two poetic autobiographies, *Bloodroot*[2] and *Poems*.[3] The latter won first prize in poetry at the University of California, Irvine, in the year of its publication. Collectively these three works demonstrate that Villanueva is a poet who senses her personal development in terms of time. In fact, among the poets discussed in this volume, she is not only the most sequential in presentation but also the only one to write a poetic autobiography, an achievement that makes her unique also among Chicano poets. Well-known male poets like Gary Soto, José Montoya,

Tino Villanueva, and Raul Salinas have indeed written personal poems that capture fragments of their lives, but none has written a sustained narrative sequence in lyric form, as Alma Villanueva has done. In *Mother, May I?* she records the important phases of her life from childhood to her early thirties.

In comparison with the other three Chicana poets, Villanueva seems to have had the most urgent need to compose an autobiographical poem. Because this literary genre necessitates a retrospective look at the author's life, including an explanation of his or her arrival at a certain point in that life, an autobiography gave Villanueva an opportunity to confront compelling questions about her personal development which stood in the way of her desired poetic vision. For instance, in *Mother, May I?* a mother's abandonment of her child is of prime concern. Of secondary importance is the issue of an unknown father: Villanueva never knew, or even saw, her father. She did not learn until later in life that he was of German descent. Although it is the search for a mother, not for a father, which stimulated the poet's quest for self-definition, the issue of her ambiguous origins is a biographical detail that conditions the outcome of the poetic peregrination.

In light of the absence of both a mother and a father, it is understandable that Villanueva's protagonist in *Mother, May I?* must achieve the birthing of a personal self, or her "I." Her search for continuous participation in a mythical, female community may stem from a deeper wish to transcend the interruptions she perceives as having marred her own relations with her real mother. The fact that Villanueva was raised by her Mexican grandmother until she was eleven years old may account for her emotional identification with Mexican culture. Since her closeness to her grandmother is part of her childhood, her Chicana, or Mexican-American, identity plays a minor role in her adult poetic persona, which lies more within a community bounded by gender than within one bounded by race or ethnicity.

When compared with the poetry of Cervantes and Zamora, Villanueva's shows the least awareness of a Chicana consciousness. Her solution of the dilemma of being both a woman and a Chicana is to respond primarily as a woman to the dominant masculine society.[4] Her primary intent is to reveal to other women an intimate record of her individual existence rather than to communicate the experiences of a communal group to a wider audience, as Cervantes does. The tension in Villanueva's poetic world is manifested at the level of a personal quest to achieve self-definition as a woman. In *Mother, May I?* her journey in search of her womanhood is also a journey in search of her poetic identity.

Although no significant conflict dramatizes the relationship between Villanueva's identities as woman and as Chicana (as it does for Zamora), they are not totally integrated with each other (as they are for Cervantes). Her two identities are juxtaposed rather than fused in her poetic voice, as shown by her shifts in focus: from past to present, from an urban to a rural setting, from linear to circular time, from a social-documentary style to a metaphoric-mythic style. In *Mother, May I?* a sequential progression of events is disrupted in favor of a more subjective reality.

As fragmentary attempts to confront the realities and desires of Villanueva's life, *Bloodroot* and *Poems* are a preparation for *Mother, May I?* In the two earlier works Villanueva seeks to explain her development as a woman and as a poet by juxtaposing a personal, documentary voice and a mythic, universal one. The first voice speaks about her social reality; the second one tells where she desires to be. In *Mother, May I?* she establishes a linear sequence in the narration of her life by using the first voice to speak of her past life and the second voice to speak of her present life.

Villanueva confesses to an early familiarity with the works of Pablo Neruda, having read (in translation) and admired his *Residencia en la tierra* and *Veinte poemas de amor y una canción desesperada* (1924), but not to a familiarity with the works of Walt Whitman. We should not be surprised, however, to find Whitmanesque influences in *Bloodroot*, for during the period 1925–1936 Whitman exerted a major influence on Neruda, especially on *Residencia*.[5] Thus in *Bloodroot*, when Villanueva speaks of her body—and by extension of all women's bodies—we hear a Whitmanesque voice in tone and imagery and especially in the theme of cosmic unity which dominates the work.[6] Whitman speaks of the human body in a celebratory tone, conferring on it cosmic proportions; the same tone is heard in *Bloodroot*. Neruda, in contrast, describes his own body in humorous terms, stressing his consciousness of its materiality.[7] When Neruda describes the female body in *Veinte* and in the erotic poems of *Residencia*, however, he too adopts a cosmic interpretation, depicting a woman's body as a microcosm of the world and a veritable force in the universe.[8] Villanueva's celebration of her body thus coincides both with Neruda's vision of the female body and with Whitman's general tone and attitude.

Although it was Neruda's works that directly influenced *Bloodroot*, it was really Whitman's voice that left its mark on Villanueva. Indeed, Villanueva's poetry reveals stronger connections with the Anglo-American literary tradition of Whitman than it does with the Latin-American and Chicano literary heritage of Neruda. The mythic tones of Neruda's description of the female body may seem more congenial with Villanueva's poetic sensibilities, but she is really tapping Whitman and her North American roots through her reading of Neruda.

In *Poems*, however, the influences are mainly from contemporary American women poets, especially Sylvia Plath and Anne Sexton, though Villanueva's poems in this collection are more loosely organized than those of either Plath or Sexton.[9] Throughout *Mother, May I?* Villanueva uses short lines, at times seemingly inattentive to where she breaks them, though occasionally a break signals an abrupt shift in focus or tone. Villanueva's stylistic devices, unlike Plath's clinical precision of image and her tight stanzaic and metrical patterns, especially in "Lady Lazarus" and "Daddy," are oral and presentational in tone. More than either Plath or Sexton, Villanueva desires to surmount the barriers between speaker and audience.

Villanueva's predominantly colloquial tone is characterized by a number of variants. One is a childish, or even infantile, language, a kind of little-girl baby talk that becomes a way of reliving the joys and pains of childhood. A second variant is the bawdy tone, most pronounced in some of the *Bloodroot* poems and in those of the Irvine collection. The bawdiness is testimony to the fact that Villanueva, like some of her Anglo women contemporaries, wants to invade traditional male linguistic preserves.[10]

As an autobiography calls for a self-conscious appraisal of the poet's "I," Villanueva is better able in *Mother, May I?* than in *Bloodroot* and *Poems* to scrutinize and analyze her persona. In this poetic narrative she reveals her growing consciousness of the development of her narrative and poetic voice, as well as of the constraints it imposes. For this reason, *Mother, May I?* is less derivative than the earlier poems. Villanueva's desire to write an autobiographical poem might have been inspired indirectly by

Whitman. At the formal level, her poetic autobiography combines Whitman with Plath and Sexton. If Whitman provided the genre, Plath and Sexton provided the mode. Villanueva employs a modified confessional mode to disclose the private and intimate details of her life.

The poetic enterprise of *Mother, May I?* is to create from concrete experience a personal myth of a universal womanhood. As an autobiography, the poem must incorporate both identities—woman and Chicana—into the poetic voice. On the first level of analysis, I treat the poem as a self-sufficient entity, freed from the context that conditioned it.[11] *Mother, May I?* is a fictional account of events and actions that explain the coming into being of the protagonist as poet. By closely reading the poem as a verbal artifact, or a string of words that echo one another, I argue that *Mother, May I?* successfully integrates the identities of woman and Chicana into the poet's "I."

The coming into being of the poetic identity is the precondition of the poem as text. In describing the process of how her protagonist becomes a poet, Villanueva also implicitly tells how she, the author, came to narrate the poem. On the second level of analysis, then, the poetic identity is not the object spoken about by a fictional narrator but rather an actual utterance by the author to a specific audience. I propose that the poem's epilogue is the enactment of the relationship between the author's poetic identity and her implied audience. As we shall see, Villanueva chooses to keep her two identities of woman and Chicana separate rather than to fuse them in a single all-encompassing identity.

BLOODROOT AND THE IRVINE *POEMS*

Bloodroot is a kind of poetic journal, a hasty jotting down of notes, impressions, and ideas. Many of its themes are cosmic. Full of carnal and elemental images (blood, womb, stones, plants, minerals, water), these poems express Villanueva's nostalgic desire for a return to an original, maternal womb from which, presumably, both women and men emerged. The female body is portrayed as a Jungian archetype. Villanueva's female speakers celebrate and rejoice in women's bodies and wombs, urging everyone, but especially men, to recognize their connection with their maternal bond. The opening lines of her poem "(wo)man"[12] are representative:

> (wo)man
>   Yes, Woman!
> I celebrate our bodies,
> our wombs,
> intact and perfect even as
> we're born
> out of our mother's
>   womb
> I celebrate
> because most   . . . If man is out
> men have forgotten   of touch with
> how to   the earth,
> he is afraid   how can he
> of us, he   touch woman)[13]
> denies us,
>   —but in the process
>   denies his own existence;
>   when will he re/learn
>   this ancient fact—

Villanueva's mythic "I" in this poem shifts into a "we" that desires to speak about, and to, all women. In the next stanza her "I" proudly asserts her body's functions ("the slick/red walls of our / wombs, / the milk of our breasts / the ecstasy of our clitoris"), whereas her "we" defines categorically the essence of women (in stanza 5):

> we are the trees of the earth
> our roots stretching deep and strong,
> the stone of the firmament,
> sister to the stars
> that gave birth to the soil.

The title poem "bloodroot" describes a woman's fantasy in which she experiences a mystic pregnancy, one independent of any interraction with a male. Using Whitmanesque tones and images, the female persona calls upon trees, wind, and birds to perform the male reproductive act. Ecstatic and exuberant, she receives, as in a trance, the "sperm" of trees and the nectar of hummingbirds. Bitterness and sweetness are conjoined in her.

BLOODROOT[14]

I grow heavy with the sperm
of trees,
with the nectar
of hummingbirds (listen to their
motor, purring)
with the journeying
wind, it
fills me
and tiny kisses cover
my eyes, my neck,
my leafy hair: roots

threaten to form;
my toes ache;
my eyes shut
and chrysalis begins. I
see the sun in a
bloody pattern: colors dance.
different eyes will open
and my roots are wise; they
love me, but not
too well.

I grow heavy with the sperm
of trees.

The speaker celebrates the awakening of a mythic female consciousness and foreshadows the creation of a primal world where the blood of woman will be the root of all life. The images in "bloodroot" suggest a parallel between the speaker's body and the earth: "my leafy hair"; "my eyes shut / and chrysalis begins." The sun is associated with blood, a source of life in women's bodies: "I / see the sun in a / bloody pattern." Since "chrysalis" is beginning, the woman is in a process of becoming mature but has not yet reached the point of full maturation. The poem externalizes a woman's inner wish to birth alone. In the title "bloodroot" Villanueva joins two words together to call attention to the indissociable relationship of their meanings in her poetic world. She uses this same technique in the poem "ZINZ"[15] by locating the creatrix in a non-Western "motherafrica." The neologism emphasizes the idea of union among all men and women.

> we were
> collectively, together
> born
> out of
> motherafricas
> womb

In the early poems of *Bloodroot* Villanueva seeks to rediscover the resonance of nature and to make her readers aware of their interdependence with the female universe. She also desires to birth independently of a male power. Villanueva repeats these themes again and again in modified ways throughout *Bloodroot.* Although they did so in different ways, her masculine inspirators, Neruda and Whitman, energetically chronicled an awakening consciousness in their countries. Villanueva attempts to chronicle an awakening consciousness of a mythical womanhood. As Whitman urges humanity to reestablish its connection with the natural universe, so Villanueva urges her audience to reestablish its lost connection with a female, magisterial cosmos.

Villanueva's poetic voice changes even as she writes *Bloodroot* and the Irvine *Poems.* A more personal and autobiographical voice emerges midway through *Bloodroot.* In "I sing to myself"[16] Villanueva takes up Whitman's dictum that poetry should lead a reader to compose a song of himself.[17] This poem gives evidence that Villanueva is beginning to confront the paradox of her objective; to sing her spontaneous, natural song of beauty and wonder, she must first confront her own feelings of bitterness and distrust. The opening metaphor of an "over-ripe / fruit" represents the feelings that keep her from speaking and releasing her song.

I SING TO MYSELF

> there is something
> I carry deep
> within me
> like an over-ripe
> fruit, one whose use is past and
> won't rot and merge
> and gags me
> now and then;
> it is the fruit
> of bitterness and distrust.
> oh yes, they planted the seed, but
> I tend the soil . . .

Later stanzas of "I sing to myself" identify in direct language the referent of *they* in line 11: a father who never loved her ("I could weep and rage / against the man who never / . . . desired me in a secret fathers / way");[18] a mother who spent all her energies needing and desiring men ("never finding a breast to rest / and warm myself"); and a self-centered husband ("who loved me at his leisure and / neglected my deepest needs"). The final stanza metaphorically foreshadows Villanueva's conversion into the new Eve, who will birth herself by swallowing and transforming the putrid fruit:

> I will swallow you whole and
> accept and transform you
> till you melt
> in my mouth.   (you/man only
>   bit the apple:
>   you must swallow
>   death—
>   I/woman give birth:
>   and this time to
>   myself)

The poem juxtaposes the two voices that later make up Villanueva's poetic identity in *Mother, May I?* In "I sing to myself" the mythical voice allows her to express a vision of herself transfigured as the new Eve, and the private voice, to express her unhappy personal life. These two voices never merge or fuse in "I sing to myself," a division that indicates the distance between where she is now and her goal of transcendence. As yet there is only talk of transformation. The parallel between Adam biting the apple and the new Eve birthing herself is also important. The act of incorporating objects by eating them becomes a sustained image pattern in *Mother, May I?*

The female persona of "in your body,"[19] another poem in *Bloodroot*, makes attempts at individuation. Its frame is mythic, but, unlike the women speakers of "bloodroot," "(wo)man," and "ZINZ," who assume the existence of a female primal cosmos, the speaker of this poem realizes that if she is to gain that paradise, she must struggle for it and earn it. The poem draws an analogy between a woman's sexual orgasm and the process of evolution. Coitus is not simply an act between one man and one woman but the recapitulation of the creation of the entire universe, or a clashing between earth and ocean.

IN YOUR BODY

in your body
   I found
the oceans of the earth
saltless seas of distant planets
lava flow of the first eruption
that created
the first mound of earth
from the waters
     the lonely stormy waters
before earth was born—
in you/me I felt creations hot hard urgency
to be
   and I slept in swirling waters
floated in stagnant seas
cradled and crushed by the tides
your salty semen rushing
over my shores, leaving me pregnant and
exhausted in its wake,
     full of you, the saltysea.

storms and seasons and shifting sun and tide find
   us separate:

and my own body
feels the tide
a relentless gentle/fierce tide
and I wait at my shore for
a perfect, whole seashell
to cast up on the tide
   aeons of time in the
     making and forming
       of this perfect

       shell

      shaped like a

star.

The poem moves from a description of the woman's sexual orgasm with the cosmic lover's body (stanza 1) into a statement of
separation (stanza 2) and, finally, into a description of the woman
waiting alone to toss up the "perfect . . . seashell." The seashell
represents either a child or a poem or both. The pattern of opening
and closing, which pervades *Mother, May I?* is suggested in "in
your body" by the tide's ebb and flow and the biological rhythm
of the woman's reproductive cycle.

The more personal, private poems in *Bloodroot*, which are

based on autobiographical incidents, describe relationships with key figures in the poet's childhood and youth: her mother, her aunt, and the Mexican grandmother who was so important to her. The fictional world of these poems is neither timeless nor universal, as is the world of the mythic poems. Rather, they describe a finite, temporal, and more overtly subjective world. Nevertheless, from its place in ordinary, everyday settings, the poetic consciousness expresses its longing for personal transfiguration. In "I was a skinny tomboy kid,"[20] for example, the persona reflects on her adolescent years when she saw herself as a fated victim because of her female identity. Consequently she desired to be a man, equating her masculinity, or tomboy activities (climbing roofs and fences; walking down streets with tightly clenched fists), with freedom, movement, strength, and hardness, and her femininity with helplessness, standing still, softness, and letting go: "I vowed / to never / grow up / to be a woman / and be helpless / like my mother." The adult persona recognizes in retrospect what she did not see years earlier: "but then I didn't realize / the kind of guts / it often took / for her [mother] to just keep / standing / where she was." Her unhappy childhood led her to create a "legendary/self," "believing in my own myth / transforming my reality." Throughout the poems of *Bloodroot*, the private voice searches for a continuous harmony that can help her overcome the discontinuous quality of her life. She often looks for that harmony in nature and in cultural objects: in the bison whose hooves remember the ancient joy ("he has fed for two springs"); in green bean sprouts "intimately connected to the earth" ("i dreamt"); in the dazzling beauty of a piñata ("Let us celebrate").

A small number of poems in *Bloodroot* express Villanueva's social identity as a Chicana. Of the forty-seven poems in the collection, five are dedicated to relationships with her Mexican grandmother and aunt. They all portray particular concrete circumstances, many of which are recognizably Chicano for an audience familiar with the locations. References to Market and Guerrero streets, to the Mission district, and to welfare lines and clinics define an urban, Chicano, working-class context in the San Francisco Bay area. In "you cannot leave,"[21] tensions between Mexican and Anglo worlds are revealed in the story of Villanueva's aunt, who tried to go to an Anglo church but found "their [Anglo] / faces . . . blank / and their / eyes / mute; they did not / recognize her." In "to Jesus Villanueva, / with love,"[22] a poem about her grandmother, the speaker claims that the main rule of Anglo society is "you lie. you push. you get." So she lies and pushes to make a doctor examine her ailing grandmother, to convince the welfare office to send her grandmother's check on time, and to persuade the landlady to spray her grandmother's house "for cockroaches." In the same poem Villanueva presents a humorous anecdote she heard from her mother about her grandmother's outwitting a border official. The "you" in this passage is the author's grandmother.

> you were leaving Mexico
> with your husband and two
> older children, pregnant
> with my mother.
> the U.S. customs officer
> undid everything you so
> preciously packed, you
> took a sack, blew it up
> and when he asked about
> the contents of the sack,
> well, you popped it with
> you hand and shouted
> MEXICAN AIR!

I assume that the grandmother told the story to her daughter in Spanish and that the mother then communicated it in English to her daughter, except for the phrase "Mexican Air." The daughter-author recounts it to us in English, translating even the phrase "Mexican Air," as her footnote states.[23] In the initial lines of "to Jesus Villanueva" she remembers naming the food products of her grandmother's world:

> my first vivid memory of you
> mamacita,
> we made tortillas together
> yours, perfect and round
> mine, irregular and fat
> we laughed
> and named them: oso, pajarito, gatito.

Although the first anecdote is transmitted by the mother, both anecdotes involving the grandmother were originally related in Spanish. The grandmother is the poet's link to Mexican-Chicano culture and the Spanish language, but the narrator recounts in English her experience of naming objects in Spanish with her grandmother.

These poems reveal a speaker who is aware of a separation between Anglo and Mexican-Chicano cultures. In *Bloodroot*, as in *Mother, May I?* the poet's voice as it relates to a Chicana identity is almost always associated with her grandmother and her early childhood. The mythical voice envisioning a female cosmic world, and the biographical voice desiring personal transfiguration, are always associated in *Bloodroot* with Villanueva's quest for a female identity. These two identities—Chicana and female—are juxtaposed rather than synthesized or fused.

Most of the poems in *Bloodroot* reveal Villanueva's preoccupation with defining her identity as woman and as poet. Whitmanesque energy, tones, and incantation help her to express and celebrate the birth and beauties of her womanhood, much as Whitman, in an earlier period, celebrated the birth and growth of a country. These mythic strains, however, do not permit Villanueva to integrate into her celebration of womanhood an expression of the particularity of her Chicana self.

In *Poems*, Villanueva turns to her two female models and adapts their literary persona of the poet-narrator as a witch, a wild and threatening woman.[24] She acknowledges her female inspirators in "The Last Words,"[25] dedicated to "Anne & Sylvia / & all those that burned before them / in Salem & other places." The theme of woman as witch continues in a somewhat altered form the mythical strain of *Bloodroot* because the tradition of woman as witch evokes mysterious and magical contexts. The identity of woman as witch/bitch is the opposite pole to the identity of woman as creatrix, the primal Earth Mother of the early poems in *Bloodroot*. Villanueva employs the witch persona to taunt and satirize men, who "claimed themselves gods and priests and oracles" ("witches' blood"). The mocking tone indicates that she has gained awareness since writing the more naive poems modeled on Whitmanesque vocabulary and imagery.

Villanueva defines her feminine "I" in *Poems* by resisting and opposing male society. In "The Last Words" she quotes the final stanza of Plath's "Lady Lazarus," the only stanza of that poem which refers explicitly to men:

Out of the ash
I rise with my red hair
And I eat men like air.

The witch as poet-narrator describes a "hysterical mob" that would like to burn her at the stake for daring to utter notions about the human condition which society wants to repress: "the hysterical mob does not like to be / reminded of their true natures— / they would like to forget women like me." Nevertheless, she must write what she must, just as

> witches' blood must flow! dry and crackle—
> sink into the mother, turn to ash—
> red fire/blood release the utterance—

Although the crowd may want to set the torch to her, the truth is that "they do not know I burn, self/imposed / in a fire of my / own making." Her fire is the "heat" or energy of love, of words, and of blood impelling her to write the poem: "my witches' secret: the poem as / my witness." Her poems, as well as those of Plath and Sexton, "cannot be destroyed. / they burn in the heart, long after / the witch is dead." Villanueva never explicitly identifies her enemies in this poem, but her use of Plath's line— "And I eat men like air"—suggests that she, like Plath, sees her enemies as men. She sees herself outwitting them with the daring ruse of self-immolation, which they do not expect.

A tone of bravado toward men is more pronounced in "witches' blood," "Of Utterances," and "Of/To Man."[26] In "Of/To Man" Villanueva boasts of woman's ability to have numerous sexual orgasms at once, since "(spiritual orgasms count, too)":

> you're limited to one
> at a time: Is that the
> main bitch?
> well man, my man—
> let's set herstory
> straight. I come IN my cunt
> IN my clit, you might say
> my whole body is IN the
> act.

At the conclusion of "witches' blood" Villanueva's female monster flaunts to the "priests" and the "oracles" her preference for a witch identity rather than the goddess identity they have given her. Taunting them with a series of directives,

> call me witch
> call me hag
> call me sorceress
> call me mad
> call me woman. do not
> call me goddess.
> I do not want the position,

she openly adores in herself what men have called unclean in women: "I prefer to gaze in wonder, once / a month at my / witches' blood." She critically denounces men who "have killed / made war / for blood to flow, as naturally / as a woman's / once a month." Villanueva shifted "witches' blood," which originally appeared in *Bloodroot*, to the Irvine collection, thus underscoring her technique of juxtaposition by placing old poems next to new poems. The technique becomes more meaningful in *Mother, May I?*

The desire to give birth to the poem becomes the compelling theme of the Irvine collection. Villanueva accepts, in "Of Utterances," Sexton's advice that a woman must become her own muse. With ribald humor she attacks the theory of poetry which cultivates the myth of woman as the inspirational source of white male poets:[27]

> the "White Goddess"
> to white men
> to poets and men of genius
>   "a source of inspiration;
>   a guiding genius . ."
> that beautiful goddess
> that legendary Angel.

She goes on to describe in parodic tones the "legendary Angel" who descends

> with her milky white limbs,
>   full breasts, rosy at the
>   tips with the milky
>   stanzas and lyrics
>   to the touch of man:
> the cunt all acceptance,   opening wide
>   to the mind of man   and
>   giving birth to their children
>   The Poem.   The Painting.   The Sculpture.

After that satiric litany she interjects:

> and I with my fetish for dark men.
> and dislike (dis-taste) for sucking (this part's o.k.—
> cocks and swallowing the salty sperm (this part's not—
> of prose and rhymes.

Villanueva raises the possibility that she too might have to copulate with a white god just as her white male predecessors have done with the "White Goddess." Acknowledgment of her fetish for dark men, however, implies awareness of herself as different from traditional white poets. She, a woman-poet with a preference for dark men, cannot accept the white male model of artistic creation. Her images of "sucking . . . cocks" and "swallowing the salty sperm" of "prose and rhymes" parody the male poet who copulates with his white muse to produce his art piece. They also suggest a self-parody because she, metaphorically speaking, had sucked upon and swallowed Whitman's cosmic imagery and tones in her earlier poetry. Her mocking tone indicates that she now has enough distance to question a white male literary tradition before naively accepting it.

Villanueva further undermines and ridicules the stylized gesture of the white male poet invoking his angelic goddess with an unexpected deviation that substitutes African black gods as muses of women poets. Her suggestion is that if black gods did exist, she might accept them as sources of creative inspiration. She flouts this gesture, however, only to gain ironic effects, because she no sooner proposes the option of black gods as women's muses than she declares it nonexistent: "we women just don't have any / dark and lovely, / descending / 'Black Gods.'" Her resolution is to use her own "resources / and imagination" and become her own "source of inspiration; / my very own genius":

> I grew my own wings, became my
> own muse.
>
> I decided to fly
> and not
> descend

Villanueva identifies with Plath and Sexton in their challenge to the white male ego and his literary discourse. She introduces the dimension of the nonwhite male and his literary tradition by suggesting the possibility of "Black Gods" as muses. She sees herself at the center of an opposition between white male and black male or between dominant tradition and minority tradition. Although her references to women contain no specific indications of race, her choice of Plath and Sexton marks an identification with white women writers. Her references to "dark men" may suggest a Chicana consciousness, as "dark men" may include Chicanos as well as black men. These references, however, may also suggest her own identification with those white women who prefer black men as an alternative to white males who do not satisfy them. Villanueva sees her poetic feminine consciousness as apart from the dominant male tradition, but she does not specify the nonwhite group of which she is a member.

Except for five poems already published in *Bloodroot*, the twenty-one pieces in *Poems* are new. These twenty-one poems are designed to elaborate Villanueva's identity as a woman. Two of the five earlier pieces are about her grandmother: "to Jesus Villanueva, / with love," and "there were times."[28] Her decision to include these two poems suggests that she continues to want them to form part of her poetic identity. Their poetic voice, however, which expresses a specific Chicana identity, remains unintegrated with the voice of the new poems which develop her vision as a woman. When the collection is viewed as a whole, the two identities remain separate and juxtaposed rather than integrated and synthesized.

2

SUMMARY OF *MOTHER, MAY I?*

Mother, May I? is about forty pages long and is divided into three parts. The first part recounts the joys and games of childhood as the protagonist grows up in a working-class neighborhood in San Francisco, with a Mexican grandmother and aunt who speak primarily in Spanish. The mother, absent for the most part, appears at strategic moments of the girl's life. In the mother's absence the girl grows up attached to her grandmother, a wise old woman who becomes her mentor and educator. To the protagonist, her *mamacita* is exceptional: a nurturing mother figure, a warm disciplinarian, a powerful human presence. The protagonist mentions her father only once: "sometimes I cried for my / father but I didn't know who / *he* was" (p. 306).[29]

At the age of six or seven the girl experiences the trauma of rape. She tells no one about it, not even her grandmother. A few years later the mother decides to put her child in an orphanage: "then she / gives me away / to strangers" (p. 314). The mother also commits the grandmother, now old and sick, to a retirement home, and eventually the girl is placed in a foster home. She confronts death for the first time when she sees her grandmother die. Part I closes with the girl at her grandmother's funeral, where she secretly drops a rose into *mamacita's* grave.

In Part II the girl escapes from her foster parents and goes to live with her Spanish-speaking aunt. At thirteen her romance with a young boy results in pregnancy, and "a child blooms / inside me" (p. 319). Her idea of romance—boy meets girl; they fall in love; they marry and live happily ever after—is ruined, however, by the boy's parents who do not allow them to marry. The girl has the child alone.

The pregnancy results in the mother's return: "my mother / keeps me." The girl experiences the pain and joy of childbirth. After a few years she does marry her childhood sweetheart and has another child. Her husband goes to fight in a war, probably in Vietnam, and upon his return conflict ensues: "he drinks too much / and / he hurts me sometimes" (p. 322). Difficult years continue as the protagonist searches to find meaning in her life. The husband, "crazy," is eventually "locked / away." As Part II ends, the young woman is looking for her grandmother's grave site. This scene marks the poem's turning point, because that is where the protagonist finds her identity as person and poet.

Whereas Parts I and II develop the woman's personal history in a causative sequence, Part III breaks the narrative line as the poem becomes more metaphoric. The part opens with the death of an intimate friend, whose husband marries the protagonist. She adopts his children and, together with her own children, retreats to the countryside. The protagonist thus experiences motherhood in both a biological and a cultural way. We imagine her speaking the rest of the poem in the country, presenting her own "*myth* (of creation)" and poetically summarizing the key events already narrated. In the epilogue the three major dramatic characters— mother, grandmother, granddaughter—speak their thoughts.

METAPHORS, OPPOSITIONS, AND TRANSFORMATIONS

Mother, May I? makes the act of a woman's birthing its central metaphor for the two other activities that motivate the protagonist in her quest for self-definition: her drive to birth herself as a woman and a person and her drive to create her poem. The creative process, or self-expression, is thus to be understood in three different contexts: (1) the reproductive cycle of coitus, pregnancy, and birth; (2) the psychological development in becoming a person; and (3) the artistic process of producing a cultural artifact, such as a poem, a film, or a painting. Since the "I" is the means by which the fictional speaker narrates her story-poem, the birthing of her "I," or personhood, is tied to the artistic act of expression.

Two central oppositions are found in the metaphors of the protagonist's quest for self-knowledge as a person and as a poet. The first is between images of taking-in and giving-out. Related to, but not perfectly parallel with, the first opposition is the second, between acts of repression, or holding-in, and acts of expression. The first terms of each opposition—taking-in and holding-in—though describing similar actions, are associated with opposite feelings. Taking-in is usually a positive act, referring often to the physical incorporation of something from the outside, by eating it, for example. The act of holding-in is always negative. Unlike the act of taking-in, which involves bringing inside something from the outside, holding-in, or repression, refers to something that is already inside and unconscious. The second terms of the two oppositions—giving-out and expression—relate to acts of expelling, except that giving-out operates in a physical context (feces, babies, words) and expression, in a psychological and artistic context. The events and actions embodying these oppositions are interwoven and interlinked throughout the poem. My discussion of the first opposition integrates examples that relate to the second and more fundamental opposition of repression and expression.

Three actions of taking-in and giving-out from three different categories of experience show how these oppositions influence significant events in the protagonist's life. The first action is biological: ingestion into the digestive tract (eating, swallowing) and expulsion from the gastrointestinal tract (defecating, expelling). These biological functions occur during the narrator's early infancy, or the anal phase in Freudian terminology.[30] Delighted by her acts of excreting, the fictional narrator as a little girl encounters the tabooed parts of her body. The child's creative impulses lead her to imitate the act of birthing by excreting her feces. She likes to swallow corn kernels and her tiny rubber doll because she loves to find these objects in her excrement, and she enjoys using the bathroom because that is the place where "you make things." In the child's naive vision the rhythmic movement of defecation, a pleasurable straining and releasing, is comparable to giving birth. For her, the process of defecation is "like having babies."

The human body's absorption of food and the excretion of waste are not exact parallels to the birthing of babies and the writing of poems. Villanueva's analogy between the birthing of babies and the writing of poems is accurate; the results of these activities are generally accepted by society as good and beneficial. Her insistence that the defecation of excrement is analogous to the other two categories, however, represents an inversion of society's norms. It is acceptable to say that her baby is her poetry, but to claim that her feces are also her poetry because they represent an act of release is to make a countercultural statement.

The little girl hears grown-ups talking about birthing—"you have to push it out / hard"—"it" meaning a baby in the adults' language. But the child comically confuses "it" with feces, reinforcing the analogy between defecating and birthing. Her tendency to confuse the meaning of words she recognizes is also an indication that she is in the anal phase of development:[31]

> I hear them talking sometimes:
> —you have to push it out
> hard.—I do that. I
> like to look at what I
> make. it even smells
> good to me. sometimes
> they're pretty, when you eat
> too fast
> and the corn comes right out.
> it makes it yellow. one
> time my aunt came in and I
> peed and pooped and I
> said—I just made a

43

salad—she didn't
look too happy. so I kept
it to myself. *(p. 305)*

Here the girl rejoices in having "peed and pooped" and verbalizes the joy to her aunt. Her imagination transforms the excrement into a beautiful salad. The verbal communication of her action, however, evokes her aunt's unhappy look, a response that encourages the girl to refrain from telling of the action, if not to hold back the action itself.

On another occasion the girl swallows her tiny rubber doll so she can "have a baby in my / poop." Again her imagination transforms her doll into a baby. The grandmother discovers her swallowing her doll and utters a loving warning, with a smile: "—it'll get stuck and grow as big / as you and you won't have any room / left.—so / I stopped" (p. 306). The child stops because the grandmother's mild threat makes her fear that she will not be able to fulfill her fantasy about having a baby.

From the poem's onset, then, the child's creative impulses are in conflict with society's rules. The family, in the persons of her aunt and grandmother, begin to socialize her, to teach her that she must obey rules and laws. The child expresses her anal impulses but she also quickly learns to control them. The woman narrator looking back on this incident tells us: "and then I learned how / to hide" (p. 306). The deictic "then" reveals that the woman narrator, now speaking in the moment of the story's telling, realizes that at this particular moment in her childhood she learned to repress, or "hide," the side of her personality which wanted to do pleasurable but tabooed things. She learned that she could not do, and should not express her feelings about, certain things.

This first development in her life occurs in the private environment of the home dominated and controlled by two Mexican women. The second development, related to the experience of male-female sexuality, takes place in the public social world. The specific incident is the protagonist's rape by an adult male, an aberration from the reproductive sexual act in which the woman takes in, or eats, so to speak, the male sperm and releases or creates a baby. The narrator, seven or eight years old, experiences the horror and trauma of male sexual abuse.

The child is playing in the park with her slightly older friend Peggy when they meet a male stranger (of unspecified race) who tells them that playing in the park is illegal. One of them, he says, will "have to go with him to / sign a book." Peggy, who points to the protagonist and says "she'll go," runs away, leaving the heroine to confront the stranger alone. The stranger "all of a sudden . . . picked / me up and he wouldn't put / me down" (p. 311). In the face of this threat the girl invents stories about her mother, naively assuming that they will influence the stranger to let her go. She reverts to arguments from play and fantasy as well as from social differences to convince the rapist to set her free:

> —see this dress? my mother
> bought it for me. she
> has lots of money. she'll
> > give you money
> > if you let me
> go. look! my dress is pretty
> and new!—I'd been showing
> off that day twirling in circles
> pretending
> I was kidnapped from a king
> and queen
> pretending
> I was rich
> because my dress was so beautiful. (p. 312)

Although her family is lower-class, the girl has assimilated the notion that sordid incidents like the one she is about to experience do not befall people with money. But her references to fantasy, status, and riches are to no avail. The man invites her to "suck something / good," an invitation that in the context constitutes an order.

> he put me down.
> he took off my dress.
> he took off my t-shirt
> he took off my panties.
> and then he said
> > —do you want to suck something
> > good?—
> and I thought it must be bad.
> it must be licorice because
> I hate it because
> he hates me and
> he wants me to eat
> something bad and maybe
> if I eat something bad

he'll let me go. so I said
—o.k.—
he put it in my mouth
and it didn't taste like anything.
it hurt my mouth but I
wouldn't cry and then
he made me lie down
and the stickers hurt
and I was getting all dirty
and I knew if I cried
he'd kill me.   *(p. 312)*

Although it is not explicitly stated, we infer that a real rape has taken place. I use the word "real" because it is important to see that "rape" is not a figure of speech meant to stand for some other kind of experience. Sylvia Plath's sense of psychological estrangement led her to create, in "Lady Lazarus" and "Daddy," for example, psychological forms where hierarchical relationships between society and individual or between father and daughter are greatly exaggerated. In "Daddy" Plath sees herself as a Jewish daughter psychologically tormented by a father whom she presents as a brutal Nazi oppressor.[32] Whereas a poet like Sylvia Plath invented elaborate configurations to capture intense psychological torment, Villanueva talks in direct, explicit terms of an actual rape.

In Villanueva's poem, the rapist forces the girl to put his penis into her mouth. The positive action of swallowing or taking-in, in the first example, is replaced in this second example by the negative action of gagging, or holding-in. The gagging also serves a metaphorical function: it represents the repression of the girl's powers of speech to tell about her experience. In the first example the child expresses her biological impulses physically and verbally, though she learns later she was not supposed to do so. In this event she is forced to experience the rape and is then intimidated into repressing it. The action of defecating in the first example, or giving-out, is replaced here by the negative action of holding-in.

When the girl promises "not to tell anyone" about her experience the stranger lets her go.

and when my aunt saw me she said
Peggy told her and the police were
finding me and I told her
—I always have to do the dirty

work.—
and I didn't cry.

it was then I decided to become a boy.   *(p. 313)*

The child cannot really communicate to anyone the words "he raped me." She probably means to have the words, "I always have to do the dirty work," taken literally. That is, rape is dirty work and I, not Peggy, had to experience it. Her words displace her original impulse to tell about the concrete act of rape; instead, she refers to a more general and more ambiguous event ("dirty work"). In this way she finds a compromise between telling and not telling: she is able to say what she wants to say but not in a way that really expresses what happened to her. She sublimates her femininity into a tomboy identity, having learned that little girls are vulnerable to males who have the physical power to oppress them. She assumes the mask of masculinity and thus identifies herself with her oppressor. Ultimately she represses the story of the rape, never telling anyone about it.

The protagonist goes through her tomboy phase, fighting the toughest boy in school, climbing roofs, fences, and even high buildings and throwing an ashtray at her stepfather when she sees him strangling her mother. Soon the biological process takes its course with the onset of menstruation. "I bled there [on a high building] the first time / and knew it was special, but / I ignored it" (pp. 313–314). The tomboy phase and the coming of puberty form a minor opposition that metaphorically varies the pattern of taking-in and giving out. On the one hand, by assuming a tomboy identity, she represses her female characteristics; on the other, menstruation brings their release.

The third experience of taking-in and giving-out is associated with a second journey to her grandmother's grave site, which parallels an earlier visit at her grandmother's funeral. The second visit is more satisfying because it brings a moment of self-knowledge as a person and as an artist. This third action occurs in a sexual but nongenital context: it involves the physical body in a figurative way. Before explaining the significance of the second graveside visit and its relation to previous events, especially to the rape incident, I briefly summarize intervening events.

Up to this point in the poem the mother has been present only intermittently in the child's life. Before the grandmother's death the mother abandons the girl to an orphanage and commits

47

her mother, the protagonist's grandmother, to a retirement home. The mother, for reasons unrevealed, is present when the grandmother dies in the retirement home, where the girl has visited her several times: "I bring her chilis and onions / and comb her hair / and rub her back" (p. 315). When the protagonist arrives with her mother and aunt to see her grandmother, the nurses announce that she is already dead. Refusing to believe them, the girl runs into her grandmother's room and sees her grandmother sit up, hears her tell in Spanish her last wish, "Alma, *no me quiero morir*" ("Alma, I don't want to die"), and then sees her die. Whether the grandmother is already dead or actually dies at the moment the granddaughter enters the room depends upon whose interpretation of events we choose to believe—the nurses' or the girl's. More important, the girl's interpretation is a complete refutation of society's view.

On seeing her grandmother die, the girl utters a cry of pain:

> she sat up
> and said
> —Alma, *no me quiero morir*—
> and then she died.
>   AIIIIIIIII MAMACITA
> mamacita
> and then I cried.   *(p. 316)*

The capital letters indicate that the girl cries out in a loud *grito* ("scream") to express the pain and sorrow she feels at losing the person who nurtured her as a child. The word "mamacita," containing the word "mama," suggests the pain the girl associates with her mother's absence.

The girl's verbal release of pain leads to a nonverbal release as she begins to cry. The grandmother's death marks a critical moment in the girl's life, as it causes her to release repressed feelings. When the nurses give her medication to make her stop crying, however, she is again forced to curb her emotions:

> and I couldn't stop crying so
> they made me stop with some medicine
> and I didn't cry again.
> I didn't cry that night
> or the next day
> or the funeral day.   *(p. 316)*

Instead she drops a rose into her grandmother's grave and feels it

48

"squish." The flower is identified with the girl, as both are "squished." The adult narrator, thinking back to this moment, says:

> and they thought I was selfish
> and stubborn because
> I dressed up in my new shoes
> and a skirt and a red shirt
> and I didn't cry.
>
> they didn't know the rose
> was me.   *(p. 316)*

The rose is the metaphoric containment of the girl's self that for the time being remains repressed. By wearing new shoes, a skirt, and particularly the red shirt, she intentionally flouts society's social codes of dress for a funeral, especially one that takes place in a conservative Mexican setting. She does not say anything, but her dress is a defiant, albeit indirect, display of her repressed self.

The years between her grandmother's funeral, when the girl is about ten, and the second visit to the grave, when she is twenty-one, are a time of mixed joy and pain. She experiences joy with an Anglo boy,[33] a bright spot in an otherwise dreary childhood:

> we walk, the
> boy and I.
> we speak, the
> boy and I.
> we laugh, the
> boy and I.
> we kiss, the
> boy and I.   *(p. 319)*

The repetition and the parallel syntax give this experience a fairy-tale tone. She enjoys sexual gratification: "we love / on rooftops, doorways, parks, alleys." She expresses herself in a positive way in bearing her first child. Years later she gives birth to a second child by the same boy, now her husband. He goes to war, "to / their armies, their guns, their prisons, their death." When the husband returns he is angry and "wants to kill / something." The fairy-tale aspect of the romance is lost, recoverable only during moments of sexual love: "but when / we make love / we are children / again."

The predominant tone of those intervening years, however, is marked by silence, frustration, and anxiety. After her rape experience and her grandmother's death, the girl feels more intensely the dissociation between an inner "unembodied" self and an outer "embodied" self.[34] She conceals the inner self from everyone: "there is / a place / inside / me they / cannot enter. that is / where / I'm hiding" (p. 318). The narrator intimated this division in her personality earlier when, as a child, she learned to conceal pleasurable acts associated with her genitals. Her body, or the embodied self, wears the social masks and complies with the wishes and desires of others. Her unembodied self maintains itself pure and authentic in its alienation from its real surroundings. Both selves are part of the heroine's repressed personality: the inner self because it is protected from all interpersonal relationships, the outer self because it remains an unrecognized part of her complete self.

As a consequence of the rape and the loss of her grandmother, the girl closes herself off to everything and everyone. Psychologically, she refuses to open up to, to take in, her surroundings, the very thing she will have to do to achieve personal release and expression. Instead, she affirms denial, a response that leads her to become an isolated, private person. Her denial is underscored dramatically when she becomes catatonic. She closes her orifices, a gesture that counters her earlier gesture of having to open her mouth to ingest the semen: "the years / my mouth would open / and no words would / speak, / my mouth locked tight. / and a loneliness grew / that I couldn't name" (p. 323). Reflecting back, the narrator realizes that she was not only separate from others—from her husband, her children, her environment—but was also separate from herself:

> I put on my masks, my
> costumes and posed for each
> occasion. I conducted myself
> well, I think, but
> an emptiness
> grew
> that no thing
> could fill. I think
>
> I hungered for myself.   (p. 324)

Her inner "I" cannot express itself as long as it remains repressed and latent. What she must ultimately do is confront her inner "I" and integrate it with the self she does not like.

That is her state of mind when she returns to search for her grandmother's tombstone. The woman's husband accompanies her and finds the grave, but he plays no part in the spiritual interaction between grandmother and granddaughter. In Villanueva's poetic universe, men are excluded from any dynamic participation in the creation of meaning:

> we look for you, my
> husband and I
> we look for you till
> I'm dizzy. are you
> here, mamacita? are you
> here? he says—here
> it is.—he's found
> you, a "13"
> in the ground. they said
> —Jesus Villanueva
> is "13".—
> I touch the
> one, the
> three.
> I begin to cry
> and no one stops
> me. I didn't
> know it but
> a seed spilled out
> and my mouth
> ate it. I think
>
> that's when the rose took root.   *(p. 325)*

The woman figuratively swallows her grandmother's "seed," a sign of a maternal source. The seed is linked with both life and death: with death because it comes out of the tomb, the terminal experience of the life cycle, and with life because it comes out of the earth. The poem's presupposition is that the earth is the archetypal, female source of all life. The grandmother, literally buried in the earth, becomes a figurative womb that provides the heroine with the seed of a new life.[35] This part of the poem echoes the dominant theme of *Bloodroot*: the earth as an archetypal mother. The connection between her grandmother and the earth as a primordial form in *Mother, May I?* is more implicit but nonetheless operative. It is a kind of buried text in the poem.

51

The woman's eating of the seed parallels her swallowing her tiny doll when she was a little girl. More important now, her eating of the seed transforms her action of encompassing the male genitals with her mouth as a child. Ingestion of the seed is positive and reverses the earlier negative action. The seed represents restoration, the phallus, loss. It is a metaphor for the nurturing grandmother and a substitute for the phallus, a metonymy for the rapist.

The passage below immediately follows the one just cited:

> when she left this man she thought
> she'd die
> but she didn't. she thought
> the sun would go out
> but it didn't.
> and she heard a voice, distant
> and small, but
> she heard it.
> and her mouth opened slightly
> and a word spilled out. the word
>
> was "I."   *(p. 325)*

The narrative strategy in the above passage emphasizes the heroine's transformation from nonperson to person. In it an implicit "I" speaks of herself as a "she" in order to dramatize her birth as an I-subject. The strategy in this passage reverses the one in an earlier passage that dramatizes the narrator's divided self.

> Dreaming
>
> the danger of flying
> is coming back. you must
> close your eyes. one
> time I didn't and I saw me
> laying there and I didn't like me
> and I didn't want to come
> back. I thought she
> was disgusting. she
> had to eat and everything. she
> Was stuck. I
> wasn't. I came
> back anyway and then she
> stood up and looked in the mirror
> and scared me
> to life.

but I kept dreaming, no matter
how stubborn
she was.   *(pp. 308–309)*

The narrator here objectifies herself as "other." The secret self she created and desired to be stands outside and looks at her false self, which she hates. Since the mother abandoned her as a child, it makes sense to assume that the child turns inward toward herself the feelings she perceives to be her mother's: "she hates me" becomes "I hate me." Seeing herself only reinforces the self rejected by the mother. The process of dreaming enacted in this passage is a means of exorcising in herself a mother's hatred.

As the narrator meditates in the present on a past moment, she reflects awareness of her divided self. The "I" is the imaginary authentic self, whereas the "me" and the "she" are the real false selves. The linguistic shifting emphasizes the lack of a secure place which results from her having lost identity with her mother. The passage on dreaming enacts the separation of the self in temporal (past-present) and spatial (here-there) dimensions. The narrator identifies with an "I" to dramatize separation and division. In the magical birth passage the narrator speaks of herself as a "she" in order to dramatize cohesion and union.

The magical birth scene and the graveyard scene together reverse the experience with the rapist in the park, completing the protagonist's transformation from nonperson to person. In the rape scene the process of taking-in and expelling was incomplete: the girl took in but she did not release. In the magical birth scene the process of taking-in and expelling is complete, as the girl takes in and expels the seed in the form of the word that spills out. The woman encounters her "I" as a woman, and implicitly as a Chicana, because in returning to her grandmother she is affirming a Mexican identity. The grandmother represents Mexican culture, a detail to which I return later.

The pattern of swallowing and ejecting the maternal seed suggests the pattern in a woman's reproductive act when she "swallows" the male sperm and eventually expels the child. It is also a metaphor for the artistic process as creation. The seed the heroine figuratively swallows and ejects is magically transformed into a word. The grandmother's seed gives the woman the power of speech, the power to express her "I," her self. The word "I" is stressed by being placed within quotation marks. As such, it

53

suggests a consciousness of the word as word, the basic raw material of a poet or a writer. The woman's "I" is both the subject of the poem and the device by means of which she narrates her story.

In contrast with the satiric representation in "Of Utterances" of the white male artist as figuratively copulating with his white muse, Villanueva dramatically rejects this genital model in *Mother, May I?* in favor of a magical and nongenital one. The seed is absorbed by the mouth, transformed, and ejected as a word by the mouth. The interaction is between woman and woman, grandmother and granddaughter. The implicit rejection of genital sexuality is also an implicit rejection of the protagonist's mother's dependence upon male attention: "she was always going away / with one of *them* [men]. / she was always beautiful / for *them* (p. 306]. This moment of self-knowledge is connected with the woman's decision to leave her husband, as if to say that she is now able to confront her life alone rather than remain in an unhappy marriage.

The language attributes an androgynous quality to the grandmother. Her name is Jesús, which in Mexican culture may be given either to a man or to a woman if the woman is named Maria de Jesús. The ambiguity of gender in the name Jesús suggests an attempt to achieve a birth outside a limited sexuality of male-female relationships. In Catholic mythology it also suggests a nongenital birth, as Christ was conceived within a woman without the aid of a human male. Because the grandmother is named Jesús, and because she is the source of the protagonist's birthing as woman and as poet, the divine associations reinforce the nongenital aspects of her birth.

Part II ends with a turning inward toward the "I." Repeating the phrase "I am here" several times to affirm the presence of her "I," the narrator qualifies it each time. Even the word "simply," which negates qualification, is attached as a qualifier:

> Inside
>
> I am here. (do
> you hear me?) hear
> me. hear me.
> I am here. birthing
> (yourself) is
> no easy task.
> I am here. (pleading)

I am here. (teasing)
I am here. (taunting)
I am here. (simply)
I am here.   *(p. 326)*

Part III, abandoning the narrative line and the urban land-scape, shifts to a more poetic style and to a country landscape. The actual location of the narrator is ambiguous. We never really know where she is, in contrast with the specific locations given in Parts I and II: the home, the school, the grave site. In Part III we imagine her speaking from the country, the place where she comes to terms with her internal contradictions. By her placing of the poet Villanueva employs the convention that portrays the country as a pastoral land, an idealized utopia, removed from the temporal and spatial complications characteristic of city life.

The recognition scene between the two selves is dramatized in the passage entitled *"Her myth* (of creation)" (pp. 328–329), where Villanueva makes self-conscious use of an underlying mythical sequence of the quest, the plunge into the unconscious, and rebirth. As she descends alone, anxious and terrified, into a netherworld, she sees "dark figures / with bleeding bodies / and staring eyes / with voiceless mouths." She confronts these de-mons when she realizes "they / were me." The symbolic ritual represents the woman's confrontation with her false self, whose acceptance earlier had threatened pain and hurt. The birthing has released her inner "I," which now looks at the very things she has refused to face: the self rejected by the mother, the dead figures, the "they," the enemies who are at once foreign and familiar, distant and close.[36] She has felt their presence through-out her life but has avoided them by objectifying them as "other." When she realizes the "dead" are really images of herself, she achieves a moment of ecstasy and transcendence (the "light [that] blinded" her, the "highest mountain"). Realizing that she is not separate from her experiences, that indeed she *is* her experiences, she accepts her life, ugly as some of it may be:

Her myth (of creation)

it was dark, so dark
I was lost, so I
lay down flat
in my fear

and dark figures
with bleeding bodies
and staring eyes
with voiceless mouths

came to me
and I lay flat
with fear
till I realized they

were me. the dead.
and when I realized this,
a light burst through
the roof (I thought

I was on the highest
mountain on earth
looking, looking
with a shift
of my eyes) and the light
blinded me, so
I closed them. then I really
saw and

I was no longer afraid.
I did not weep.
I did not laugh.
I was not old.
I was not young.
"I am here."
I said.

Specifically, Villanueva's mythic ritual echoes the female archetype of the Demeter-Kore story of a violent separation and then a reunion between a mother (Demeter) and her daughter (Kore or Persephone). Villanueva belongs to a group of women poets who, preoccupied with female-female relationships, have employed the Demeter-Kore myth to help them recover a lost community of mothers, daughters, and sisters. As Alicia Ostriker notes, they have used this myth, as well as others, for differing purposes, as Villanueva does here by inverting the ascents and conquests of male heroism. In Kate Ellis's "Matrilineal Descent" it is the poet (Demeter) who descends into the dark world to recover a lost daughter.[37] Villanueva also shares with some modern women poets their preoccupation with giving birth unaided to themselves, becoming, so to speak, their own mothers and authors of their poems. With a sense of her own experiences, identity, and voice, the poet now takes control of her life, giving birth to the girl-child and the woman-adult who is herself. As the act of birthing may be read as a metaphor for female creativity, she births her "I," her poem, her text. In her own words, "birthing / (yourself) is no easy task."

SOCIAL OPPOSITIONS

Like much of Chicano prose and poetry, *Mother, May I?* portrays a dual rather than a multicultural society of different nationalities and ethnic origins. The social categories that structure the heroine's society are drawn from Mexican-Chicano and Anglo worlds. The central social oppositions have to do with race and gender.

The racial identity of Villanueva's protagonist does not depend upon a conflictual relationship between herself as a member of a social group and the larger society. Such conflict does, however, characterize the literary personae of Lorna Cervantes and Bernice Zamora, who, despite differing poetic strategies, reveal strong social identities as Chicanas. Villanueva, in fact, never opposes the dominant society on the basis of race. Her protagonist's racial identity rests on the projection of a nostalgic world of childhood which she associates with her Mexican grandmother. Although the search for her womanhood and her personhood involves a negation of self, no comparable struggle defines her Chicana self. The Chicana part of the poetic identity remains fixed in childhood. The feminine part of the poetic identity challenges the larger society, moving and changing as it does. The basis of her social conflict is thus gender, not race.

The protagonist remembers her grandmother fondly. The diminutive *mamacita* connotes love and affection. The opening scene of *Mother, May I?* plays on a light-dark (good-evil, life-death) contrast, a device intended to set up her readers' expectations about the characters.The narrating consciousness simulates a mind of childhood opening up to the sensitivities of physical light, movement, and joy. As the narrator tries to make us see what she saw and feel what she felt as a child, the grandmother is the first person she recalls, associating her with the light and

the joys of childhood. Only her grandmother knew her secret of
extracting joy from light:

> I was always fascinated
> with lights then,
> with my hands
> with my fingers
> with my fingertips, because
>
> if I squinted my eyes at them
> lights sprayed off
> burst off
> and a joy burst inside me
> and it felt good on my
> eyes to see it, so
>
> I squinted my eyes at
> everything in this manner
> and everything had joy
> on it, in it. it was
> my secret. only
>
> my grandma knew. I knew
> she knew by the way
> she looked at things
> long and slow and peaceful
> and her face would shine, lights
> all over, coming out of
> her tiniest wrinkles;
> she became a young girl.
> there were things that could not
> shine lights. we
> avoided these. these things
> took joy. these things
> could make you old. I didn't
> know it then, but
>
> these things were death.   *(pp. 303–304)*

The *mamacita,* then, and also the aunt who cares for the
heroine after the grandmother dies, are presented as positive—
nurturant, responsive, kind—figures. The grandmother is linked
with the Spanish language not only because it is her own language
but also because she has taught the girl the Spanish she knows.
References to the Spanish language recall the nurturing aspects
of the girl's education. When the girl laughs at her grandmother

who is frantically searching for the hat that all along has been on
her head, the grandmother gently reprimands her for her rudeness:

> and she spat—*grosera*! ["rude"]—and it
> made me laugh harder and she gave
> me the hand that meant a spanking
> (and she never spanked me)
> and she laughed too.   *(p. 308)*

The narrator's memories of her grandmother evoke love, warmth,
joy, and peace:

> . . . we
> go to movies and chinatown and shopping.
> she holds one side of the shopping bag, I
> hold the other. we
> pray and dunk *pan dulce* in coffee. we
> make tortillas together. we
> laugh and take the buses
> everywhere. when we
> go to the movies she cries and
> she dances when she irons. I
> comb her long hair and rub her
> back with alcohol.   *(p. 307)*

Because the grandmother is described in terms of habits and
thoughts more typical of a preliterate society than of a literate
one, we may assume that she comes from a predominantly oral
culture. Her modes of thinking and behavior accord with Walter
Ong's definition of formulary devices as standardized verbal expressions, such as epithets, adages, and proverbs,[38] which are typical of oral cultures. The grandmother, for example, relies on
patterns of expression and behavior which she has known all her
life and which probably came to her by word of mouth. When the
girl goes outdoors without wearing panties, her grandmother tells
her she must wear long pants under her dresses so that the wind
cannot smell her. The grandmother assumes an empathetic relationship between nature and the body, implying that nature can
fertilize the girl if she is not careful. She uses animistic arguments
from an oral tradition to persuade the child to modify her behavior. Another example is her explanation of how she knew
when her children were dying: "they always / pointed up with
their fingers." The grandmother has standardized, well-defined
meanings for and responses to certain events, which she recalls
and applies to specific situations when she needs to.

The grandmother's world—preliterate, preconscious, utopic —is one pole of the oppositional dyad of race. The antagonistic force is the public world and its institutions. The characters connected with the public world are seen as negative—insensitive, impersonal, and hostile. They are the rapist, the white female schoolteacher who tolerates no Spanish in her classroom, the nun at the Catholic school who slaps the girl's hands with the ruler (pp. 310–311), the nurses, and the doctor who keeps looking at the clock while the protagonist gives birth (p. 322). These characters, representing the Anglo world, are portrayed as defective primarily because they stand for values associated with traditional masculine culture: the repression of spontaneous feeling; the supremacy of mind over matter, of reason over body, of technology over nature; the devalued occupation of women as mothers and nurturers.

That the primary impulse motivating the protagonist's conflict with society is sexual and not racial is clear from specific events, such as the rape incident. At other times the heroine experiences a male world by way of women who behave as female enforcers of male authority. For example, the nurses at the retirement home suppress the flood of tears that overwhelm the girl when her grandmother dies. A release of emotion through tears is permitted women in most male-oriented cultures, whereas men are not permitted the same release. When the nurses give the girl medication to stop her uncontrollable weeping, the poem exposes how well the nurses have internalized a male value holding that tears are an undesirable sign of weakness.

A clearer picture of the way women function as female enforcers of male values emerges from reflection upon the characters, actions, and symbols presented in section 5 of the poem:

> the nun asked to look at
> my hands. I thought she thought
> they were beautiful, so I
> put them out
> and she hit them with
> a ruler. it hurt it hurt
> and she told me to
> put them out
> again and I wouldn't and she
> tried to grab my hands so
> I grabbed the ruler and hit
> her and ran

home and my grandma let me
stay when she saw
my hands. there was
a beautiful young nun who
spoke spanish and english and she
sat in the dark on the other
side of the cage. the metal was black
and cold and beautiful. it had flowers
and I loved to put my face on it, it
felt so good and cold.
and when she came and sat and spoke
her voice was very warm. she
said she came from mexico. I
bet she didn't let them shave
her head. this boy who was
very bad sat behind me
and he put his fingers in my *nalgas*
when we prayed and when I turned
and stared at him, he'd
smell them and smile. he
whispered one time in the yard
—they all have bald heads.—   *(pp. 310–311)*

This passage offers two versions of a Catholic nun: a bad nun
who functions as an agent of male power, and her antithesis, a
good nun. When the bad nun asks to see her hands, the girl
naively supposes that the nun wants to see them because she
thinks them beautiful. The child quickly learns her mistake. We
perceive this nun as negative because she hits the child's hands
with a ruler for no apparent reason. When the girl says of the good
nun, "I / bet she didn't let them shave / her head," the poet is
suggesting that the bad nun is bald. Another implication is that
the bad nun is an agent of the Catholic church, the "them" who
shave women's heads. The good nun has a sense of self-autonomy.
    The presupposition about hair, a conventional one, is that it
is a symbol of sexuality. A shaven head therefore suggests the
absence of sexuality, and, by extension, the repression of sexual
thoughts. By its shape and its austerity a bald head may connote
phallic associations. The bad nun is a masculine, phallic-headed
nun. The ruler linked with the same nun is also a phallic sign
giving her a masculine identity. The hand she slaps, when contrasted with the ruler, suggests femininity by its shape and its
open position. The striking of the girl's hands with the ruler is
thus a kind of symbolic rape forshadowing the real rape that

61

follows immediately. If the ruler is accepted as a masculine symbol, the nun who wields it represents an extension of masculine society, a female enforcer of masculine authority.

The good nun is a fusion of two opposing states. Unlike the conventional bald nun, she has hair on her head, thus suggesting sexuality. Yet she is a nun, presumably a virgin and a celibate. She has sexual potency because she is a virgin, but as a celibate she has chosen to deny herself sexual intercourse with men. Thus in the beautiful young nun a biological, natural code of virginity is fused with a cultural code of celibacy. This harmonious fusion of sexuality and celibacy, reinforced by the fact that the nun comes from Mexico and speaks both English and Spanish, is the objective the poem's narrating consciousness strives to attain. It does so in the epilogue.

To realize her dream vision, the daughter must reconcile herself with her mother, a process that addresses tensions in the mother-daughter relationship rather than racial attitudes in second and third family generations. The narrator's closing words in the epilogue suggest, nonetheless, a symbolic harmonization of the paradoxes and ambiguities in the mother's attitudes toward race.

Ethnically the mother is Mexican but socially and culturally she has assimilated the values of the mainstream. Although the grandmother's and the aunt's identities clearly fit into a Mexican world, the mother lies ambiguously between the Anglo and Mexican worlds. In "legacies and bastard roses," a poem in *Bloodroot* echoed explicitly in *Mother, May I?* Villanueva says that the mother, despite her family's advice to "marry a good mexican boy," found Anglo men more attractive: "the sun on a / gringo's hair makes me / worship / them." When she returns in *Mother, May I?* at the time of her daughter's first pregnancy, she claims that "we women stick together." The tragic irony is inescapable, for earlier she had given her daughter away "to strangers." When she accompanies her daughter to the clinic, she defends the latter's decision to have the child alone, but she does so from self-righteous motives. She tells the clinic secretary: "*she* didn't want to marry *him*." The emphasis given the two pronouns suggests that the mother knows the boy's family has forbidden the marriage because the girl is Mexican.

> —I [the boy] can't marry you. they [the boy's family]
> won't let me. they

```
    say
she'll have 12 more
kids in 10 years, you
know those people.
they
say
NO.—                                    (p. 319)
```

Instead of acknowledging that her daughter has been the victim of racial discrimination, the mother denies it, entertaining the fantasy that her Mexican daughter rejected the Anglo boy. The mother believes Anglo is better than Mexican. Her aspirations, after all, were to marry Anglo.

In the epilogue the poet presents her utopian vision of the merger between woman and Chicana. Neither the grandmother nor the aunt can function as a model for the protagonist. Although she admires these women, she cannot fulfill herself in the same way they did. Theirs is a world gone by, in which women of their social class were limited to the domestic sphere. Neither does her mother, a more public, more active, woman, offer her a satisfying model. Although her poetic "I" includes an awareness of both first- and second-generation women in her family, it also represents a transformation of each. She affirms the contribution that each has made to the creation of her personal identity:

Epilogue

```
as in all
stories, there is a
story within a
story. there is the
story of my friend (the
one who walked
with me to the
hospital; she was why
I beat up the
toughest boy in school,
because he was going
to beat her up; she was my
best friend since 12; she still
is) who somehow
is always
there. her soft
eyes always
recognize
me.
```

(mom)

men come
and go. your friends

stay. women
stay. mom
said. perhaps

this is a story of
women raging against
women; of
women loving
women; of
women listening to
women, because
men don't have time
to because
men move
on, because
men haven't learned
how to
listen, to
speak as
women; so

the thread, the story
connects
between women;
grandmothers, mothers, daughters,
the women
the thread of this
story

(mamacita)

when a man opens a woman, she
is like a rose, she
will never close
again.

ever.

(me)

pistils. stamens.
wavering in the sun.
a bloom on the bush.
a mixed bloom.
they wonder at it.
a bastard rose.

a wild rose.
colors gone mad.
a rupture of thorns.
you must not pluck it.
you must recognize
   a magic rose
            when

you see it.

(excerpted from my poem
Legacies and Bastard Roses)

The mother appears transformed within a network of continuity and relationship with other women. She has learned that only women can provide other women with friendship.

(mom)

men come
and go. your friends

stay. women
stay. mom
said.

The order in which the speakers are presented is not generational—grandmother, mother, granddaughter—but rather mother, grandmother, granddaughter, an arrangement suggesting that the poet feels closer to her grandmother than to her mother. The sequence also reinforces the grandmother's role as a mediating agent because she nurtured the girl in the absence of her real mother. The grandmother played the same role metaphorically at the magical grave scene by offering the heroine a way to move from a negative to a positive life. *Mamacita*'s text in the epilogue is the source from which the poet's own text emerges.

By juxtaposing her own passage and the grandmother's, however, the poet reveals the difference between them. She tells us that she is a rose, just as her grandmother does, but her use of "rose" has a different sense from her mamacita's use:

(mamacita)

when a man opens a woman, she
is like a rose, she
will never close
again.

ever.

The grandmother holds the traditional view that virginity is desirable in a woman. Her words communicate a nostalgia for the loss of the ideal "closed" rose in her system of values. They also posit a reliance on an outside male agent to initiate a woman's growth and development: "a man opens a woman."

In the closing fragment expressing her own identity "(me)," the heroine's rose echoes her grandmother's rose, but whereas the grandmother's rose, once opened, will never close again, the poet's rose is open: "pistils. stamens. / wavering in the sun." Alone, content, and self-sufficient, she does not depend upon any outside agency for her maturation. An open rose means rebirth, power, and beauty in Villanueva's poetic scheme. The poet hears her grandmother's statement about the traditional rose in a way no one else does:

(me)

pistils. stamens.
wavering in the sun.
a bloom on the bush.
a mixed bloom.
they wonder at it.
a bastard rose.
a wild rose.
colors gone mad.
a rupture of thorns.
you must not pluck it.
you must recognize
   a magic rose
         when

you see it.

The poet's fragment also recovers other images used in the autobiography. The image of the sun, for example, recalls the mother who in "legacies and bastard roses" worshiped the "sun on a / gringo's hair." In Part II of *Mother, May I?* the poet refers to her first husband, who was Anglo, as her "sun": "he is my sun, I / turn and turn toward / him" (p. 322). When she decided to leave him "she thought / the sun would go out / but it didn't." In the poet's speech in the epilogue the image of the sun does not suggest female dependence upon men, as it does in the other two speeches. Instead, the language flaunts the speaker's independence of a social world of real men and women. The poet celebrates the feminine and masculine aspects of herself ("pistils.

stamens.") within the context of a mythical, magical world. The placement of "pistils" and "stamens" on the same line suggests equality and harmony rather than the sexual asymmetry that characterizes woman's experiences in the social world.

The images also reflect a racial context; "a mixed bloom," "a bastard rose," and "a wild rose" suggest the botanical phenomenon of hybridization, or a mixing of strains. The images may be extrapolated from a botanical to a social context, where hybridization suggests racial mixtures, a form of *mestizaje*. Race is "colors gone mad." The poet is giving positive meaning to "bastard," which is considered negative in most cultures. She is literally a bastard child because she never knew who her father was. Furthermore, "bastard" ties in with "Chicano," as Chicanos are unlegitimated in the United States. Thus the poet, unlike her mother, affirms her Mexican-Chicano self in a positive way.

Villanueva perceives herself to be the unusual rose. Earlier in the poem the protagonist flaunts her person at her grandmother's funeral by wearing new shoes, a skirt, and a red shirt. In the epilogue, however, she speaks metaphorically, thus producing a self-definition that harmonizes feminine with masculine, Chicana with woman. Symbolically, she fuses race and sex.

3

THE READERS IN *MOTHER, MAY I?*

My reflections on *Mother, May I?* are based on the assumption that the text is not an autonomous artifact, but rather that it has status within a determinate context.[39] As such, it describes a relationship between an utterance and the situations of utterance. It presupposes a certain kind of reader to whom it conveys a message. Because the poetic identity is also the text of *Mother, May I?* or the result of narrating a life, the poem elucidates the relationship between Villanueva's poetic voice and her implied audience. The argument in this section is that the two identities of woman and Chicana, which seem to be integrated when the text is read simply as a succession of words, remain separate but juxtaposed when the text is seen as an utterance spoken to someone.

Before analyzing the implied audience in Villanueva's poem, I want to explain in more detail how I understand this concept. In composing a written work, a writer makes certain assumptions about his or her audience: that its members belong to a specific linguistic and cultural community, for example, or that they share certain beliefs and values about the world because they are linked by common bonds, such as gender, race, and social class. Writers assume that their audiences are familiar with certain social and literary conventions. They make literary decisions based on assumptions that their readers will understand the meanings of the words used and that they will accept the linguistic, cultural, and literary conventions that governed the composition of the text. These assumptions about an audience are, of course, embedded in the language employed in this instance by the poet to write the poem. The notion of the implied audience, then, refers to the addressee or the reader characterized, directly or indirectly, in the text. This fictionalized reader is a construct of the text, who may or may not correspond to the actual or real reader. The reader characterized by and in the text may be defined as a composite of attitudes, background, and values which the text presupposes.[40]

In composing *Mother, May I?* Villanueva has made few concessions to the Spanish-speaking public. She writes in English, thus making the poem available to all who read and understand it, Anglos as well as Chicanos, men as well as women. She assumes a reader with little or no formal acquaintance with literary forms and figures, though her poetry is certainly not outside the scope of literary influences and traditions. Yet in contrast with Bernice Zamora's poetry (see chap. 5), which at times almost demands a familiarity with specific literary works, Villanueva's poems are intended more for the uneducated reader. Zamora's image patterns and allusions assume an educated reader even in Spanish, though she does employ linguistic codes from an everyday Chicano vocabulary. In contrast, Villanueva's vocabulary and situational references, though presented in English, are closer to everyday discourse than they are to academic or poetic discourse.

Thus the nature of the implied audience in *Mother, May I?* does not require shifts from English into Spanish or from Spanish into English as it does in Zamora's poetry. Rather, the shifts in *Mother, May I?* are shifts in voice in Villanueva's poetic identity as it addresses its implied audience. They are embedded in the speaker's forms of utterance, her frame of imagery, and some-times, as in the epilogue, in the arrangement of the words on the page. They make up the slants and biases that determine the emphasis of an argument and fix the status of a particular kind of reader. I submit that the epilogue is the enactment of the relationship of Villanueva's poetic identity with her implied audi-ence. Villanueva chooses a strategy whereby she juxtaposes her addressees rather than synthesizes them: she apposes rather than integrates the identities of woman and Chicana and their implied social contexts, Anglo and Chicano.

The epilogue dramatizes Villanueva's technique of creating meaning. Made up of passages from an earlier poem, the epilogue is the result of choices that have displaced other possibilities. Some lines are new whereas others are repeated verbatim from "legacies and bastard roses," a poem that had already appeared in *Bloodroot*.[41] By disclosing that the epilogue is excerpted from "legacies and bastard roses," Villanueva makes it clear that she is not ending her autobiographical poem with a new passage composed precisely for the occasion but is reverting back to an earlier work. The device of quoting herself is an enactment of self-display. She is acknowledging to her audience that she is revising herself.

The final fragment of the epilogue, which first appeared in *Bloodroot*, is now to be read as the closing statement in the story of Villanueva's life. By quoting herself Villanueva invites her readers to compare her voice of the past with her voice of the present. The epilogue does on a small scale what *Mother, May I?* does on a larger scale. *Mother, May I?* revises the personal biog-raphies already presented in *Bloodroot* and in the Irvine *Poems.* Villanueva does the revision by juxtaposing old words with new words, by taking bits and pieces from an old poem and inserting them into a new poem. By putting them in a new context, she gives them new meaning. Setting "legacies and bastard roses" and the epilogue side by side reveals what material has been excluded and what included.

> Legacies and Bastard Roses/
> (to mom and mamacita)
>
> I thought of you last night
> after
> I washed my face, my skin

is dry now so
I add oil to soften it or
I crack and
I remember you applying
and reapplying oils
to your face and neck, you
always told me
a girl could never be
too careful.

(mom)

don't forget. men come
and go. your friends

stay. women
stay. I
heard this at 7
and never forgot.

(mom)

he raped me
and I never told
anyone,
not even mi
mama, I
was so ashamed, I
lay in the tub
for hours
emptying
the tub and
refilling
it, crying
softly.
my tears fell
softly,
into the
dirty
water.

(mom)

he passed me on the road
that day in Louisiana
that day I walked all
the way to town
carrying you
carrying a suitcase
in the heat

that day
he passed
that uppity Mexican
that day.

(mom)

my family
always
said, "marry a good mexican
boy"—
    but the sun on a
gringo's hair makes me
worship
them

(mamacita)

when a man opens a woman, she
is like a rose, she
will never close
again.

ever.

(me)

pistils. stamens.
wavering in the sun.
a bloom on the bush.
a mixed bloom.
they wonder at it.
a bastard rose.
a wild rose.
colors gone mad.
a rupture of thorns.
you must not pluck it.
you must recognize
    a magic rose
            when

you see it.

The closing passage of *Mother, May I?* is identical to the one that terminates the earlier poem. Similarly, the grandmother's discourse remains intact. Only the mother's utterance has been changed. Not only is it shorter but it reappears in a new context, intermixed with new words that represent the narrator's voice. The poet has excluded the passages that connect her mother with a specific cultural setting. References to the mother's rape by, presumably, "that uppity Mexican," to her family's advice on whom to marry, and to her own preference for Anglo men are omitted. Instead, Villanueva places the mother in a network of relationships with other women, a transformation that implies a decision to reevaluate the mother. And the poet has done just that in her autobiographical poem. By placing words representing her own voice as narrator next to her mother's words, the poet emphasizes her newly found connection with her mother.

Together, the mother's shortened speech in the epilogue and the author's narration presuppose a modern female audience whose members believe that women can be spiritual mothers to one another. They express women's commitment to women to follow through with responsibilities in a way that men do not. Their words form a hymn in celebration of women: their anger, their love, their strengths. They speak as women to women. The repetition of the word "women" six times in the narrator's text is an endorsement of women, seeking as it does to build feelings of community among them. The repetition and parallelism give the discourse the effect of a litany, or an incantation, in praise of women. The breaking of lines between a preposition ("of") and a noun ("women") further stresses the idea of womanhood:

> this is a story of
> women raging against
> women; of
> women loving
> women; of
> women listening to
> women.

If Chicanas relate to the attitudes and values put forward in this discourse, their identity will be based on gender and not on race or cultural difference. They will react primarily as modern women who share the goal of building a community of women helping one another in times of need, rather than as members of a social group with a particular history and culture.

The message of the grandmother's text is less modern. Her words sound like an adage or a proverb that carries the weight of a long oral tradition. More traditional in form than the mother's and the narrator's, her discourse has a more standard syntax: its two complete sentences are loosely joined together by a comma.

The line breaks more conventionally between noun and verb rather than between preposition and object.

These two forms of discourse, the mother's and the narrator's on the one hand, and *mamacita*'s on the other, reflect two opposing attitudes about women; they are spoken to two different groups in the same implied audience. By quoting her grandmother's discourse the poet implies an audience that respects a speaker who calls to mind the traditional values of a Mexican grandmother. The words lamenting the loss of virginity might alienate the implied addressee of the mother's discourse, but in quoting them the narrator honors women who sprang, as her grandmother did, from a particular cultural community and who contributed to the historical development of a modern woman's identity. To the extent that the narrator commemorates a Mexican grandmother, she is speaking to Chicanas as members of a cultural community. The other group of modern women in the implied audience overhear the sentiments expressed in this passage, but they will respond to them only if they respect a speaker who celebrates a traditional woman.

As noted above, the implied audience comprises two groups of addressees. The poetic voice speaks first to one group and then to the other. The poet's recognition of a modern feminine community marks her own present identification as an adult woman, and the celebration of her Mexican grandmother stresses her past identification in childhood. The poet's manner of addressing the two groups suggests that she sees them as separate from each other rather than as integrated into the same community of women.

The final passage presenting the poet's self-definition emphasizes a sense of difference from both her mother and her grandmother. Her mother's and her grandmother's discourses are presented in a narrative style, whereas her form of utterance is lyrical. Her text communicates its message by way of images instead of statement. Evoking and suggesting through metaphor, it emphasizes the expression of the lyrical self rather than the communication of a message.

The narrator's form of utterance when seen as an exchange between a speaker and an addressee is different from those of her mother and grandmother. Thus it too suggests a different audience, hypothesizing a mythical community of women rather than a socialized audience of either women or Chicanas. Her poetic fragment as a statement of her autonomy communicates the sense of an "I" speaking to a "you" who listens. Her statement might be regarded as a placard she is holding up to the recipient of the message, the "you" repeated three times at the end: "you must not pluck it. / you must recognize / a magic rose / when / you see it." Who is this "you"? To whom is the discourse addressed?

Emile Benveniste asserts that the third-person pronoun may function as a sign of the person who is absent from an instance of discourse.[42] Following Benveniste, I see the "they" of "they wonder at it" outside the communication situation. In Villanueva's poetic world, "they" often refers to society, to men, to women who are like the nun, the nurses, or the schoolteacher—to all those outside her value system. Only the "I" and the "you" are inside the circuit of communication. The "you" refers to those who can inject themselves into the discourse by identifying with either the "I" speaking or the "you" to whom the "I" speaks. First and foremost, the "you" designates women. It may also include men who can acknowledge their femininity and become like women, like mothers and daughters everywhere. As the poem includes a Mexican grandmother and makes references to a form of traditional Mexican culture, the "you" also includes Chicanas. The poetic consciousness orients itself more toward woman (gender) than it does toward Chicano (race). Villanueva's primary inclination is to establish bonds among categories of gender instead of race.

Villanueva's form of address, defining herself in relation to her mother and her grandmother, makes clear that her "I" is separate from the "you." In the final analysis she sees herself as separate from both Anglo and Chicano societies. In the epilogue the three voices are heard separately; they are like three different melodies played one right after the other: "mom," "mamacita," "me." The three audiences—a community of modern women, a community of Chicanas, and a community of abstract, mythical women—are not meshed into a single voice. The epilogue produces the effect of a collage, a tissue of several voices and audiences, inviting the viewer to witness different textures and forms at once. The epilogue juxtaposes one voice with another voice, one kind of compositional quality with another. In the end it makes the reader more aware of differences, boundaries, and demarcations than of similarities, overlappings, and convergences.

Villanueva directs her poetic voice alternately to women and to Chicanos, a separation also present in other parts of the autobiography. The "I" in the poem fluctuates between an "I" that speaks in a little-girl voice and an "I" that speaks as an adult woman. As it fluctuates, it orients itself more to one audience than to the other. In passages where the "I" recounts her childhood, the "I" is speaking more to Chicanos than to women. For example, when the narrator says in her little-girl voice, "you can't speak / spanish here," the colloquial "you" means / either herself or anyone, though the context of the passage orients the "you" more to Chicanos than to Anglo men and women. The references to the Mexican grandmother, to the white schoolteacher who permits no Spanish in the classroom, to a character who says she can read, count, and recite poems in Spanish, and to traditional Mexican food (*pan dulce* and tortillas) derive specifically from Chicano cultural codes. Furthermore, the specific references to language in this passage presuppose members of a social group who have the desire, the need, or the linguistic competency to speak Spanish. The Chicanos addressed here are, of course, readers who, like the narrator, may have experienced a socialization process whereby they have lost the original language. Thus they experience the events described just as the author who writes about them does, that is, in the language that replaced the maternal tongue. The Anglo women and men in the audience also hear the message, but they are not the privileged recipients of it.

The narrator's statements expressing her alienation from a white Anglo society are also heard by the Chicanos in the audience. In a few key places the "I" exposes certain myths that United States society has entertained about its Latino population. Although these statements may be familiar to a general audience, Anglos as well as Chicanos, they carry nuances that relate in a specific way to Chicanos. For example, the family that adopts the girl checks her hair for lice and accuses her of stealing. The family of her teenage lover believes that Mexican women have too many babies and, furthermore, that they have them indiscriminately. To capture the full elocutionary force of these passages, readers must belong to a community of socialized Chicano readers who are aware, for example, that American perceptions that Mexicans have lice in their hair and bear numerous children have led to social humiliation. This community shares the view that Anglo society has fostered, and may still foster, such notions about Chicanos. In these passages Villanueva reflects on social conventions familiar to a Chicano audience.

The narrator's "I" that speaks of childhood and adolescence also refers to experiences unique to the female anatomy, such as menstruation and pregnancy. References to these natural biological functions and to the girl's rape imply a female audience rather than an exclusively Chicano audience. The important point, however, is that material particular to a Chicano audience is seldom part of the narrator's voice as an adult woman.

When the narrator as an adult woman directs her "I" to a female audience she usually employs lyrical language. Whereas processes unique to women, such as menstruation, are simply narrated as facts in the early part of the poem, later on they are given symbolic value and are intended to evoke magical and mythical feelings about women. The identities of mothers and daughters in these metaphorical passages are undefined in terms of racial and class categories. For example, in the section entitled "*the thread* (the amputation)," Villanueva reevaluates her separation from her mother. Speaking as a woman to women, she recounts her relationship with her mother and her own daughter in the context of a mother-daughter pattern she sees everywhere, for she has listened "to mothers / and daughters / everywhere."

the thread (the amputation)

the thread is bloodstained. I
gave it to you, as my
mother to me, as her
mother to her
and it is thick with
blood, with life
and we are thick with
each other, my
daughter, my

daughter, my
girl; you
stand, staring
with your knife's
amputation: your
hands bloody: it
is your amputation—I

took it from my
mother: you
take it from
me—blood, my
daughter. love, my
daughter. life, my
daughter: life. now,

go and play.
become your
own mother
and spin your own lovely

thread.   *(pp. 331–332)*

The poet's reconciliation with her mother is the muted story in the poem; it is never witnessed by the audience. Presumably it has taken place primarily for two reasons: first, because the narrator never expresses anger or resentment toward her mother; second, she could not celebrate the closeness between mothers and daughters, as she does in the poem's final passages and epilogue, had she not first resolved her differences with her own mother.

The use of pronouns in the above passage about the paradox of continuity and separation in the mother-daughter bond[43] suggests woman's double identity as both daughter and mother. The poet employs the image of the thread to reinforce this theme on three levels: (1) as a metaphor for the physical connections (umbilical cord, menstruation) between mother and daughter at the time of birth and later: "the thread is bloodstained"; (2) as a metaphor for the meanings her own daughter will create in life; and (3) in the epilogue, as an explanation of the meaning of the story she has just told: "the thread, the story / connects / between women; / grandmothers, mothers, daughters, / the women / the thread of this / story." The repetition of "daughter" at the end of the first stanza of *"the thread"* and at the beginning of the second has a rhetorical purpose: to mark the transition from the theme of continuity in the first stanza to the theme of separation in the second stanza and to emphasize the feelings of the mother as she sees her daughter, the child, become her daughter, the woman.

The key symbol in the second stanza, "amputation," refers not only to the physical cutting of the umbilical cord at the time of birth but also to the psychological and emotional separation of the daughter from the mother. Villanueva links her own mother to the idea of amputation, not to continuity, thus suggesting that she associates the memory of her mother with the violence of separation. In contrast, she links herself with both the joy of continuity and the pain of separation. Her daughter now stands before her with her "knife's amputation" as she once stood before her own mother with her "knife's amputation." Given the conventional phallic symbolism of "knife," the knife's amputation alludes to the choice made by the daughter to leave her mother and go with her husband. The narrator is saying that separation is what allowed her to become her own mother, as she now tells her daughter to do: "become your / own mother / and spin your own lovely / thread." In this context "thread" means one's own life.

In a similar passage Villanueva speaks in the third person about the rebellions and the jealousies in a mother-daughter relationship. The "I" is implicit but the "you" is explicit in this passage from section 26:

> . . . they mouthed
> the same curses
> she and her mother
> mouthed "bitch, whore" the
> unnameables, the
> unutterables you say
> to those you love, to
> your mother, that bitch, to
> your daughter, that whore
>   of a girl
>
> I love you. (p. 330)

In both passages cited the identities of the pronouns and the frame of imagery offer limited possibilities. The audience, which includes Anglo women and men, Chicanas and Chicanos (and possibly members of other ethnic groups who read English), must identify with the "I"-mother or the "you"-daughter. As there are no ethnic or cultural features to orient the message to a socialized community of Chicana readers, Chicanas must identify with it in terms of gender rather than of cultural differences. The implication for men, regardless of race, is that they must become like mothers or daughters. If they cannot relate to or empathize with the sentiments expressed, they will have difficulty understanding or appreciating the text. The emphases of the arguments imply an audience of women linked by the common bond of gender. As noted above, the audience is not defined in terms of race or social class.

Many of the passages in *Mother, May I?* are implicit attempts to recreate the mother-daughter bond. Several examples that relate to the theme of "playing" are illustrative. Playing is stressed on several levels throughout the poem; in fact, its title is the name of a children's game. Activities such as defecating, dreaming, and birthing are all forms of play for the heroine. Playing is her way of filling the gaps and of forgetting the discontinuities in her life. At its most fundamental level, playing is represented by the physical gestures and body movements the little girl makes with her doll. The child's play activities allow her to achieve an imaginary cohesion that compensates for the unsatisfactory relationship with her mother. At times she assigns her own identity to her doll and she, in turn, becomes the mother. She thus makes the doll a "you" and her "I" a mother, an event that enacts her fantasy to become her own mother.

The following passage is one of two that are entitled "playing."

> playing
>
> I am little and I sleep with you.
> we pretend.
> we pretend, I'm the mother
> and you're the little girl
> and you cry for me cause I
> have to go to work and you
> have to stay. I
>
> laugh at you, big cry baby. I
> go away and you pull me back
> by my leg and we
> laugh and laugh
> till it's time to
> get up.   *(pp. 306–307)*

The other passage describes the bed as the ideal microcosm of the world, where the child orders the relationships between her mother and herself. She even fantasizes that she becomes her mother's mother.

PLAYING

the pretend
place
is bed, we
lay together, you
tell me stories
about when you were
little and you were
bad, I
laugh and laugh
and we
are both 5
and no one's
the mother. we
hide from the
grown ups,

playing.

I think one time we
never switched
back and I stayed
your
mother and I stayed
bigger and I stayed
stronger, to take
care of you,
mother, we

forgot the world is bigger than
our bed.   *(pp. 309–310)*

As she grows up, the protagonist plays at being someone else, adopting different masks and different personae. She births her first child "dreaming" so as to avoid the pain of knives and the needles used by the nurses to give her injections.

The act of playing also functions at a metatextual level. As the subject of the poem is also the "I" of the poet, the poet plays by writing: she plays with words, with language, with images. She plays by mixing old words with new words. Her final utterance at the end of the epilogue illustrates another kind of playing with words: she makes the rose magical, much as a child would, telling us to respect it because it is special. Writing allows her to fantasize and dream as an adult, much as playing with dolls did as a child. Writing as a means of play often relates to her desire to achieve harmony in the mother-daughter relationship, as is aptly illustrated by the following passage:

> I watch you put lipstick
> on, red and beautiful, you
> press your lips together
> to make it stick
> and I
> grab you
> and kiss you
> on the lips with my
> mouth open—is this
>   how they do it,
> mother?—
> I ask
> I wish
> to be closer
> to you
> than lips or lipstick
> or skin
> I wish
> to kiss
>
> your womb.   *(p. 309)*

As one theme of the poetic narrative is the absence of the poet's mother during early childhood, such expressions of the child's desire to be close to her mother emphasize the act of writing as a means of reliving and reshaping the experience of childhood. Through her writing the narrator-poet makes her mother play with her as she never did in real life. Through the process of writing her life she now "kisses" her mother.

By reconstituting the lost mother-daughter bond, Villanueva forces her readers to identify as mothers and/or daughters. The relationship between the text and the reader is analogous to the one between the heroine and the mother figure described by the narrator, who seeks to create a bond between text and reader by sensitizing him or her to the dynamics of the mother-daughter relationship. The text, by asking its readers to become mothers and daughters, is the mother of its readers who are daughters. Through her writing Villanueva relives and recreates her experiences as well as reshapes and redefines those of her readers. She makes them unlearn past identifications and assume newer, more positive, attitudes about the mother-daughter bond.

For Villanueva, writing is a way of releasing what she has repressed, a positive act with therapeutic value through which she reexperiences herself as a child, as an adult, and as a woman. As she notes just before the epilogue, "I / was always / good at / make believe. all / I ask is / may / I play?" In an earlier passage (in *"life cycle"*) she writes: "I'm / a juggler. / I'm a juggler." And in her text Villanueva has indeed juggled themes of life and death, past and present, dream and reality, child and adult, subject and object, mother and daughter. She has juggled different voices—a little girl's baby talk, a young woman's despair, an adult woman's maturity—as well as her social and mythic voices. And ultimately she juggles the two groups in her implied audience.

To integrate her audience Villanueva would have to speak with a poetic voice that united the two identities, woman and Chicana, much as Lorna Cervantes does in "Beneath the Shadow of the Freeway" (see chap. 3). Cervantes not only integrates these two identities; she also creates a lyrical moment in a narrative and discursive poem. It is important to understand, however, that Villanueva chooses juxtaposition instead of integration because she wants to emphasize the alienation she feels from both Anglo and Chicano societies. Neither group's experiences typify hers. She identifies with an Anglo tradition of women and desires to identify with Chicanas, but she maintains herself separate from each social group.

There are objective grounds for Villanueva's alienation from Chicano society. A literal definition of "bastard" highlights the ambiguity of her origins. She knows a Mexican-Chicano community socially only from her grandmother, but she cannot be certain of her Chicano origins. For this reason the poetic voice hesitates to identify with *La Raza*. In contrast, the obvious physical differences between men and women make her absolutely certain of her gender.

The autobiography, as well as the poems in *Bloodroot* and in the Irvine collection, brings to light no evidence of integration with Chicano males, one important indicator of a Chicana's social identity. Although Anglo men also do not play a dynamic role in the autobiography, other indicators of language, culture, and literary influences make clear that Villanueva's context is an Anglo tradition. The references to Mexican-Chicano culture permit her to assert her differences with and her alienation from an Anglo world, but she does not assign a central role in her poetry to her separation from that world.

The other notable feature indicating a lack of integration with a Chicano community is the absence of the Spanish language. The few Spanish words Villanueva does use are familiar enough to the English reader: for example, tortillas, *pan dulce*, and *mamacita*. The longest Spanish phrase in *Mother, May I?* is "*Alma, no me quiero morir*," and Villanueva translates that in a footnote (p. 316). The passage describing Villanueva's return to her grandmother's grave is a discursive interchange between her "I" and her *mamacita*, the "you." In this passage *mamacita* is clearly understandable by Anglo women and men. Even the girl's cry of pain at her grandmother's death, "AIIIIIIIIII MAMACITA," does not necessarily imply a Spanish-speaking audience. Because the linguistic combination "AI" may also be used in English to express a woman's moan or wail, it has a place in English phonetics.[44] *Mother, May I?* as well as the poems of *Bloodroot* and the Irvine collection, would have to contain more Spanish to be addressed to a Spanish-speaking community of Chicano readers, but not so much as to exclude the English-reading community. Nevertheless, the poetic voice shares in a Chicano experience because it speaks in English about events that took place before the maternal tongue was lost to the language of the dominant society.

The core of *Mother, May I?* is not the portrayal of contest and struggle in the identities of "woman" and "Chicana," as it is in some of Zamora's poems. Rather, its core is a disjunction in the sequential presentation of the experience of being a woman and the experience of being a Chicana. The poem reveals a discontinuity in the poetic voice between a consciousness of a past life and a consciousness of a present life. The poetic voice examines its past in relation to its present in order to show where the poet began and how she came to be where she is today. The poetic voice of the past speaks from a position that marks the specificity of her cultural roots. The voice of the present speaks from a position that marks the result of a life process. This second voice articulates and celebrates women's reproductive powers to create children and their creative powers to write poems. It urges women to recognize the particularities of their female anatomy, to become spiritual mothers and daughters to one another, and to reconstitute a lost family of women.

The most powerful and dramatic passages in the latter part of the poem are those with mythic overtones: for example, the passage that recounts the heroine's encounter with her "other" self in the netherworld, the section entitled "*the thread* (the amputation)" stressing the daughter's identification with and separation from the mother, and the poet's final utterance. These passages presuppose a mythical community, not a social community, of women (and men), whether Anglo or Chicano. It seems to me a telling factor that the process of the protagonist's finding her poetic identity is never placed in a sociocultural matrix. The poem is oriented to women solely on the basis of biological similarities. Although the phenomenon of blood in terms of menstruation and childbirth is a very real factor in women's lives, placing the female anatomy at the center of a quest to define a female identity must be regarded as mythical.

By juxtaposing the two identities of "woman" and "Chicana," Villanueva is at once expressing a hope for their reconciliation and asserting her inability to achieve a synthesis between them. She chooses a mythical community of women because she is thereby permitted to speak to alienated women everywhere, regardless of race. The consequence of her choice is the silence of her poetry on the subject of Chicana experience. In a curiously paradoxical way, Villanueva shows that the search for a female identity is especially complex when considered in relation to a Chicana self-definition. She challenges her readers to discover how to include a Chicana identity in a female identity.

III

THE CHICANA AS SCRIBE

Harmonizing Gender
and Culture in
Lorna Dee Cervantes'
"Beneath the Shadow
of the Freeway"

1

I am a poet
who yearns to dance on rooftops,
to whisper delicate lines about joy
and the blessings of human understanding.

I believe in revolution
because everywhere the crosses are burning,
sharp-shooting goose-steppers round every corner,
there are snipers in the schools . . .

These two verses express two radically different perspectives on
the world. Irreconcilable as their substance may seem, their origin
is one single poetic voice, the voice of Lorna Dee Cervantes. The
above lines, from "Poem for the Young White Man Who Asked
Me How I, an Intelligent Well-Read Person Could Believe in the
War between Races,"[1] present the two conflicting but central
positions in Cervantes' poetry. The first passage expresses her
desire for an idealized, utopian world, possibly called into being
by the visionary power of poetry. The second counters this view
with a realistic perspective that sees a world fraught with social
problems, a world where social revolution is necessary because
"sharp-shooting goose-steppers" hide in every corner. These two
contradictory attitudes shape Cervantes' poetic sensibility. Given

85

the marked differences between them, one desiring a peaceful harmonious world and the other recognizing a violent polarized world, the reader may anticipate her poems to be expressions of tension between desire and knowledge.

The two perspectives stem from Cervantes' dual identity: she identifies herself primarily as a poet and as a Chicana. In comparison with Villanueva, whose identity as poet oscillates between woman and Chicana, that is, between gender and social identity, Cervantes' identity oscillates between Chicana and poet. Her voice as a poet represents her inner utopian self who desires to believe that social tensions can be reconciled by poetry, and in it Cervantes, a Chicana, speaks primarily as a poet. Her voice as a Chicana corresponds to her outer social self who feels that the world can be changed only by social revolution, and in it Cervantes, a poet, speaks primarily as a Chicana.

The social dimension of "woman" is also present in Cervantes' poetic voice. When the main identity energizing the poem is her Chicana self, as in "Poem for the Young White Man," her woman identity is implicit. When she chooses to emphasize her identity as a woman, as in "Beneath the Shadow of the Freeway" and "Uncle's First Rabbit," she usually does so within the boundaries of a specific Chicano environment.[2] As a female poet, Cervantes is critical of Mexican-Chicano culture, which has traditionally given authority and power to the Latino male; she questions the privileges accorded the male at the expense of the female. This perspective is most evident in the family poems: "Uncle's First Rabbit" and "Beneath the Shadow of the Freeway." Her two social identities, however, are rarely in conflict.

The same coordinates of the triad that characterizes Villanueva's poetic identity—woman, poet, Chicana—also structure Cervantes' poetic identity. In Cervantes' poems, however, the tension among these coordinates is localized at different points of the triad. In reading Cervantes' poetry we must shift our focus from tension between the identities woman and Chicana, which frame Villanueva's work, to tension between the identities Chicana and poet.

Cervantes' solution to the double dilemma of being a woman and a Chicana is to respond primarily as a Chicana, a decision that interferes with her desired utopian vision. When she decides deliberately to suppress her Chicana and female voices and respond as a poet, specific discontinuities interfere to mar the harmony of her poetic vision. Almost all Cervantes' poems express the paradoxical relationship between these dual identities. And although the images of a Chicana poet and a poet-visionary do not merge easily, her poems are dramatic enactments of a desire for integration and harmony between a collective, communal voice and an individual, personal voice.

With few exceptions, among them "Beneath the Shadow of the Freeway," "Refugee Ship," and "Freeway 280,"[3] most of the poems in *Emplumada*, Cervantes' first published collection, appeared there for the first time. She wrote most of these poems while a fellow in poetry at the Fine Arts Work Center in Provincetown, Massachusetts, in 1979–80. As Cervantes came originally from San Jose, California, the Provincetown sojourn gave her the opportunity to meet writers and artists from different cultural backgrounds and literary orientations. In San Jose, for several years before her experience at the Fine Arts Work Center, Cervantes edited, published, and printed *Mango*, a successful small-press journal which published primarily Chicano and Chicana poets. Thus she has had direct literary and cultural experiences with both Anglo and Chicano groups.

In this chapter, I postulate that the two main audiences of her poetry are Anglo and Chicano readers. On the one hand, Cervantes' identity as a Chicana posits a Chicano readership that expects the poet to speak to the issues of social justice and community. As a Chicana she feels an overriding need to respond to the authority of La Raza because she feels that a Chicana should write for and to her own community. She probably developed this concept through her participation in the social movement of the 1960s, which aimed to express the particularities of a Chicano experience. On the other hand, her identity as a poet assumes a readership with the conventional notion that poets are or should be responsible only to their art. In poems such as "In January," "Starfish," and "Moonwalkers," she would seem to be expressing the part of her which, as she confides in "Poem for the Young White Man," does not want to write about political issues and revolution: "I am not a revolutionary. / I don't even like political poems." These two rival sets of reader expectations implied by Cervantes' poems shape and determine her themes and stylistic strategies.

Cervantes' characteristic themes and stylistic strategies come back again and again to the tensions between two worlds: one real, one desired; one violent and divisive, the other peaceful and harmonious. These thematic oppositions generate her two basic poetic modes: (1) a discursive "hard" mode where she examines and evaluates the conflicting attitudes in a series of logical, causative steps; (2) an imagistic "soft" mode that attempts to evoke contemplative and meditative moods. Poems such as "Poem for the Young White Man" and "Visions of Mexico" are discursive because they are spoken by an identifiable Chicana speaker who talks about real social struggle within a historical world. They are dialogic in tone, unfolding in a pattern of statement and counterstatement. Poems such as "Starfish," "In January," and "Shells," which are spoken by a disembodied lyric speaker, rely more on loose associations suggested by concrete images than on logical connectives between ideas. The two modes, discursive and lyrical, are not mutually exclusive; depending upon the individual poem, they intersect and traverse each other, reflecting different gradations of the same poetic voice. This intermixing reinforces the notion of continual conflict between them.

In "Beneath the Shadow of the Freeway," Cervantes' richest and most complex poem, her two poetic modes are mingled. She alludes to herself as a "scribe," a translator and recorder of female experiences. In the analyses that follow I use Cervantes' image of scribe to define her Chicana voice as a translating, or a mediating, voice between her community's experience and a larger audience. "Beneath the Shadow of the Freeway" also contains a variant of her lyrical voice, a self-conscious poetic "I" involved in the act of self-discovery. Cervantes' discursive "I" as scribe stresses the communicative function of language, conducting a struggle between an inner and an outer world. Her "I" as lyric poet emphasizes the expressive function of language, attempting to externalize her inner utopian world where the self may enjoy a harmonious relationship with the natural landscape. Whereas the scribe explains and asserts through propositional statements, the lyric poet presents and describes through images. Of all the poems in *Emplumada*, "Beneath the Shadow of the Freeway" is the most dynamic revelation of the conflict between the two literary modes that characterize Cervantes' poetic universe.

2

The poetry of both Villanueva and Cervantes emerges from an experience of alienation, but, whereas Villanueva assumes aliena-tion and responds to it primarily as a woman in search of her poetic voice, Cervantes makes the experience of alienation the subject of her poems. Two of her discursive poems, "Poem for the Young White Man" and "Visions of Mexico While at a Writing Symposium in Port Townsend, Washington," dramatize the dual conflict between a historical and an utopian vision and between community and poetry. In each poem Cervantes, as scribe, trans-lates the experience of a Chicana's alienation from both history and utopia to a larger audience. Whereas her Chicana speaker explains in the first poem what it means to exist between a Chicano community and a white society, in the second she reflects on her relationship to Mexico and the United States. Cervantes chooses to embody the paradoxical nature of her con-flict between community and poetry in several concrete opposi-tions: Chicano-Anglo, South-North, Mexico–United States, and oral-written.

POEM FOR THE YOUNG WHITE MAN
WHO ASKED ME HOW I, AN INTELLIGENT
WELL-READ PERSON COULD BELIEVE
IN THE WAR BETWEEN RACES

In my land there are no distinctions.
The barbed wire politics of oppression
have been torn down long ago. The only reminder
of past battles, lost or won, is a slight
rutting in the fertile fields.

In my land
people write poems about love,
full of nothing but contented childlike syllables.
Everyone reads Russian short stories and weeps.
There are no boundaries.   *10*
There is no hunger, no
complicated famine or greed.

I am not a revolutionary.
I don't even like political poems.
Do you think I can believe in a war between races?

I can deny it. I can forget about it
when I'm safe,
living on my own continent of harmony
and home, but I am not
there.   20

I believe in revolution
because everywhere the crosses are burning,
sharp-shooting goose-steppers round every corner,
there are snipers in the schools . . .
(I know you don't believe this.
You think this is nothing
but faddish exaggeration. But they
are not shooting at you.)
I'm marked by the color of my skin.
The bullets are discrete and designed to kill slowly.   30
They are aiming at my children.
These are facts.
Let me show you my wounds: my stumbling mind, my
"excuse me" tongue, and this
nagging preoccupation
with the feeling of not being good enough.

These bullets bury deeper than logic.
Racism is not intellectual.
I cannot reason these scars away.

Outside my door   40
there is a real enemy
who hates me.
I am a poet
who yearns to dance on rooftops,
to whisper delicate lines about joy
and the blessings of human understanding.
I try. I go to my land, my tower of words and
bolt the door, but the typewriter doesn't fade out
the sounds of blasting and muffled outrage.
My own days bring me slaps on the face.   50
Every day I am deluged with reminders
that this is not
my land

and this is my land.

I do not believe in the war between races

but in this country
there is war.

In designating a white man (and by extension, the dominant society) as the addressee, the title suggests that the "I"-speaker is different in race and gender from the addressee. This expectation is borne out by lines 29 and 31—"I'm marked by the color of my skin" and "They are aiming at my children"—from which we learn that the speaker is a woman of color. The intelligent, well-read person of whom the white male has asked a question is female and belongs to a racial minority. At the beginning the poem seems to be the response of the woman implied by the title, an assumption reinforced by the possessive adjective "my" in the first line, which must refer back to the first-person pronoun in the title. There is one small problem, however. The title suggests that the "I" believes in the existence of racial conflict. Yet the "I" implicit in the first sentence states, "In my land there are no distinctions"—racial distinctions, that is. The title leads the reader to expect one thing but the poem seems to deliver another.

The speaker of the first two stanzas describes a fairy-tale place, a land where racial tensions, it seems, have been overcome. The only visible sign of any past conflict is a "slight / rutting in the fertile fields." The title encourages the reader to think that the young white man does not believe in racial strife, for if he asks the "intelligent" and "well-read" woman how she can believe in the war between races, it must be because he, an intelligent and well-read man, does not believe in it. For him, intelligence is incompatible with a belief that racial discrimination exists. The content of these two stanzas would seem to point to him as the speaker. Yet the "I" who believes that racial conflict exists is speaking.

The lines opening the third stanza—"I am not a revolutionary. / I don't even like political poems"—are consistent with the views of the first two stanzas which sound more like a fairy tale. The rhetorical question of line 15, "Do you think I can believe in a war between races?" would make perfect sense if the young man were the speaker. But the next phrase, "I can deny it," assures us that he does not speak these words, for why would he deny racial war if he does not believe in it in the first place? The "I" speaking drops her assumed mask in the phrase, "but I am not / there."

This "I" partly identifies with the young white man's land of harmony, for to say "I am not there" implies some knowledge of his land and an admission of having been there. Within the same sentence the "I" shifts from "my own continent of harmony / and home" to a negation of this land. The pronoun "my" reinforces the woman's identification with her interlocutor's fairy-tale land. The shifting intimates that the "I" of "but I am not there" is the same "I" that is supposedly in the white man's land. As soon as the "I" establishes an identification with his land, however, she begins to dissociate herself from it, triggering the retreat from a dreamland into a fragmented world. This is one of Cervantes' favorite stylistic strategies. She describes the dream and establishes her identification with it; she then inserts a conjunction—"but" in this instance—which initiates the shift away from the desired dream toward the reality. She uses the same technique in the poem's final three lines, where the "but" separates racial harmony and racial war.

Stanza 4 puts into motion the antagonist-realist voice that challenges the utopian voice of the earlier stanzas. The "I" now speaks like someone who believes in the war between races. After line 4 the speaker interrupts her narrative with an aside to her interlocutor. The preceding ellipsis may suggest that, although he has listened attentively so far, he now makes a disapproving gesture to indicate that the speaker's discourse about social violence is a cliché or a "faddish exaggeration." The fact that the speaker's statement to him is placed within parentheses heightens the conflict between them. The woman cannot speak to him from her place in this real land in the same way she did from her place in the utopian land of the preceding three stanzas. Her perspective has shifted from inside to outside his land.

She and her "children," that is, her racial community, are marked by ethnic color and bullets are aimed at them. Because the white man is not so marked, the "goose-steppers" do not shoot at him. The woman's words are definite, sharp, and direct: "These are facts." Real, physical violence produces psychological and spiritual "wounds": a "stumbling mind," an "'excuse me' tongue," and the classic feeling of inferiority shared by oppressed peoples. By her "'excuse me' tongue" the speaker means several things, all pointing to the ambiguities of her social position. For one thing, she means the English language, because as a Chicana she sees Spanish as her authentic language. She must use English, however, to express her Chicana self to a white audience that, in most instances, would not understand her if she used her own language. English is her "'excuse me' tongue" because she must use it to apologize for her situation (in the sense of explain and defend). Second, the "'excuse me' tongue" refers to her situation as a woman. She ironically supposes that a woman does not have the right to speak, that to speak is to intrude into the conversation. Third, the phrase also suggests that Cervantes as a poet must use a discursive kind of language to communicate to an audience that has different expectations about the nature of poetic language. She expects her general audience, like the young white man, to disapprove of her direct, factual expression. In any of these meanings the phrase accentuates the speaker's, and by extension Cervantes', subordinate place in society as Chicana, as woman, and as poet.

The question posed in the poem's title implies that a person of intelligence, culture, and literacy should not entertain ideas about racial struggle. Cervantes' response inverts what we might expect to be the roles of rational argumentation and lyrical expression. For example, in the lines, "bullets bury deeper than logic" and "Racism is not intellectual," her discursive, factual argument is guided by the heart's voice rather than by the mind's. The "wounds" she feels are impervious to reasoned discourse that would deny them. The vision of harmony which the young man believes to be reasonable is in her poetic universe the expression of lyrical, counterfactual longing.

The final stanza reiterates the speaker's conflict between desire and knowledge. Associating poetry with the "inside," or the personal and subjective, she desires to write poems that might blot out the angry muffled sounds on the "outside," or the real world. Ironically, to communicate lofty gestures and sublime thoughts, she has to "bolt the door." She seeks isolation with her typewriter in a room away from the world's noise. It is the conventional notion of the poet composing the text alone in an ivory tower ("tower of words"), insulated from direct interaction but ostensibly communicating with everyone. The outside world of action and commitment is associated with sublinguistic phenomena: loud sounds and noises, "muffled outrage." The conflict between poetry and community remains present to the end:

> Every day I am deluged with reminders
> that this is not
> my land
>
> and this is my land.

The deictic "this" is ambiguous. In the poem it has only the immediate context of "land" in line 47—"I go to my land, my tower of words"—to provide a referent. In this sense her land is the metaphorical territory of poetry because she is a poet. Yet it is an illusion to believe that she inhabits only the world of poetic creation because insistent reminders tell her she cannot write solely about sublime thoughts and gestures: "to dance on rooftops" and "to whisper delicate lines about joy." The word "land," however, also means a real country in the context of the poem. Yet even in this sense "land" is ambiguous because it refers to a territory that, though now part of the United States, formerly belonged to Mexico. The young man of the title assumes that he and the speaker are citizens of the same land. She, in contrast, does not share the same sense of certainty about belonging to this country. These lines thus also express the historical dilemma of identifying with a homeland that itself treats Chicanos ambiguously.

The final three lines realistically incorporate the unresolved logical paradox between the visionary ideal ("I do not believe in the war between races") and the material reality ("in this country / there is war"). Her inner utopian "I" wants to believe that poetry can reconcile racial hostilities, but her outer social "I" knows that the battle must be fought in the historical world. It is obvious that Cervantes finds it difficult to compromise on matters of race. The pulls between her lyric "I" and her discursive "I" remain conflictual to the end. On reading "Beneath the Shadow of the Freeway," however, we will see that she finds it easier to compromise on matters of gender. Her scribe voice in "Beneath the Shadow," responding as a woman within the boundaries of her barrio, mediates, or compromises, the two incompatible views about men bequeathed to her by her mother and her grandmother. Her scribe voice in "Poem for the Young White Man" does not mediate; rather it explains the incompatibility between the desire to write the way she thinks a poet is expected to write and the reality that defines her community's relationship with the outside world. Or, to put it another way, Cervantes expresses the dilemma of wanting to be an American poet without compromising her identity with and her loyalties to the Chicano community.

"Visions of Mexico," divided into two parts, shows that Cervantes understands that her identity as a Chicana is defined by

an ambiguous relationship not only to the dominant society in
the United States (the young white man) and to written poetry
(her "tower of words"), but also to Mexico and to an oral poetry.
"Visions of Mexico," in defining the conflict between oral and
written poetry more sharply than does "Poem for the Young
White Man," highlights Cervantes' role as an intermediary between two cultures and two literary traditions.

VISIONS OF MEXICO WHILE
AT A WRITING SYMPOSIUM IN
PORT TOWNSEND, WASHINGTON

Mexico

When I'm that far south, the old words
molt off my skin, the feathers
of all my nervousness.
My own words somersault naturally as my name,
joyous among all those meadows: Michoacan,
Vera Cruz, Tenochtitlán, Oaxaca . . .
Pueblos green on the low hills
where men slap handballs below acres of maiz.
I watch and understand.
My frail body has never packed mud   10
or gathered in the full weight of the harvest.
Alone with the women in the adobe, I watch men,
their taut faces holding in all their youth.
This far south we are governed by the law
of the next whole meal.
We work and watch seabirds elbow their wings
in migratory ways, those mispronouncing gulls
coming south
to refuge or gameland.

I don't want to pretend I know more   20
and can speak all the names. I can't.
My sense of this land can only ripple through my veins
like the chant of an epic corrido.
I come from a long line of eloquent illiterates
whose history reveals what words don't say.
Our anger is our way of speaking,
the gesture is an utterance more pure than word.
We are not animals
but our senses are keen and our reflexes,
accurate punctuation.
All the knifings in a single night, low-voiced
scufflings, sirens, gunnings . . .
We hear them   30
and the poet within us bays.

Washington

I don't belong this far north.
The uncomfortable birds gawk at me.
They hem and haw from their borders in the sky.
I heard them say: Mexico is a stumbling comedy.
A loose-legged Cantinflas woman
acting with Pancho Villa drunkenness.
Last night at the tavern
this was all confirmed
in a painting of a woman: her glowing
silk skin, a halo   10
extending from her golden coiffure
while around her, dark-skinned men with Jap slant eyes
were drooling in a caricature of machismo.
Below it, at the bar, two Chicanas
hung at their beers. They had painted black
birds that dipped beneath their eyelids.
They were still as foam while the men
fiddled with their asses, absently;
the bubbles of their teased hair snapped
open in the forced wind of the beating fan.   20

there are songs in my head I could sing you
songs that could drone away
all the Mariachi bands you thought you ever heard
songs that could tell you what I know
or have learned from my people
but for that   I need words
simple black nymphs between white sheets of paper
obedient words   obligatory words   words I steal
in the dark when no one can hear me.

as pain sends seabirds south from the cold   30
I come north
to gather my feathers
for quills

The major structural device of this poem is the theme of
migration, and the central image is the migrating bird that is
always in transit between one home and another. The theme of
migration has strong implications for a Mexican-Chicano community whose history has been shaped by patterns of migration,
both internal (within Mexico and within the United States) and
external (between Mexico and the United States). Like the migrating bird, the speaker hovers between two homelands, Mexico and
the state of Washington, identifying with each place but also

alienated from each. In another poem entitled "Como lo siento," the speaker, witnessing the image of a crow spiraling and drifting, reflects: "I thought of the circle / my own life made, and how / at heart I'm a hoverer." The speaker in "Visions" hovers between two extreme points of the circle in the migratory cycle, desiring to find the harmonizing midpoint. The image of the hovering bird, like the image of scribe, connotes transition, uncertainty, and suspension between one home and another. Cervantes' real homeland, California, is the geographical midpoint between the two extremes of Mexico and Washington. Again in this poem, as in "Poem for the Young White Man," the "I" fluctuates between the desire for a utopian land and the knowledge of a real land of conflict and struggle.

Although nothing explicitly indicates that the speaker in "Visions" is a woman, the reader infers that the speaker is the female persona of Lorna Cervantes. At a writing symposium in Washington State, she looks south, thinking about her relationship to Mexico. The words of the first stanza correspond to her lyrical, inner "I" which desires to see Mexico as more utopian than it is. She immediately sees herself in a harmonious relationship with Mexico, implicitly comparing herself with birds and reptiles that shed their feathers and skins for new growth. These images of reptiles, birds, and feathers suggest Quetzalcoatl, the plumed serpent-god of pre-Columbian Mexico, an association reinforced by three of the names defining the historical landscape. Michoacan, Oaxaca, and Tenochtitlán, the Aztec name for Mexico City, are specific sites of the pre-Columbian empire. The pre-Columbian association is further buttressed by the image of men playing handball, recalling the ancient ball courts of an indigenous era.

When the speaker says in the opening lines, "old words / molt off my skin, the feathers / of all my nervousness," the "old words" represent the English language, which she imagines herself casting off as naturally as reptiles and birds shed their skins and feathers. They give way to her "own words" which "somersault" as effortlessly as her name. Since her name is Spanish, we assume she sees herself speaking Spanish, pronouncing the pre-Columbian names with ease. The English language is like a hard exterior, a "shell," to use one of Cervantes' favorite images, which covers the soft part underneath, her own language, Spanish. In her vision of Mexico her nervousness about speaking Spanish leaves her, as she is able to speak it gracefully when she is that far south.

The image of speaking Spanish with grace and facility clashes with the one Cervantes gives us in "Oaxaca, 1974" and in "Refugee Ship," two poems in which she wrestles with that very issue. In the former poem she says, "My name hangs about me like a loose tooth," and in the latter, "I'm orphaned from my Spanish name. / The words are foreign, stumbling on my tongue." In these two poems Cervantes presents a more realistic portrait of her relationship with Mexico in the speaking and understanding of Spanish. In "Refugee Ship," she confides, "Mama raised me without language," meaning her mother chose to teach her English (which she views as the absence of language) but not Spanish (the presence of language).

In "Visions of Mexico," then, Cervantes' vision of herself speaking Spanish gracefully has an ironic dimension. The irony is compounded when we note that not only does she speak Spanish with facility, but she also pronounces the indigenous names with ease. The presence of the Spanish name, Veracruz,[4] among other pre-Columbian names contributes to her ambiguous relationship as a Chicana to Mexico. Veracruz is a city-port founded by the Spaniards. Cervantes' speaking Spanish and yet pronouncing the pre-Columbian names with grace recalls ironically at once both conqueror and conquered. Although, for the Chicano, the Spanish language is the language of an oppressed group in relation to United States history, in relation to Mexican history it represents the language of the oppressor.

Mexico is presented as an agrarian society, with meadows, green pueblos, acres of *maíz*, and adobe homes. Proof that Cervantes romanticizes Mexico is found in the lines following line 9: "I watch and understand." Her speaker is too frail to perform the heavy physical labor of the village. She remains inside the adobe house with the village women, watching the men doing the harvesting and packing mud. From the line, "Alone with the women in the adobe," the reader may infer that the native women are also frail. One of Cervantes' blind spots in these lines is that she overlooks the sexual inequalities in this society. Her speaker appears content to sit inside with the women watching the men. This portrayal of the village women suggests a sexual inequality which would surely trouble Cervantes in her own context. In

"Crow," for example, she says that the women of her community taught her self-reliance:

> Before men came they whispered,
> *Know good polished oak.*
> *Learn hammer and Phillips*
> *Learn socket and rivet.*

In a more realistic vision of a rural Mexico, the village women would be performing hard physical labor along with the men.[5]

A second blind spot is that her speaker's attitude rationalizes the hard, physical aspects of primitive life. Even though she perceives the men with "taut faces" and recognizes that life in this village means a severely limited existence ("we are governed by the law / of the next whole meal"), she refrains from taking issue, directly or indirectly, with a social structure implied by inequalities such as poverty. Again, Cervantes' romanticized view of a rural existence is incompatible with her view of an urban existence in, say, "Cannery Town in August," where the situation, tone, and images convey an awareness of hard, physical struggle for survival.[6]

The speaker's relationship to Mexican history and culture is clarified by the word *corrido* in line 23. The *corrido*, an oral ballad, a pristine spoken form, was cultivated in the late nineteenth century by Mexican communities with limited access to the printed word for purposes of disseminating information about events that were important to preserving their history.[7] The *corrido* as a literary form has characterized the experiences of the Mexican population in the Southwest, especially along the United States–Mexican border. It usually tells a story that is either unarticulated or presented in negative form by traditional United States history.[8] Originating as a spoken attempt to capture the events and actions of a community, it remains an oral form for a long time before it is put into print. As a literary form it is discursive and narrative rather than lyrical and suggestive.

Like any Chicana who writes, Cervantes is alienated from the *corrido*, with its gestural elements and other aspects, such as acoustic and sound qualities, which cannot be expressed by written discourse. The speaker recognizes her alienation from the oral world of her ancestors ("My sense of this land can only ripple through my veins / like the chant of an epic corrido") at the same time that she accepts her connection with it ("I come from a long line of eloquent illiterates"). Cervantes, like the historical scribe, is in a middle position between an identification with and an estrangement from an oral world. Because she sees herself as a scribe, her image as poet is closer to a *corridista* (someone who recites or sings the *corrido*) whose primary intent is to translate experiences to an audience, than it is to a poet who creates meaning. Like the *corridista*, she too is more a vehicle for the experiences of others than a composer-creator of personal experience.

Because of the proximity of the sentence, "I come from a long line of eloquent illiterates," to the word *corrido*, the eloquent illiterates are her own Mexican-Chicano ancestors who depended upon gestures, actions, and the spoken word to communicate their history. The words "eloquent illiterates" also echo the pre-Columbian references in the first stanza and hence include, though more remotely, the rich culture of an indigenous Mexican population which the Spanish conquerors reduced to a mute gesture. Cervantes' image of herself as a scribe is appropriate here too: as a scribe she extracts texts from different historical eras—both ancient and modern—and makes them part of contemporary culture.

Stanza 2 contains a mixing of voices from two planes of expression: language (written and spoken) and paralinguistic forms of communication (gestures, emotions, reflexes). The chant and the epic *corrido*, primarily spoken and sung forms, are juxtaposed with the poet-speaker's own written form, the poem itself. The mixing of linguistic with paralinguistic forms occurs specifically in the line, "the gesture is an utterance more pure than word." Gestures are precisely the paralinguistic signs of communication which escape written discourse. They are not usually designated as utterances, a classification reserved for denoting spoken and, less commonly, written discourse. Yet in this line the verb "is" syntactically links "gesture" with "utterance," with the comparative "more pure" separating them. The speaker's reference to "reflexes," or gestures, as "accurate punctuation" is another example of mixing. Punctuation is a specific convention of printed language. Yet the speaker equates this feature of writing with precisely those expressions, "reflexes," which escape it. As in "Poem for the Young White Man," Cervantes here links the world of her community with loud, violent noises and sounds: "All the knifings in a single night, low-voiced / scufflings, sirens, gunnings." On hearing these noises the poet, a person of words, "bays" in empathy with the community.

The loud noises suggest an urban setting. The disjuncture between the urban image and the rural images of stanza 1 accentuates the poem's theme of migration from a rural to an urban context. The interplay of the two images also suggests an ambiguous quality in the poet's relationship with her community. It invites comparison with the scribe who in a medieval context marked a transitional moment in history when European society moved from an oral to a print culture.[9] In an analogous way the disjuncture between rural and urban suggests a transitional moment in the modern history of Chicanos, as they move from a culture that has used oral forms of expression in a modern context—and still does, to some extent—to a culture that begins to express itself in literary forms (novels, poems, short stories).

The second part of "Visions of Mexico" shifts to the Washington scene and continues the theme of migration. In the south, migrating seabirds from the north reminded her of "mispronouncing gulls / coming south / to refuge or gameland." The image of "mispronouncing gulls" is probably a reference to American tourists who descend upon Mexico, mispronouncing Spanish as they move toward their vacation resorts, seeking "refuge" and "gameland" from their tax obligations. The speaker is like the migrating bird who leaves the warm southern climate to come north to build its nest. More inclined toward the south, however, she feels herself in alien territory among the "uncomfortable birds" of the north ("I don't belong this far north") where nothing appears natural. She is a strange bird in a strange land whose presence makes the other inhabitants uncomfortable. They show their discomfort by gawking and by hemming and hawing at her. She is neither seen nor heard by them.

In the north she hears only negative depictions of Mexico: "a stumbling comedy. / A loose-legged Cantinflas woman / acting with Pancho Villa drunkenness." The reference to the characters of Cantinflas and Pancho Villa suggests that Mexico is known through the images reflected in the media, a technological extension of print culture. The speaker offers a specific example as proof: a painting portraying Mexico as a blond-haired woman with dark-skinned men "drooling" after her.

The penultimate stanza states the poem's central paradox. To erase the sounds of the touristic mariachi bands, the speaker wants to sing authentic songs about her people, who knew only the oral word, to an audience that relates only to words on the page, the "you" in the first line of this stanza. This "you" includes all those, Chicanos as well as Anglos, who do not know her ancestors' history as she would like them to know it. The paradox is that in order to sing those songs she needs "words / simple black nymphs between white sheets of paper." The sexual innuendos in the references to "nymphs" and "sheets" reinforce the theme of a desire to give birth to the poet's songs. Although the content here necessitates the presence of "simple" and "black" nymphs, nymphs are traditionally white and Greek. As such they echo a schema that belongs to the symbolist tradition of Anglo-American modern poetry, a tradition that, according to Charles Altieri, contemporary poets have attempted to challenge.[10] And although the thrust of Cervantes' poetry shares in this attempt to find an alternative to the symbolist model that valorized the mythological modes of a Judeo-Christian order, the presence of these mythical nature goddesses in this poem only deepens the implication of a Chicana poet in two literary traditions: an oral, Mexican-Chicano tradition and a written, Anglo-American tradition.

As mediator between an oral people and an audience that reads, this poet steals "words . . . / in the dark" when no one hears her. The synesthesia of mixing visual and auditory modalities heightens the paradoxical relationship between oral and written. The implication of her stealing words is that these words are not hers. She furtively steals the words of others to employ them in a way they are not employed by those who own the words. To obtain these words she comes north, "to gather my feathers / for quills." Whereas birds travel south to escape the pain of cold, she comes north toward the pain. In order to write, she must accept the pain of reality associated with the north rather than the nostalgia of romance associated with the south because the north is a print culture. She comes north to gather her "feathers" to build her nest—words she needs to write poems. The repetition of "songs" in lines 21–24 and of "words" in lines 26–28 stresses the urgency the speaker feels about fulfilling her objectives as a mediator between an oral people and a reading audience. Small but important deviations in the writing of these lines create rhetorical effects of urgency and immediacy: multilevel, run-on

sentences, the absence of grammatical punctuation, and spacing
to separate syntactic units:

> but for that   I need words
> simple black nymphs between white sheets of paper
> obedient words   obligatory words   words I steal
> in the dark when no one can hear me.

The final stanza once again echoes a pre-Columbian civilization. Feathers, plumage, and quill are images relating to the
theme of writing in Cervantes' poetry. The name of the volume, *Emplumada*, is a feminine adjective meaning "feathered in
plumage." The word *pluma* in Spanish means "pen." Because
of its associations with birds and flight, *emplumada* connotes
the image of someone who sees herself singing beautiful songs
with graceful ease. The image of feathers in *Emplumada*, as in
"Visions," is also tied to Quetzalcoatl, a pre-Columbian god who
represented the union of *quetzal* or "bird" (feathers) and *coatl* or
"snake" (earth), a union joining flight and land. The unifying of
two extremes in the mythic bird suggests that Cervantes wants
to resolve tensions between poetry and community, oral and
written, high and low, north and south. "Beneath the Shadow of
the Freeway" offers the geographical midpoint of California between the two poles of north and south, which circumscribe
Cervantes' cultural identities.

3

Cervantes' lyric poems express a desire to be free from the pressures of social commitment and responsibility. Spoken by disembodied lyric speakers, they reveal her need to speak in a voice
that deliberately tries to avoid claiming a social consciousness.
As such they are less dependent than the discursive poems upon
a familiarity with the subtleties and innuendos of the interrelationships among Mexican, Chicano, and Anglo cultures. In
contrast with the dialogic structure of the discursive poems in
which the speaker explores both sides of an issue, the lyric poems
have a monologic structure in which a speaker attempts to exter-

nalize inner experiences. They are attempts either to capture specific scenes in the natural landscape, as are "In January" and "Starfish," or to express a personal and private philosophy, as is "Shells." They require readers who, of unspecified ethnic background or gender identification, can make connections between the images and the outside world.

The associations evoked by Cervantes' images are not radical leaps. Cervantes does not take the "long floating leap" advocated by the American contemporary poet Robert Bly in his essay, "Looking for Dragon Smoke."[11] Cervantes' images remain anchored in the concrete world, directed outward toward the historical landscape instead of inward toward an unconscious psychological landscape. They do not represent surreal leaps into the unconscious by which the poet attempts to make visible the latent and dormant aspects of human experience.

Although Cervantes relies on the poetic image to suggest contemplative and meditative moods in these poems, she never decomposes, never fragments or shatters, the poetic surface; words are almost always organized into complete sentences or into phrasings with rhetorical connectives and grammatical punctuation.[12] Her most radical deviations include an "I" in the act of self-discovery, an absence of punctuation, and paratactic phrasing—all elements that appear in her discursive as well as in her lyrical poems. An analysis of three lyric poems, "In January," "Starfish," and "Shells," shows that even when Cervantes speaks in her lyric voice, she does not achieve a vision of harmony and integration. Image patterns or gradations in tone intrude to suggest futility, sadness, and death. With the exception of "Beneath the Shadow of the Freeway," Cervantes writes no celebratory poems—only poems that desire celebration.

IN JANUARY

That old man at the corner
keeps casting his rod.
What can he possibly snag
in this invisible season?
He reels it in.
He is all smile and bulging pockets.
His gray eyes are glazed
with the iridescence of his age.
His cheeks hold the last ash.
And though his daughter

is bringing him pillows and tea
and the handsome son-in-law
bends the line, a slow thing
stirs in the shadow of the bougainvillea.

This poem is a series of concrete images. All the sentences work well syntactically, some of them specifying actions and others describing the principal character, the old man. The narrator is a detached observer who speaks in the present tense about a succession of events taking place in the natural landscape. There is a slight ambiguity about the poem's pragmatic situation. Where are we and how do we know? Words and phrases, such as "casting his rod," "snag," and "reels it in," suggest the activity of fishing, which is usually associated with the country, near a lake or by a seashore. The phrase in line 1, "at the corner," seems to be a contradiction because it suggests an urban context: "at the corner" of a street or a house. The phrase, however, does not totally eliminate the possibility of a country setting because it could refer to the corner of a pier, placing the old man closer to a body of water than to a city street. As the poem continues, the first syllable of the word "season" momentarily suggests that the old man is at sea, but the suggestion is immediately negated by the second syllable, *son*. The image of the daughter "bringing him pillows and tea" seemingly puts the old man in his garden and not at the seashore. The image of "invisible season" also suggests an urban context, where the seasons are less well defined than in a rural setting. We may assume, then, that the old man entertains a fantasy that he is actually fishing. The daughter and the handsome son-in-law who "bends the line" also participate in the old man's world of make-believe.

The poem's images establish a pattern of rising hope and skeptical realism. A pattern embracing romance and reality also characterizes the discursive poems, but there the pattern is established more by the force of statement and assertion than by the relation among images, as is true here. The old man keeps casting his rod, an action suggesting hope, for he does it again and again. The next sentence reveals the narrator's skepticism about the old man's success in this "invisible season." The images describing the old man's demeanor, "all smile and bulging pockets," soften the skepticism. The next image is one of old age transforming the old man's dismal ("gray") eyes, giving them an iridescent quality, a transformation enacting the conflict between gloom and hope.

The conflict is decided in favor of gloom, possibly death: "His cheeks hold the last ash."

The grammatical syntax of the final sentence suspends and compresses the conflict between the two attitudes of romance and reality. It communicates a sense of deficiency in the old man's world of fantasy and make-believe. In spite of his family's supportive actions ("And though . . ."), something else ("a slow thing . . .") is happening. The final image, "a slow thing / stirs in the shadow of the bougainvillea," evokes mystery and ominous threat. This obscure image of a slow thing stirring echoes, albeit faintly, the mood and tone of Yeats's "The Second Coming":

> somewhere in sands of the desert
> A shape with lion body and the head of a man,
> A gaze blank and pitiless as the sun,
> Is moving its slow thighs . . .

Yeats's images, in keeping with the tone of doom in his poem, are far more exaggerated and overtly sinister than are Cervantes'. Yeats is foretelling the overthrow of an entire civilization. Cervantes' mysterious portent, however, may be said to be all the more enigmatic because it comes in the enclosed space of the old man's home and garden, amid the apparently delicate and beautiful bougainvillea.

The final sentence also breaks with the earlier precise images to suggest an unnameable abstract presence ("thing") stirring beneath the surface of life. Its length contrasts sharply with the one- and two-line sentences preceding it, a feature that further emphasizes the rupture. The longer sentence slows the pace and heightens the significance of the final image, contrasting the gloom of "shadow" with the iridescent colors of "bougainvillea." The poem's implicit terminal point is loss and futility.

"In January" represents the traditional family in its three characters. The daughter and the son-in-law suggest the potential to continue the family line through the institution of marriage. Some biographical detail about Cervantes will enrich our understanding of this poem. Like Villanueva, Cervantes comes from a father-absent family in which three generations of women play the dominant role. The narrator of "In January" reflects Cervantes' distrust of the traditional family as utopia. The implication is that the family ought to be sufficient, but the "slow thing" stirring, interrupting and ruining the perfect image, intimates otherwise.

In "Starfish" Cervantes is seeking a lyric moment that can offer an escape from the social world. The poem describes the speaker's encounter with nature on the beach: it frames, isolates, and centers on a very ordinary object, the starfish.

STARFISH

They were lovely in the quartz and jasper sand
As if they had created terrariums with their bodies
On purpose; adding sprigs of seaweed, seashells,
White feathers, eel bones, miniature
Mussels, a fish jaw. Hundreds; no—
Thousands of baby stars. We touched them,
Surprised to find them soft, pliant, almost
Living in their attitudes. We would dry them, arrange them,
Form seascapes, geodesics . . . We gathered what we could
In the approaching darkness. Then we left hundreds of
Thousands of flawless five-fingered specimens sprawled
Along the beach as far as we could see, all massed
Together: little martyrs, soldiers, artless suicides
In lifelong liberation from the sea. So many
Splayed hands, the tide shoveled in.

The hardness of minerals ("quartz" and "jasper") is mixed with the softness of "sand." The usually colorless and transparent quartz is juxtaposed with the opaque and colorful jasper. The details emphasize nouns rather than verbs: "seaweed, seashells, / White feathers, eel bones, miniature / Mussels, a fish jaw." The images of eel bones and fish jaw, connoting dismemberment and death, mar the harmony suggested by "seaweed, seashells / White feathers . . . miniature / Mussels." Lines 5 and 6 dramatize the process of the narrator's consciousness, catching the immediacy of the moment: "Hundreds; no— / Thousands of baby stars." The image of baby stars captures an inversion of high and low, heaven and earth, where the sand becomes a reflecting pool of the stars in the sky.

The next six lines establish a linear structure of consecutive events: "We touched them"; "We would dry them"; "We gathered"; "Then we left hundreds of / Thousands." The speaker and her companions leave the vision of the beach to return to the social world. The images in the final three lines suggest that the

starfish are the casualties of war: "little martyrs, soldiers, artless
suicides / In lifelong liberation from the sea. So many / splayed
hands." The metonymy of the starfish as "splayed hands"
forebodes disintegration and disharmony instead of the peace
and illumination that would more likely accompany a lyrical
moment. Like the image of the family in "In January," the encounter with nature in "Starfish" is also insufficient as a transcending force. If anything, the last lines of "Starfish" convey a
feeling that relates to Cervantes' wish of liberation for her people.

SHELLS

I string shells
put an order
to my life

I find in shells
the way I live
everything I touch

is fragile
but full of color
or brine

I can't
hold back
from touching

§

stranger
not my husband
you offer

seabirds
cleft surf
the sun

ripping apart
the fog-strewn
shoreline

§

I am young
balloon-mad
the child in me

scatters down the coast
off the pebbled beach
of Point Reyes

that was another time
I bordered my pale life
with the colors

of hallucinogens
every pebble
was a wonder

I could name
only by color
jade   vermilion

sandstone   buff
or the inexplicable
azure glass

I was alone
gathering
the polished stones

I still hold
dear—for me now
every joy

measures itself
against the brilliance
of that time

§

you said
you suffered
a sheltered life

I want to scratch
that envy
from your voice

I take refuge
in the fact
that every

pleasure
I've worked myself
like the fireplace

my grandmother built
still standing
all these years

every stone
set furiously
in place

§

I dust pebbles
turn them
to sheen

what I want
is an unnamed
thing

when you have gone
I wonder at the way
I let you go

without touching
you, wonder
at seagulls, the

danger in their willful
lines—for them
life is nothing

but picking
the coast clean
all they love

is a flicker of bread
or the opening
of another hand

"Shells" has a lighter tone, a more compressed form, than the
two preceding poems, partly owing to its short stanzas and lines.
In the twenty-nine three-line stanzas the three- or four-syllable
line predominates, with the longest line containing seven syllables. A second reason for the lighter, more compact tone is the
absence of punctuation and of explicit connectives. The only
mark of punctuation is the dash, which is used twice to stress
fluidity and rapid shifts in thought. The absence of punctuation
makes "Shells" stand out among the poems in *Emplumada*. Only

one other poem, "Lots: II," the last two stanzas of "Visions of Mexico," and one section of "Beneath the Shadow" are totally without punctuation. The sections in "Shells" are separated not by numbers or subtitles, as in other poems, but by the less conspicuous marking of §, a third feature contributing to the poem's lighter quality. Yet a fourth feature is the linking of isolated images by juxtaposition rather than by grammatical connectives, as in stanzas 5 and 6 of section 3:

> jade   vermilion
>
> sandstone   buff

Even though punctuation and connectives are missing, the reader is clear on rhetorical pauses, which occur at different points in a stanza. Whereas the thought in some sentences is suspended by enjambment, in others it clearly stops at the end of a stanza. For example, the clause ending stanza 2 in section 1, "everything I touch," is left suspended, to be completed in the following stanza with "is fragile"; however, the phrase "of Point Reyes," the third line of stanza 2 in section 3, terminates the thought. Sometimes the pause occurs in mid stanza, as in stanza 2 of section 1: "I find in shells / the way I live."

A second feature differentiating this poem from "In January" and "Starfish" is that "Shells" presents more information about the narrator's personal background and history, making her more of a subject than are the narrators of the other two poems. Although this poem does not overtly express any social content that is of specific interest to women as women, we know for certain that the speaker is a woman, from "stranger / not my husband." We receive a sense of her life in the past as opposed to the present moment. The loose linear structure opens in the present, makes a rapid shift to the past ("I am young," section 3, stanza 1), and then returns once again to present time ("for me now," stanza 8, section 3). Although the speaker withholds direct comment, we feel her presence, saying just enough to let us know how she feels about her life. We also feel the presence of her interlocutor, the "you," who is probably an intimate friend since he confides to her that he regrets his "sheltered life" (stanzas 1 and 2, section 4).

As the speaker strings shells, putting an order to her life, the reader can piece together a meaning for the poem by associating its images. "Shells" also offers more opportunity than does "In

January" or "Starfish" for seeing intertextual relations with some of Cervantes' other poems. Hence what may appear casual and momentary in this poem yields significance when its images are related to similar images in other poems, especially in "Beneath the Shadow of the Freeway."

Although Cervantes' maternal sources are more clearly seen in "Beneath the Shadow of the Freeway," they are also present by implication in this poem. "Shells" understandably echoes the poet's mother and grandmother when the speaker expresses her philosophy toward life, a philosophy that evolves from the interplay between the divergent views of the two women. Whereas "Beneath the Shadow" enacts their conflict within the speaker, "Shells" only suggests their presence, presupposing the reader's knowledge of certain image patterns and expressions.

The image of dusting pebbles and turning them to sheen (section 5, stanza 1) succinctly expresses the speaker's philosophy. Essentially she transforms negatives into positives: dullness into luster. The image of the shell is emblematic of the two opposing textures she wants to blend together: the hard exterior and the soft interior. Stanzas 2 and 3 of section 1 mix sensations of softness ("everything I touch / is fragile") with the hardness of "brine," an image that suggests the salty sea, hence bitterness. The interplay of the fragile with the hard is an image that recurs in the fragile softness of the grandmother and the hard bitterness of the mother in "Beneath the Shadow."

The narrator mentions the grandmother explicitly in section 4. The references to the "fireplace," to building, and to "seagulls" (section 5) are also significant images surrounding the figure of the grandmother in "Beneath the Shadow." The image of the fireplace creates a tension between soft and hard or between the pleasure and the labor the speaker is alluding to in section 4 of "Shells." From what she says to her interlocutor in the first four stanzas, we may infer that he envies the quality of her life: while he claims he has "suffered / a sheltered life," he assumes hers is adventurous and full of romance. She assures him that underneath the appearance lies hard, furious work. She, like her grandmother, has toiled for her pleasures. The harmonious composition of the fireplace once it is built ("every stone . . . in place") is deceiving, giving the impression of ease, but the achievement of this harmony is the result of strenuous labor ("furiously").

The seabirds are an ambivalent image for the speaker. As we

read "Beneath the Shadow," and even "Uncle's First Rabbit," we shall understand the connection of the seabirds to the grandmother's life and their implications for the speaker. The speaker admires the trust and confidence the seagulls demonstrate in approaching humans for food. At the same time she knows that "for them / life is nothing / but picking / the coast clean / all they love / is a flicker of bread / or the opening / of another hand" (section 5, stanzas 5–7). In going after whoever or whatever offers them security, seagulls are scavengers of human garbage. They suggest the soft grandmother who found a false security at the cost of living with a violent man for twenty-five years. The seagulls represent a dangerous temptation ("the / danger in their willful / lines") to the speaker-poet.

"Shells" gives some indications that the stranger is to be linked with the false security of seagulls. In section 2 he offers "seabirds / cleft surf / the sun / ripping apart / the fog-strewn / shoreline." The speaker then recalls her experiences on the northern California shoreline at Point Reyes, likening them to touchstones by which she measures her joys in the present. In the final section the repetition of the word "wonder" linked with the stranger and with the seagulls suggests that the stranger too offers a false security. The speaker rejects the stranger, recognizing that her life is a process of self-invention, relying on her own experiences, past and present. The poem ends on a note of quiet restlessness that keeps alive her desire for the "unnamed / thing."

4

In this section I return to Cervantes' discursive voice by way of her family poems, "Uncle's First Rabbit" and "Beneath the Shadow of the Freeway." I classify these poems as discursive because they treat the theme of social conflict. In contrast with "Poem for the Young White Man" and "Visions of Mexico," which deal with social struggle from the perspective of ethnicity, these two poems deal with it from the perspective of gender. By addressing the subject of male-female tensions, they reveal Cervantes' identity as a woman. As noted earlier, however, Cervantes' identity as woman is inextricably tied to her identity as

Chicana. Her response in these poems is specifically grounded in the setting of Chicano culture.

"UNCLE'S FIRST RABBIT"

Based on specific events, "Uncle's First Rabbit" contains elements of narrative. It is heavily descriptive, attempting to explain how a specific phenomenon such as violence becomes interiorized within a male psyche.

UNCLE'S FIRST RABBIT

He was a good boy
making his way through
the Santa Barbara pines,
sighting the blast of fluff
as he leveled the rifle,
and the terrible singing began.
He was ten years old,
hunting my grandpa's supper.
He had dreamed of running,
shouldering the rifle to town,   10
selling it, and taking the next
train out.
       Fifty years
have passed and he still hears
that rabbit "just like a baby."
He remembers how the rabbit
stopped keening under the butt
of his rifle, how he brought
it home with tears streaming
down his blood soaked jacket.   20
"That bastard. That bastard."
He cried all night and the week
after, remembering that voice
like his dead baby sister's,
remembering his father's drunken
kicking that had pushed her
into birth. She had a voice
like that, growing faint
at its end; his mother rocking,
softly, keening. He dreamed   30
of running, running
the bastard out of his life.
He would forget them, run down

the hill, leave his mother's
silent waters, and the sounds
of beating night after night.
  When war came,
he took the man's vow. He was
finally leaving and taking
the bastard's last bloodline   *40*
with him. At war's end, he could
still hear her, her soft
body stiffening under water
like a shark's. The color
of the water, darkening, soaking,
as he clung to what was left
of a ship's gun. Ten long hours
off the coast of Okinawa, he sang
so he wouldn't hear them.
He pounded their voices out   *50*
of his head, and awakened
to find himself slugging the bloodied
face of his wife.
    Fifty years
have passed and he has not run
the way he dreamed. The Paradise
pines shadow the bleak hills
to his home. His hunting hounds,
dead now. His father, long dead.
His wife, dying, hacking in the bed   *60*
she has not let him enter for the last
thirty years. He stands looking,
he mouths the words, "Die you bitch.
I'll live to watch you die." He turns,
entering their moss-soft livingroom.
He watches out the picture window
and remembers running: how he'll
take the new pickup to town, sell it,
and get the next train out.

  "Uncle's First Rabbit" is probably Cervantes' most despairing
poem. As in "Visions of Mexico," nothing directly indicates a
female speaker, but I assume that the narrating consciousness is
the persona of Lorna Cervantes. In the poem Cervantes reflects
on the beginnings of female suffering in her family. The focus is
on "mother's brother,"[13] who is often the father substitute in a
matriarchy. The tone of the poem, spoken by a narrator to an
unidentified auditor, is reflective and meditative. Although this
poem represents Cervantes' only attempt to penetrate a male
consciousness, she does not directly assume a male voice; that

is, she does not make a statement tied to an "I"-narrator. A somewhat detached speaker using mainly the third-person pronoun, "he," recounts an important event in her uncle's life when he was ten years old.

We learn that "he" is the speaker's uncle in line 8 when the niece changes from third to first person, saying "my grandpa's supper" instead of "his father's supper." This is the only place in the poem where she changes person, a shift that corresponds to the fluctuating "I" that we have observed in "Poem for the Young White Man" as well as in "Visions of Mexico," and that also appears in "Beneath the Shadow." The shifting reveals ambiguities, at levels of both content and form, about where the "I" wants to position itself: inside or outside the discourse; inside or outside dominant society.

In the story, the uncle as a young boy must fulfill his father's command to hunt for the family supper. The family has to survive and the boy reluctantly obeys his father's command. To obtain the food he shoots a rabbit (ll. 4–5), the poem's central image. The poem enacts once again the conflict between the "soft" and the "hard" seen in other poems. Here it is embodied in the tension between the rabbit (the soft natural object) and the rifle (the hard cultural artifact). Nature is a mirror for events in the world, but instead of the harmonious relationship between the natural and human worlds which the grandmother's attitude celebrates in "Beneath the Shadow," this poem reflects an antagonistic tension between them.

"Uncle's First Rabbit" assumes a mode of reading in which the shooting of the rabbit is seen as an iconic image for a prior and more tragic event in the uncle's family. The act of shooting, which the uncle associates with the female, triggers in his mind the image of his drunk father beating his mother, who was pregnant. The brutal beating caused the premature birth of a baby girl who died soon after. The poem makes clear that the newborn child was the uncle's baby sister. The brutality of man against woman is therefore the original experience witnessed by the uncle, and the rabbit "keening" under the rifle's butt is a copy, an afterimage of that experience.

The conflict in the natural world reflects the deeper conflicts in the human environment. The sounds made by the dying rabbit are linked in the uncle's mind with the cries of his dead baby sister: "She [baby sister] had a voice / like that [the rabbit's], growing faint / at its end." The shooting of the rabbit initiates for the uncle the "terrible singing," a metaphor for the painful experience of watching his father beat his mother. As long as he lives, the uncle cannot forget the "terrible singing." He dreams of running to escape his father's beating of his mother: "He would forget them, run down / the hill, leave his mother's / silent waters, and the sounds / of beating night after night." The uncle transfers his death wish for his father to himself. He enlists in the armed services: "When war came, / he took the man's vow" to destroy "the bastard's last bloodline." No matter where he goes or what he does, he is always haunted by the "terrible singing." At the end of the war he still connects the image of the suffering rabbit with his dead baby sister: "At war's end, he could / still hear her, her soft / body stiffening under water / like a shark's."

Although "Uncle's First Rabbit" is a narrative poem, it differs from the two examples of discursive poems analyzed earlier in this chapter. It is especially striking for its technique of compression and condensation. At least three levels of experience are mingled indistinguishably within the uncle's mind: shooting the rabbit, his father's kicking his mother, and the dead sharks he probably saw in his war experiences at sea after the boats had been torpedoed, "as he clung to what was left / of a ship's gun." The compression is expressed graphically in the ambiguous lines, "her soft / body stiffening under water / like a shark's." The image of the rabbit and the baby sister are condensed into one, the "soft body" in the ocean. The image of water also refers back to his mother's "silent waters," or the embryonic fluid of the placenta. The sensation and the sight of the stiffening shark also merge with the images of the dead rabbit and the baby girl.

The presentation of man beating woman is circular: how things were, how things are, and how things will be in the future are all the same. When the uncle returns from the war he continues the same activity: he "awakened / to find himself slugging the bloodied / face of his wife." Unable to understand, much less transform, the voices singing in his head, he breaks out of the torment by "slugging" his wife. His tragic song—a far cry from a melodious, creative enterprise—is the beating he inflicts on his wife. In "Uncle's First Rabbit" the protagonist achieves no integration. The poem ends on a note of realistic rupture: after fifty years of wishing to run away, he keeps dreaming only of taking "the next train out."

A striking feature is the cluster of noises, sounds, and voices. The alliterative repetition of numerous participials—a total of eight in stanza 1 ("making," "sighting," "singing," "hunting," "running," "shouldering," "selling," "taking")—creates a haunting effect that lingers throughout the poem, an effect reinforcing especially the violent physical actions of beating, slugging, and kicking. Sounds are linked to the victims: the rabbit, the dead baby girl, the uncle's mother, and his wife. The rabbit's keening is referred to as a "voice." It is associated with the mother ("his mother rocking, / softly, keening") and with the cries of the dead baby sister (ll. 23–24). Ironically, the mother and the wife— women with the ability to articulate words—make noises: the mother keens and the wife hacks in bed. The uncle pounds the feminine voices "out of his head." These voices are not human voices but sublinguistic forms of noise. In contrast, the uncle articulates words: "he took the man's vow." He has the only lines of dialogue in the poem, though his words are probably mumbled more to himself than to the person for whom they are intended: his father ("That bastard. That bastard") and his wife ("Die you bitch. / I'll live to watch you die").

The conflict between male and female is reinforced by the oppositions between hard and soft images, as in the metonymy "blast of fluff," to stand for the rifle and the rabbit, the male and the female. The family atmosphere of bitterness and brutality is countered by the irony of the "moss-soft livingroom." The uncle's tears are opposed to his slugging. The Santa Barbara pines provide an ironic background for the family tragedy.

The reasons for the uncle's actions are not clear. Does the war experience turn him into a brute? The narration makes clear that he was a good boy; he never wanted to inflict pain on anyone. He brings the rabbit home "with tears streaming / down his blood soaked jacket," and he "cried all night and the week / after." Or are we to think that men, as young boys, are gentle, but that when they are grown, especially if they go to war, they will turn into brutes? Or is it that the uncle is simply condemned in a fatalistic way to continue his father's brutal habits? The poem, I think, does not yield enough information to form a judgment. Cervantes' strategy in "Uncle's First Rabbit" is to present a situation with no direct commentary. Her main intent is to explain, not why but how a phenomenon of this sort becomes interiorized in one man.

The resolution of the woman's dilemma in "Uncle's First Rabbit" depends upon the male. The male has two options: to stay or to leave. For the woman, it will be better if he leaves, for if he stays he will not change his behavior. Yet he will not leave. The decision is up to the man for the women are completely passive and silent. "Uncle's First Rabbit" presents an aspect of the sexual dilemma which Cervantes finds abhorrent: the silent submission of women who endure male brutality. In "Beneath the Shadow" Cervantes breaks her grandmother's "silent waters," not as her mother does by condemning the good in her grandmother, but by transforming the uncle's "terrible singing" into a "hymn of mockingbirds." These are the two sides of Cervantes' dual perspective: the "terrible singing" and the beautiful songs she says she wants to sing in "Visions of Mexico." The first gathers together the dissonant noises of reality: the "blasting and muffled outrage" in "Poem for the Young White Man"; the "low-voiced / scufflings, sirens, gunnings" in "Visions of Mexico"; and the clashing, grating noises in "Uncle's First Rabbit." The second relates to the peaceful, serene moods of the lyrical poems and specifically to the harmonious singing of the mockingbird in "Beneath the Shadow of the Freeway."

"BENEATH THE SHADOW OF THE FREEWAY"

Each publication of "Beneath the Shadow of the Freeway" showed minor changes.[14] I analyze the version in *Emplumada* because I think it is the most definitive one. It is among the few early pieces Cervantes included in *Emplumada*, and the only poem in which she tries to capture two character voices, juxtaposing and counterposing them throughout the poem. "Beneath the Shadow" presents an exchange of statement and rejoinder, a pattern of thought demanding that in the end a choice must be made. The "I" narrating the story is detached, apparently trying to describe the course of events from the outside. Yet the "I," presented as a character taking part in the action in one section of the poem, is involved as well as detached, inside as well as outside.

BENEATH THE SHADOW OF THE FREEWAY

1

Across the street—the freeway,
blind worm, wrapping the valley up
from Los Altos to Sal Si Puedes.
I watched it from my porch
unwinding. Every day at dusk
as Grandma watered geraniums
the shadow of the freeway lengthened.

2

We were a woman family:
Grandma, our innocent Queen;
Mama, the Swift Knight, Fearless Warrior.
Mama wanted to be Princess instead.
I know that. Even now she dreams of taffeta
and foot-high tiaras.

Myself: I could never decide.
So I turned to books, those staunch, upright men.
I became Scribe: Translator of Foreign Mail,
interpreting letters from the government, notices
of dissolved marriages and Welfare stipulations.
I paid the bills, did light man-work, fixed faucets,
insured everything
against all leaks.

3

Before rain I notice seagulls.
They walk in flocks,
cautious across lawns: splayed toes,
indecisive beaks. Grandma says
seagulls mean storm.

In California in the summer,
mockingbirds sing all night.
Grandma says they are singing for their nesting wives.
"They don't leave their families
borrachando."

She likes the ways of birds,
respects how they show themselves
for toast and a whistle.

She believes in myths and birds.
She trusts only what she builds
with her own hands.

4

She built her house,
cocky, disheveled carpentry,
after living twenty-five years
with a man who tried to kill her.

Grandma, from the hills of Santa Barbara,
I would open my eyes to see her stir mush
in the morning, her hair in loose braids,
tucked close around her head
with a yellow scarf.

Mama said, "It's her own fault,
getting screwed by a man for that long.
Sure as shit wasn't hard."
soft she was soft

5

in the night I would hear it
glass bottles shattering the street
words cracked into shrill screams
inside my throat   a cold fear
as it entered the house in hard
unsteady steps   stopping at my door
my name   bathrobe   slippers
outside a 3 A.M. mist heavy
as a breath full of whiskey
stop it   go home   come inside
mama if he comes here again
I'll call the police

inside
a gray kitten   a touchstone
purring beneath the quilts
grandma stitched
from his suits
the patchwork singing
of mockingbirds

6

"You're too soft . . . always were.
You'll get nothing but shit.
Baby, don't count on nobody."

—a mother's wisdom.
Soft. I haven't changed,
maybe grown more silent, cynical
on the outside.

"O Mama, with what's inside of me
I could wash that all away. I could."
"But Mama, if you're good to them
they'll be good to you back."

Back. The freeway is across the street.
It's summer now. Every night I sleep with a gentle man
to the hymn of mockingbirds,

and in time, I plant geraniums.
I tie up my hair into loose braids,
and trust only what I have built
with my own hands.

"Beneath the Shadow" is an utterance of a single speaker. Within it are mingled two voices that represent two different belief systems. The poem oscillates between these two voices: the romantic-idealist voice of the grandmother, and the pragmatic-realist voice of the mother. In my reading of the poem, the Mexican grandmother participates in the domestic realm while the mother, in the father's absence, fulfills the role of breadwinner, going out into the world to support the family. Based on this point, and on what Cervantes says in "Refugee Ship" about her mother's teaching her English but no Spanish, my reading links the mother with the more acculturated generation in the family.

The mother and the grandmother have antithetical philosophies toward men. The poem dramatizes the speaker's efforts to come to terms with the conflicting voices of the two women. It is important to stress that neither the grandmother's nor the mother's attitude toward men is sufficient. Although the speaker listens to each voice, her own voice represents a compromise that stands in opposition to each of the other two voices.

Since the girl's family is matriarchal ("We were a woman family" [section 2]), it is not surprising to find the presence of many feminine attributes. Softness, imagination, birds, and myths are associated with the grandmother. These attributes make up her voice. They contrast with the properties of hardness, noise, activity, and fragmentation which characterize the mother's voice. At times, these two modes or ways of being intersect or crisscross. For example, the girl describes her mother as a "Swift Knight," a "Fearless Warrior," epithets suggesting masculine behavior; she also notes, though, that her mother really wanted to be a "Princess instead. / . . . Even now she dreams of taffeta / and foot-high tiaras." Inversely, the girl describes her grandmother as "our innocent Queen" who cooks and sews, activities that are traditionally feminine, but she also points out that her grandmother labored strenuously to survive: "She built her house, / cocky, disheveled carpentry" (section 4).

As the cynical and embittered mother believes that men will take advantage of soft women, she manifests a hard veneer to them. The grandmother is soft and gentle, too soft, in the view of the mother, since she lived "twenty-five years / with a man who tried to kill her." From her vocal and assertive manner the girl learns the importance of being hard, but she does not want to hear her mother's cynicism and resentment. She admires her grandmother's softness but not her submissiveness. Her portrait of the grandmother recalls the image of the seagulls in "Shells": trusting, but also dependent upon whoever or whatever offers them security. These extreme positions are the girl's legacy from her maternal sources. The girl-narrator has internalized these two conflicting attitudes, and now, in the poem, she attempts to externalize in language what is inside her.

Her own conflict is an inability to decide ("Myself: I could never decide" [section 2, stanza 2]) between "Queen" and "Knight . . . Warrior," between a feminine and a masculine style. The "So" in the next line implies a link between the girl's inability to decide and her momentary solution: "So I turned to books, those staunch, upright men." She becomes a scribe, a translator, an interpreter; she pays bills, fixes faucets, does "light manwork." Although she chooses neither "Queen" nor "Knight," she inclines toward activities traditionally attributed to males.

The girl paints a fairy-tale picture of her family, likened to a medieval hierarchy. The relationships among the three family members are well defined and clearly established. Her images of "Queen," "Knight . . . Warrior," and "Scribe" suggest a preliterate, preindustrialized society, one in transition from oral to literate modes of communication. The sexually ambiguous image of the scribe fits her state of indecision: "Scribe" is male but does not conjure up the image of the actively aggressive knight slaying the dragon. Furthermore, "Scribe" is ironical because the speaker is a female recorder of the experiences of the Mexican-Chicano women in her family. As a scribe she captures in print what her maternal predecessors have orally transmitted to her.

These medieval images of "Queen," "Knight . . . Warrior"

and "Scribe" contrast sharply with the image of the freeway, an indicator of the American dream and of a complex technological society. They also emphasize the disparity between the Chicano community and the larger society: one an urban community with vestiges of the oral and rural; the other an advanced, modern society. The parallel suggested is that the speaker's Chicano community is to the modern society what European medieval society was to the world of print, when print began to dominate. The parallel, of course, is not exact, for the speaker's world is an urban barrio in northern California. As noted earlier in the discussion of "Visions of Mexico," the important point suggested by the historical parallel is that a Mexican-Chicano community in transition from a rural to an urban context begins to participate more fully in a literate society by articulating what has so far not been said in the literary world.

Despite the ambiguity characterizing the girl's attitude, she still valorizes her grandmother positively as someone desirable to imitate. To the grandmother, the first character the girl recalls to memory (section 1), is assigned the highest place in the medieval matriarchal hierarchy, a queen among knights and scribe. The grandmother's presence, more than the mother's, permeates the girl's memory. Sections 3 and 4 elucidate in more specific ways the contrast between an inner, dreamy, soft voice and an outer, cynical voice.

Images of birds—mockingbirds and seagulls—and myths are the standards by which the grandmother assesses people and events. The grandmother's way of thinking is formulaic, a feature characteristic of an oral culture.[15] She still lives by standards connected more with an oral way of life than with a culture dependent upon writing. She thinks in fixed standard expressions and speaks in metaphors. The arrival of seagulls means storm. Mockingbirds sing for their wives who nest. By explaining what mockingbirds do the grandmother negatively alludes to the behavior of human males: "They [mockingbirds] don't leave their families / borrachando." Her metaphor is prescriptive: human males should be on hand to care for their wives and children, but instead they leave their families to *borrachar* ("get drunk"). The grandmother respects the way birds "show themselves / for toast and a whistle." As in "Uncle's First Rabbit," nature is a kind of mirror, but here it reflects the ideal patterns of behavior which should govern the way men live. The analogy between birds and men offers a slight hint that the grandmother thinks men devious. Negative, unflattering statements about men can only be inferred. The mother's mode of expression is different: direct, crude, and satiric. The mother mocks and condemns the grandmother for putting up for twenty-five years with a man who brutalized her. "It's her own fault, / getting screwed by a man for that long. / Sure as shit wasn't hard." The mother's quoted statement undermines the positive qualities the girl has attributed to her grandmother; for the mother, the grandmother is too soft. The pun on "hard" reveals her satiric, mocking attitude. The grandmother was not hard with men; hence, it was not hard for men to victimize her. Although hearing her mother's words, the girl turns her attention once again to the grandmother's softness in the next line: "soft she was soft." A more meditative tone marks these words, which also have a nice ironic quality. They convey the girl's agreement with her mother, but they also reveal affection for her grandmother.

In section 5 the poem shifts from a contemplative, serene evocation of the grandmother to a violent, noisy, loud outburst. The images now evoke disruption and divisiveness instead of harmony and peace: glass bottles breaking in the streets and words cracking into shrill screams. The lyrical subject becomes more involved, as though experiencing the situation in a present moment. The language creates emotive effects: fear, confusion, danger. It also becomes ambiguous. Who are the referents of the pronouns? Is the "I," for instance, the same girl-narrator who now focuses on her experiences with her mother? Or is the "I" the mother herself now stepping to the foreground to tell her experiences with her own mother? And what is the referent of the impersonal "it" that now intrudes into the scene?

Possibly "it" refers to the nonpersonal force of the freeway, already designated by "it" in section 1, line 4, or the phenomenon of noise: the glass bottles breaking, the shrill screams. The context suggests quarreling, fighting, perhaps even physical abuse. Both components, freeway and noise, are outside. Presumably the speaker is inside the house, an inference derived not from any explicit statement but from the context: "bathrobe   slippers / outside a 3 A.M. mist heavy." When the "I" says "it entered the house in hard / unsteady steps   stopping at my door," the "it" takes on a more precise identity: "hard / unsteady steps" and "a breath full of whiskey" are metonymic references to a male per-

son. The sounds of the freeway, the noise, and the male all displace themselves from the outside to the inside. We are not told
precisely who this male is.

The referent of "it" changes again when the speaker says,
"stop it   go home   come inside / mama if he comes here
again / I'll call the police." Grammatical syntax eliminates the
possibility that the "it" is a quarrel between the mother and the
male. The speaker says "come inside" to her mother and not to
the man, for he has already entered the house. Furthermore, the
tone and the mood of these lines make it unlikely that she says
"come inside" to the man. The mother has to be outside for the
directive to make sense. The "it," then, does not refer to a quarrel
between the mother and a male, for if the male is already inside
and the mother is outside, this line makes no sense. The "it"
probably designates the man's sexual advances which threaten
the speaker: "mama if he comes here again / I'll call the police."
Whoever and whatever the "it" is in the latter part of this stanza,
the pronoun refers to a threatening force coming in from the
outside associated with maleness and the mother.

Both the male and the freeway are associated with the outside
world, and both can be sources of influence: the male on the
family and the freeway on the barrio. The freeway in Cervantes'
poetry is an ambivalent image. On the one hand she reveals an
acceptance of this particularly Southwestern invention as part of
a Chicano experience. On the other, she sees it as an invader of
the more private spaces of Chicano communities in the Sun Belt
states. The freeway in "Beneath the Shadow" is not the disruptive
force of, say, "Freeway 280," where it "conceals . . . [the barrio]
all beneath a raised scar." Rather, in "Beneath the Shadow" the
freeway defines and limits the speaker's community. A linguistic
detail reinforcing the freeway's association with a masculine force
is the gender it is given in the bilingual codes of Chicano Spanish:
freeway is "*el* freeway" and not "*la* freeway."

To return to my earlier question, is "mama" in section 5 the
grandmother, that is, the mother's mother, or is she the girl's
mother? Although this section is ambiguous, I think the speaker
is the girl-narrator who has witnessed her mother's experiences
with men. One might argue that the narrator is really the girl's
mother speaking about her own mother because it is the grandmother who is soft toward men: men take advantage of her. The
mother, in contrast, is hard toward men and therefore says to her

mother, "mama if he comes here again / I'll call the police." According to this interpretation, the first stanza of section 5 is the mother's reenactment for her daughter of her own mother's softness toward men and its meaning for her.

This interpretation, implying that the male comes to visit the grandmother, is at odds, however, with what the girl-narrator has told us earlier about her grandmother: "She built her house . . . after living twenty-five years / with a man who tried to kill her." This sentence has a ring of finality. The male was not present when the grandmother built her house: either he had left or he was dead. Section 5 contains markers of transiency pointing to a man who comes and goes: "mama if he comes here *again*" [my emphasis] and "go home." The mother would not say "go home" to the grandmother's partner, who is probably her husband, and therefore, I assume, the mother's father.

My interpretation, therefore, argues that this section refutes the mother's position. In other words, the mother's aggressive personality may be an improvement over the grandmother's submissive nature, but both suffer the male's physical abuses. The narrative force of section 5 is derived from the fact that it comes between the mother's two speeches wherein she advocates hardness toward men (stanza 3 of section 4 and stanza 1 of section 6). Its very placement exposes the contradiction in the mother's position.

In stanza 2 of section 5 the girl-narrator withdraws from the outside—the disturbance and confusion of her mother's life with men—into the inside, into the quiet, calm world of her grandmother's quilts and mockingbirds. The phrase "from his suits" refers to the man the grandmother lived with, not to the male who visits the mother in the preceding stanza. The stanza marks a thematic break with the first stanza because the girl moves from outside to inside on two levels: literally from outside to inside the house, and metaphorically from her external to her internal consciousness. All the images in this stanza are soft, suggesting peace and harmony. What the girl means is that inside herself there is a softness (a "gray kitten"), which functions like a "touchstone" to help her assess the authenticity of relationships with men. Just as her grandmother collected the scraps and pieces discarded by men ("from his suits") to make a quilt, so too the girl will create order out of disorder. The quilts stitched from the patches of men's suits, and the mockingbird's songs composed of disparate sounds ("patchwork") of other birds, are like mosaics, the piecing together of unlike elements to form a continuous whole. Like her grandmother and like the mockingbird, the girl-narrator wants to harmonize the dissonant voices of her grandmother and mother to establish her own voice and her own attitude toward men.

In section 6 the girl, in effect, steps into her grandmother's place. The mother directly criticizes her daughter for being too soft, warning her that her softness will be an open invitation to men to take advantage of her:

> "You're too soft . . . always were.
> You'll get nothing but shit.
> Baby, don't count on nobody."

The girl inwardly agrees ("—a mother's wisdom") by affirming that she *is* soft on the inside, like her grandmother, but she also notes that she has grown "more silent, cynical / on the outside," like her mother. The next two stanzas constitute the girl's answer to her mother:

> "O Mama, with what's inside of me
> I could wash that all away. I could."

> "But Mama, if you're good to them
> they'll be good to you back."

The "I could" is repeated to stress her insistence to her mother that she could wash "that" (the "shit") away. The insistence suggests that she is trying to overcome her own doubts. She wants to believe that with the springs of warmth inside her she will find the magnanimity to rise above men's injuries. She also wants to believe that if she is good to men, men will be good to her, and hence she will not have to "wash that [shit] all away." Her point is an implicit criticism of her mother: men weren't good to you, mother, because you weren't good to them. With this argument the daughter undermines the mother's style of relating to men.

If the daughter means these words seriously, she comes across as an idealistic naive young girl, because all men will not be good to women simply because women are good to them. Rather, her words are ironical because she knows her grandmother's life disproves this philosophy. These words express her desire for what relationships between men and women ought to be and not her knowledge of what they are.

The insertion of "back" in "But Mama, if you're good to them / they'll be good to you back" suggests a child's language. The rhetorical emphasis on "back" as the last word of her answer stresses the idea of reciprocity. Her inner voice desires smooth relationships between men and women. When "back" becomes the first word of the next stanza, its effect is to pull the girl out of the reverie, the dream, and return her to the poem's points of origin: the freeway and her grandmother. The inclusion of the verb "is" in the sentence, "The freeway is across the street," makes the tone more emphatic than it was in the first line of the poem: "Across the street—the freeway." The girl recognizes the existence of the freeway, defining her barrio and setting its limits.

The two final stanzas embody the daughter's resolution of the two extreme positions of her mother and grandmother. Her compromise represents a reversal of our expectations about the benefits she might derive from her maternal sources. We would expect her to learn softness and trust from her grandmother. Instead she learns a kind of mistrust: "and trust only what I have built / with my own hands" is a direct echo of the grandmother's behavior (section 3, stanza 4). Indirectly the phrase is also a positive echo of what the mother said earlier to her in a negative form: "Baby, don't count on nobody" (section 6, stanza 1). Similarly, we would expect her to derive hardness from her mother. Instead she learns gentleness: "Every night I sleep with a gentle man." The "gentle man" stands in direct opposition to the mother's macho visitor who struts in at three o'clock in the morning. The images of "gentle man," "hymn," and "mockingbirds" in the night evoke a scene of order and harmony, in direct contrast with the loud noisy nights of her mother. The pun on *hymn* and *him* suggests a harmonization of male-female tensions. These lines also echo, albeit more faintly, the presence of the grandmother because "mockingbirds" and "summer" are linked with the grandmother's life. The irony of the narrator's mediation—trust in self from the grandmother and gentleness from the mother—demonstrates that the narrator comes up with her own reading of their lives.

In the final stanza the girl envisions herself in the future ("and in time" as opposed to "It's summer now"), harmonizing the three voices: her grandmother's, her mother's, and her own.

Her voice and her grandmother's dominate. She inserts herself ("I") within the pattern of activities her grandmother performed. She, like the mockingbird, mimes and imitates the same actions. The language of this stanza implies repetition and circularity. The girl is still in the same place as she was when the poem began, that is, within the defined boundaries of her environment. She has not crossed the street to the freeway. She is also bounded by her grandmother's pattern of life: summer, mockingbirds, geraniums, loose braids, and the will to survive. The girl does not mean that she will literally return to her grandmother's ways, for that would be a return to the past. There is a slight ambiguity in the phrase, "and in time." It may allude to the future, but it also means "in history." In other words, while her grandmother planted geraniums and believed in myths and birds to escape historical time, the girl performs her actions with full acceptance of the here and now.

The girl's attraction to her grandmother also reveals her desire to assert her Chicana identity and culture. Hence her compromise allows her to affirm several identities: her identity as a Chicana, as a woman, and as a poet. As a poet she transforms the elements of her grandmother's and mother's voices into the substance of her poetry. Cervantes does not build houses or cultivate the earth. Instead she belongs to another generation that inscribes its own cultural identity in writing and thus gives value to the words and actions of her ancestors.

In its final stanzas the poem momentarily achieves a breakthrough into a lyrical moment, an integration between desire and knowledge, utopia and history, in which Cervantes' persona imagines a harmonization in male-female relationships. Envisioning an agrarian utopia with matriarchal overtones, the woman ("I") is in control, planting the earth and wearing her hair in loose braids. Her hairstyle evokes an image of a rural, Mexican woman, but not the traditional one dependent upon a man. This woman trusts in her own abilities. The girl-narrator expresses an immanentist[16] philosophy oriented toward an experiential order rather than a timeless transcendent realm. She will rely on herself, trust only her own tangible experiences, and find meaning not in already existing schemata and patterns, but in the dynamic qualities of her own secular experiences.

The irony is that in the entire body of her poetry Cervantes achieves her one lyric moment in a poem that is primarily discursive and narrative. There is no such moment in any of her lyrical poems. "Beneath the Shadow of the Freeway" communicates a dialogic struggle taking place within the protagonist who wants to reach a compromise between mother and grandmother. Yet the poem offers no clear mapping of how a real harmonization in male-female relationships is to be effected. It communicates no comparable struggle in how the narrator achieves a relationship with a "gentle man." The process of how the narrator transforms the macho male in section 5 to the gentle man in the penultimate stanza (section 6) is not explained. The poem does, however, imply—in the phrase "in time," in history—the presence of struggle and conflict. In making this suggestion I do not mean to imply that the poem should explain this process; rather I want to stress that its culminating moment is an inner one in which the protagonist expresses her utopian, lyrical sentiments.

5

"Beneath the Shadow of the Freeway" not only confronts the question of Cervantes' existential voice as a woman and as a Chicana, but it also brings out the conflict between her two literary voices: a discursive one and a lyrical one. By juxtaposing these two poetic voices, "Beneath the Shadow of the Freeway" combines the principal elements of Cervantes' style, thus suggesting that it also confronts the question of her literary voice.

The poem's first four sections are written in a discursive mode. Section 5 interrupts this mode by moving into the softer lyrical mode, a shift that accommodates the specific content. Ironically, the more violent, chaotic content of section 5 necessitates the softer lyrical mode, whereas the peaceful, harmonious content of sections 1–4, and later 6, requires the harder discursive mode. The reverse has been true of the other poems where the discursive style is used to present a speaker in a struggle with a social, sometimes violent, world, and the lyrical style, a speaker with no stated social identity, searching for personal expression. In "Beneath the Shadow" the speaker of section 5 is concerned with self-expression, which is integrated with a social world. The speaker of the other discursive sections finds her moment of inner illumination. The two styles crisscross and intersect, just as certain qualities of the soft grandmother and the hard mother crisscross at the poem's thematic level. To understand the interplay between these two verbal strategies, I associate the discursive style with a mimetic or referential voice, and the lyric style with a more self-conscious, self-referential voice, one associated with certain modern techniques.

Mimetic voice, derived from verbal imitation, refers primarily to the representation of spoken speech in a written text.[17] It gives the illusion of a human voice speaking and enunciating words. In "Beneath the Shadow" three levels of mimetic voice characterize sections 1–4 and 6: (1) dialogue, or a character's speech acts (the words in quotation marks which the girl-speaker attributes to her grandmother, her mother, and herself); (2) indirect discourse, or paraphrasings of another speaker's words; and (3) narrative, or storytelling by an identifiable narrator, the girl who documents her family's past events and sayings. The first two, dialogue and indirect discourse, give facticity to the reality imitated, the speaker's psyche. They convey the impression that these words were actually spoken in the same order and form as they are rendered to us. The third kind of mimetic voice—storytelling by an identifiable narrator—predominates in these first four sections, whereas a combination of the first and third kinds makes up the final section. The third kind of mimetic voice predominates throughout Cervantes' poetry.

In her voice as narrator, Cervantes splits herself into narrator and one of the characters in narration and recounts in a present moment the activities of her family and barrio in a past moment. Her manner is detached and objective: "I watched it"; "We were a woman family"; "I turned to books." She functions as an eyewitness narrator, telling rather than showing. In section 2 the poet-narrator describes herself as scribe, translator, and interpreter. At a stylistic level, these three terms situate the poet, because they indicate how she envisions herself with respect to her subject matter and her audience. These three writing activities do not include the primary creation of a text; instead they transform one kind of text into another. They suggest some "middle person" who mediates between an oral speaker or writer and an audience.

The language of the poem is appropriate to someone who documents memorable events and sayings. The majority of lines making up the narrator's discourse are cast in complete sentences, structured according to conventional patterns: subject, verb, and object-clause. The human origins of particular sayings are clearly identified: "Grandma says / seagulls mean storm"; "Mama said, 'It's her own fault.'" The narrator uses parallel phrasing which facilitates understanding and recall: "She likes . . ."; "She believes . . ."; "She trusts . . ." The lines are easy to follow, even when the poem is read or heard for the first time. The language and the phrasing imply that the text functions as an exchange between its message and an audience that is primarily, although not exclusively, a listening audience.

In section 5 Cervantes' narrating voice, especially in the first stanza, does not recount events solely in the storytelling voice of the earlier sections, where she tells about events and people. She now makes the "I" the center of the action, speaking in the voice of someone who is experiencing an event. We feel that these threatening events are happening to someone. More emotionally involved, the voice communicates urgency and rapidly accumulating sensations: visual (darkness), auditory (freeway traffic, glass bottles breaking, "hard / unsteady steps"), olfactory ("a breath full of whiskey"), and emotional (fear, anger).

Whereas narrative discourse is distinguished from speech utterances in the preceding sections (for example, section 3, stanza 2, lines 4–5, and section 4, stanza 3), in section 5 narrative and speech discourse are run together. No quotation marks separate the mother's words to her mother or to the male from the narration. Specific conventions of printed language are deliberately violated. The absence of capitalization and of any kind of punctuation breaks with the earlier style, which obeys standard grammatical rules. The wider spaces between words are also a new feature.

Rhetorical connectives are omitted to suggest confused and rapid processes of thought at moments of emotional turmoil. Examples are the paratactic phrasing and the spacing in section 5, stanza 1:

> inside my throat   a cold fear
> as it entered the house in hard
> unsteady steps   stopping at my door
> my name   bathrobe   slippers
> outside a 3 A.M. mist heavy
> as a breath full of whiskey
> stop it   go home   come inside

These shifts in mood and tone are apparent when the poem is recited, for two reasons: (1) the conventions of mimetic voice—an identifiable character narrating and articulating speech, for example—provide continuity; (2) certain elements of graphic scoring, particularly the absence of punctuation and the spacing, are signs instructing us how to recite these lines. Their function is to convey the agitation and emotion felt by the speaker. The spacing gap on the page is the analog to the gesture in spoken discourse, a gesture inevitably lost in written discourse. In this particular context the gap corresponds to the speaker's gesture of heavy and broken-up breathing to communicate fear and urgency. Cervantes captures the gesture forever lost to the written word.

A curious paradox emerges here. The scoring of this section captures the "I" in the performance of the event, dramatizing the "I" in the act of self-discovery. In this sense the passage is closer to an oral experience than the passages of sections 1–4 because it stresses the immediacy of the gesture and the emotions of the narrator. Yet the only way we know that we must recite this passage so as to communicate the gesture and the emotions is by seeing, by reading, the text. The ability to convey the "I" in the performative act presupposes a reader who has a relationship with the written text, who can read a "voice" on the page. What the eye must note is the sudden change in the notation of language, in spacing and punctuation, for example. Such changes register language itself as performative, attempting to generate signification on the printed page.

In stanza 2 of section 5 the poet eases out of the threatening situation and returns to the inner secure world of the grandmother: the "gray kitten . . . purring," grandma's quilts, "the patchwork singing / of mockingbirds." Like the preceding one, this stanza uses no capitalization; even "grandma" is lower case. Yet, unlike stanza 1, it uses only one spacing gap. Generally, stanza 2 opposes a soft inner world to the hard outside world of stanza 1, but the opposition occurs within the lyrical-suggestive mode.

The conflict suggested by these two voices is the one between "Scribe" and the lyrical "I." Sections 1–4 are oral in the sense that they depict an "I" that sees itself as mediating between a community and a larger audience, performing a similar role to that played by the poet in a traditional oral culture. Paradoxically, the role of mediator is dependent upon typographical markings.

In contrast, in section 5, the poet is being more oral than in the previous sections because she captures the "I" in its performative act. Paradoxically, the orality is dependent upon the activity of reading. The conflict between a spoken voice and a voice on the page helps to reinforce the idea that a modern poet's "I" can never be an unmediated phenomenon, a totally oral experience, not even for a Chicana poet as consciously rooted in her community as is Cervantes.

The final section seems to resolve the poet's paradox in favor of the discursive style. Stanza 1 repeats the exact words once spoken to her by her mother. Stanza 2 interrupts the girl's answer to her mother, which follows in stanzas 3 and 4. The interruption reveals the girl's inner thoughts as she reflects upon her mother's words. Yet the girl's words, which are directed inward toward herself, are couched in the language of her storytelling voice, which up until now has reported on events related to the outside—her environment and her family. The use of quotation marks in stanzas 3 and 4 suggests that she articulates her thoughts and sentiments aloud to her mother. The presentation of these words as direct speech utterances corresponds to Cervantes' outer discursive voice. Their content, however, expressing her desire for peace and harmony in male-female relationships, corresponds to her lyrical vision. Furthermore, the "I" speaking in stanzas 3 and 4 clashes with the "I" speaking in stanza 2, which represents itself as silent and cynical on the outside, because the direct speech utterances of the former stanzas do not represent the voice of a cynic. The word "Back" in stanza 5 achieves the return to the outer, real world where she ironically succeeds in expressing a utopian vision "in time" in her discursive and narrative voice. The intermixing of a discursive style with a lyrical vision intimates Cervantes' desire to hold the tension between outer and inner, public and private, hard and soft, history and vision, in a dynamic, creative relationship.

"Beneath the Shadow of the Freeway" highlights Cervantes' social voice as a Chicana and as a woman in its struggle with a stylistic voice. The poem is the best example of the mixing of her two dominant modes. She moves in and out of these two modes, showing us what it means to be a Chicana, a woman, and a poet in the contemporary world. Whether she is expressing a personal identity through a disembodied lyric speaker, or a social identity either as a Chicana or as a woman who is a Chicana, Cervantes desires to integrate public and private, discursive and lyrical. The salient feature of Cervantes' conflict between scribe and poet, mediator and creator, is that she does not find her inner moment of harmony in either of the two polarities: a personal expression or a social expression as a Chicana. These two identities remain polar opposites in her poetic universe. Instead, she finds harmony in the expression of her feminine consciousness as a Chicana in relation to her community.

Alma Villanueva and Lorna Dee Cervantes come from similar personal backgrounds. Both were raised in father-absent families living in urban, working-class environments. Two generations of women—grandmother and mother—played a central role in their personal development. In spite of these similarities, Villanueva and Cervantes are two very different poets, both in their choice of themes and in their poetic strategies.

As poets, Villanueva and Cervantes make different responses to the dilemma created by their social situation as women and as Chicanas. Although the triadic identity of woman, Chicana, and poet exists in a relationship of conflict and struggle in the poetic worlds of both, they differ in the nature of the relationship. Villanueva, responding to the dilemma with a strong feminist voice, succeeds in smoothly integrating her identity as a woman with her identity as a poet. The single, most important issue for Villanueva is to make her divided self cohere as a woman. Strongly identifying with alienated women everywhere, she never assigns markers of race, culture, or class to the women who constitute her audience. Because she sees herself as culturally consonant with alienated women everywhere, she acknowledges no social barriers between herself and other women, or among other women themselves. The time and energy Villanueva devotes to elaborating her poetic "I" as a woman as contrasted with her poetic "I" as a Chicana are evidence that she speaks from a feminist position within Anglo white culture, taking issue with the masculine principle that defines women as subordinate and marginal. Villanueva's decision to give priority to her identity as a woman—that is, a gender identity—may perhaps be explained by the circumstances of her birth. If we take her reference to "bastard" seriously, her protagonist may not know positively the identity of her father, a detail that would make it impossible for her to know his ethnicity. Thus the protagonist may have a social certainty, but not a biological certainty, about being a Chicana. In contrast, she is totally certain of her gender. This sociological factor provides objective grounds for Villanueva's ambiguous relationship to "Chicano." And though there is evidence that she desires to be part of a social community, her autobiographical poem expresses conflict between a longing to reach an audience of alienated women everywhere, regardless of race, and a longing to communicate with a more particularized Chicano readership. What is unsaid in *Mother, May I?* is a hungering for a reconciliation between the two audiences and an inability fully to achieve it.

The situation is quite the contrary with Cervantes, who responds to the dilemma with a strong historical and social voice. The problem, as she conceives it, lies not in the expression of her personal poetic "I," as it does for Villanueva, but in the expression of a historical collective community. Whether she looks out toward the white dominant culture, as in "Poem for the Young White Man," or looks at what she envisions as Mexico in "Visions of Mexico," she speaks as a poet who identifies culturally and ethnically as a Chicana. The barrier preventing her integration with Anglo or Mexican culture is one determined by culture and not by gender, as it is for Villanueva. For Cervantes, the term "Chicana" encompasses both gender and ethnicity because her identity as a woman is inextricably bound to her Chicana self.

The conflict among the three identities of woman, poet, and Chicana in Villanueva's poetic universe is reversed in that of Cervantes. The two entities that remain juxtaposed in Villanueva—woman and Chicana—are the very two identities that find a synthesis in Cervantes. Inversely, the two entities synthesized by Villanueva—woman and poet—are the very two identities that remain juxtaposed in Cervantes—Chicana and poet. What is unsaid in Cervantes' poetic world is the desire to harmonize a social voice as a Chicana with her voice as a poet who has concerns other than social ones. Cervantes, therefore, does not integrate community and poetry, history and utopia, when she speaks from a position of race. Rather, she integrates them when she speaks from a position of gender. It is easier for her to envision harmony between men and women than to envision harmony among different racial groups.

Although both these Chicanas choose English as their pri-

137

mary vehicle of expression, they use it for different purposes. Villanueva wants to communicate the personal quest for her poetic "I" to a universal audience of women. She makes sparing use of Spanish words and phrases; when she does use them, she translates them in footnotes.[18] Cervantes, on the other hand, uses English because she intends to translate the experiences of her community to a larger audience. She feels no need to justify her world to an Anglo audience. Instead, she records, explains, and memorializes it. In *Mother, May I?* Villanueva wants to express how prior generations of women contributed to the development of her "I." Cervantes, the scribe, wants not only to explain what prior generations of women contributed to the formation of her "I," but also to record their own history. In this sense, Cervantes records the thoughts and sentiments of her maternal predecessors which previously were absent in written discourse.

When we consider these Chicanas' poetic endeavors from the standpoint of publication and distribution, the results are contrary to our expectations. Since Villanueva is the poet who sees herself as communicating with a female audience everywhere, it would be logical for her poetry to be published by a major press. The fact is, however, that her three collections were published by small presses, oriented toward a Chicano community. In addition, she was recognized by the Chicano academic community of the University of California, Irvine, which was responsible for publishing *Poems* and awarding her first place in poetry. In contrast, whereas Cervantes sees herself as documenting a specific cultural experience and transmitting it to a particular audience, she is, ironically, the only Chicana thus far to be published by a major press.

IV
PROHIBITION
AND SEXUALITY IN
LUCHA CORPI'S
PALABRAS DE MEDIODIA /
NOON WORDS

1

Unlike the other three poets discussed in this book, who were born and socialized in the United States, Lucha Corpi's socialization as a woman took place in Mexico. In 1965, a short time after her marriage in San Luis Potosí, Mexico, Corpi emigrated with her husband to the San Francisco Bay area.[1] Five years later she and her husband were divorced, a difficult and painful experience. Her son Arturo was born in Oakland, California, where they have lived ever since. Lucha Corpi obtained a bachelor's degree from the University of California, Berkeley, and a master's in comparative literature from San Francisco State University. She has served on the board of Aztlán Cultural, a Chicano organization. In 1970–71 she was vice-chairwoman of the Chicano Studies Executive Committee, and from 1970 to 1972 she served as coordinator of the Chicano Studies Library at the University of California, Berkeley. Her poetry and short stories have appeared in Chicano journals, such as *Fuego de Aztlán*, published in Berkeley, and *De Colores*, published by Pajarito Publications in Albuquerque, New Mexico. The Chicano poet Tino Villanueva selected a few of her poems for *Chicanos*, an anthology compiled in Spanish and published in Mexico. Corpi has taught English as a second language in the Oakland Adult Education program since 1973.

The emigration and the divorce, two central events in Corpi's life, ruptured to some extent her identification with the values that define the status of women in Mexico. Life in the United States led her to question her culture's definition of woman as man's property, with little or no freedom to choose her own feminine and sexual destiny. Although United States culture inspired her to seek freedom from the constraints on women's sexual expression in Mexico, Corpi could not fully embrace the options open to women in the United States, such as the possibility of remarriage after divorce or sex without marriage. Neither could she return to her country of origin, for there she would bear the stigma of having transgressed two taboos of her culture: she would be perceived by her family and her society as a woman who had abandoned her country and who had been abandoned by her husband.

Given these circumstances, Corpi chose to identify herself as a Chicana. As noted above, she became involved in a Chicano community. Another indication of her Chicana identity is the publication by *Fuego de Aztlán* of a bilingual edition of her collection of poems, *Palabras de Mediodía / Noon Words*, in 1980.[2] Furthermore, she has presented readings of her poetry to audiences composed of Anglos as well as Chicanos in various places in the Southwest. In 1982 Corpi was one of the key speakers at the Tenth Annual National Association of Chicano Studies Conference in Tempe, Arizona. She has thus been accepted by the poetic circles of the Chicano community with which she has chosen to associate.

Written in Spanish and translated into English by Corpi's friend, Catherine Rodríguez-Nieto, the poems of *Palabras de Mediodía* are indirect expressions of the conflicts that followed from Corpi's ambivalence about crossing the boundaries between Anglo-American and Mexican cultures. Although the poems do not overtly manifest those conflicts, they are nonetheless shaped and influenced by specific biographical and cultural pressures. Corpi's poetry also reflects her life in a modern culture that permits women to express themselves in writing. It is noteworthy that she did not write until she began living in the Chicano community. Although living, writing, and publishing in the United States, socially and culturally Corpi remains a Mexican woman in her poetry, where she orders relationships between men and women according to traditional Mexican values. Her decision to identify herself as a Chicana in the United States manifests her desire to fuse two distinct cultural experiences, which in a sense she both accepts and rejects.

In *Palabras de Mediodía*, Corpi makes a conscious attempt to dramatize a woman's search for passionate love free of the constraints placed on female sexual desires in her culture. One rule of sexual behavior prescribed by traditional Mexican culture is that a woman must be a virgin and must find sexual fulfillment in marriage. Corpi's poetic world, then, is conditioned by the tension between a woman's desire for passionate love and the restrictions that limit her freedom to choose her sexual future. Ironically, the same conflict is embodied in her name: the word *lucha* means "struggle" and *corpi* ("corpus," "corps") suggests "body"; hence "the struggle of the body" (*la lucha del cuerpo*). Corpi's poetic works imply that sexual gratification is a model against which to judge the fulfillment of a human being; yet they contain no overt references to sexual activity. Instead, Corpi's poems allude to sexual activity by means of the erotic codes and conventions of a Mexican romantic, lyrical tradition. For example, the image of a seed fertilized by the sun and rain suggests the insemination of the ovum by the sperm; the cutting (*cortar*) of a fruit or a flower from the vine suggests the action of a man possessing a woman.[3] Read from the perspective of a modern culture with fewer sexual restrictions on women, Corpi's erotic passages seem to manifest an unconsciously sublimated or displaced desire. In her poetry the object longed for but never defined in explicit terms is a sublimated wish for sexual gratification. Paradoxically, these erotic codes and conventions derive from a literary tradition whose values imply the very constraints on women which Corpi would like to eradicate.

In Corpi's poetry the expressive features of language are more prominent than the communicative features. Her poems progress by way of images that evoke meaning rather than by statements that make logical connections. The lyrical metaphors that imply sexual activity, the rhetorical arguments that suggest a tragic mood instead of addressing the heart of the problem, and the use of ellipses imbue her poetry with a dimension of "silence," as she attempts to inject a female emotional consciousness into a male literary tradition that has not permitted women to speak.

Yet the unconscious fantasy of Corpi's poetic persona in *Palabras de Mediodía* is a dream impossible to realize. In the United States she cannot transform herself into a new and liber-

ated woman without surrendering the values that defined, and repressed, a woman in Mexico. I see her pulling between the two
opposing pressures of a desire for sexual liberation and a knowledge of cultural prohibition on several levels. In the first part of
this chapter I analyze Corpi's autobiographical and allegorical
short story, "Tres Mujeres,"[4] in order to establish the cultural
constraints imposed upon her as a Mexican woman, constraints
primarily related to issues of nationality and gender. In the second
part of the chapter I elucidate the pervasive imaginative structure
of Corpi's poetic universe through a discussion of poems in various categories. In a set of landscape poems Corpi reflects upon
her childhood and adolescence in Mexico in order to show that
her poetic universe is split between a desire for sexual experience
(rebellion, expression) and a knowledge of prohibition (repression,
silence). Next I address the poems that talk about the prohibition,
the frustrated desire of the poetic persona, and show how un-
realized desire leads to sublimation. The next category comprises
poems that enact the process of sublimation. They are important
because they reveal Corpi's identification with the erotic codes
and conventions of a romantic and lyrical tradition. The last
group of poems reveal traces of Corpi's attempt to challenge the
social laws of her culture which limit women's freedom to choose
for themselves. My analysis of them shows that the erotic codes
and conventions through which Corpi sublimates her desire for
sexual liberation are the same as those that reinforce the values
of the society that represses women's freedom. This contradiction
mitigates and diffuses her criticism of that society.

"Tres Mujeres" / "Three Women"

"Tres Mujeres," Lucha Corpi's first attempt at writing, appeared
in *La Cosecha*, a special edition of *De Colores* devoted to creative
expression by Chicanas. Written in 1970 and published in 1977,
approximately three years before Corpi's poetry appeared, the
story is significant because it addresses the lacunae that characterize her poetry. "Tres Mujeres" is a direct revelation of what
can only be inferred from the poetry: Corpi's inability to embrace

fully either the culture she had known in Mexico or the culture she had to live within the United States.

The bridge (*el puente*) is a recurrent image in *Palabras de Mediodía*. On one level this bridge is, of course, the historical border between Mexico and the United States which Corpi crossed with her husband in 1965. Her description of the crossing in "Tres Mujeres" suggests that the couple entered the United States with proper documentation and left Mexico because the husband, dissatisfied with life there, sought better economic and educational opportunities. Symbolically, he looks beyond the bridge: "El veía hacia adelante, hacia aquella cuidad . . . más allá del puente" (p. 81). ("He looked ahead, toward that city . . . beyond the bridge.") Corpi's protagonist and double, Juana María, on the other hand, is not so eager to leave her native land: "Ella volteaba hacia . . . atrás . . . y silenciosamente dos gotas de despedida rodaban y caían" (p. 81). ("She looked . . . back . . . and, silently, two teardrops rolled down and fell.") On a higher level the bridge is a metaphorical border between two identities: Corpi's already internalized identity in Mexico and the new identity she once sought in the United States. Her ambivalent attitude toward both countries forced her to live, whether in the United States or in Mexico, always on the bridge, always in a space between. As a work dramatizing Corpi's dilemma, "Tres Mujeres" clarifies her relationship to the two cultures.

In "Tres Mujeres" Juana María must decide between the two histories she perceives are available to her: "pertenezco a la historia ya escrita y a la que vendrá" (p. 75). ("I belong to a history already written as well as to one yet to be written.") Juana María sees a clearly defined past and looks to an imprecise future. Corpi's technique of creating an ambiguous geographical location helps to dramatize a liminal space, in both a temporal and a spatial dimension. Like most traditional allegories, "Tres Mujeres" is based on the convention of a journey. Juana María is a traveler in search of her destiny. On the advice of her grandmother, she follows the flow of a river that leads to a house where the three women of the title await her. Although the river and the house are never precisely located in either Mexico or the United States, the description specifies that the river divides the territory into two sections ("el río . . . divide en dos las tierras morenas") and that the northern part of the river is preferred by the birds that are searching for food. In the context of the story, a river dividing a northern land from a southern land suggests Mexico and the United States, and yet the two lands are "tierras morenas" ("brown lands").

Corpi enhances the illusion of a border location by introducing objects and people connected with both countries. For example, the house the granddaughter is to find is associated with her future destiny. When Juana María arrives at the house, she is surprised to meet Daniel, a character we later learn is her son: "¿Qúe hace él aquí? Con seguridad se le escapó a la abuela y me siguío" (p. 75). ("What is he doing here? For certain he snuck out on his grandmother and followed me.") Corpi's account of the border crossing by Juana María and her husband suggests that Daniel was born in the United States, for he did not participate in the emigration. By juxtaposing an ancestral Mexican grandmother and a great-grandson whose life is linked to the United States, Corpi mixes past and present, life in Mexico with life in the United States.

A second example concerns Rosa Catalina, who welcomes Juana María before her meeting with the three women. Rosa Catalina reminds the protagonist of the circumstances of their initial meeting (p. 76):

> —Como le iba diciendo, nos conocimos hace mucho tiempo. Quizá recuerde a aquel estudiante, Juan Ramón Gómez, que mató a otro campañero de escuela con una navaja por accidente. Era mi hijo. A pesar de los esfuerzos de usted y de otros de sus compañeros el juez lo condenó a prisión perpetua.

> —As I was saying, we met long ago. Perhaps you'll remember that student, Juan Ramón Gómez, who accidentally killed another boy in school with a knife. He was my son. In spite of your efforts and those of his friends, the judge sentenced him to life in prison.

This passage describes a familiar event in working-class Chicano barrios in the United States. It helps to create cultural ambiguity because it suggests a character who in the past knew life in the United States and who is presently on a journey that seems to be taking place in Mexico. This temporal and spatial ambiguity underscores Juana María's state of mind: Is she here or there? Is she in the past or the present?

On entering the house Juana María confronts the two histories defining the extremities of her existence. They are embodied in the allegorical figures of Guadalupe for Mexico and Amerina for the United States. The third woman is Justina, a double image of the woman Juana María now is and the woman she seeks to become. While Guadalupe urges Juana María to return to her original homeland, Amerina tries to persuade her to settle in the United States. Justina, on the other hand, simply tells Juana María that she will have to decide for herself.

Guadalupe embodies the ideal of the *mujer sufrida*,[5] the long-suffering Mexican woman who fulfills herself by sacrificing for others, usually men. As the story makes clear that Juana María has already left Mexico, Guadalupe may be seen as the fulfillment of the woman she might have been had she never left Mexico: "Soy consuelo del que sufre y anhelo del que ama; la columna íntegra en donde descansa la familia. . . . Regresa a mí, hija" (p. 81). ("I am the solace of he who suffers and the desire of he who loves; the pillar where the family rests. . . . Return to me, daughter.") Guadalupe awakens within Juana María feelings of guilt about leaving Mexico as well as nostalgia for the security of her former way of life: "a ese regazo tibio de donde quizá nunca debería haber salido . . . volver a ser . . . la joven que sabía su lugar y desempeñaba su papel entre su gente" (p. 82). ("to that warm breast that I, perhaps, should never have left . . . to be once again . . . the young girl who knew her place and performed her role among her people.") Although Juana María would like to accept the identity offered by Guadalupe ("Hubiera querido regresar a Guadalupe"), she knows it is impossible: "ya no soy ésa de entonces. . . . No puedo dejar de llorar" (ibid.). ("I am no longer the one I was then. . . . I cannot stop crying.")

Her Mexican dream now dead, Juana María looks to Amerina: "Amerina se levanta y desde su pedestal me mira poderosa" (ibid.). ("Amerina gets up and from her pedestal, looking powerful; she sees me.") Although Juana María notes how different she and Amerina are, "Somos tan extrañas la una a la otra" (ibid.), she recognizes that Amerina offers her the opportunity not only to question the life of self-effacement that Guadalupe represents but also to choose her own destiny: "Lo que yo te ofrezco es una vida rica y libre; eso no es lo que tenías antes. Siempre has vivido por o para alguien más. Nunca para tí misma" (p. 83). ("What I offer you is a rich and free life that you did not have before. You have

always lived through or for someone else. Never for yourself."]
Juana María accepts this criticism: "Cuanto de cierto hay en sus
palabras. No puedo desmentirla" (ibid.). ("How true are her words.
I cannot deny them."] The tête-a-tête with Amerina discloses
that Juana María's ambivalence about accepting the United States
as her new cultural homeland is rooted in reasons that are as
much sociopolitical as sexual. Confessing to having once believed
in Amerina's promise of liberty and equality (p. 82), "He aquí mi
tesoro—el poder, la igualdad, la felicidad, la libertad" ("Here is
my treasure—power, equality, happiness, and liberty"), Juana
María now knows it to be mere empty words (p. 83):

> Su oferta atrae, pero he visto la mirada demudada
> en algunos de sus hijos prendidos siempre a la
> esperanza de algún día poder alcanzar esa
> libertad y felicidad. Sólo los escogidos pueden
> disfrutar de ello. Aquellos encerrados en cortezas
> encaneladas, ojos cubiertos por el polvo de sus
> tierras, esos se requiebran sobre la tierra y la
> humedecen con sus gotas salinas hasta que la sangre
> se les agolpa en los corazones y surge violenta como
> torbellino. Ellos no son los escogidos. Desde su
> pedestal Amerina los mira y sonríe. Esa poderosa
> visión, seductora; lo ofrece todo pero lo absorbe todo.

> Her offer attracts me, but I have seen the distraught
> look in some of her children, always hoping for the
> day when they can have liberty and happiness. Only
> the chosen can enjoy the dream. Those who are imprisoned
> in dark skins and whose eyes are covered by the dust of
> her lands break their backs on it, wetting it with their
> salty sweat until their blood beats in their hearts and
> surges violently like a whirlwind. They are not among
> the chosen. From her pedestal Amerina sees them and
> smiles. Her powerful vision is seductive; she offers
> everything but she absorbs everything she offers.

Corpi, aware of a Latino community's situation in the United
States, fears that by accepting the United States she too would
be considered among those "encerrados en cortezas encaneladas."

Juana María also has personal and dramatic reasons for
finding fault with Amerina. Ironically, she reaches the epitome
of happiness with her husband in the United States: "Era marzo
y ya no llovía. Y lo anaranjado de los ocasos de invierno iba
dejando paso al dorado. El sol brillaba con una intensidad mágica.

Eramos felices" (pp. 82–83). ("It was March and it didn't rain anymore. The orange of winter sunsets was becoming a golden color. The sun shone with a magical intensity. We were happy.") Juana María believes she can realize her dream of fulfilling herself as a woman in the United States: "Amerina me dejó jugar con la esperanza" (p. 83). ("Amerina let me play with hope.") The rupture of the marriage brought disappointment. Juana María's questions to Amerina suggest that she blames her for the unwanted divorce, possible in the United States and far more unlikely in Mexico: "¿Quién entonces se llevó el fuego? ¿Quién sacudió las flores del cerezo antes de tiempo y lo dejó todo desnudo? ¿Quién se bebió toda su savia? Y ahora en medio del campo yermo sus ramas desnudas gritan y nadie escucha" (ibid.). ("Who then took the fire? Who shook the flowers from the cherry tree before its time and left it naked? Who drank its sap? And now in the midst of a dry field its naked branches shout and no one hears.") In this extended metaphor the fire is the passion of the marriage, the tree is Mexican tradition, and the flower is the woman. Juana María's point is that by making the divorce possible, the United States took from the Mexican tradition its romance and passion before she could fully realize her dream.

The more reticent Justina simply points to a *gruta* ("grotto") that Juana María must enter: "En esa gruta . . . hay un camino escondido. Búscalo" (p. 86). ("In that grotto . . . there is a hidden road. Find it.") In the end the woman enters the *gruta*, which I take to be Corpi's symbolic representation of her acceptance of an uncertain future. Left without external models of authority and faced with her own breakdown, Corpi presents through Justina the identity she seeks but cannot as yet obtain. She is still the empty space between the rejected alternatives of Guadalupe and Amerina.

The images associated with each woman help to highlight the protagonist's ambivalence toward the two cultures. Each woman is linked with a specific color. Guadalupe has black eyes and hair, dresses in black, and sits on a black bench. The blue-eyed, blond Amerina dresses in white and sits on a white bench. Between the two extremes of a "black" Guadalupe and a "white" Amerina is the "gray" Justina: "Justina es una mujer triste" (p. 75). ("Justina is a sad woman.") The color gray in Corpi's poetry means sadness, absence, and silence.

The details about Guadalupe suggest that she stands for the

historical succession of three cultures: pre-Columbian, European, and Mexican. Juana María remembers Guadalupe when she dressed in white and when (p. 75) "un guerrero velaba su historia. Era la princesa que dormía en el volcán" ("a warrior guarded her story. She was the princess who slept in the volcano"). This description presupposes the popular Mexican legend about a pre-Columbian woman, Iztaccíhuatl (*íztac* means "white"; *cíhuatl* means "woman"),[6] whose name also identifies one of Mexico's highest volcanoes. Woman and mountain are thus locked together as one in the Mexican popular imagination. Iztaccíhuatl is a sleeping princess because the outline of her reclining body is, even today, imaginatively traced in the physical form of the mountain. The warrior guarding her, according to the legend, is Popocatépetl (*popoca* means "smoked"; *tépetl* means "mountain"), the name of another volcano situated beside Iztaccíhuatl. Juana María next recalls: "Después su imagen resurgió vestida de azul y con rosas en las manos" (p. 75). ("Later, her image was reborn, dressed in blue and with roses in her hands.") The princess in this context is the European Virgin Mary introduced into Mexico by the Spaniards. The Mexican context, which synthesizes the two images, is suggested by the name "Guadalupe." Indigenous to the Americas and typically Mexican, this name invokes the legend of the Virgen de Guadalupe who appeared at Tepeyac to Juan Diego, a young Indian, and thus fuses pre-Columbian and Catholic elements. The context in which Guadalupe is presented also includes the legendary and phantasmic figure of the Wailing Woman, who searches by night for her lost children. Commonly known in Mexico and the Southwest as La Llorona, the Wailing Woman may also represent the fusion of Aztec and Spanish elements in Mexican culture. Her origin may date back to pre-Columbian times.[7] Certainly her legend has existed since the time of the Spaniards and is still alive today in Mexico and the Southwest. Juana María associates with Guadalupe some verses that her grandmother taught her as a child, which connect the name with the figure of the mourning mother (p. 80):

> ¡Guadalupe, Guadalupe
> A dónde vas?
> —Voy a buscar a mis hijos
> Los que dejé en el lugar

Donde el río arrulla a las garzas
En su camino hacia el mar (p. 80).

Guadalupe, Guadalupe
Where are you going?
—I am going to search for my children
whom I left there
where the river lulls the herons
on their way to the sea.

The three cultures—pre-Columbian, Spanish, and Mexican—represented in the name Guadalupe highlight the various transformations of a woman as symbol of purity, virginity, and motherhood from one cultural context to another.

Guadalupe's farewell gesture is to offer Juana María a ring (una sortija): "Tómala, Juana María, llévala siempre contigo" (p. 82). Juana María finally envisions Guadalupe as the sleeping princess: "La princesa viste de blanco una vez más: su imagen se pierde entre las cimas nevadas de dos gigantes" (ibid.). ("The princess dresses in white once again: her image is lost between the snowy peaks of two giants.") This vision of Guadalupe refers back to the pre-Columbian context or Iztaccíhuatl and Popocatépetl. It also implies, albeit indirectly, the male as a warrior. Together these images—"princess," "white dress," "warrior"— conjure up a scene of innocence, chivalry, and romance. Because the pre-Columbian period predates the European and Mexican periods embodied in the figure of Guadalupe, these images also suggest nostalgia for a former, and supposedly a purer, existence. The portrayal of pre-Columbian culture in mythic terms as an uncontaminated stage of Mexican history before the Spaniards introduced corruption has been a literary convention in both Mexican and Chicano literatures.[8] In Corpi's story these images and their connotations, along with that of the ring as a traditional symbol of marriage, suggest Juana María's attraction to the idea of being wedded once again to a romantic image of womanhood. That is, she would like to be the woman she once was ("una vez más") before becoming the woman she now is. Implied is a desire to return to an uncontaminated condition, a desire operative on the levels of both gender and nationality: to be a virgin and an authentic Mexican woman.

The imagery surrounding Amerina relates to a different culture. Juana María imagines Amerina as a Helen of Troy with crystalline eyes and golden hair: "la poderosa razón por la que los hombres mataron sin titubeos" (p. 75). ("The powerful reason why men killed without vacillation.") She is also the Statue of Liberty: "Flor de Mayo, el velero que surcó los mares y la depositó [Helena de Troya], antorcha en mano, en las playas solitarias de una costa brava. Amerina orgullosa y seductora en su pedestal promete sin intención de dar" (ibid.). ("The Mayflower, the ship that plied the seas and placed her [Helen of Troy], torch in hand, on the solitary beaches of a brave coast. Proud, seductive Amerina, who on her pedestal promises with no intention of giving.") The use of the word *seductora* within a context of liberty may suggest that Corpi was attracted by the image of a woman radically opposed to the feminine ideal of her own culture. Whereas Corpi's Guadalupe is a woman who realizes herself by sacrificing for others, her Amerina, linked with a mythic Helen of Troy, is a woman who fulfills her desires at any cost.

Although associated in the above passage with the seas of Europe and North America, "Amerina" suggests another name and another context. Similar in sound in Spanish to Amerina is *Marina*, meaning "sea." Thus the name "Marina" suggests the ocean crossed by Cortés to reach the New World where he met the Indian woman, Malintzin Tenépal, whom the Spaniards renamed Doña Marina. She is now pejoratively called La Malinche by Mexicans for her participation with the Spanish in the conquest.[9] As the woman who favored the foreigner and betrayed her people, Marina became a cultural symbol of treachery. Lucha Corpi has strong objective reasons for identifying with Marina, and that she does so is evident in the four poems in which she purportedly speaks for Marina. The similarity in sound between Amerina and Marina in "Tres Mujeres" suggests that Corpi may see in her allegorical figure of Amerina some trace of Marina, of the woman who, according to the myth, abandoned her people. Amerina-Marina may represent the potential threat of giving up one's original culture to assume a foreign identity.

The "gray" Justina is less clearly drawn than the other two women. The protagonist cannot see her face: "no puedo verle la cara." Her voice is like the murmur of an autumn rain: "como cuando hay que vivir días de callada existencia" (p. 75). ("as when one has to live days of quiet existence.") Justina radiates no sense of history; no cultural associations surround her as they do Guadalupe and Amerina. As her name suggests, she is an abstraction—the justice and the balance that the protagonist seeks. Justina is both Guadalupe and Amerina without being either one: "Justina se aleja de mí, una ráfaga de aire la envuelve. Gira alrededor de sí misma y al encontrarme con su cara es Guadalupe; una vez más y es Amerina" (p. 86). ("Justina distances herself from me, a gust of wind surrounds her. She swirls around and on seeing her face she is Guadalupe; another swirl and she is Amerina.") Compared with the other two women, who make long speeches to Juana María, Justina hardly speaks. She and Juana María communicate, instead, by way of gestures and sensations (p. 84):

> Justina me da su mano y salimos a un patio
> interior. . . . Pone su otra mano en mis cabellos y
> los acaricia. Y poco a poco recorre con ella toda mi cara.
> La detiene en mis ojos, en mi nariz, en la boca. Y la
> regresa hasta mi sien y ahí la deja.

> Justina gives me her hand and we go out to an interior
> patio. . . . She puts her other hand in my hair and caresses
> it. Little by little she touches my entire face. She holds her
> hand on my eyes, my nose, my mouth. She returns it to my
> forehead where it remains.

With Justina's hand on her head and as though in a mystical trance, Juana María sees a transfigured Justina (pp. 84–85):

> Sus ojos que antes carecían de color se transforman en color
> de miel ante mi incrédula mirada. Cae el manto que cubre
> su cabeza y sus cabellos se descrubren de color jengibre
> obscuro. Toda ella resplandece con una hermosura
> insuperable.

> Her eyes once lacking color are transformed to the color of
> honey before my unbelieving eyes. The cloak that covered
> her head falls and her hair is a dark ginger color. Her
> beauty is unsurpassable.

In a vision that foreshadows the story's ending, Juana María sees an immense grotto (una gruta inmensa) open in front of her. From the grotto she hears music and a child's voice reciting verses of poetry. The child in the cave represents the rebirth of a new identity that Juana María must now confront.

Without actually saying so, Corpi suggests that Juana María's new identity is to be a blend of the two alternative cultures she knows but cannot fully embrace. To understand the significance of the imagery, which suggests a blend of the United States and Mexico, it is necessary first to summarize Juana María's discussion with her grandmother in Mexico before her marriage and subsequent departure. The story's events move forward in a linear pattern interspersed with a series of flashbacks. The story traces Juana María's arrival at the house, her conversation with the three women, and the ensuing events. The flashbacks proceed from the earliest to the most recent events in the heroine's past: the heroine's conversation with her grandmother, the border crossing, and conversations between Juana María and her husband in the United States. The grandmother appears in both the ongoing story line and in the first flashback.

From the dialogue recounted in the first flashback, the grandmother clearly recognizes that the norms of Mexican society give the man final authority in marriage. Her own experience has led her to conclude that for a woman marriage is a prison. Given these circumstances, the grandmother advises Juana María never to marry. Although marriage will provide her with the illusion that her husband and children are hers, in truth she will be alone. In accepting marriage Juana María would accept the role designed for the woman, the role of living completely for her husband. If the marriage succeeds, she may find happiness. If not, she will be forced to break with the role and make her life alone: "Pero recuerda que una vez que des un paso fuera de ese camino, tendrás que seguir adelante y no es fácil" (p. 77). ("But remember that once you set foot outside this path, you will have to go on and it won't be easy.") Instead of marrying, the grandmother counsels, Juana María should live with her lover.

In having her propose this option, Corpi presents the grandmother as a character who knows that her granddaughter's life will be different from her own. The prescient grandmother already sees Juana María's odyssey beginning. She believes that Juana María will preserve her freedom of choice by living with her lover. That way she will keep her self-autonomy and her lover will remember her as the woman who offered him freedom. The grandmother states the ancestral taboos that Juana María will in due time break: "Casarse es malo; pero casarse e irse lejos de su patria de uno es sacrilegio. No te cases, Juana María, no te cases" (p. 77). ("To marry is bad but to marry and go far away from one's country is sacrilege. Don't marry, Juana María, don't marry.")

Juana María's answer to this advice assures her grandmother that her marriage will be a satisfying one. To Juana María's "Adiós Abuela," the grandmother responds: "No adiós, Juana María, nos volveremos a ver. Adiós se dice sólo cuando ya no hay remedio" (p. 77). ("No, not farewell, Juana María, we'll see each other again. Farewell is said only when there is no more hope.")

In the forward-moving plot the grandmother arrives at the house before the heroine does and leaves with Justina a gift for her granddaughter. The gift is a *paliacate rojo* ("red handkerchief"). Juana María opens the handkerchief and finds a chain and a medallion (p. 86):

> En él [el medallón] un sol y tres caminos que
> convergen en uno hacia una gruta. La figura de
> una niña triste y pensativa en espera a la entrada.
> En la mano izquierda una pluma de águila y en la
> derecha una ramita de albahaca. En el borde del
> pañuelo hay cinco letras grabadas: ADIOS.

> On the medallion one sun and three roads converging
> into one leading to a grotto. The image of a sad
> and pensive little girl waiting at the entrance.
> In her left hand a feather of an eagle and in her
> right a small branch of basil. Five letters are
> engraved on the border of the handkerchief: ADIOS.

The three roads leading into the grotto seem to represent the three women who reflect the choices open to the heroine. The grotto represents the convergence of these identities, or the point at which the protagonist can no longer postpone a decision. She is, therefore, sad and pensive because she faces the unknown and must decide. The eagle's feather in her left hand evokes simultaneously the United States and Mexico, as both countries use the eagle as a symbol. According to an ancient myth, the Aztecs were told by their gods that they would find Mexico-Tenochtitlán, their city, where they would see an eagle spreading its wings upon a cactus and devouring a serpent.[10] The image of the *pluma* (meaning both "feather" and "pen") may be seen as an integrating symbol, standing for the writing the woman will do in the United States which will reflect her life in Mexico. The little branch of basil in the girl's right hand represents a plant historically acclimated to Mexican soil and used traditionally by Mexican people as a seasoning in popular dishes. Thus it may be thought of as prefiguring the presence of Mexican traditions and customs in Corpi's poetry. The separation of the two—the pen (for writing) in the left hand and the basil (for tradition) in the right hand—foreshadows the fragmentation of the self in Corpi's writing. The edges (*el borde*) of the handkerchief are emblematic of the boundary between her past life in Mexico and her future life in the United States. It must be remembered that Corpi, in choosing to live in the United States, moved into a community whose linguistic resources allow *el borde* to designate not only the edges of something (in this instance a handkerchief) but also the international border between the United States and Mexico. In the Southwest, owing to the influence of the English language, *el borde* is "the border." The grandmother's ADIOS engraved on *el borde* (the edges) is synonymous in this context with *el borde* (the border), because, in the grandmother's view, once Juana María crosses the international boundary all hope of returning is lost: "Adiós se dice sólo cuando ya no hay esperanza."

The woman's entrance into the grotto marks the end of the story. From the beginning the woman has feared the arrival of what she refers to as *la bestia nocturna*: "Prefiero . . . que nunca llegue la hora de la bestia nocturna" (p. 74). ("I prefer that the hour of the nocturnal beast never arrive.") The nocturnal beast may represent a variety of states: silence, darkness, physical or spiritual decay. Essentially, it represents the paradoxical notion of "the core of a void" to which the protagonist feels herself condemned. The hour of the nocturnal beast arrives when Juana María enters the grotto. When associated with the contours and the shape of a grotto, the image of the *bestia nocturna* suggests that Juana María is entering the "belly of the beast," an action that satisfies physical hunger but nothing else: "La bestia nocturna mata para saciar el hambre, nada más" (p. 88). ("The nocturnal beast kills to satisfy hunger, nothing else.") The "belly of the beast," especially when associated with a Latin American, is a symbolic reference to the United States[11] and has both spiritual and political implications.

The word "grotto," however, also connotes "shrine," for the Catholic Virgin often appeared in a cave. The image of "shrine" is congruent with the historical context of Guadalupe as virgin and mother. The image of *gruta* in a Mexican context suggests such notions as mother, virgin, and womb. In entering the *gruta*, Juana María accepts her confrontation with the void that may lead to new life. The tripartite image of mother, virgin, and womb is appropriate to Juana María. First, she affirms her role as mother to her son Daniel, who accompanies her into the grotto: "Nos detenemos a la entrada de la gruta. Daniel me da su mano. Le doy la mía" (p. 89). ("We wait at the grotto's entrance. Daniel gives me his hand. I give him mine.") Second, Juana María is symbolically virgin because she searches for a new identity. Third, the grotto serves as a symbolic womb from which a new life will evolve. These mixed impulses of desire and terror associated with the grotto or cavern image reveal Juana María's ambivalence about forging a new identity in a foreign territory that historically is hostile to Mexican people. The story ends with the single word, *Entramos* ("We enter").

With these details in mind, we can better understand the biographical and cultural constraints that made it impossible for Juana María/Lucha Corpi either fully to accept or reject an identity as a Mexican or an Anglo-American woman. "Tres Mujeres" dramatizes the moment between past and present, between Mexico and the United States. In that historical moment Corpi found herself living in the United States after her separation and divorce. In actuality she could not return to Mexico, because she would bear the double stigma of divorce and emigration, the first bringing more social ostracism to a woman than the second. Another constraint was imposed by the birth of her son, for a return to Mexico would mean separating father and son. "Tres Mujeres" makes it clear that the husband, who appears in flashback, was committed to his decision to live in the United States. Furthermore, the grandmother's advice to Juana María to remain in Mexico suggests that Corpi felt guilty about leaving her homeland and therefore would want to spare her son the same kind of suffering. These biographical details help to explain why Corpi would prefer the United States.

Nevertheless, Corpi, though choosing to live in the United States, could not fully accept Anglo-American culture. Attracted by the identities of both Guadalupe and Amerina but unable to embrace either one, her only option is to accept Justina as her model. The character of Justina gives Corpi the opportunity to blend what she retains of her own Mexican culture with what she gains from her experience in the United States, that is, to blend the ideals of womanhood instilled by her own culture with the desire inspired by United States society for freedom from the old cultural restrictions. The blending is implied in Corpi's conscious decision to identify herself as a Chicana. "Tres Mujeres" reveals her alienation from both the Mexican and Anglo worlds while at the same time indicating her attraction to both. The poems in *Palabras de Mediodía* make clear her wish to integrate the twin desires: to enjoy sexual gratification and to choose her own sexual destiny. Yet, as analysis of the poetry reveals, Corpi's adherence to the erotic codes and conventions of a literary tradition denying women sexual freedom prevents her from fully achieving the smooth integration of her desires.

2

The recurrent images making up the imaginative structure of Corpi's poetic universe in *Palabras de Mediodía* fall into four basic categories or areas of human experience: (1) the natural world of trees, fruits, rocks, sea, earth, and wind; (2) the cultural traditions of Mexico, both pre-Columbian and Catholic-European; (3) the pagan world in both its European and its Mexican contexts; and (4) the world of artistic expression, or poetry and writing. The images associated with these geographical and cultural landscapes reveal the tensions between a desire for sexuality and a knowledge of strict prohibition. The tensions dramatize Corpi's self-division into the open, free woman she desires to be (future) and the closed, repressed woman she was socialized to become (present). The motifs of opening and closing which characterize the poems here discussed are pervasive throughout *Palabras de Mediodía*.[12]

The natural world emerges from two different geographical terrains Corpi knew as a child and an adolescent in Mexico. At one pole is the tropical, sunny, green environment of Jáltipan, Veracruz; at the other is the dry, arid, rocky environment of San Luis Potosí. Jáltipan, in the middle of the jungle, is the land of Corpi's birth and early childhood. Corpi's family moved to San Luis Potosí, a city in central Mexico in the state of San Luis Potosí which adjoins Veracruz, when she was nine years old. There she lived until her marriage at the age of nineteen and her emigration to the United States. To Corpi, the people of Jáltipan are lighthearted, carefree, and frank; those of San Luis Potosí are conservative, hyper-Catholic, critical, and suspicious of one another. She notes that in San Luis Potosí grillwork protects the windows of houses, and doors are closed all the time.[13]

These two geographical landscapes generate the next group of images. Corpi uses the tangible products of a pre-Columbian cultural tradition to weave the world of Jáltipan and those of a Judeo-Christian tradition to weave that of San Luis Potosí. The third set of images consists of references to mythical women—some explicit, some implicit—taken from both classical Western and popular Mexican contexts. Figures from the classical tradition are vestal virgins: the prophetess Sibyl who wrote her divine intuitions on leaves and on fragments of bark;[14] the phoenix, symbol of death and rebirth; and the mute Philomela who wove her tragic story of rape into a tapestry. In Corpi's allusions to popular Mexican tradition, two figures recur in her poetry: La Chaneca (a Veracruz variant of La Llorona) and *la lechuza* (the owl), a companion of witches in Mexican folklore. The point of intersection between these two worlds—pre-Columbian and Catholic Mexico, classical and popular Mexico—is embodied in the powerful image of Doña Marina, the historical character who symbolically fuses the encounter between the two civilizations in the conquest of Mexico.

The fourth set of images, concerning writing and poetry, confirm the identification of Corpi's poetic persona with the passive rather than the active artifacts involved in the process of writing. For example, in the Marina poems, a woman's name is represented as the object written and not as the agent writing. In "Quedarse Quito" / "Keeping Still," the second poem in *Palabras de Mediodía*, Corpi identifies herself with a blank page, thirsty for a drop of ink, as it pleads with the pen to write on it.

Y por segundos
todo se vuelve
a la primera página
innumerada
blanca
sedienta
de una gota de tinta
que le recuerde
la impureza
del tiempo viviente
y que parece murmurar

"Escribe en mí
escribe
Qué terrible
morir limpia!"

And for an instant
everything turns back
to the first page
unnumbered
blank
thirsty
for a drop of ink
to remind it
of the impurity
of living time
it seems to whisper
"Write on me
write
How horrible
To die clean!

This metaphor has sexual implications: the blank page is the woman as virgin, the pen is the metaphorical penis, and the drop of ink is the semen or creative fluid. Writing, according to this sexual metaphor, is the activity of sexual penetration.[15] Corpi's persona as a blank page pleads with the phallic pen to write on it so that she will not die a virgin (*limpia* ["clean"]). The irony is that Lucha Corpi, simply by writing, is violating the traditional codes and conventions that she ultimately defends in her poetry.

The topography of Veracruz and San Luis Potosí is the nexus of images that establish the metaphors for the conflicting pressures between sexuality and prohibition. Corpi divides her inner landscape into two, linking her desire to be open and free (sexuality) with Veracruz, and her awareness of closure and repression (prohibition) with San Luis Potosí. She employs a predominantly imagistic mode to explore her past experiences in order to understand how she has been socialized. The poems "Lluvia" and "Solario" are set in Jáltipan; "San Luis" is set in San Luis Potosí.

VERACRUZ AND SAN LUIS POTOSÍ: LANDSCAPES REVISITED

Images of *prole de Tlaloc* ("people of Tlaloc") and *canción de Teponaztle* ("song of Teponaztle") appear in "Lluvia" / "Rain," set in Jáltipan. Tlaloc, the Aztec god of rain, and *teponaztle,* an indigenous musical instrument,[16] give the poem a pre-Columbian flavor. La Chaneca appears in "Solario," a poem of nine vignettes. The fifth vignette describes the open plazas of Veracruz where the Tehuana women (from the Isthmus of Tehuantepec, taking in parts of Veracruz and Oaxaca) meet to sell their goods. They call to their prospective buyers with "marimba voices." The marimba, a kind of xylophone indigenous to Veracruz, suggests pleasure and joy. It is also an indicator of Veracruz's African cultural roots, since the marimba was introduced to the New World by African slaves the Spanish imported into Mexico by way of the port of Veracruz. The eighth vignette tells of Jarocho, the generic name for the campesino of Veracruz, to whom, so the poet confesses, she never wrote a note of love. The sunlit houses of Jáltipan with their large, wide patios are full of musical sounds and noises: outside, the loud screams of parrots (*la gritería de los loros*), the sounds of flute, marimba, and harp (*el arpa*), the ringing of bells in the plaza; inside, the voice of Francisco Gabilondo Soler, the singing cricket who sang to children on the radio on Sunday afternoons.

The smells of flowers and the tastes of foods contribute to the tropical jungle setting: orange, mango, ceiba, and cashew trees, thin reeds (*juncos delgados*) and cornfields (*los maizales*). Afternoons of rain bring the aromas of "dulce de calabaza y atole caliente" ("squash cooked with sugar and hot *atole*").[17] In the seventh vignette, visual and gustatory sensations become mixed because the sensual delights of the cashew tree are so intense in this jungle that even the eyes "taste" the sweetness of its fruit:

> La exquisita y sensual
> esencia del marañón
> cuando los ojos apenas
> si saborean la delicia
> de una primer mordida
> que se ha dado mil veces
> antes de darse entera.
>
> The exquisite, sensual
> essence of the marañón
> when one's eyes barely
> tasted the delight
> of the first mouthful
> given a thousand times
> before the whole giving.

The synesthesia of eyes tasting is important because it fore-shadows the dominance of the visual over the other senses. In the context of childhood, these lines suggest the small "bites" of life taken by a child (*de una primer mordida*) without yet having to assume the responsibilities of adulthood (*antes de darse entera*). In the context of sexuality they highlight the poet's method of coping with sexual desire. She has tasted the *delicia* a thousand times (*mil veces*) but has never experienced it to its fullest (*antes de darse entera*).

The opening lines of "Solario" imbue the secular landscape with a liturgical quality: orange trees put away their bridal gowns for morning; mango trees stretch like green cupolas of jungle cathedrals; crickets sing the ritual of their divine office:

SOLARIO

I

Anochecía

Ya los naranjos habían guardado
sus trajes de boda para mañana
los mangos como cúpulas verdes
de catedrales selváticas
solemnemente presidían
el oficio nocturno de los grillos.

Me senté junto al arroyo
y me lavé los pies enlodados
mientras La Chaneca desde
el fondo de la noche
me observaba cavilante,
sus largas trenzas de azabache
prendidas sobre el pecho
con la Cruz del Sur.

Seguí camino del olvido
y sorprendí al tecolote
en la ceiba dormido
con los ojos abiertos.

A quién buscas hoy?
El rayo en el poniente
me preguntó.
Busco un solario de amor.
Amor . . . El viento repitió.

SUNSCAPE

I

Night Was Falling

The orange trees had put away
their bridal gowns for morning.
Mango trees like the green cupolas
of jungle cathedrals
presided in solemnity
over the night ritual of crickets.

I sat down beside the creek
and washed the mud from my feet
while Chaneca watched
hesitant
from the depths of the night
her long, jet-black braids
pinned across her breast
with the Southern Cross.

I went on toward oblivion
and surprised an owl
sleeping wide-eyed
in the ceiba tree.

The last ray of the setting sun asked:
What are you searching for today?
I am looking for a place
filled with sunlight and love.
Love . . . echoed the wind.

The introduction of La Chaneca (ll. 10–15) contributes more secular magic to the scene. Presented as the constellation Canis Major,
her braids are the lines connecting each star in the north with
Sirius in the south. Like a shadow at night in the astral landscape,
she watches as the speaker sits by the stream to wash her muddied
feet. The poet, like La Chaneca, wanders at night. La Llorona, a
figure reminiscent of Medea, was cursed to roam at night in
search of the children she killed to prevent her Spanish husband
from taking them away. When the sun's ray asks, "¿A quién
buscas hoy?" ("What are you searching for today?"), the implication is that the woman's night wanderings in search of someone
or something are a familiar sight. Like her symbolic, cultural
ancestor, the poet too is restless, searching for something to complete her. The sun asks, "Whom do you search for?" but the poet's

answer reframes the question in terms of a place: *un solario de amor* ("a sunscape of love").

In several key places Corpi uses ellipses as linguistic devices to mark meaningful silences that cannot be filled with words. In this instance an ellipsis follows the word *Amor*, significant because love is simultaneously everything and nothing for the poet: everything, because it is what she most desires; nothing, because she can never obtain it. Here, as elsewhere, the ellipsis signals a point of extreme emotion. It creates the effect of suspension, as the echo of the wind's voice lingers before vanishing into the landscape.

In the third vignette of "Solario" the poet recalls Tirso, her family's water carrier (*el aguador*), who taught her to swear when she was three years old. By repeating the curses in the company of others she delighted Tirso and his people but outraged her family who washed her mouth out with laundry soap.

III

Tirso se llamaba
el aguador.
Me enseñó a mal decir
cuando apenas tres años
angostos pero hondos
se abrían paso
entre el verde añejo
de las sabanas.

al oirme decir aquello
que era extraño
a mis labios
la mitad del mundo
lo celebró con risas
y la otra mitad
me podó la selva
de la lengua
con navaja de lejía.

III

Tirso
was the water-carrier's name.
He taught me to swear
when barely three years
(narrow but deep)
were opening their way

between the ancient greens
of the savannahs.

When I said those things
so strange to my lips
in company
half my hearers
laughed;
the other half
pruned the jungle
on my tongue
with the razor
of laundry soap.

In this episode the world divides into two social groups: one that enjoys the child's blasphemies and one that punishes her naive spontaneity. Tirso has contaminated the child by teaching her words that the family castigates her for uttering. We obtain an image of a proper, decent family that prohibits its little girl from cursing and swearing. The poetic consciousness pinpoints an early experience that introduces the counterpressures of expression and repression.

The fourth vignette, about the poet's grandmother, is significant precisely because there is no speech between poet and grandmother. Although the grandmother plays a key role in "Tres Mujeres," even uttering the words that constitute a central taboo broken by the granddaughter, she is, except for this passage, absent from *Palabras de Mediodía.*

IV

Voy mirando sus manos y su boca
tranquilos los ojos que me miran
como faroles al final de la vereda
de un bosque de mechones y sonrisas.

Mi abuela junto al fogón viejo
trenzándose el cabello.

IV

I watch her hands and mouth,
her eyes watching me, tranquil
as lamps at the end of the path
through a forest of hair and smiles

My grandmother, sitting beside the stove,
braiding her hair.

While the poet observes her grandmother's gestures, the two women seem to communicate by way of their eyes. The grandmother's action of braiding her hair introduces an important motif in Corpi's collection. Corpi's women characters are silent, without words. Like their creator, they are cultivators of the unsayable,[18] communicating feelings with their eyes or by gestures. In this vignette the poetic consciousness attempts to "read" her grandmother's eyes or gestures, as if the grandmother by braiding her hair was "weaving" a message for the poet.

Corpi suggests a link between the actions of braiding and weaving in the second vignette. Her poetic consciousness desires to find the thread (un hilo) or the strand of hair (un cabello) which ties up all those small things heaped up inside herself from years ago, discarded as one might consign useless objects to the attic. Her poetic goal is to find this thread, this hair, and untie the knot of all those things piled up inside the "attic" of her spirit:

> Hay un hilo, un cabello
> quizá, de tan delgado
> imperceptible que ata
> las mil cosas pequeñas
> que en alguna edad
> del espíritu
> quedaron arrumbadas
> en el desván
> de la conciencia.
>
> A thread, a hair perhaps,
> so thin as to be
> imperceptible
> ties together
> a thousand things
> left heaped
> during some age of the spirit
> in the attic
> of the mind.

"Solario" builds up to a key statement in which Corpi links the image of the seas of Veracruz with a restlessness that may lead to freedom. She closes "Solario" with images of inquietude (las aguas inquietas), bitterness (salada), and rebellion (emancipación), thus intimating that she retains something (Algo) from a childhood experience which moves her to rebel and to search for a more open life.

IX

Algo del mar
se me quedó en las venas:
La salada emancipación
de las aguas inquietas.

IX

Something of the sea
stayed in my veins:
The salty freedom
of restless water.

The image of salt, recurring often in Corpi's poetry, suggests that
her search for liberation will be neither sweet nor easy.

In "Solario Nocturno" Corpi articulates the images that describe the side of her that mourns, the melancholy and silent side.
In this poem, in contrast with the Veracruz poems, Catholicism
and its Lenten rites submerge Corpi's retrospective look at the
region:

SOLARIO NOCTURNO

I

San Luis
con su alma de piedra
cincelada
por los cascos indómitos
del sol
tenía
la hipnotizante
melancolía
de un tambor de cuaresma
y el misterio enlutado
del violeta
bordado en el sayal
del corazón.

II

Buscaba el verde
entre las grietas
de las canteras
y sólo encontraba
el gris del futuro
enclaustrado
por los altos muros
coloniales.

III

Era la hora extendida
del oficio vespertino,
lisa, lisa, alisada,
monótona y ténebre,
con sus diálogos
letánicos y fríos.

Las torres caían
consecutivas,
las azucenas
se desplomaban
en cadena
sobre las cabezas
de los pobres
que seguían siendo
pobres a la salida.

Y yo me preguntaba
si éste era el misterio
que guardaba el cielo.

IV

El campesino hurgaba
la tierra
con sus manos
de cuero deslustrado
y ella dura y seca
lo burlaba de su amor.

V

Ahí conocí
por primera vez
el terrible pecado
del silencio.

NOCTURNAL SUNSCAPE

I

San Luis
with its soul of stone
chiseled
by the untamed hoofs
of the sun
possessed
the hypnotic
melancholy
of a Lenten drum

and the somber mystery
of violet
enbroidered on the sackcloth
of its heart.

II

I searched for green
in the cracks
of quarried hillsides
and found only
the gray of the future
enclosed
in high colonial
walls.

III

The hour of Vespers
was lengthening,
smooth, smooth, polished,
tenebrous, monotonous,
with the cold responses
of its litanies.

Towers fell
in sequence
lilies
dropped chains
of petals
on the heads
of the poor
who left
poor as they had come.

I wondered
if this was the mystery
guarded by heaven.

IV

The peasant dug
at the earth
with his scuffed
leather hands
and the earth, hard and cold,
gave him nothing for his love.

V

It was there
I first discovered
the terrible sin
of silence.

The San Luis landscape is dry, hard rock, with no greenery. The Lenten season, with its violet colors and its rituals of mourning, sacrifice, and self-effacement, pervades the atmosphere. San Luis, the saint, functions as metaphor for the external landscape, which is a reflection of the poet's inner state. A "mystery draped in mourning" (el misterio enlutado) has been embroidered, not on the saint's cassock (el sayal), but rather on the "cassock" of the saint's heart. The word enlutado, from en luto, literally means "in mourning." By extension it is "embroidered" in the heart of the landscape and by implication in the heart of the poetic self.

San Luis, a center of mining since the colonial era, does not offer the speaker the fertile, tropical lands of Veracruz. She searches for greenery in the spaces between the rocks on the hillsides but finds only the "gray of the future" (recall Justina of "Tres Mujeres"). The tedious litanies (diálogos) of the long hour of Vespers go back and forth in a monotonous question-and-answer pattern. The land is silent, making no response to the laborer's efforts. In the closing statement, parallel to the one at the end of the Jáltipan poems, the poet, from a perspective of achieved knowledge, remembers learning the "terrible sin / of silence." Only the vague deictic Ahí ("there") pinpoints this experience. The deictic itself confirms a "silence" because it fails to specify where in exact terms. Corpi uses the adverb "there" again and again to refer to physical and spiritual places that have to do with emptiness and loss.

"COFRADÍA DE INSERVIBLES" AND "LA CIEGA": PROHIBITION OF SEXUALITY

Both "Cofradía de Inservibles" and "La Ciega" are meditations on desire and the failure to fulfill it. In "Cofradía de Inservibles" Corpi attempts to define an internal room where she has stored "things" that remain unfulfilled, unexpressed, or incomplete, which are las mil cosas pequeñas ("the thousand small things") mentioned in "Solario." "La Ciega," a parable, dramatizes the process of self-fragmentation. Paradoxically, both poems affirm and deny the visual sense as the center of activity.

COFRADÍA DE INSERVIBLES

En la vastedad
del estrecho espacio
entre espíritu y mente
he formado una cofradía
de inservibles
         fantasías fragmentadas

poemas inconclusos
    rituales interrumpidos
hazañas que no llevé a cabo
         deseos de marinera frustrada   *10*
    estrías de luz color música
diálogos monolingües
         viceversas de una sola dirección
recuerdos de la hija que no tuve
         pequeños pedazos de muerte

         De vez en cuando
         me refugio ahí
         ausente de mí misma

como una mancha de tinta   en el papel indiferente
como una estrella atrapada   en un gran hueco sideral   *20*
    sin manos   sin piel   sorda
              y muda
         y presido sacerdotisa
              nocturna
         la ceremonia diabólica
         de todas las cosas rotas
         e inconclusas de mi vida

SECRET SOCIETY OF FAILURES

In the vastness
of the narrow space
between spirit and mind
I have formed a secret society
of failures
         fragmented fantasies

unfinished poems
    interrupted rites
deeds undone
         desires of a land-bound sailor   *10*
    strips of light   color music
monolingual dialogues

                    one-way vice versas
           memories of a daughter never born
                 little pieces of death

                              From time to time
                              I take refuge there
                              absent from myself

        like an ink-stain   on indifferent paper
        like a star trapped   in a great sidereal hole   *20*
           without hands   without skin   deaf
                                    mute
                           and I preside, nocturnal
                                 priestess
                           over the diabolic ceremony
                           of all the broken, unfinished
                           things in my life.

Corpi's society of failures is made up of shadows, of dreams
that might have been but never were. Desires are dismembered,
interrupted, unfinished, fragmented. The poet catalogues her ruptured fantasies, a strategy that emphasizes the pointing and listing
of experience instead of conveying a participation in unity and
wholeness. She has stored her "fragmented fantasies" (ll. 7–15)
between mind and spirit, a reference to "el desván / de la concien-
cia" ("the attic / of the mind") in "Solario." At the beginning of
the poem the reader confronts "En la vastedad" ("In the vastness")
but then is immediately forced to take in "del estrecho espacio"
("of the narrow space"). The deflation from vastness to nar-
rowness is one manifestation of Corpi's poetic strategy: from
everything to nothing, from promise to loss, from abundance to
emptiness.

The poet's self-fragmentation is evident when she says (ll.
16–18) that she finds sanctuary within this internal room, "absent
from myself." Ironically, she finds a haven in the very place (*ahí*)
where all her broken dreams are. The word *misma* in Spanish is
an intensifier. The phrase *mi misma* here (literally, "me myself")
suggests that the speaker separates herself from the person she
feels herself to be. She describes the separation in terms of two
entities that should enjoy cohesion and harmony: the paper is
indifferent to a blot of ink; a huge astral hole traps a star. In her
internal room she lacks corporeal presence, alienated from her
physical body, its sensations and passions. The lines that follow

deny touch (*sin manos*), feeling (*sin piel*), hearing (*sorda*), and speech (*muda*), thus alluding to the repression of speech and all senses except the visual. The physical energy and sensation lost in olfactory, auditory, kinesthetic, and speaking realms are sublimated in a visual experience. Sight is the only sense affirmed: "y presido sacerdotisa / nocturna."

The poet's image of herself as priestess of the night recalls the night owl in the ceiba tree in the first vignette of "Solario":

Seguí camino del olvido
y sorprendí al tecolote
en la ceiba dormido
con los ojos abiertos.

I followed the road to oblivion
and surprised an owl
sleeping wide-eyed
in the ceiba tree.

The juxtaposition of the two images—the owl in the ceiba tree and the poet as a nocturnal priestess—produces an ironic effect. Like her friend the owl, the speaker is all eyes; but like the owl that, even with eyes open, is really asleep, she too is asleep because she presides over basic voids or lacks: "todas las cosas rotas / e inconclusas de mi vida" (ll. 26–27).

The image of the priestess of the night also strengthens the religious connotations of the word *cofradía*, a community or brotherhood sharing common spiritual goals. The speaker's rituals, however, are diabolical because they celebrate the horror of dismemberment rather than the beauty of wholeness. The irony of the religious connotation is reinforced by the placement of the words on the page, which seem to establish the contour of an altar or a temple, with lines 1–6 the raised platform and lines 7–15 the foundation. The remaining lines repeat the shape with variations. A further irony is that the priestess, who should be in front of the altar, is down below, as though supporting the dead weight of her broken dreams. The "diabolic ceremony" refers to Corpi's writing as a ritual that again and again makes the memory of failure one of its primary subjects.

Whereas Corpi presents herself in "Cofradía" as a subject who is speaking, in "La Ciega" she speaks about herself as a subject. The poem thus reveals her own fragmentation. She divides herself into narrator, character (*ella*), the character's reflection (*la sombra*), and the character as "other" (*la otra*). "La Ciega" is a concatenation of reflections:

LA CIEGA

A mediodía anticipaba la redacción de su sombra
sobre el pavimento. Todo oscilaba, se mutaba
mientras el sol acumulaba sus granos de luz.
Mas ella fija esperaba a la otra.

Las dos de la tarde consumieron su propio fuego.
Y al mirar al suelo el deslinde de la sombra ya
no era ella.

Levantó entonces los ojos. Del racimo se
desprendieron dos gotas de sangre. Y quedó ahí
fija y ciega.

El viento murmuró: "Ciega, la sombra es una ilusión,
una ilusión . . ."

THE BLIND WOMAN

At noon she waited for her shadow
to be composed on the pavement. Everything wavered,
changing, while the sun accumulated grains
of light. But she remained fixed, waiting for the other.

Two o'clock consumed its own fire.
And when she looked at the ground the border of the shadow
was no longer herself.

Then she raised her eyes. Two drops of blood
fell from the cluster. And she stayed there
fixed and blind.

The wind murmured: "Woman, the shadow
is a lie, a lie . . ."

At the height of the day (*mediodía*, "noon") a woman anticipates the reflection of her shadow on the street. The shimmering, vibrating setting ("Todo oscilaba, se mutaba") suggests an open future, full of potential. The verb *anticipar* connotes hope and expectation. The sun, now gathering its "grains of light," will write (*redacción*) her shadow on the pavement. The *mas* ("except" or "but") of line 4 introduces a shift away from a vibrating environment to a protagonist who is "fixed," in the sense of being rigid or unbending. The verb *esperar* expresses a sense of something the woman knows is coming but without the attitude implicit in *anticipar* of looking forward to it. These lines imply that the narrating consciousness and the woman (*ella*) know already that one shadow is anticipated but another will appear.

Within several hours the day's fire has come and gone. The statement in line 5 is somewhat ambiguous because grammatically the possessive pronoun *su* must refer back to "Las dos de la tarde." Yet the woman is also its referent. The *su* therefore functions as a marker for both the subject of the sentence ("dos de la tarde") and the woman about whom the narrator is speaking. Before the woman even knows what has befallen her, her passion (*fuego*) is consumed. Upon looking down and seeing a shadow different from the one she expected to see, the woman encounters *la otra*. By noting that "el deslinde de la sombra ya / no era ella," the narrator is really saying that *ella* has become *la otra*. With a twist similar to those found in a *cuento fantástico* by Borges or Cortázar, Corpi denies that *ella* is *la otra*, since *ella* was the shadow that the sun wrote and the afternoon consumed, but she also affirms that *ella* is *la otra*. The reflection the woman desired to see is lost in space and time.

The woman now turns to look in the opposite direction where she sees a *racimo* ("cluster"). The word *racimo* presupposes a tree or a vine with clusters of fruit or flowers from which one might extract sweet juices or smell sweet perfumes: "un racimo de uvas" ("grapes") or "un racimo de flores" ("flowers"), for example. Instead, the cluster releases two drops of blood, one for each eye, which cause the woman's blindness. She is now not only *fija* but *ciega* too. The two drops of blood are a sign of extreme suffering and pain. In the last sentence of stanza 3 Corpi reinforces the impression of stasis and fixity three times, as though the woman were nailed to the ground: *quedó, ahí, fija*. The wind, which now speaks, represents an inner voice belonging to the character. In addressing, or naming, the woman as *ciega*, the wind confirms that she is "La Ciega." Corpi divides her narrator into a character who is *ciega* and externalizes an inner voice that knows better, that sees beyond the endless turnings of the mind which lead nowhere, as in "Cofradía" (ll. 12–13): "diálogos monolingües / viceversas de una sola dirección" ("monolingual dialogues / one-way vice versas." The wind, associated with passion and love in Corpi's poetry, is wise, functioning as an agent with powers to see the situation from the outside.

"La Ciega" is a parable for the pattern of events that characterize women's lives in Corpi's poems: promise, tragedy, and ultimate loss. Corpi's aspirations as a woman from "Tres Mujeres" suggest that the *sombra* of line 1 may refer to the glorified image about womanhood her culture instilled in her. The image is apt for a woman taught to become a reflection of her husband. Socialized in such a culture she would probably see the woman as the mirror of the man, who is the ideal. Given the ruptures in Corpi's life, this woman came and vanished before she could develop and mature. The reflection of *la otra* is the woman she did become, but whom she denies as real. The "drops of blood" or the pain may refer to the *mujer sufrida*, epitomized by Guadalupe in "Tres Mujeres." Pain blinds the woman who suffers for others and never considers her own wishes. She suffers in the name of an ideal: the perfect wife, woman, and mother prescribed by her culture.

The moral that the *sombra* is an illusion (a deception, a falsity) has a double meaning. If the *sombra* of the penultimate line is the same as the *sombra* of line 1, the moral is that the woman should not accept as valid her culture's traditional values about women. But if it means the *sombra* of line 6, the moral is that the woman she did become is unreal and she, in turn, must not interpret this image as a reflection of her authentic self. The irony is that the image she refuses to recognize as authentic is really herself. The paradox, according to the wind's words, is that this reality is an illusion. The ellipsis ending the poem points to an unfinished story, or to a story yet to be written. For if the woman is fixed because she believes in the shadow and if something within tells her that the shadow is an illusion, then where or to whom does the poetic consciousness turn? The next two poems attempt to fill the silence.

"PUENTE DE CRISTAL" AND "PASIÓN SIN NOMBRE": SEXUAL DESIRE SUBLIMATED

"Puente de Cristal" ("Crystal Bridge") and "Pasión sin Nombre" ("Passion Without a Name") present two different views of the persona's sublimation of sexual desire. They create an inner vitality in order to compensate for an essentially lonely and empty life. In "Puente de Cristal" the sexual act is consummated, whereas in "Pasión sin Nombre" it never takes place. The creative energy impelling these poems comes from the erotic codes and conventions of a Mexican lyrical tradition. In "Puente de Cristal" the natural cycle of a larva becoming a caterpillar and then a butterfly implicitly denotes the sexual growth and maturation of a woman; the night succumbing to the sieges of war is a metaphor for a woman surrendering herself to a male lover. In "Pasión sin Nombre" the image of the *potro* (a young horse) is a metaphor for the wild, unbridled passion of the lover.

In "Puente de Cristal" Corpi disguises a story about sexual liberation with a story about political liberation. Codes of social struggle intersect with codes of sexual struggle to create ambiguity. The struggle (*la lucha*), however, is more sexual than political. "Pasión sin Nombre" contains less displacement of sexual desire because Corpi represents the object of desire as a man.

PUENTE DE CRISTAL

Caminábamos dóciles
en un puente de cristal
y la lucha nos encontró.

Se desgarró el capullo
y a punto cero calculado
el ojo sibílico apuntó.

Grito de lucha
en el campo
en la fábrica
en mi yo
en el tuyo
al extraño
al compañero

Sólo entre el silencio
preciso de dos puertas
pueden mantenerse
crisálidas eternas.

Caminábamos dolientes
en un puente de cristal
entre dos puertos.

Abrió sus piernas la noche
El arco ofendido cedió
y se fertilizó
la semilla guerrillera
entre el abrir y cerrar.

Giró el humo rojo
en la médula del viento
formando punto a punto
el fénix dialéctico.

Y yo por primera vez
dejé que mi palabra
apuntara hacia esenciales.

THE CRYSTAL BRIDGE

Obediently we walked
over a crystal bridge
and discord found us.

The bud tore loose
and the sybil's eye
aimed at zero.

Battle cry
in the fields
in the factory
in my self
in yours
to the stranger
to the friend

Only in the precise
silence of two doors
can the chrysalis
sleep forever.

Painfully we walked
over a crystal bridge
between two doors.

Night opened her legs
The wounded arch gave way
and the seed of war
quickened
between the opening and the shutting.

Red smoke whirled
in the medulla of the wind
forming, point by point,
the dialectic phoenix.

And for the first time
I allowed my word
to turn to essentials.

The first stanza of "Puente de Cristal" establishes the setting. The plural verb *caminábamos* suggests a group of two or more travelers, but it may also point to a speaker who travels in the community of her dreams and illusions. Since the bridge is "crystal," it represents a tenuous boundary that can break at any moment. At a metaphoric level it has two possible readings: in images of war, we may read a sexual struggle; in images of sex, we may read a political struggle. The word *dociles* ("soft") suggests travelers who are easily led, who are even unaware of their surroundings. The travelers are confronted by *la lucha,* taken as a reference to social struggle until the reader remembers that Lucha is the poet's name. The poet is playing with her name for the ambiguities it allows. If indeed we take *la lucha* to designate the poet, then the poem is a metaphoric description of an encounter with herself. The poet's strategy of punning on her name is also a convention of a popular lyrical tradition.[19]

The second stanza shifts from descriptive language to a language that is more metaphoric and lyrical. It also shifts from an "I" that speaks of itself as subject (*caminábamos*) to an "I" that speaks of itself as object, or the *capullo.* The reader's attention is deflected from the real subject of the discourse to something else. The shift from an "I" as subject to an "I" as object is a recurrent strategy employed by Corpi. The *capullo,* a metaphor for the bud of a flower or the cocoon of a butterfly, becomes the vehicle for describing the result of the encounter with *la lucha.* Essentially, a silky tissue or covering is torn. Our attention is directed to the natural process of the ripping of the cocoon in order to describe a woman's entrance into physical sexuality. These lines are prophetic of the events described in stanza 6. The sibylline eye points with a calculated aim to the target (*punto cero*). The commotion and confusion of struggle are felt by everyone in the fields and factories. The line *Grito de lucha* again plays with the ambiguity of the poet's name: the cry of a community's struggle or the cry of a woman who encounters her sexuality for the first time. The shift from *en* to *al* in stanza 3 suggests that the cry reaches the *extraño* ("stranger") and the *compañero* ("brother"). Since both are preceded by the preposition *al*, they would seem to be regarded as equal. In a political context it makes no sense to equate "stranger" or "enemy" with "brother" because they take different sides in the struggle. In a sexual context the male lover may be a stranger or an enemy if he is feared, or a *compañero* if he is loved. Depending on the context, the word *compañero* means either a comrade or a lover/husband. The context here suggests the latter.

Stanza 4 shifts back into the more contemplative mode of stanza 2. Now the poetic consciousness realizes that only in some utopian realm ("entre el silencio / preciso de dos puertas" ["the precise / silence of two doors"]) can "chrysalis," or a condition of purity, exist. Stanza 5 reflects a change in consciousness because now the travelers are *dolientes* instead of *dóciles*. They experience the pain that awareness brings. The bridge they travel connects two ports or places of safety; it is the position between, emphasizing the peril of the journey.

The next stanza describes the consummation of the sexual act through images of war. The stanza also has a political connotation: the arch under attack (*ofendido*) surrenders to the enemy and under cover of night the seeds of guerrilla warfare or of revolution are sown. The erotic images suggest that the sexual struggle is more intensive than the political one.[20] The night serves as a metaphor for the woman surrendering to her lover. The *arco* ("arch") is traced by the position of the woman's legs which open to receive the sperm. The arch, a metonymy for the woman's sexual organ, is *ofendido* in the sense of "offended" or "hurt." There is another disguise in that *arco* as a masculine noun requires a masculine adjective: *ofendido* instead of *ofendida*.[21] The verb *cedió*, the preterit of *ceder*, is more appropriate in a context of a town under siege which ultimately surrenders. The sound of *cedió*, however, suggests *se dió* ("to give oneself"), from the reflexive *darse*, a more suitable verb when a woman gives herself to a man. Sexual codes are couched in political terms. The *semilla guerrillera* in a sexual context is the poet's impulse (*fertilizó*) to rebel and seek her sexual liberation.

The result of the sexual act in the following stanza is the "Red smoke," or the passion. Now realized, it forms the phoenix.

The phrase "en la médula del viento" ("in the medulla of the wind") points to the core of the passion: *médula* suggests "core," and "wind" in Corpi's poetry is the epitome of passion or love. The process of death and rebirth evoked by the image of the phoenix reinforces the transformation that has taken place within the poet. The dead embers of her passion have been stirred and transformed into passionate love.

In the final stanza the speaker inserts herself directly into the poetic discourse for the first time. After the sexual experience comes catharsis, and the poet—"por primera vez" ("for the first time")—can speak about essentials. The use of the preterit *dejé* ("allowed") and of the subjective *apuntara* ("that my word may point") places the statement at the level of desire rather than of fact. The poet sees herself in an imaginative space speaking directly without disguises. The implication is that the poetic consciousness knows that, until sexual desire is gratified, her words cannot describe things for what they are.

A comparison of "Puente de Cristal" and "Pasión sin Nombre" suggests that the poet can describe the consummation of the sexual act according to romantic conventions when it is presented in figurative terms, but not when it involves the woman's physical body. Although "Pasión sin Nombre" is certainly not free of some disguises Corpi uses to describe the sexual act between a man and a woman, it leaves no doubt that the gratification of sexual desire lies at the center of the poet's quest. The title of "Pasión sin Nombre" is ambiguous, pointing either to a passion so intense that it is impossible to name or to a passion that comes to no fruition (*sin Nombre*). A close reading confirms that the poem allows for both possibilities.

PASIÓN SIN NOMBRE

Desdoblé el miedo
y observé al potro
desbocado de tu amor.

Quería que su crin
brillara entre
luciérnagas ocultas;

que tus manos
se cerraran en mi cuerpo
y desataran el nudo
ciego del viento dormido.

Mas no llegó el potro
con su crin brilante,
ni el roce de tu mano,
ni tú, antiguo amante.

Y mi cuerpo se quedó
muy quieto, centrado
en el blanco vestal
del viento huracanado.

PASSION WITHOUT A NAME

I unfolded my fear
and watched
the unbridled horse of your love.

I wanted his mane
to shine with
hidden fireflies;

Your hands to close around my body,
untie the blind knot
of the sleeping storm.

Yet the horse did not arrive
with its shining mane
nor the touch of your hand,
nor you, my love.

And my body became
very quiet, centered
in the vestal robe
of the hurricane.

This poem divides into two parts, with the first three stanzas expressing the speaker's ardent desire and the last two confirming its nonfulfillment. The speaker unfolds (*desdoblé*) her fear and dares to see (*observé*) the lover's passion. The speaker is a passive participant in the passion; she does not say *sentí* ("I felt") or *me dí* ("I gave myself"), for example. Again the focus on the eyes: she observes from a distance. The male lover's wild passion is personified by the *potro*, a young male horse before its first mating. The second stanza continues to direct the reader's attention to the *potro*, the object spoken about, rather than to the *tú*, the person addressed. It concentrates on one aspect of the young horse—*su crin* ("its mane"). This stanza reveals the woman's socialization established in "Tres Mujeres," where all the woman's goals and motivations are projected to the male. As Amerina told Juana María, "Siempre has vivido por o para alguien más. Nunca para ti misma" (p. 83). ("You have always lived through or for someone else. Never for yourself.") The speaker in "Pasión sin Nombre" wants the male to shine in glory, to outshine even the *luciérnagas ocultas* ("hidden fireflies").

The third stanza continues to elaborate on this theme, but now the focus veers from the third person *su* to the second person *tú*. The lines "que tus manos / se cerraran en mi cuerpo" marks Corpi's closest approach to expressing an undisguised sexual desire, as her persona now talks directly to the lover, telling him she desires his hands to close within her body (*en mi cuerpo*), an especially strong image. The word *en* in this instance means *dentro* ("inside"). The poet does not say "around my body" (*alrededor de mi cuerpo*), as the English translation has it.[22] The phrase *en mi cuerpo* obviously suggests "within" or "inside" the body. The next two lines, though advancing the speaker's desire, begin to hint that its realization is impossible. The *viento dormido* ("sleeping wind") is the latent passion, or "nudo / ciego" ("blind knot"). By saying "el nudo / ciego del viento dormido," Corpi affirms the presence of a "knot" so tight and blind that it is impossible to undo.

Stanza 4 marks the unbridgeable gap between the speaker's desire and its consummation. Corpi's speaker carefully negates each item that functions as an object of desire. Nothing has materialized: the *potro* did not come; nor did its manifestation (*crin*), the lover's manifestation (*el roce de tu mano*), or the lover himself (*ni tú, antiguo amante*). The addressee is an *antiguo amante* ("ancient lover") simply because he has been desired for so long. The result is that the speaker's body is left totally immobile, silent, and still. With different words, the poet conveys immobility three times: *quedó* ("was left"); *muy quieto* ("very still"); *centrado* ("centered," "fixed").

The final two lines express the sublimated desire. The word *vestal* suggests the vestal virgins of classical mythology who vowed to remain chaste and guard the fire of the hearth. The poet, like the vestal virgins, sees herself dedicated to the service of a higher ideal, or, as she puts it, the *viento huracanado*. The classical virgins guarded a hearth fire; the speaker as vestal virgin guards a hurricane. The hurricane is an energy image highlighting the intensity of her passion. The irony is that, whereas the vestal virgins chose to remain pure in order to fulfill their vow to the goddess Vesta, the speaker seems to have no choice.

The word *blanco*, used as an adjective, means "white," hence purity, but as it is preceded by the masculine article *el* it may also connote the "target" or the "center" of the service. The speaker's passion has been transformed from a *viento dormido* to a *viento huracanado*. In the midst of the very passion itself she cannot obtain it. The connotations of "vestal"—fire, hearth, and altar—suggest the sanctity of the home to which the woman may dedicate herself. The poet's writing is also a sublimation of sexual desire because in it she acts out her service to passion, the subject of her poetry.

The focus of "Pasión sin Nombre" is on the speaker's disappointment over the lover's failure to arrive. She is simply left at the altar of a violent wind to soothe and care for her devouring passion.

3

In the next set of poems Corpi embeds her own story in the fictional stories of three women: Marina in the Marina poems, Veronica in "Romance Tejido," and Guadalupe in "Romance Negro." In the guise of an account of their repression, Corpi expresses her desire for sexual fulfillment. The pattern of these women's lives is similar to the pattern of the poet-narrator's life as described in earlier poems: the promise of a full life ends in total loss and deep sorrow. Like the poetic persona in "Puente de Cristal" and "Pasión sin Nombre," these women's lives are structured by the tension between sexuality and prohibition.

The reader is never told in clear, direct terms what tragic events have befallen Marina, Veronica, and Guadalupe to make them so sad and silent. For example, Veronica in "Romance Tejido" mentally weaves her story of passion as she executes a design in an actual embroidery. The audience must disentangle the threads in the warp and the woof of her design in order to decipher her story. As none of these three women ever speaks, and as they are never questioned as to their feelings about themselves or as to what has happened to them, the poet-narrator's task is to build a bridge between them and their society.

Corpi metaphorically alludes to the sexual act as the root of these women's problems. The descriptions of the sexual acts are ambiguous, though rape is suggested by adjectives in the Marina poems and verbs in "Romance Negro" connoting violence. Yet the metaphorization of the events in all three poems works against the presentation of the sexual act as rape. The poems all pursue society's reaction to the women's participation in sexual acts. Apparently Corpi wants to protest not so much the sexual act itself as the rejection of the women by their families and their culture.

THE MARINA POEMS

Corpi's poems on Marina tell the story of the young Indian woman who served Hernán Cortés as guide, interpreter, comrade-in-arms, mistress, and mother of his son. Three different forms of her name—Marina, Malintzin, and Malinche—are referred to in the analysis of "Tres Mujeres." Malintzin Tenépal, so named by her parents, was the daughter of a cacique or chief of the province of Coatzacoalcos, where Marina was born. Doña Marina is her Spanish name, the title of respect having been conferred on her by Cortés and other Spaniards who knew her. Marina is the symbolic mother of the Mexican people. Malinche is the name given to Marina by some modern Mexicans and understood by all in Mexico and the Southwest to mean the traitress who knowingly and willingly betrayed her Indian civilization by allying herself with Cortés and the Spaniards. The term is still used in those areas to designate anybody corrupted by foreign influences.[23] To this legacy of names may now be added a fourth, Chingada, the central figure in the writings of Octavio Paz and Carlos Fuentes in the modern period.[24] Octavio Paz describes the Chingada as the violated native woman and mother, a symbol of the violation of "the very flesh of Indian women."[25] According to Paz, Marina, fascinated by Cortés and, by extension, by the Spanish male, allowed herself to be seduced, giving herself voluntarily. Even so, Paz sees her as a figure representing all Indian women who were not only fascinated or seduced, but also violated or raped, by the Spaniards. For Paz, "every woman—even when she gives herself willingly—is torn open by the man, is the Chingada."[26] Marina is the symbol of betrayal because she allowed herself to be "opened," or "penetrated," by the Spanish male.

In her four poems about Marina, Corpi attempts to reverse the image given to Marina by modern Mexican writers such as Paz.[27] She presents Marina not as a woman who betrayed (*se vendió*), but as a woman who was betrayed (*fué vendida*) by husband, lover, and son. Implicitly, she was also betrayed by family, culture, and country. As in Paz's cultural discourse, the focal point of Corpi's poetic discourse is sexual. But unlike Paz, who portrays a Marina eager to jump into bed with the Spaniards, Corpi, in "Marina Madre," the first of the four poems, shows Marina as an unwilling participant. Yet Corpi's Marina does not actively resist the rape. Rather, the reader must presuppose a reluctant Marina who felt she had no other choice but to submit, as men would force sex upon her in spite of her objections.

I. MARINA MADRE

Del barro más húmedo la hicieron,
al rayo del sol tropical la secaron,
con la sangre de un cordero tierno
su nombre escribieron los viejos
en la corteza de ese árbol
tan viejo como ellos.

Húmeda de tradición, mística
y muda fué vendida . . .   8
de mano en mano, noche a noche,
negada y desecrada, esperando el alba
y el canto de la lechuza
que nunca llegaban.
Su vientre robado de su fruto;
hecha un puño de polvo seco su alma.

Tú no la querías ya y él la negaba   15
y aquel que cuando niño ¡mamá! le gritaba
cuando creció le puso por nombre "la chingada."

I. MARINA MOTHER

They made her of the softest clay
and dried her under the rays of the tropical sun.
With the blood of a tender lamb
her name was written by the elders

184

on the bark of that tree
as old as they.

Steeped in tradition, mystic
and mute she was sold—   8
from hand to hand, night to night,
denied and desecrated, waiting for the dawn
and for the owl's song
that would never come;
her womb sacked of its fruit,
her soul thinned to a handful of dust.

You no longer loved her, the elders denied her,   15
and the child who cried out to her "mamá!"
grew up and called her "whore."

II. Marina Virgen

De su propio pie, junto al altar
del dios crucificado se hincó.
Como ella te amó, veía solamente
al ser sangrante. Y amaba en él
tu recuerdo secreto y enlutado.

Había querido lavar su pecado   6
con agua bendita. Y arropaba
su cuerpo con una manta gruesa y nítida
para que no supieras que su piel
morena estaba maldita.

Alguna vez te detuviste a pensar
en dónde estaba su alma escondida.
No sabías que la había sembrado
en las entrañas de la tierra
que sus manos cultivaban—   15
la tierra negra y húmeda de tu vida.

II. Marina Virgin

Of her own accord, before the altar
of the crucified god she knelt.
Because she loved you, she only saw
the bleeding man, and loved in him
her secret and mourning memory of you.

She tried to wash away her sin   6
with holy water, then covered her body
with a long, thick cloth

so you would never know
her brown skin had been damned.

Once, you stopped to wonder
where her soul was hidden
not knowing she had planted it
in the entrails of that earth
her hands had cultivated—   15
the moist, black earth of your life.

III. LA HIJA DEL DIABLO

Cuando murió, el trueno se reventó en el norte,
y junto al altar de piedra la noche entera
el copal ardió. Su mística pulsación para
siempre calló. Cayó hecho pedazos el ídolo
de barro sucio y viejo, y su nombre se lo llevó
el viento con un solo murmullo ronco:
su nombre tan parecido a la profundidad
salina del mar. Poco quedó. Sólo una semilla
a medio germinar.

III. THE DEVIL'S DAUGHTER

When she died, lightning struck in the north,
and on the new stone altar the incense burned
all night long. Her mystic pulsing
silenced, the ancient idol
shattered, her name
devoured by the wind in one deep growl
(her name so like the salt depths of the sea)—
little remained. Only a half-germinated seed.

IV. ELLA (MARINA AUSENTE)

Ella. Una flor quizá, un remanso fresco . . .
una noche tibia, tropical,
o una criatura triste, en una prisión
encerrada: de barro húmedo y suave:
es la sombra enlutada de un recuerdo   5
ancestral que vendrá por la mañana
cruzando el puente con manos llenas—
llenas de sol y de tierra.

IV. SHE (MARINA DISTANT)

She. A flower perhaps, a pool of fresh water . . .
a tropical night,

or a sorrowful child, enclosed
in a prison of the softest clay:
mourning shadow of an ancestral memory,   5
crossing the bridge at daybreak,
her hands full of earth and sun.

In her vision of Marina, Corpi draws on images from the four
categories of experience: (1) the natural world; (2) the Judeo-Christian world; (3) popular Mexican myths; and (4) the world of artistic expression (writing/poetry). The first three poems in the
series depict the central roles usually contained in the symbolic
representation of Marina as woman: (1) mother, (2) virgin, and
(3) condemned woman, or whore. The fourth poem signals a new
"presence" yet to come.

As the poet-narrator refrains from directly assuming the consciousness of Marina throughout the four poems, Marina has no
power of speech. In this respect Corpi's characterization goes
counter to the historical figure of Marina who, in facilitating
communication between Moctezuma and Cortés, served as the
linguistic bridge between the two cultures. She knew various
dialects and was said to have learned Spanish rapidly. To the
Spanish chroniclers she was known as *la lengua* ("the tongue").[28]
Corpi's narrator is a mediator between a wordless Marina and an
audience that listens to the narrator express and interpret
Marina's sentiments.

Once again, Corpi's poetic strategy is to shift from a form of
address implying a general audience to one that implies a direct
interlocutor, as she does in "Pasión sin Nombre" and other
poems. In certain places she makes her audience concrete by
shifting to a *Tú* ("you"). For example, in the final stanza of
"Marina Madre" the narrator's audience, familiar with the legend
of Marina, yields its privileged position to Hernán Cortés, the
referent of *Tú*, and remains outside the discourse to overhear the
rest of the sentence. This time the audience links *él* with Cortés's
lieutenant, Juan Jaramillo, whom Marina married, according to
Bernal Díaz, an eyewitness and a chronicler of the conquest.[29] The
aquel ("that one") is Martín, Marina's son by Cortés.[30] In "Marina
Virgen," the second poem, the narrator shifts from one audience
to the other, the first two lines implying a general audience but
the next four lines implying the direct interlocutor *Tú*. In stanza
2 the first three lines again address the general audience, whereas
the final two lines address the *Tú*. The third stanza maintains the
focus on *Tú*. In "La Hija del Diablo" and "Ella," the third and

fourth poems, the narrator speaks once again to her general audience, which thus functions as her direct interlocutor except in those places where its members overhear the words she ostensibly speaks to Cortés.

In "Marina Madre" Corpi uses natural images of an indigenous world to portray Marina's origins. The first stanza evokes a creation story: the human person, here a woman, is created from mud or clay. The clay is a metaphor for Marina, mother and fertile earth. The description seems to suggest Malintzin Tenépal, as she and not Marina comes first in the historical discourse. The image of moist clay seems especially appropriate for Malintzin as she was born in Coatzacoalcos, a tropical region in the state of Veracruz, on the Bay of Campeche. Nevertheless, the poem's title clearly indicates that the protagonist is Marina. The discontinuity of a description that calls to mind Malintzin but really refers to Marina suggests that Corpi identifies not so much with Malintzin as she does with Marina, the woman who knew Cortés and who straddles both cultures and worlds. Marina's name is written in the *corteza de ese árbol.*

Unlike the pre-Columbian gods represented by figurines of rock and marble, Corpi's Marina is made of a soft, fragile substance. Clay can be shaped according to the maker's will, but once dried it hardens in the form molded. Features of clay suit the image Corpi wants to convey of Marina, who was formed by others according to their design and, once made, had no choice but to live out the roles they assigned to her. For them, Marina was a pliable, purely physical object.

"Marina Madre" recounts a series of actions of which Marina is the recipient rather than the agent: *la hicieron* ("they made her"); *la secaron* ("they dried her"); *su nombre escribieron* ("they wrote her name"); *fué vendida* ("she was sold"). Line 4 of stanza 1 identifies the agents as the old men (*los viejos*) who fashion her of the "softest" clay and dry her in the tropical sun. The relationship between "clay" and "sun" symbolizes the relationship between female and male. The sun acts on the clay by drying it, completing the process of creation. Likewise, the old men "act" on Marina: they give her a name and they write it with the blood of a tender lamb on the bark of a tree. The image of the innocent lamb killed for its blood foreshadows the events in Marina's life described in the next stanza: she too loses her innocence and virginity. The tree represents tradition and history; hence Marina's name is fixed in writing. Drawing from images of the natural world, Corpi is depicting the creation of a Mexican woman by men and the beginning of a tradition inscribed by men for all time.

The phrase *fué vendida* echoes the story of Malintzin Tenépal because she was literally sold by her family to itinerant Mayan merchants from Xicalango, an ancient center of coastal trade. The merchants, in turn, traded her to the Indians of Tabasco, who later made a gift of her to Cortés.[31] The phrase "de mano en mano, noche a noche" gives an impression of Marina as a sexual object passed from one man to another. The first part of the phrase is used conversationally in Spanish to designate a woman who engages in sexual activity with many men, as in "esta mujer ha pasado de mano en mano" ("This woman has been with many men"). The presentation of a Marina sexually exploited by men indicates that *fué vendida* is to be interpreted figuratively, but Corpi makes no absolute distinction between a pre-Columbian and a European usage. In fact, because *fué vendida* refers to the selling of Marina before she knew Cortés, it suggests that the Spaniards continued rather than began Marina's exploitation by men, sexual or otherwise.

The ellipsis (l. 8) produces the effect of a pause. It momentarily diverts attention away from the forward movement of the sentence and thus arouses even more interest in what follows. The ellipsis suggests that the ensuing material is especially difficult for the narrator to put into words. She feels Marina's pain. The repetition in "mano en mano, noche a noche" conveys monotony and routine. Marina endures these sexual nights only because she has to. The consequences are devastating, since her personhood is negated (*negada*) and desecrated (*desecrada*), stripped of its sanctity. The two words *negada* and *desecrada* refer implicitly to Marina's rape. Their rhyme links them to the final word of the poem, "chingada." The fact that they are past participles contributes to the impression of a passive Marina, a victim of men's sexual lust. Each night Marina awaits the morning because it may release her from her obligations: "esperando el alba / y el canto de la lechuza / que nunca llegaban." The belief that the song of the *lechuza* ("owl") presages death originates in Mexican popular sayings and beliefs. The message is clear that under these circumstances death would be a relief for Corpi's Marina—but death never comes.

Corpi's portrait of Marina makes clear two things: (1) Marina does not choose to engage in sexual activity with the Spaniards; (2) she passively submits to their lust. In fairness to Corpi's Marina, we might assume that Marina submits for one of two possible reasons: (1) she faces the risk of being killed, or (2) the Spaniards will override her objections and force her to submit. Since Corpi also suggests by her reference to the *lechuza*'s song that Marina would welcome death in this situation, we wonder why Marina does not refuse, even at the risk of incurring death. If death is not a risk, then with even more reason we wonder why she does not refuse. Corpi's cultural paradigm leaves readers no alternative but to accept a passive Marina who can do nothing about her situation.

In line 15 the narrator changes the focus of her narration from a meditative discourse spoken to a general audience to a direct statement to a specific *Tú*. By so doing, Corpi attributes ambiguity and richness to the *Tú*. The *Tú* is more than just Cortés. Implicit in *Tú* is the Mexican male. As the referents of *Tú, él,* and *aquel* are Cortés, his lieutenant, and Marina's son by Cortés, these men's roles correspond to Marina's tripartite role of mistress, wife, and mother. Since all three men negate her, Marina's personhood is negated on all three levels. The import of the final two lines is that Marina's son, sent by Cortés to be educated in Spain, returns and does not recognize her. Instead of calling her "¡mamá!" as he once did as a child, he now sees her as the Indian woman his father had raped, or the Chingada. In the historical context of the conquest of Mexico, the *aquel* designates a mestizo population, sprung from sexual encounters between Spanish men and Indian women. When the son, and implicitly a mestizo people, call her Chingada, they humiliate their own mother. Marina is once again named and defamed by a man, and thus another layer of definition is imposed upon her. She has not chosen these names for herself.

Rather than capitalizing the words La Chingada, Corpi lower-cases them and uses quotation marks ("la chingada"). By so doing she shifts the expression from its place in popular, oral language into written discourse. Although she does not similarly shift the word "mamá," the context indicates that it is also translation from oral speech. Had Corpi used capital letters instead of quotation marks for Chingada, she would have given more emphasis to the word. Her decision to place it within quotation marks, thus distancing and containing the expression, may suggest her desire to treat this defamation of woman as something "other," something that is foreign to her language. Although Corpi portrays a Marina who is Chingada, she cannot incorporate the word into her poetic discourse. Corpi's phrasing of the two final lines instructs the reader to shout the word "¡mamá!" but the quotation marks and the initial lowercase letters of the defamation instruct the reader to pronounce it softly.

Corpi begins her series of poems with Marina as *madre*, not with Marina as *virgen*. The more logical order, however, would be to speak about Marina as virgin first and as mother second. The general assumption in the cultural discourses concerning the figure of Marina, as in those of Paz and Fuentes, is that Marina was a virgin before the conquest. The conquest is Marina's deflowering, and also the land's and the nation's.[32] The discontinuity between Marina the traditional cultural symbol and Corpi's Marina hints that Corpi writes to vindicate herself as well as Marina. Corpi's life fits the pattern of becoming first a mother and then a symbolic virgin, since cultural constraints would prevent her from expressing her sexual self after the breakup of her marriage. Temporal and spatial indicators in "Marina Virgen" point to a Marina already abandoned by Cortés.

"Marina Virgen" expands upon the theme of the Chingada but places it within a Judeo-Christian context. The image of the tree in "Marina Madre" is replaced in the second poem by the Christian cross on which Jesus Christ, the divine Redeemer and Savior, suffered and died. Marina willingly kneels before the cross (*De su propio pie*). Stanza 1 suggests the tableaux of the holy women kneeling and gazing up at the cross. The gesture of kneeling implies the subjugation of the one who kneels to the one who remains standing. Marina Virgen is modeled on the image of the *mujer sufrida*, or the long-suffering Mexican woman.

Corpi's Marina cannot distinguish between the man she loved and the Catholic religion he imposed on the New World. When Corpi says "Como ella te amó, veía solamente / al ser sangrante," she suggests that Marina sees in Christ the Redeemer only a bleeding and humiliated Christ. And in the victimized Christ she sees a transfigured image of her own identity. Because Cortés has abandoned her, she too is a *ser sangrante*. Marina's love for Christ is a sublimation of her love for Cortés, for in the service of a higher ideal (Christ) she guards her secret and mourning memory of Cortés. The suffering Christ mirrors an image of herself as a person who suffers, much as Marina mirrors to Corpi an image of herself.

In the second stanza, the word *pecado* must be interpreted according to sexual and racial codes. Marina has assimilated the notion of "sin," a Christian, not an Indian, notion. Marina's sin is that she allowed herself to be violated, an event inextricably tied to the fact that she was Indian. Her gesture of covering herself with a thick, clear cloth, which she does to keep Cortés from seeing her dark and damned skin, suggests grieving and self-effacement. Lines 6 and 7 suggest that, had she been able, she would have washed away her sin with the trappings of Western civilization: the *agua bendita* ("holy water"). Marina's dark skin, or her body, was damned because she was a victim of a violation. But there are also racial overtones: Marina belonged to a race whose skin color condemned it to an inferior social rank.

Stanza 2 is told from Marina's perspective: she believed her sin was her violation. The narrator, however, interprets Marina's reason for wearing the thick shawl: "so you would never know / her brown skin had been damned." Stanza 3, with its sharp turn to the *Tú*, reveals more clearly the narrator's sentiments. The sin for the narrator is not Marina's violation, but rather the failure of Cortés to acknowledge that Marina had a soul. What bothers the poet-narrator is not so much that Marina was used as a sexual object as that the man she loved abandoned her, never even aware that she sacrificed her life for him. Implicitly, Marina is abandoned by family, culture, and country.

In the first two lines of stanza 3 the narrator is being mildly charitable to Cortés, for she gives him credit for once stopping to wonder where Marina's soul was hidden. As the translator points out, *Alguna* may mean "Once." This sentence also may ambiguously imply that Cortés never stopped, even once, to wonder about Marina. The ambiguity lies in the absence of a question mark at the end of the sentence. Whichever way we choose to interpret *Alguna*—as "once" or "never"—the fact remains that both meanings are a negative reflection on the man.

The final four lines of "Marina Virgen" return to images of nature, but they deviate from the cultural myth of Marina as mother earth which began the poem. Marina "plants" her soul in the earth she cultivates, but the black, moist earth is presented as a metaphor for the life of Cortés: "la tierra negra y húmeda de tu vida." The narrator reproaches Cortés because he never realized how completely Marina loved him. She "cultivated" a life for him and never one for herself. Cortés's life, then, fertilizes her life. The dash ending line 15 indicates a momentary pause before the final line, which repeats the *tierra* of line 14 in order to make its identity more precise.

In recounting Marina's death, the third poem, "La Hija del Díablo," continues the parallel with Christ's passion, for the setting is the natural landscape: "el trueno se reventó en el norte." Marina is once again the ancient idol (*ídolo*) which now falls and breaks into pieces. The *barro* is Marina's skin, now dirty and old, the same skin that was *maldita* in "Marina Virgen." The desire here is to undo the image of Marina as a *mala mujer*, an evil woman ("Hija del Diablo"), so that a new Marina can arise, as the phoenix does in "Puente de Cristal." The wind erases her name, as if to cancel it forever. The phrase *salina del mar* recalls the bitterness of the restless seas in "Solario" which pointed to rebellion and emancipation. In "Hija del Diablo," to intensify the finality of the events, Corpi uses the technique of accenting the letter o: *murió, reventó, ardió, calló, cayó, llevó*. Marina disintegrates into the natural elements originally used to compose her. The only sign of a presence to come is a seed half-alive.

The fourth poem, "Ella (Marina Ausente)," prefigures the birth of a new woman, whom Corpi simply calls *Ella* ("She"). The title captures the paradox of a Marina who is present, in the sense that her remains are in the earth, yet who is also absent because she is dead. The first four lines suggest the possibilities of what "Ella," the half-alive seed of "La Hija del Diablo," may become: a flower, a pool of fresh water, a tepid, tropical night. These images recall Corpi's Veracruz and point to a desire to return to the past and begin anew. On the other hand, "Ella" may be a sad child enclosed in a prison made of wet, smooth clay (*de barro húmedo y suave*), suggesting Corpi's San Luis Potosí, the other option available in a return to the past. Corpi has used this image of a prison made of clay to describe Marina's skin and body; the prison is thus a metaphor for Marina's body, or the body of the *criatura triste*. As the body is made of the natural elements of the Mexican earth, it also suggests Marina's and Corpi's Indianness, their *mexicanidad*.

Line 5, beginning with *es la sombra enlutada*, affirms that "Ella" is a shadow of an ancestral memory enshrouded in mourning. The significant words in Corpi's formulation are "shadow" and "memory." The "new" Marina is a "shadow," but she is not a reflection of a real person. Rather, she is a "shadow" of a "memory" (*un recuerdo*). The abstract definition of Marina is twice removed from a concrete order, evoking Corpi as much as it does Marina. It evokes Marina because she is a cultural ancestor of the Mexican people, the word *ancestral* suggesting a pre-Columbian past. The definition also suggests Corpi because *recuerdo ancestral* harks back to the words of her grandmother who urged her, in "Tres Mujeres," to remain in Mexico. The ancestral memory is the cultural taboo Corpi violated. The definition projects the desire to get rid of the taboo and find transformation as a new woman.

Implicit in the statement of what the shadow will become is a reference to La Llorona, also a shadow in mourning. Yet these lines point to a transformation. In contrast with the traditional *llorona*, who in legends usually appears at night, this *llorona* crosses the bridge in the morning with her hands full of sun and earth, as if relieved of her burdens. We see a glorified *llorona*, a glorified Marina, and a glorified Lucha. The verb in *que vendrá* ("that will come") projects the event into the future, emphasizing the notion that this new woman is yet to be born. Marina/Corpi desires a new beginning with abundance (*con manos llenas*): no longer a "shadow" (*enlutada*) in mourning but a person who comes by morning (*por la mañana*). If Marina is a figure parallel to Corpi, the boundary symbolically crossed is that between Mexico and the United States. The new Marina is not the old Marina. Rather, the new Marina signals what is yet to come in a Chicano community.

The images of *sol* and *tierra* include Marina as the earth and also Cortés, since he too is equated with the earth that Marina cultivated with her hands ("Marina Virgen"). In herself—the earth—Marina sees only Cortés, as she has no other identity than the one he reflects back to her. In Marina's and Corpi's hands there is now plenitude, or completeness, a sexual desire consummated. The same images (*sol* and *tierra*) also mark another transformation. "Ella" sees herself as a self-sufficient woman with both the sun, the fertilizing agent, and the earth, the substance fertilized, in her possession. The force of this transformation is mitigated, however, by the reader's awareness of the traditional meanings of these words. These images return to the beginning, when the sun, by drying the clay, completed the process of Marina's creation. Corpi's transformation is still dependent upon the codes that governed the world responsible for Marina's ruin.

There are objective reasons for identifying Lucha Corpi with Marina. First, as Corpi herself explains, history and popular legend trace Marina's origins to Corpi's hometown: "The town is a few kilometers from Tabasco, and they say Marina was from the tribe of the Tabasqueños. It is possible that the Tabasqueño empire extended to my town, because it is so close. Marina could be from there."[33] Second, Marina lost her son when he was taken by Cortés to Spain; Corpi feared losing her son through the divorce: "With my divorce there was a question of whether my son would live with my ex-husband or with me. For the first time I was confronted with the possibility of my son growing up away from me." A third reason may be added to the two suggested by Corpi. Marina straddles three cultures: Indian, Spanish, and Mexican. Fully accepted by none, the legendary Marina was an outcast in all three cultures. Corpi herself also straddles three cultures: Mexican, Chicano, and United States. To some extent she must feel herself marginal in all three. Her experience in the United States prevents her from regarding herself as an authentic Mexican. In the past, upon reflecting on the possibility of returning to Mexico, Corpi has said: "Things were no longer the same; I couldn't go back to being *una hija de familia* ["a family's daughter"]." The constraints of her personal Mexican development keep her from embracing the social values of United States culture regarding feminine behavior. Finally, though Corpi embraces a Chicano identity and is active in the Chicano community, she maintains an emotive identification with traditional Mexican culture.

4

"ROMANCE TEJIDO"

Corpi calls four of her poems romances: "Romance Liso," "Romance de la Niña," "Romance Tejido," and "Romance Negro."[34] They are not classical romances in the technical sense of having eight syllables in a line with patterns of assonant rhyme falling on the even-numbered lines. Rather, "romance" here refers to the theme of love and its loss. Both "Romance Tejido" and "Romance Negro," the poem most reminiscent of a García-Lorquian mood, relate tragic events in women's lives. Written primarily in lyrical, evocative language, "Romance Tejido" suggests a parallel between Veronica, its fictional protagonist, and the poet-narrator. As Veronica imaginatively weaves her story, so the poet-narrator tells a story by weaving images into a poem.

ROMANCE TEJIDO

Verónica
Rosa de fuego blanco

Qúe brizna astral se oculta
tras el chal negro de tu mirada?
Qué detalle de pasión primera
entretejes en el bordado?

Verónica
Pasión apenas si amante

Qué buscas en los pequeños
momentos del ayer sin tiempo?
Qué diseño dejaste incompleto
en el bastidor del sueño?

Verónica
Vestido de cuaresma

Qué bestia fiera entró de lleno
sin advertir esencia ni presencia?
Qué revolotear de mariposas
pasó de largo hacia la ausencia?

Verónica
Luto azul de rosa blanca

Qué esencia de nardos ahogó
el humo sagrado del hogar?
Quién te dejó el corazón
inundado de olvido y de silencio?

Verónica
Rosa de fuego pálido
Pasión si amante apenas, ya consumida

Luto blanco en el baúl
de la esperanza.

WOVEN ROMANCE

Veronica
Rose of pale fire

What star-splinter hides
behind the black shawl of your gaze?
What detail of first love
is woven into the design?

Veronica
Passion barely loving

What are you looking for in the small
moments of a timeless yesterday?
What design is incomplete
on the frame of your dream?

Veronica
Lenten dress

What fierce beast came bursting in
Ignoring essence and presence?
What butterfly's wing
passed on the way to absence?

Veronica
Blue mourning of a white rose

What spikenard scent was stifled
by the sacred smoke of home-fires?
Who left your heart
flooded with oblivion and silence?

Veronica
Rose of pale fire
Passion barely loving, yet consumed
White mourning
    in the hope chest.

The events in "Romance Tejido" are presented in an alternating pattern of statements and questions. In the statements (stanzas 1, 3, 5, and 7) the protagonist's name is followed by an image that describes Veronica. In the even-numbered stanzas (2, 4, 6, and 8) the poet-narrator addresses two consecutive questions to Veronica, her direct interlocutor. Each statement contributes to our knowledge of Veronica, and each series of questions intensifies the conflict within the poet/narrator. Like "Romance Negro," "Romance Tejido" ends with a statement revising the images already presented.

Implicit in the character of Veronica projected by Corpi's narrator are two other women who come from Catholic and pagan traditions: St. Veronica and Philomela. St. Veronica, one of the women present at Christ's passion, offers Christ her veil to wipe his face. On the veil is left the imprint of his face. The name Veronica connotes the image of a woman who mourns at Calvary. The second woman, Philomela, is raped by a wicked king who cuts off her tongue to keep her from talking about his transgression. For years she perseveringly tells her story without words by weaving an account of her rape into a tapestry. She sends the finished cloth to her sister, the wife of the wicked king, who obtains her own and Philomela's revenge by punishing her husband. Both Veronica and Philomela silently perform acts that result in creative products. Corpi's Veronica recalls both women: the mourning St. Veronica and the mute Philomela.

The oxymoron of Veronica as a "rose of white fire" (fuego blanco)[35] captures an image of a passion so intense that it is white, and as such it recalls "el blanco vestal / del viento huracanado" in "Pasión sin Nombre." The juxtaposition of these two images, fire for passion and white for purity, suggests their role as twin forces of creation and destruction. Purity is Veronica's essence, and its loss is her undoing. Similarly, her passion is a creative force but its realization is also her undoing. At the beginning of the poem the virginal Veronica is potentiality (fire and passion). The first question (lines 3–4), juxtaposing brizna astral (a small piece of a star) and chal negro (black shawl), recalls the image of the trapped star in the great astral hole of "Cofradía de Inservibles." Veronica's gaze is a black shawl, a sign of prohibition of pleasure which hides a "star splinter," an inner radiance. The next question (lines 5–6) places Veronica within the confines of domesticity. She is embroidering, mentally weaving a dream of passion while she does so. The word bordado refers to an embroidery; entretejes, to the action of weaving or knitting. Because these metaphors refer to two different kinds of sewing—one does not "weave" an embroidery—entretejes here denotes a mental exercise. The young Veronica sublimates her dream of passion by acting it out in the motions of embroidering. The embroidery is the only visible articulation of the dream of passion.

The second image of Veronica (stanza 3) tells us she barely (*apenas*) begins to feel sensual passion. The next pair of questions create feelings of anxiety: Veronica is restless, searching. Something as yet unstated has caused her to leave her dream of passion incomplete. The *bastidor* is the wooden frame tightly holding the embroidery. When the narrator says "bastidor del sueño" ("frame of your dream"), she confirms that Veronica is indeed imaginatively weaving dreams. In the next image Veronica is a purple dress, a sign of Lenten sorrow. Passion or desire is transformed into sorrow or mourning. The set of questions that follow convey that some "wild beast" (*bestia fiera*) has descended upon Veronica without taking into account who she is (*esencia*) or what her attitude toward the whole event was (*presencia*). The only trace of the event is the fluttering of butterflies (*mariposas*) as they immediately pass on their "way to absence." The *mariposas* suggest that Veronica's once bustling imagination is now transformed into absence, into an empty place. The next image (stanza 7) makes Veronica the "Blue mourning of a white rose" instead of the rose of white fire (lines 1–2) she is at the start of the poem. The blue mourning is a middle point between the black (or purple) mourning and the "White mourning" that ends the poem.

The metaphor of the *bestia fiera* is ambiguous. It creates innuendos of rape, but it could also refer to a man, a ferocious animal, overtaken by passion. In this last sense it recalls the image of the *potro*, used by Corpi in "Pasión sin Nombre," which contains no hint of rape. In "Romance Tejido" the male expends his passion on the woman's body and exits, leaving only a heart flooded with oblivion and silence.

The final set of questions (stanza 8) mark the climax of the narrator's probing. The *nardos* are Easter lilies. As the flowers that young Mexican girls carry to the altar when they make their first Holy Communion, they are a conventional symbol of innocence and purity. The English translation distorts the sense. The scent of lilies is the active agent that stifles (*ahogar* literally means "to drown") the sanctity of the home and family rather than the passive agent stifled by home fires, as the translation indicates. The images and their connotations in the two lines, "Qué esencia de nardos ahogó / el humo sagrado del hogar," suggest that someone's obsession with purity (*esencia de nardos*) kept Veronica from enjoying her function as mother, wife, and mistress of the home.

The second question in stanza 8 shifts the focus from "*qué,*" which has so far begun each question, to "*quién.*" The change suggests a narrator less interested in "what is done" than in "who is responsible." Coming at the end of a series of questions, *Quién te dejó* communicates a sense of urgency: Who did this to you? The *te,* a reflexive pronoun, conveys a stronger sense of Veronica as tragic victim than do the previous questions. Stanza 8 introduces ambiguity because it makes us wonder whether the tragic event is the sexual act itself or a family's obsession with virginity which leaves Veronica's heart so empty. This deliberate ambiguity underscores the narrator's indecision about the direction in which the process is moving: Is male desire or the family's excessive preoccupation with virginity responsible for woman's undoing? The narrator can neither identify in precise terms the party responsible nor directly attribute blame where it is due. The fact that the narrator even mentions the sacred fires of the home inclines the answer toward the second possibility. The relationship between Veronica and her implied family is similar to the relationship between Guadalupe and her family in "Romance Negro."

The last stanza of "Romance Tejido" revises the poem's earlier images. No longer a "rose of white fire" ("fuego blanco") but a "rose of pale fire" ("fuego pálido"), Veronica's passion has been dampened. It no sooner barely begins to love when it is consumed. The pattern of a great passion (*fuego*) extinguished before its time recalls Juana María's complaint to Amerina in "Tres Mujeres," where Juana María blames Amerina for making a divorce possible, thus extinguishing her passion before it has an opportunity to realize itself. The image of *Luto blanco* refers to the white matrimonial dress which may connote mourning if a woman has participated in illicit sex or has been sexually violated or raped. The white dress lies useless in the family trunk (*baúl*). Ironically, the conventional receptacle for family mementos contains the white dress, now a forbidden item because matrimony is now impossible for Veronica.

The effect of the poem's ending would have been different had Corpi closed it with the questioning attitude of stanza 8 or had she pursued the questioning into further stanzas. We would thus have been left with the force of the question, "Who is responsible?" though perhaps still without knowing the identity of the one responsible. Instead, Corpi returns once again to images reminiscent of the poem's beginning (Verónica, Rosa, Pasión, Luto) which convey a desire to tie things up and prevent the poem from ending on a discordant note. Ultimately, the description phrased in terms of statements rather than questions implies a tone of resignation.

"ROMANCE NEGRO"

"Romance Negro" combines dramatic narrative with lyrical meditation. In the former mode it describes a succession of events related by cause and effect; in the latter mode it establishes a relationship between the events and the narrator. "Romance Negro" describes a sexual event in the life of a young, beautiful girl and its effect on her and her family in a rural Mexican village. Images of luscious fruits, of sweet smells and tastes (oranges, cacao, sugarcane, vanilla, cinnamon), establish a tropical setting and climate in the Americas. The girl's name is Guadalupe. After having a sexual experience while bathing in a stream one Sunday afternoon she has to confront her family. The poem gives no evidence of Guadalupe's voluntary participation, yet it makes no clear statement that her participation was involuntary. "Romance Negro" is unclear about what happens because Corpi excludes the girl's response to the sexual act itself.

ROMANCE NEGRO

Hay sabor de vainilla
en el aire dominical.

Melancolía de la naranja
que aún cuelga de la rama,
brillante y seductora,
sin esperanza de azahar.

Guadalupe se bañaba en el río
muy de tarde en un domingo.

Promesa de leche en los senos

201

Vainilla el olor de los cabellos   *10*

Canela molida el sabor de los ojos

Flor de cacao entre las piernas

Ah, la embriaguez de la caña
entre los labios.

El se acercó y la miró así
rodeada del agua
inundada de tarde

Y en un instante arrancó la flor

Estrujó la leche hasta cambiarla
en sangre

Desparramó la vainilla por el   *20*
silencio de la orilla

Bebióse el candente líquido
de los labios

Y después . . . después desapareció
dejando sólo un rastro de sombra
lánguida al borde del agua.

Su madre la encontró y al verla
sacó de su morral un puño de sal
y se la echó por el hombro.

Y a los pocos días su padre   *30*
recibió una yegua fina de regalo.

Y Guadalupe . . . Guadalupe colgó
su vida del naranjo del huerto
y se quedó muy quieta ahí
con los ojos al río abiertos.

Hay sabor de vainilla
en el ambiente de la tarde.

Una nostalgia ancestral
se apodera de la mente.

De la rama cuelga una naranja   *40*
todavía sin promesa de azahar.

DARK ROMANCE

A flavor of vanilla drifts
on the Sunday air.

Melancholy of an orange,
clinging still,
brilliant, seductive,
past the promise of its blooming.

Guadalupe was bathing in the river
that Sunday, late,

a promise of milk in her breasts,

vanilla scent in her hair,   *10*

cinnamon flavor in her eyes,

cocoa-flower between her legs,

and in her mouth a daze
of sugarcane.

He came upon her there
surrounded by water
in a flood of evening light.

And on the instant cut the flower

wrung blood from the milk

dashed vanilla on the silence   *20*
of the river bank

drained the burning liquid
of her lips

And then he was gone,
leaving behind him a trail of shadow
drooping at the water's edge.

Her mother found her, and at the sight
took a handful of salt from her pouch
to throw over her shoulder.

A few days later, her father   *30*
accepted the gift of a fine mare.

> And Guadalupe . . . Guadalupe hung her life
> from the orange tree in the garden,
> and stayed there quietly,
> her eyes open to the river.
>
> An orange clings to the branch
> the promise lost of its blooming.
>
> Ancestral longing
> seizes the mind.
>
> A scent of vanilla drifts   *40*
> on the evening air.

I divide "Romance Negro" into three structural segments: (1) the abstract, or summary, of the general proposition that the narrative develops (ll. 1–6); (2) the narrative proper, describing the main events (ll. 7–36); and the coda, or the section terminating the poem (ll. 37–42).[36] The coda echoes the abstract and recapitulates the ultimate effects of the story's events. The second segment may be divided into three smaller units: (a) the description of Guadalupe (ll. 7–14); (b) the entrance of the male, his rape of Guadalupe, and his departure (ll. 15–27); and (c) the family's reaction to the seduction: mother's, father's, and Guadalupe's, in that order (ll. 28–36).

The poem generates the central oppositions that impel Corpi's poetry: giving-withholding, softness-hardness, opening-closing. The basic tension in these oppositions is seen in the contrasting connotations of the two words in the title; a romance between a man and a woman with the potential for fulfillment leads to darkness and loss.[37] The oppositions may be compressed into the central meaning of Corpi's poetic work. Guadalupe's desire for sexual gratification (giving, softness, opening) is transformed into loss and emptiness (withholding, hardness, closing). The fantasy of sexual gratification is evoked in the poem's abstract: "Hay sabor de vainilla / en el aire dominical." The flavor of vanilla drifting in the Sunday air evokes romance, fullness, and sweetness. The sounds of *vainilla* and *aire dominical* are light and airy, intended to suggest promise and hope. Lines 3–6 introduce tension between the promise of a ripe, brilliant orange and its unfruitfulness; the image of a melancholic orange still clinging to the vine initiates the movement away from promise toward loss, a movement heightened by *sin esperanza de azahar* ("past the promise of its blossoming").

These lines are spoken by a narrator who in a present moment—*Hay* ("There is"); *cuelga* ("hangs")—tastes the sweetness of the Sunday air. A melancholy mood seeps in as the narrator reflects upon a brilliant, seductive orange that, although still (*aún*) hanging from the vine, has no hope of blooming. The word *azahar* is important. If stanza 2 is interpreted according to the laws of nature, seemingly the only paradigm available, it engenders an impossible desire. In a purely natural process an orange cannot return to its flower stage (*azahar*), as the orange of this stanza seems to desire. It can do so, however, in a natural process involving humans, if someone plucks it, eats it, and plants its seed in the ground. In time the seed will become a tree and the tree will blossom. The stanza expresses a desire to return to a previous stage and redo a process while at the same time recognizing the impossibility of doing so (*sin esperanza de azahar*). The wish to return to an earlier time calls to mind an actual event in "La Hija del Diablo," the third Marina poem: Marina is "erased" and returns to the stage of a "seed half-alive." When the process is resumed in "Ella (Marina Ausente)," Marina/Corpi is a woman reborn.

A second reading of "Romance Negro" helps the reader to understand why the orange has no hope of blooming. The word *azahar*, designating the flowers that Mexican women carry in their wedding bouquets, may also stand for the promise of marriage. The second reading reveals that Guadalupe is the seductive and alluring orange without hope of marriage, as explained in the narrative proper. On a first reading, however, the phrase *sin esperanza de azahar* cannot refer to Guadalupe, for the lines that follow make clear that Guadalupe has every hope for marriage. If applied to Guadalupe, the phrase *sin esperanza de azahar* is directly contradictory to the thrust of the lines that describe Guadalupe (ll. 9–14).

The description of Guadalupe in the first unit of the narrative proper, beginning with stanza 3, effects two shifts, from present to past tense and from an abstract to a concrete setting. These lines follow the literary convention of presenting the woman in a beautiful garden as a luscious fruit to be eaten and enjoyed. The poet does not talk about a real garden but uses natural imagery to talk about a woman. Just as Marina was the earth, so Guadalupe is this garden. Through a metaphoric elaboration, parts of Guadalupe's body are fused with the smells, tastes, touch, and sights of tropical food: vanilla, cocoa, and sugarcane. Guadalupe delights in these sensual smells of her body. The absence of verbs in these phrases is the poet's strategic device for emphasizing the presence of Guadalupe's body in the plants and fruits. Her hair is vanilla-scented, her eyes are "cinnamon flavor," her lips are the rapture of sugarcane, and so on. In other words, Guadalupe is untrammeled nature.

The poet tries to create an imitative environment of sensual delights through sounds. Clusters of soft, open-ended vowels are repeated: "Promesa de leche en los senos"; "Vainilla el olor de los cabellos; "Flor de cacao entre las piernas." We are invited by reading the lines aloud to imitate with our lips the gestures of kissing, sucking, and blowing, thus participating in the sexual experience. We round our lips to produce the ending sounds of *senos, cabellos, ojos,* and *labios,* and open our lips to produce the ending sound of *piernas.* We do the same with a phrase like *Flor de cacao,* rounding the mouth on *Flor,* opening it on the a's, and then closing it around the final o. The muscular actions in reading the lines match the sensual experience the poet wants to create.

The second unit of narrative proper, beginning with line 15, effects yet another shift, this time to the male's perspective. Having set up the metaphoric equivalence between the girl's body and the perfumes of flowers, spices, and plants, between a human and a natural order, the poet then describes the sexual act in terms of these vehicles rather than in terms of the female body. The male now acts on the flower, the milk, the vanilla, and the sugarcane. As noted earlier, metaphors representing the woman as a fruit, a flower, or a vegetable to be "cut" (*cortar*) and hence possessed by the male abound in Mexican songs, sayings, and ballads.

The preceding unit dedicated to Guadalupe is marked by an absence of verbs. The second unit describing the male's actions is replete with strong, active verbs: *arrancó, estrujó, desparramó, desapareció.* They seem to tell the story of a rape. Within the literary tradition of presenting the woman as a flower, a fruit, or a vegetable to be possessed by the man as the keeper of the garden, the verb *arrancar* is important: "Y en un instante arrancó la flor" ("And in an instant he plucked the flower"). *Arrancar,* "to pull out by the roots," implies force and violence. The verb "cut" used by the translator does not. "Cut" is the equivalent of possession whereas *arrancar* is the equivalent of rape. *Estrujó* ("wrung"), when used in the context of a man's "wringing" a woman's breast to the point of drawing blood, connotes force. The verb *desparramó* ("to scatter in a disorderly fashion") also conveys harshness in an act performed by someone who does not care how or where the scattered object falls. The effect of the accent on the last ó of these verbs is one of closure, indicating the finality of actions in the past. Action is felt as sexualized, but it is also felt as violent and abrupt. If we emphasize the violent aspects of the description, then, we tend to think of the encounter between man and woman, not as a seduction, but as a rape.

Yet if we interpret the lines as a description of rape, another disturbing issue arises. The Guadalupe rejoicing in her body's delights earlier in the poem is noticeably absent in the description of the rape. The male is a full participant in the action; the woman is totally passive. The verb *bebióse* emphasizes that the man consumes the liquid. Its accented ó is softened by the suffix *se*, indicating the reflexive nature of the action. The encounter between man and woman is a unilateral contract; only the man enjoys full sensual gratification. Only he is involved in a process that has a beginning and an end. If we contrast this finished process with the one suggested in the abstract, we see that the orange as trope is fixated with no hope of realizing what it desires (*azahar*). Guadalupe, too, is also fixated. For just as a real orange in the natural cycle is to be eaten and tasted, so the natural culmination of a woman's development in a society like Guadalupe's is marriage. The event may be intended as a rape, but the description mitigates the effect of rape as event by portraying rape as metaphor.

Since Guadalupe is totally passive and since the entire experience is seen from the man's perspective, we do not know what she feels. The textual indicators suggesting violence might be taken as a statement about a traditional culture, in this instance Mexican, where strict social norms forbid women, especially in rural villages, the freedom to say no to men who want to force their will upon them. A similar ambiguity about rape is seen in Corpi's rendition of Marina. Corpi portrays a Marina who implicitly chooses to submit while at the same time portraying a Marina who thinks death a preferable alternative to the monotonous nights. Even though the connotations surrounding a cultural discourse of the magnitude of the conquest do not appear in "Romance Negro," it seems to me that Guadalupe behaves under the same constraints that condition Marina's response. Guadalupe, like Marina, passively acquiesces because she feels she has no choice. "Romance Negro" describes a social rape, where woman's freedom of choice is severely restricted.

The poem goes on to say that marriage for Guadalupe is impossible. The *Y* of the final stanza of the second unit connects what follows with what has happened before. The ellipsis in *Y después . . . después* suggests that the narrating consciousness hesitates, as if to reflect: "And after? What happens after?" The reality is that the male leaves after satiating himself and Guadalupe is faced with the "after." The word *sólo* communicates that the man has taken everything he wants, leaving only a vestige of a drooping shadow (*un rastro de sombra*) at the water's edge. Guadalupe, formerly her family's glory, has become not only a shadow but a "trace of a shadow." She is now potentially the ruin of her family. The promise in Guadalupe's and her family's future are now deflated into a sense of loss, lack, and disturbing quietness.

The third unit of the narrative proper, beginning with line 28, recounts the family's reaction. By dedicating a stanza each to the mother and the father, Corpi reveals her concern with the effects of the rape on Guadalupe's family. The mother's reaction on meeting Guadalupe is to take a handful of salt from her pouch and throw it over her shoulder, an action conveying that she sees in Guadalupe an omen of evil.[38] This gesture implies that the mother is more concerned about consequences than about her daughter's feelings. Metaphorically, the mother is expressing a wish to undo what the male has done, as if trying to wash away the ill deed.

The connector *Y* in *Y a los pocos días* again serves as a link between the family reaction and the rape, between the present and the past. Presumably the man who raped Guadalupe sends the father the gift of a fine mare (*una yegua fina*) to atone for the insult to the father. In the same literary tradition that portrays the woman as flower or fruit and the man as keeper of the garden, the fine mare metaphorically stands for a woman, connoting her fertility. In a traditional culture the exchange of an animal between a man and a woman's father may be equivalent to a promise of marriage. As this particular situation seems to concern rape, it is unlikely that the gift of a *yegua fina* is intended as an offer of marriage. More likely this gift of significant value is intended to make restitution to the father for the loss of his daughter's virginity, a woman's exchange value in a traditional society. That the father accepts the mare is clear from the verb *recibió*. In contrast, with the English verb "receive," the Spanish *recibir* carries the implication that one "accepts," say, a person's visit or gift. In this kind of system women are undervalued, considered the equivalent of domestic animals. The rules of the society permit the rapist to offer the animal and the father to accept it. To the father, the fine mare means more than avenging his daughter's honor.

The symbolic connotations of *yegua fina* in this context, however, must not be ignored. *Yegua fina* undercuts the need for the parent's worry, as it suggests that the male desires the woman. It also works against the poet's intention to communicate a rape, for rape would make a woman useless, even disgusting, in most traditional communities. The image of *yegua fina* implies an identification with the very social mores the poet wants to challenge. The words are probably chosen for their melodic, lyrical qualities, but their symbolic connotations hardly fit coherently and smoothly into stanzas that seem designed to communicate the poet's dissatisfaction with the treatment of the woman as object. The image of the *yegua fina* is the poet-narrator's misplaced sexual desire.

Whether the literal or the figurative meanings are emphasized, *yegua fina* represents a desire to make restitution. The movement toward restitution is undermined in the following stanza, however, when Guadalupe's reaction expresses loss. Here is the first sign of Guadalupe's response to the rape, in that she performs an action. Lines 25–27, though focused on Guadalupe, are purely descriptive; they make no statement as to her feelings. By placing the stanza describing what Guadalupe does (ll. 33–36) after the one telling about the gift of the mare, the poet suggests that Guadalupe's reaction has more to do with her father's acceptance of the gift than with the rape experience. Guadalupe's reaction also suggests that *yegua fina* is to be understood in a literal sense, because the symbolic connotations of *yegua fina* as fertility conflict with her negative reaction. According to the rules of her society, a woman ought to be happy if a man sees her as desirous and seductive. Guadalupe reacts as she does, *colgó su vida* ("hung her life"), because her father prefers accepting the gift to avenging her rape. The exchange for restitution takes place between rapist and father, totally excluding Guadalupe.

The description of Guadalupe's reaction is ambiguous. The stanza may give the impression that she commits suicide, since she remains very still with her eyes fixed on the river. Suicide is certainly an understandable alternative if the loss of virginity means the abandonment of all hope for a woman to have a meaningful life. The idea of suicide, however, would be clearer had the poet said, "Guadalupe se colgó / del naranjo del huerto." Because *colgar* is used as a transitive verb, the phrase *colgó / su vida* suggests that Guadalupe "hung her hopes," meaning that her aspirations for marriage are destroyed. The popular meaning of the verb *colgar* is "to be left hanging or suspended." For example, a Spanish speaker could say "me quedé colgado(a)" after trying hard to court someone who never responded. The phrase produces humorous effects in an amorous context. This comic expression, of course, makes Guadalupe's situation all the more tragic because her life has ended.

The semantic relationship between the orange and the tree—*naranja* denotes the fruit, *naranjo* the tree—suggests the hierarchy in female-male relationships. The orange is the symbol for Guadalupe who hangs suspended from the tree in her father's garden. Guadalupe is the product of a masculine order that has defined her only value as her virginity. With her virginity lost, Guadalupe is useless. Like the brilliant, seductive orange, she becomes a symbol of fixity and stagnation. Guadalupe is chosen in a way that precludes her own free choice.

The coda, beginning with line 36, shifts back once again to the present tense, repeating the abstract with some modifications.[39] Its first distich replaces the elegant *aire dominical* with the more mundane *ambiente de la tarde*. The next distich suggests that the telling of Guadalupe's story has aroused a nostalgia that grips the mind—whose mind, though, is not known. It may be the narrator's, but no conclusive proof exists that it is. The Spanish language allows for the impersonal adjective to be used with certain nouns relating to the body, hence *la mente* ("the mind") instead of *mi mente* ("my mind"). Within Corpi's poetic scheme, however, the word *ancestral*, especially when associated with nostalgia, here a longing for one's home, evokes memories of her native land.

The final stanza of the poem compresses the four lines of stanza 2 of the abstract into two lines. The main transformation concerns the word *todavía* ("still," "yet"). Whereas "sin esperanza de azahar" in the abstract gives the impression that hope is definitively impossible, "todavía sin promesa de azahar" in the coda suggests that satisfaction is yet possible. Because the word *azahar* appears at the end of the story, it may denote marriage as well as a return to the blossom stage. It is unlikely that *azahar* in the sense of marriage refers to Guadalupe, however, because her final gesture implies that she has abandoned all hope of it. Ironically, she hopes for marriage in the beginning but not at the end. The narrative consciousness, in contrast, speaks of an orange in the beginning with no hope of returning to its blossom stage. At the end it speaks of an orange that yet (*todavía*) hopes for *azahar*, in the sense of both marriage and the blossoming of a flower. Implicit in these lines is the notion that someone has been longing for sexual fulfillment for a very long time, fulfillment that can be obtained only by returning to a purer state, in both a physical and a national context.

"Romance Negro," like "Romance Tejido" and the Marina poems, is characterized by ambiguities and discontinuities. Its various elements do not form a harmonious whole. Read in terms of a romantic, lyrical tradition, the poem wants to communicate a rape, yet the metaphorization of Guadalupe's encounter with the male diffuses the impact of a rape experience. The use of the convention of *yegua fina*, especially in stanzas that reflect the poet's dissatisfaction with the family's treatment of Guadalupe, does not integrate smoothly with her protest and her intent to communicate a rape. In the context of the other poems discussed here, the use of *yegua fina* expresses the poet's sublimated desire for sexual gratification.

These discontinuities in the description of Guadalupe's sexual experience and of the family's reaction suggest the fragmentation of the poetic consciousness. They express the poet's horror at a social practice that gives women limited choice in determining their own sexual fulfillment, while they also establish her identification with a literary tradition that legitimates this social system. Corpi's adherence to the codes and conventions of a

Mexican romantic tradition which assumes that women are objects of male desire impedes her from articulating Guadalupe's attitude toward her experience. This gap is ultimately the poem's silence. Implicit in "Romance Negro" is Corpi's unconscious fantasy for women to engage in sexual relationships with the blessing of a traditional social order.

The fragmentation of the poetic self at the level of subject matter—opened versus closed, traditional versus liberated, fulfilled versus lacking—is mirrored at the level of the presentation of the poems in *Palabras de Mediodía*. As a Chicana poet, Lucha Corpi reveals an awareness of the need to communicate with both Spanish- and English-speaking audiences. She writes her poems in Spanish, but she makes a gesture to her English-reading audience by offering translations of all the poems. The original Spanish and the translation are placed on facing pages, suggesting a juxtaposition rather than a resolution of tensions between two cultures. The two audiences of a society familiar with two languages remain separated rather than integrated within one bilingual audience.

Lucha Corpi's statements about the translations make clear that she works hand in hand with her translator. She discusses with Catherine Rodríguez-Nieto the poems, their translations, and their imagined impact in both languages. So, although Corpi conceptualizes and writes her poems in Spanish, she is not unaware of what the poems, once translated, will communicate to her English-speaking audience. She has in fact indicated that if a poem cannot be translated into English so as to capture the thought of the Spanish original, it is not to be published.[40] Translation, then, is her response to a language difference between the two cultures that compose her audiences.

Lucha Corpi's bilingualism is different from that of Bernice Zamora, who mixes the two languages in her poems. Although some of Zamora's poems presuppose bilingual readers who know the meanings and can understand the implications of words in both languages, Corpi's do not do so in a strict sense. In searching for a broad audience, Corpi is aware of a dual readership, making her poems accessible to an audience that reads Spanish, but not at the expense of her English-reading audience. Her form of bilingualism is realized by her placement of poem and translation on facing pages.

A second point is that Lucha Corpi's poetry presupposes an audience of women, but it does so in a different way from the poems of Villanueva and Zamora, which contain specific textual markers to indicate a female readership. In contrast, Corpi's method of implying an audience of women is more indirect than direct, as are also her poetic strategies: she speaks to and implicitly for her female characters rather than permitting them to speak for themselves. In her poetry she attempts to articulate a woman's personal feelings and to inject these into a literary tradition that conventionally has ignored them. Some of Corpi's poems (not discussed here) establish domestic situations showing how a woman's time is occupied during the hours of the day when the man is usually absent.[41] The imagistic questions of "Romance Tejido" which reveal a woman's state of mind; the imagistic arguments of the Marina poems, whose effect depends more upon our understanding of the metaphors than upon any direct statement; the strongly imagistic progression of most of her poetry— all suggest that Corpi's main concern is to represent the consciousness of women. These features of her poems move toward the delineation of a female consciousness absent in dominant poetic discourse.

THE DRAMATIZATION OF A SHIFTING POETIC CONSCIOUSNESS

Bernice Zamora's
Restless Serpents

> You insult me
> When you say I'm schizophrenic.
> *My* divisions are
> Infinite.
>
> —"So Not To Be Mottled" from *Restless Serpents*

Bernice Zamora, my fourth and final central figure in Chicana poetry, traces her cultural roots to a different area of the American Southwest. Unlike Alma Villanueva and Lorna Dee Cervantes, who as native Californians were raised in predominantly urban environments, Zamora was born in Aguilar, a small village in southern Colorado located at the foot of the East Spanish Peak, where her ancestors had lived and worked as farmers for several generations. The farmlands around Aguilar and the coal mines near Trinidad and Valdez formed Zamora's environment until she was seven, when her father moved the family to Denver. Preferring a rural over an urban life, however, he chose Pueblo, Colorado, a median point between Denver and Aguilar, as the family's permanent home.[1] More than the geography of Denver, more than even that of Pueblo, where Zamora lived most of her life before moving to California, the brutal landscapes of southern Colorado and northern New Mexico loom largest in her poetry. Zamora remembers returning to the farms and mountains of Aguilar during her summers while in school. The volcanoes, mountains, and rivers, and the traditional ceremonies of these areas, mapped the natural borders of Bernice Zamora's childhood. They also form one extreme of her polarized poetic landscape. The works of poets, particularly male poets of the English and American tradition, represent the borders of Zamora's academic education. She received her formal education in Pueblo, attending mostly Catholic schools. She pursued degrees in English, obtaining a bachelor of arts degree at Southern Colorado University and a master's at Colorado State University. In 1963, at the age of twenty-five, Zamora moved to California and continued her studies, working for a doctorate in English and American literature at Stanford University. While at Stanford she began to write poetry. Becoming better acquainted with English and American poets, she interwove literary figures of this tradition into her poetry. Together these two landscapes—one natural and regional, the other academic and literary—represented Zamora's polarity between a Mexican-Chicano and an English-American literary tradition.

The natural environment of southern Colorado and northern New Mexico, and the academic milieu of Stanford University, are not as far apart as they may seem at first. Ironically, Stanford, the Ivy League institution and bastion of the intellectually elite on the West Coast, is only one hour by car from Carmel and the Monterey peninsula. The proximity is important because Carmel and Monterey are the land of Robinson Jeffers, the American poet who probably exerted the most significant literary influence on Zamora and who provides a link between the two poles of her poetic landscape. That Zamora chose Jeffers over other poets for her main literary inspiration is no accident. On the one hand, Jeffers gives Zamora an opportunity to express allegiances and loyalties to her natural and cultural roots because he writes about a land similar in its harshness to the land of her rural origins in Colorado. On the other hand, Jeffers, though a minor poet in the canons of American literary tastes, has textual roots in mainstream United States literature. Zamora's intertextuality[2] with Jeffers represents the conflict between her positive identification with a poet whose subject is California and its land, and a critical perspective on his masculine assertions about nature and woman in his poetry.

Zamora's response to Jeffers primarily engages her identities as a woman and as a poet, with her identity of Chicana present but subordinate to the other two. The polarized settings, cultures, and traditions that appear throughout Zamora's poetry—a natural landscape and a literary landscape—imply the identities of Chicana and poet. These two identities—the first rooted in a cultural-ethnic base, the second in an intellectual, academic base—overlap with her strong identity as a woman, which moves back and forth between the two landscapes and traditions. I assume that Zamora acquired this identity from her experiences in the larger society—the impact of the woman's movement during the 1960s and 1970s—as well as from her experiences in the Chicano movement. The strong sexual bias of the Mexican-Chicano male observed and felt by Chicanas inspired and encouraged their resistance to the cultural tradition of male superiority and authority over women.[3]

In *Restless Serpents*[4] Bernice Zamora offers a qualitatively different scenario of the relationships defining the identities of woman, Chicana, and poet from those offered by any of the other poets discussed in this volume. For this reason I have chosen to present her last. Of the four poets whose works I analyze, Zamora best exemplifies my hypothesis of a triad of conflicting identities. As opposed to the other poets, who have chosen one identity over the others, Zamora in her poetic works reveals a shifting consciousness that dramatizes a strong tension among the three identities. She is the most conscious of all three identities at once. Her poetic voice articulates conflict and tension rather than striving for synthesis and resolution.[5] Sometimes this conflict is dramatized in a single poem. In "Gata Poem," for example, she attempts to respond to both a Mexican-Chicano sociocultural context and an English-American literary context. At other times we hear in the juxtaposition of several poems the multiple voices of the poetic consciousness, as it expresses in one poem a positive relationship to Mexican-Chicano culture and in another defines itself in critical opposition to the Chicano male. Zamora also reveals a shifting perspective toward the dominant literary tradition, now identifying with its poets as writers she admires, now criticizing them as males whose traditions exclude women.

To understand Zamora's poetry, then, we must shift our perspective so as to see the reverse side of the triad of woman, poet, and Chicana, thus bringing to the surface the implied counterparts of woman and Chicana, that is, male and Chicano. Zamora confronts in a direct and explicit way the male dimension only implied by the struggle in Villanueva's *Mother, May I?* and indirectly alluded to in Cervantes' "Beneath the Shadow of the Freeway." What distinguishes Zamora's poetic universe from that of the other poets, then, is her vigorous desire to master the male.

Zamora's poetic persona encounters the male adversary in both traditions. In fact, her literary persona finds it hard to conceive of its struggle with the male as independent of either one tradition or the other. Like Villanueva's, Zamora's response to the dilemma is to reenact the history of woman's oppression without compromising her autonomy as a woman and a poet. Unlike Villanueva, who seeks an abstract community of women with no real concrete basis in either the Anglo or the Chicano society, Zamora articulates a male-female conflict in the specific contexts of the Chicano male and of the English-American poet. Whereas Villanueva's female consciousness does not—perhaps cannot—contain the social specificity of a Chicana consciousness, Zamora's female consciousness enters into sharp conflict with a desire to assert her Chicana ethnic self. Her strong feminine consciousness leads her to distrust the traditional Chicano male and inspires her to conduct a sexual battle against him. Her distrust prevents her from identifying with him in a racial struggle against the dominant society, a struggle that inevitably includes herself as a member of the same community.

Zamora's decision to restrain the expression of her Chicana self to the dominant society suggests a major difference between herself and Lorna Dee Cervantes. Cervantes refuses to compromise her ethnic identity; Zamora refuses to compromise her female identity. In "Beneath the Shadow of the Freeway" Cervantes envisions a future when male-female relationships will be harmonious, thus obtaining a lyrical moment. My analysis of this poem reveals a gap in the transition from the macho male of her grandmother's and mother's generations to the "gentle man" of her own generation. Zamora, unlike Cervantes, cannot envision such a transition. Instead, she insists on "fighting the fight," on filling in the gaps and mapping out the concrete details of the struggle to transform the macho into a gentle man.

Zamora's strong feminine consciousness also leads her to conduct an intertextual battle against the literary masters who are responsible—at least in part—for her identity as a poet. Of all the Chicanas discussed in this book, Zamora is the most academic, the most intellectual, the most obviously influenced by poets of the dominant tradition, most of whom are male. As a woman and as a poet, Zamora revises her masters' stories and constructs new ones that include herself and, implicitly, other women like her. In this sense, even her intertextuality is a form of feminism, for in responding to male poets such as Jeffers and her other literary precursors she also makes a statement of what it means to be a woman. In Zamora's world women speak for themselves and revise the canon of established literary tastes. The intelligibility of Zamora's poetry, then, depends not only upon the presence of a sexual or male text but also upon the presence of a literary text. Zamora's desire to master the male and gain autonomy in her relationship with men is also implicitly connected to a desire to master the dominant culture. If the poetic consciousness can accomplish this twofold task, perhaps it can also eliminate the barriers that keep it from asserting a Chicana identity to the dominant culture.

I suggest that the primary determinant of Zamora's poems in *Restless Serpents* is sex, in the double English sense of gender and the erotic. The poems that follow represent attempts to redefine sexual relationships between men and women as well as relationships between a text and its literary source. At both sexual and intertextual levels, they articulate statements in male-female discourse which women have not expressed to men, or which men have not permitted women to say, or which men themselves traditionally have not said. These statements are therefore linked to problems of both sexuality and textuality. Thus Zamora's poetic voice is constantly rotating on the triad of identities, never really finding a single fixed point on which to position itself. No matter which option it momentarily chooses, the decision almost always implies an awareness of at least one other alternative for a Chicana poet.

1

I begin with "Gata Poem."[6] It is the paradigm for the poems of *Restless Serpents*. In it are the two dominant poetic modes employed by Zamora to construct her poetic universe: dialogue and narrative. The poem also includes practically all the important sets of categories, or codes, that define the major poles or oppositions of her poetry. As a paradigm, "Gata Poem" sets up a system of relationships among several sets of conflicting codes. Thus it is a site of tension where opposing codes coming from two distinct literary and cultural traditions—English-American and Mexican-Chicano—interlock and traverse each other.

"Gata Poem" is the expression of a poetic voice that is striving to define its place in these two main traditions. The poem dramatizes a Chicana's struggle to confront both an internal and an external dilemma. The internal dilemma concerns the fictional speaker's desire to hold fast to her identity as a woman within a Mexican-Chicano tradition that bestows privileges on the male over the female. The external dilemma concerns her desire to reject the English-American larger society and thus to assert her ethnic identity as a Chicana. The major thematic opposition, then, is a struggle between sex and race, an opposition that can be translated into the question the poem attempts to answer: Can I assert my ethnic Chicana self to the larger society and still affirm my autonomy as a woman within my minority culture? Zamora's intent to assert both these identities at once makes "Gata Poem" a unique work in *Restless Serpents*. In no other poem in the collection does she attempt so overtly to integrate these two identities into her poetic persona.

The poetic frame of "Gata Poem" is Mexican-Chicano culture, a frame that Zamora seldom privileges over the English-American culture that governs so much of her poetry. Zamora's decision to write "Gata Poem" in Spanish[7] is important because only two other poems of the fifty-eight in *Restless Serpents* are in the same language—"El último baile" and "A tropezones en Stanford"—except for "Stanford" in the title of the latter. The major difference between "Gata Poem" and these other two pieces is that in the former Zamora responds as a Chicana whereas in the other two she emphasizes her consciousness as a woman. That "Gata Poem" displays an awareness of the English dominant tradition is evident from the bilingualism of the title and the shift from Spanish into English in stanza 1. Because most of its lines are in Spanish, "Gata Poem" seems to favor a Mexican-Chicano, rather than an Anglo, poetic register. In asserting her Chicana persona in Spanish, the language of the minority culture, Zamora is ostensibly rejecting the dominant literary tradition. She writes in Spanish as a Chicana, but nonetheless is poetic. In contrast with the other poems discussed here, such as "Sonnet, Freely

Adapted," written in imitation of Shakespeare, and the poems that directly allude to Jeffers, "Gata Poem" presupposes no previous literary text. "Gata Poem" thus demonstrates a form of negative intertextuality. The text in "Gata Poem" is Mexican-Chicano culture. The translation that follows the original is mine.

Gata Poem

Desde la cima me llamó
Un hombre perfecto, un chicano
Con cuerpo desnudo y tan moreno que
He glistened in the sun like a bronze god.

—Ven, mujer.
Ven conmigo.

Se me empezó a morir como una gata
    en la noche
Y yo misma era gata vestida de negro.

—¿Qué quieres, señor?   10
¿Qué quieres conmigo?

—Quiero cantar eternamente contigo
    lejos de la tristeza.
Quiero enseñarte un sol tan brillante
    que debemos verlo con alma escudada.
Quiero vivir contigo por los nueve mundos.

—Ven, gatita.
Ven conmigo.

       Y me fui

Cat Poem

From the summit he called me
A perfect man, a Chicano
Naked, and so brown that
He glistened in the sun like a bronze god.

—Come, woman.
Come with me.

He began to die on me like a cat
    in the night.
And I also was a cat dressed in black.

—What do you want, sir?   *10*
What do you want with me?

—I want to sing with you eternally
    somewhere far away from sadness.
I want to show you a sun so brilliant
    that we must see it with a guarded soul.
I want to live with you in nine worlds.

—Come, kitten.
Come with me.

And I left *or* And I went

"Gata Poem" is marked by a continual slippage of the poetic voice, as the reader finds it impossible to pinpoint the identity of the speaker's voice. In the poem's latter half (ll. 12 ff.) the voice constantly vacillates, slipping back and forth between the feminine speaker's voice and her male addressee's, between the gender identity of male and female. Thus the poem creates an ambiguous poetic space. In reality, the poet is striving to create a new identity—the dual assertion of a Chicana self and a female self. In the end she does not achieve that goal. I propose that what the poem means is what it does. Its meaning is the uncertainty as to the identity of its voice.

"Gata Poem" portrays sexual rivalry in terms of verbal play between a Chicana and a Chicano, the goal of which is to determine who decides the rules of the sexual contract. The epitome of male machismo is the Chicano on the summit. The pun on *cima* ("pinnacle") / *sima* ("abyss") enriches the poem. If the reader's experience with the poem is purely auditory, the Chicano's location is ambiguous: Is he above or is he below? Only by reading the poem does one know for certain that the Chicano is above.

The ambiguity as to the Chicano's location suggests a consciousness that desires to question the social rules defining boundaries between men and women in a Mexican-Chicano context. According to the social conventions of the traditional serenade in Spanish and Latino cultures, for instance, the man's place is below and the woman's is above. The poet's impulse is to invert these positions by placing the man above and the woman below. This transposition of traditional gender roles is consonant with the dominant themes of Zamora's poetry. The impression that the Chicano is below is a possibility only on the poem's oral level; the issue is settled at the poem's written level. From the outset tension is established between two antagonistic codes pulling in opposing directions: the oral code says "Chicano may be above or below"; the written code says "Chicano is above." This interplay between oral-aural and written-visual codes recurs in several of Zamora's poems.

The first three lines of "Gata Poem" are narrative, presupposing a speaker and an implied addressee. The Chicano at this point is outside the circuit of communication between speaker and addressee, for he is the subject spoken about by the narrator. The narrative language has an ambiguous quality: it could belong either to a speaker who is telling somebody else about the Chicano's call, or to a speaker who is silently pondering the event. That the speaker is a woman is clear from the relationship implied in the phrase, *Desde la cima me llamó* ("From the summit he called me"), and the ensuing line of dialogue, *Ven, mujer* ("Come, woman"). The woman is reflecting in present time upon an occurrence in past time. The temporal sequence—the narration of the call followed by the event of the call—suggests that the narration is a silent meditation rather than a spoken description.

The purpose of these three lines is to present the myth of the Chicano as a "bronze god." The lines in Spanish produce seductive effects. The repetition of soft vowels (*e*'s, *a*'s, and *o*'s) and the soft labials (the *c* of *cima* pronounced like an *s*, the *m*'s and the *ll* of *llamó*) give the lines melodic tones that the English translation does not convey. The hard sounds of *p*, *f*, and *t* in *perfecto*, the *ch* in *Chicano*, and the hard *c* sounds in *con cuerpo*, offer a contrast because they alter the rhythm and help to project these words to the foreground. In other words, it is important to note that this male is "perfect" and is a "Chicano" and that he has physical, sensual qualities. In making this distinction between the languages I am not suggesting the popular but, nonetheless, unfounded notion that Spanish has a propensity to be soft and musical and English to be hard and harsh. Rather, I am suggesting that Zamora elects to write in Spanish because Spanish, more easily than English, evokes for her an involvement with the romantic myth.

The speaker's abrupt shift into English (l. 4) interrupts the flow of her preceding phrases (up to the word *que*) constructing the romantic, sexual image of the Chicano. The shift to English at this strategic point disrupts the romantic effect achieved by the opening lines. The English sentence sounds vapid and dull. The crescendo effect of the lines in Spanish is destroyed by the English line. The relative pronoun *que* prepares the reader for the high point, but instead of fulfilling expectations by continuing the approach to a romantic climax, the English line is merely a slogan. The slogan, which sounds more jargonistic in English than in Spanish, provides the only clue that the Chicana is critical of the romantic rhetoric by which the Chicano can imagine himself as a "bronze god." In the opening stanza the speaker thus moves from a position of an involved narrator (the lines in Spanish) to a position of a distanced narrator (the line in English) who is critical of the situation.

Dialogue first appears in stanza 2 (ll. 5–6). The man utters an abrupt, straightforward directive to the woman, indicating his position of power over her. The lines in dialogue reveal the communication situation between the speaker and the addressee, now the Chicano and the Chicana, respectively. Even more directly, the dialogue stresses the effect the Chicano wants to make. He hopes to generate a specific action on her part, to persuade her to follow him.

Stanza 3 (ll. 7–9) suspends the dialogue and returns to the woman's meditative, romantic narrative. Although these lines, separating his command in stanza 2 from her question in stanza 4 (ll. 10–11), are part of her internal narrative, they are on a different level of signification. They suggest a surreal scene through the juxtaposition of disparate images: death, a cat, blackness, night, a woman and a man. The description produces erotic effects of a sexual fantasy. Through an elaborate metaphor, the woman transforms the Chicano into a feminine animal. The man dies as a female cat would die in the night. In a Chicano-Mexican context, associations link *gata* to a stray female cat wandering the streets, indiscriminately mingling and copulating with any male cat. The image transmitted is one of the Chicano expiring on the Chicana as a female cat would expire in the night. The word *morir* in line 7, then, means what "to die" means in sixteenth- and seventeenth-century literature—the sexual orgasm.

Line 9 links male and female in the common symbol of *gata*, for the woman speaks of herself as also being a *gata*, thus identifying with the Chicano. The phrase that identifies the woman as a *gata—vestida de negro*—suggests a woman in mourning. Traditional norms of Mexican-Chicano communities dictate that women dress in black to mourn the death of a close family relative. These lines therefore suggest that the woman of the poem identifies with the traditional woman of her culture, someone whom she imagines obeying traditional rules. The traditional rule here is that the woman succumb to the sexual pleasures the male has to offer her.

The image of *gata* also brings to mind the creature evoked by the title of the collection, *Restless Serpents*, and by several other poems. The image of the serpent in "Gata Poem" is indirectly suggested in the image of a cat performing the rhythmic movements of a snake, gliding and circling in and out with the motion of waves. In other poems the image of the snake is presented directly (as in the title poem, "Restless Serpents," or in "Stone Serpents"), or is evoked by the poem's spatial design (as in "El último baile," where the image of the serpentine dance [*baile*] suggests on a kinesthetic level the movements of a snake). The snake image operates in both its Judeo-Christian and pre-Columbian contexts: it is both a negative and a positive image. As a classic phallic symbol it has the usual Freudian negative implications of male power over women. In the pre-Columbian context it relates to Quetzalcoatl or the Plumed Serpent, a positive deity who intimates a connection with artistic achievement. The poetic persona of *Restless Serpents* is restless, always struggling to define its authentic place in relation to its cultural and literary traditions. At the metatextual level in "Gata Poem," the cat/snake image also relates to the poetic voice slipping in and out between two genders and among various formal codes.

Unlike the dialogue in stanzas 2 and 4, the narrative in stanza 3 is not intended to persuade. Rather, stanza 3 expresses the thoughts of a mind in silent meditation, a mind losing itself in a dream. Its effect is to invite readers to interpret it, to find the relationships and connections among its images. In stanza 4 the woman answers the man with a question. Here again, as in stanza 2, these lines of dialogue stress the oral communication between woman and man. Her question seeks to generate a specific action on his part; she wants him to tell what he desires of her. Her manner of answering him suggests that she too has some measure of power. She is not responding to his command without questioning it. Whereas stanza 3 is couched in self-conscious, reflective language, the language in stanzas 2 and 4 is persuasive and argumentative.

In stanzas 5 (ll. 12–16), 6 (ll. 17–18), and 7 (l. 19) it becomes difficult to distinguish the speaker from the addressee, male from female. Interpreting the poem loosely, one might argue that the rules of exchange in a conversation dictate that the Chicano enunciates stanzas 5 and 6. In this interpretation, the content of stanza 5, an answer to her question, and the dash preceding *Quiero* (l. 12), are elements suggesting the presence of a male voice. Possibly threatened by the woman's stern tone in stanza 4, possibly softened by the sexual encounter in stanza 3, he changes his formerly terse style to a softer, more endearing tone. He then repeats the command in stanza 6, only this time he uses the diminutive *gatita*. The parallel syntactic structure between this stanza, *Ven, gatita. / Ven conmigo*, and stanza 2, *Ven, mujer. / Ven conmigo*, is another formal feature indicating that the Chicano is the speaker. Following this line of argumentation, the gender ending of *gatita* would imply a male speaker.

If the Chicano actually does speak these lines, her answer, *Y me fui*, has two possible meanings. The juxtaposition of stanzas 5 and 6—stanza 5 a commitment in elaborate language and stanza 6 a directive in direct language (except for the metaphoric elaboration of *gatita*)—suggests that the Chicano, though promising poetic floweriness, still prefers giving commands. If the Chicana sees the words *Y me fui* as a contradiction, they most likely mean that she rejects the Chicano and goes off without him. The poem's typography reinforces the latter idea. The argument against this interpretation, however, is that the diminutive *gatita* softens the commanding tone and turns the command into an invitation. The inviting tone adds power to the fantasy of the male as someone capable of fulfilling the woman. *Y me fui* is then more likely to mean that she goes with him. It is important to realize that this phrase, as my translation indicates, can communicate either meaning: "I went" suggests that the Chicana decides to submit to the Chicano's sexual call; "I left" suggests that the Chicana asserts her separateness from him.

As Zamora thinks primarily in English, *fui* may also be—as sometimes happens in her poetry—a literal translation into Spanish of "come," used in popular speech to designate the sexual orgasm. This connotation of *fui* ("came") suggests that, in all probability, the Chicana imagines herself surrendering sexually

to the Chicano. If the Chicana does surrender, her language reveals enough consciousness to make the reader suspect that she
does not surrender uncritically.

If one looks closely at the voice and gender changes in stanzas
5 through 7, however, one must conclude that the communicative
circuit breaks down because it becomes impossible to distinguish
between speaker and interlocutor, between man and woman. The
Chicana may be the speaker in stanza 5, for, though presented as
dialogue, it is couched in romantic, flowery language. No prece-
dent exists for the Chicano's employing this kind of language,
whereas she has used impassioned narrative in the first three
lines of stanza 1 and in stanza 3. Stanza 5 may very well correspond to her dream of what she would like the Chicano to promise
her—eternal songs and brilliant suns. It is as though her voice
has absorbed his voice; he may speak, but only as an imagined
voice within her. Even though the Chicana is critical of the
romantic myth of the Chicano as a "bronze god," the myth is
also her fantasy because it is presented in sentimental, flowery
language which corresponds to her imagined voice.

The gender changes also create ambiguities in stanza 6. Since
both male and female are *gatas* in stanza 3, either one could call
the other *gatita*. In stanza 3, however, the Chicana performs the
metaphoric reversal of *gata* on him, not he on her. The reversal
represents her sexual transformation of him into a *gata*. If, then,
stanza 6 is actually a spoken communication, as I assume stanzas
2 and 4 are, only she can call him *gatita*, as she is the only one
who has employed the term by thinking it. Even if stanza 6 is
spoken by the Chicano, he can call her *gatita* only in her imagined
dialogue. If he says *Ven, gatita*, the male voice is therefore within
herself. The Chicana has moved into the masculine position:
earlier he says *Ven*, but now, in language exactly parallel to his,
she says *Ven*. She has transformed the male's abrupt order by
using the diminutive *gatita*, which softens the commanding tone
and turns the order into an invitation. The woman is offering the
relationship to the Chicano under new terms: an opportunity to
accept his femininity. According to this reading, the woman has
renegotiated the traditional contract so that she, not he, defines
its terms. The final phrase, *Y me fui*, would then mean that she
leaves without him.

The poem's consciousness communicates a desire for equality between male and female, Chicano and Chicana. The word

conmigo ("with me") is important. In Spanish it is one word, not two as in English and French. Repeated three times in the poem, twice by the first voice and once by the second voice, it suggests a desire to have male and female dissolve into one, especially in stanza 6 where the ambiguities in voice and gender are heightened. The sexual transformation of the male into a *gata* also suggests a desire to find an equality between the two genders so that there will no longer be a "low" and a "high."

The crucial issue is to determine what occurs in the interval between the enunciation of *Ven, gatita. / Ven conmigo,* and the final line, *Y me fui.* There are at least two possibilities. The first is that the male will accept his new identity of *gatita* and follow her, instead of holding onto his macho identity, more fittingly suggested by the masculine *gato. Y me fui* would then mean that she goes off without him, open to the possibility that he will follow. The second and, I think, the more radical possibility is that in the silence between the softened command and the final decision the woman herself realizes that the revision of the traditional contract ultimately represents a closed cycle, because Chicana and Chicano have only changed places instead of altering the substance of the relationship. No one can win. The only way she can redefine the contract is to lock herself into the macho role. Realizing the circularity of the situation, she decides to break away and go off alone without the male.

My reading of "Gata Poem" suggests three options: (1) the woman goes with the traditional male; (2) she accepts the male under a redefined contract; (3) she rejects the entire process of renegotiating the contract and goes off alone. The first, for me, is the least credible because the poem conveys too much consciousness for her to accept the traditional male on his terms. Its intent is to change and transform the male. But even if we choose either the second or the third option, we cannot decode the poem with complete satisfaction, because no matter which of the two we argue for, there are always indications of the credibility of the other one. The undecidability of the consciousness is the poem's meaning. When both identities of Chicana (race) and woman (gender) come together, the consciousness finds it impossible to integrate the two into one harmonious unit. The consciousness strives to speak from the point where these two identities of Chicana and woman meet. In the end it does not achieve what it sets out to do.

"Gata Poem" is also paradigmatic of Zamora's other poems at the intertextual level. The literary and social values, norms, and conventions that the poem, or any literary work, presupposes imply a particular kind of literary and cultural reader. If the readers of "Gata Poem" are seen as a continuum, at its two extremes are monolingual English and monolingual Spanish readers. In between is the bilingual reader, who is the ideal reader of Zamora's poetry. Only the bilingual reader is able to bring together the two different traditions from which Zamora's poems emerge and to which they respond.

As all but one of the lines in "Gata Poem" are in Spanish, it would seem that the Chicano reader is privileged over the Anglo reader. That the poem nonetheless presupposes two kinds of cultural readers is manifest on the surface, at least, in the bilingualism of the title and in the shift from Spanish into English in stanza 1. Yet even within the Spanish lines there is conflict between the dominant literary tradition and an oral, popular poetic language. The interpretation of stanza 3 depends upon the decoding of two words—*morir* and *gata*—and that in turn depends upon the presuppositions of cultural and literary conventions. The modern reader must shift from the current usage of *morir* ("die") to an archaic, literate usage (sexual orgasm). Through her study of English literature Zamora is fully aware of the latter usage. Her poem, "Sonnet, Freely Adapted," presupposes an acquaintance with Shakespearean conventions. Neither reader at the two extremes of the continuum can make the shift into English, though the Spanish monolingual reader has the advantage of being able to associate *morir* with the sexual orgasm. Such an association exists in the Spanish repertoire of associations with *morir* in a literary context.[8] The English reader, however, cannot make the association because the initial word is *morir*. Paradoxically, however, the poem makes an indirect appeal more to the English than to the Spanish reader. The assumption, then, is that the reader will shift first from Spanish into English and then link "die" with the sexual orgasm. The only reader who can easily effect this switch is the bilingual reader.

The second important presupposition necessary to understand stanza 3 is that the reader will know the meaning of *gata*, which comes not from a literate English-speaking tradition but from an oral, popular Spanish-speaking Mexican-Chicano tradition. *Gata* colloquially designates either "prostitute" (*puta*) or "servant," both of which connote a subservient position for women. To interpret stanza 3 the reader must know these meanings of *morir* and *gata*. The connotations of these two words are far apart: the first from the dominant tradition is literary and archaic; the second from the minority tradition is oral and popular. Here again, only the bilingual reader has the potential to join the two together.

A secondary conflict in the Spanish lines is a tension between narrative and dialogue. Through stanza 4 the two alternate: narrative, dialogue, narrative, dialogue. The narrative discourse is presented as romantic and meditative (except for l. 4) or as unspoken narrative reflecting the Chicana's internal state of mind. The dialogue is presented as spoken discourse. Like the two genders, these discourses are difficult to separate in stanzas 5 and 6. The language of stanza 5 is romantic hyperbole, but its form of presentation insinuates spoken discourse. Stanza 6 seems to be spoken but the insertion of *gatita* links it to the romantic narrative of stanza 3. Until this point the narrative has been presented as unspoken. The last line, *Y me fui,* retains the direct quality of the lines in dialogue, yet it is not dialogue. It also retains the nonspoken, meditative quality of the lines in narrative, yet it is not romantic. The line's position on the page suggests the poet's desire to separate it from the conflict of the prior language. The fact that the line is narrative without being romantic narrative also suggests a desire to reject the poetic floweriness of the prior language. The conflict between narrative and dialogue modes, however, is present to the end, for the line retains and rejects features of both.

The subject matter of "Gata Poem" is its own poetic consciousness. It contains within itself its own contradiction that does not allow it to come together and close. For Zamora, "Gata Poem" is the suggestion of autonomy as a woman and assertion of a Chicana ethnic self. To reach this goal the poetic persona attempts to transform the Chicano, for as long as he remains in his traditional form there can be no hope for harmony between them. The consciousness remains in a liminal state in the end, for we do not know if she decides to accept the male she has transformed, thus proving her mastery, or to reject him in the knowledge that her desire to master the male remains circular and ultimately goes nowhere.

Zamora's ambivalent relationship to the Chicano is the

dynamic force behind the poem. "Gata Poem" bumps up against its own contradiction. The desire to master the male becomes at once the recognition that without him there can be no writing. The integration of the two identities of woman and Chicana into one poetic voice makes this contradiction all the more intense. Implied is the recognition that the Chicano male, unlike the male of mainstream society, is a brother in a racial struggle against the dominant society and also a sexual oppressor in her culture. For this reason "Gata Poem" is unable to achieve closure. Hence, the poetic consciousness of *Restless Serpents* asserts itself in one context or the other, as a woman or as a Chicana.

2

The fixed point of Zamora's poetic voice in the poems discussed in this section is its identity as female. Her poetic voice slips in and out of two different cultural contexts, responding as a woman either to a Mexican-Chicano tradition or to the dominant English-American tradition. In my analysis of "Notes from a Chicana 'COED'" and "When We Are Able" I argue that when Zamora responds to a Mexican-Chicano tradition, her woman identity is never one with her Chicana identity, as she desires in "Gata Poem." My analysis of "Sonnet, Freely Adapted" shows that when she responds to an English-American tradition she does so in a literary and academic context. These poems are developed around the single continuum of dialogue, one of the dominant modes of "Gata Poem." The two extreme points of this continuum are oral and literary. Whether Zamora grounds the poems in the socially based context of "Notes" and "When We Are Able," or in the literary, learned context of "Sonnet, Freely Adapted," her language always creates ironic effects.

The female speakers of these poems respond directly to prior utterances or actions by males. Since the intent of the speakers is to convince their male addressees to alter their behavior and discourse, their rhetorical strategies are argumentative and persuasive rather than descriptive or meditative, as are the rhetorical strategies of the poems structured around the continuum of narrative, discussed in the next section. In each of these poems

Zamora employs different kinds of diction and syntax—from direct and explicit to flowery and elaborate—to persuade the male to change. The directly implied addressees of "Notes from a Chicana 'COED'" and "When We Are Able" are Chicano males; the male addressee of "Sonnet" is racially unspecified.

"Notes from a Chicana 'COED'"[9] is a powerhouse poem revealing Zamora's perspectives on the Chicano male and on poetry which are found in many of her other poems. Unlike the more tightly organized, more lyrical poems in *Restless Serpents,* "Notes from a Chicana 'COED'" expresses its message directly and explicitly, though not without producing ironic effects. Its lack of control allows some of Zamora's main concerns to surface. Although the poem does not appear in *Restless Serpents,* I include it here because it clarifies Zamora's relationship to the male in Chicano culture.

NOTES FROM A CHICANA "COED"

To cry that the *gabacho*
is our oppressor is to shout
in abstraction, *carnal.*
He no more oppresses us
than you do now as you tell me
"It's the gringo who oppresses you, Babe."
You cry "The gringo is our oppressor!"
to the tune of $20,000 to $30,000
a year, brother, and I wake up
alone each morning and ask,   10
"Can I feed my children today?"

To make the day easier
I write poems about
pájaros, mariposas,
and the fragrance
of perfume I
smell on your collar;
you're quick to point out
that I must write
about social reality,   20
about "the gringo who
oppresses you, Babe."
And so I write about
how I worked in beet fields
as a child, about how I
worked as a waitress
eight hours at night to

get through high school,
about working as a
seamstress, typist, and field clerk   30
to get through college, and
about how, in graduate school
I held two jobs, seven days
a week, still alone, still asking,
"Can I feed my children today?"

To give meaning to my life
you make love to me in alleys,
in back seats of borrowed Vegas,
in six-dollar motel rooms
after which you talk about   40
your five children and your wife
who writes poems at home
about *pájaros, mariposas,*
and the fragrance of perfume
she smells on your collar.
Then you tell me how you
bear the brunt of the
gringo's oppression for me,
and how you would go
to prison for me, because   50
"The gringo is oppressing you, Babe!"

And when I mention
your G.I. Bill, your
Ford Fellowship, your
working wife, your
three *gabacha guisas*
then you ask me to
write your thesis,
you're quick to shout,
"Don't give that   60
Women's Lib trip, mujer,
that only divides us,
and we have to work
together for the *movimiento*
the *gabacho* is oppressing us!"

Oye carnal, you may as well
tell me that moon water
cures constipation, that
penguin soup prevents *crudas,*
or that the Arctic Ocean is *menudo,*   70
because we both learned in the *barrios,*
man, that pigeon shit slides easier.

Still, because of the *gabacho*,
I must write poems about
pájaros, mariposas, and the fragrance
of oppressing perfume I smell somewhere.

The speaker and her addressee, a mistress and her lover, are academic Chicanos: she is a coed and he is a recipient of a Ford Fellowship who is supposed to write a thesis. The male text is the political slogan the Chicano lover continually repeats to his Chicana mistress: "It's the gringo who oppresses you, Babe." In attempting to answer, the woman has to decide whether to engage in a struggle against the gringo, her racial oppressor, or against the Chicano, her sexual oppressor. As he puts it, her choice is between "women's lib" and the *movimiento* (ll. 60–65). If she chooses the former, she asserts her womanhood but presumably betrays the movement in the eyes of her Chicano addressee. If she chooses the movement, she embraces the Chicano's racial struggle, but she incurs the liability of sexual inequalities imposed on Chicanas by Chicano men. Zamora's speaker exposes the contradictions of the Chicano's simplistic slogan. The real struggle is too complex, she argues, to be reduced to an opposition between herself and the gringo.

The Chicano's slogan impresses the speaker as a vague abstraction (ll. 1–3). In contrast, the hardships she endures, especially when compared with the privileges he enjoys, constitute the reality of her everyday existence. To escape this reality she writes romantic poetry: birds, butterflies, and the fragrance of perfume on the Chicano's collar. The Chicano disapproves of her poetry and urges her to write about social reality, or the white man's oppression of Chicanos, male and female (ll. 18–22). The effect of the *so* in her response—"And so I write about / how I worked . . ."—gives the reader or listener the impression that the Chicana agrees to write what he wants her to write. The lines that follow (23–25), however, are not those of a Chicana raging against her gringo oppressor. Rather, they provide concrete testimony of her own social reality: a woman who must work as a waitress and a seamstress ("two jobs, seven days / a week") in order to change the condition of her children starving to a condition of her children eating. The Chicano, in contrast, enjoys the comforts and security of his GI bill and his Ford Fellowship.

Since the Chicano's wife also writes romantic poems about

birds and butterflies and smells the "fragrance of perfume" on his collar, wife and mistress are bound together. Rather than attribute to the speaker the emotions of jealousy and hatred for the wife, responses that might be expected of her, Zamora links wife and mistress in a common identity. Whereas he talks about his wife and children to his mistress, Zamora transforms his response into the mistress's sympathy for the other woman. Both are poets; both are frustrated. We recall that in "Gata Poem" Zamora uses this technique of establishing an identity between the traditional woman and the woman who is aware of contradictions. In Zamora's poetic world, the second kind of woman seems to presuppose the first kind.

Stanza 3, "To give meaning to my life . . . ," is a parody whose effects depend on the technique of attributing to the Chicano actions that undermine the seriousness of his slogan. He makes love to the Chicana in alleys (this image conjures up the *gatas* in "Gata Poem"); he talks about his wife and children; and then he boasts of his sacrifices for the Chicana. The presentation of these actions one right after the other produces a satiric effect because it highlights the contradictions in the Chicano's behavior which seem to escape him so conveniently. A similar parodic effect is produced in stanza 4, where the Chicana amasses evidence to show him his contradictions: his privileges, his "working wife," and his *gabacha guisas*, or Anglo "chicks." His sexual activity with Anglo women is behavior that is hardly suitable to a Chicano who makes so much of the racial issue. Instead of confronting the inconsistencies in his behavior, he adds injury to insult: "then you ask me to / write your thesis," and so forth and so forth. The joke is on the Chicano, for the poem's audience can hardly ignore these contradictions. The effect of the *Oye carnal* ("Listen brother") (ll. 66 ff.) causes the audience that can capture the elocutionary force of these and following words (*crudas* ["hangovers"]; *menudo* ["tripe"]) to ready itself for the punch line. The series of hyperboles accompanied by the climactic line about "pigeon shit sliding easier" is the final criticism of the Chicano's hypocritical behavior and discourse. In essence, she puts him in his place, telling him to restrain his useless, absurd rhetoric because they both know the hard, crude life of the barrio.

The effect of *Still* (meaning "in spite of everything I've said") in the final stanza suggests that the Chicana now apparently retreats from her criticism and succumbs to an acceptance of the

Chicano's philosophy. These last lines, however, express the poem's neat rhetorical reversal. They contain a double irony: (1) it is not "because of the *gabacho*" that she writes, as she claims, but because of the Chicano; and (2) she does not write poems about what she claims she must write about—birds, butterflies, and perfume—but about concrete social existence. The fragrance recedes into an ambiguous location of *"somewhere"* instead of the specific location of "your collar," for the first time becoming "oppressing." The woman's resolution is to phrase her words so that she may criticize the Chicano. The kind of poem she says she writes is not the kind of poem she has written. She projects an image of a passive, submissive woman whom the Chicano thinks he deludes, and of a poet who says she must write about *pájaros* and *mariposas*. The reality is that she is not a naive woman but a strong Chicana capable of exposing the contradictions of her *compañero*. Also, she is not a poet who espouses the lyricism of perfume and butterflies but a poet who uses these romantic images to speak about the lives of people in a specific context.

In "When We Are Able" Zamora uses a more subtle form of irony, saying less and implying more. The speaker's use of *querido* as her form of address implies that her interlocutor is a Chicano. Depending on the context, *querido* may designate, as it does in this poem, the male in the amorous relationship.

WHEN WE ARE ABLE

When we move from this colony
of charred huts that surround
our grey, wooden, one-room house,
we will marry, *querido,*
we will marry.

When the stranger ceases to
come in the night to sleep in
our bed and ravish what is yours,
we will marry, *querido,*
we will marry.   *10*

When you are able to walk
without trembling, smile
without crying, and eat without fear,
we will marry, *querido,*
we will marry.

In responding to the implied question asked by the *querido*, "When will we marry?" the *querida*, or the mistress, lays down a series of conditions that must be fulfilled before the marriage can take place. Each stanza states one condition and each condition is followed by the refrain, "we will marry, *querido*, / we will marry." Each condition incriminates the Chicano more and more deeply. The argument moves from an implication of mutual responsibility between *querida* and *querido* in the first stanza to an attribution of blame to the *querido* in the third.

The second stanza raises the poem's central question: Is the *querido* powerless to prevent the stranger's intrusion into their "one-room house," or does he simply look the other way? The poem's ironic tone suggests that the answer is the second alternative. The ironic effect is created by two unexpected deviations. The first shift occurs when the focus changes from "our bed" to "ravish what is yours" (l. 8). The reader or listener expects something different, for example, "ravish what is ours." The shift to "yours" marks a logical paradox because "yours" contradicts what "our bed" affirms.[10] "Yours" implies that what the stranger "ravishes" is "not mine." The shift into second person contradicts what "our bed" and the four preceding uses of "we," including the one in the title, suggest. This shift indicates a divided consciousness. On the one hand, the consciousness accepts the terms of the traditional contract with the male, making her his possession and, on the other hand, it also sees itself as outside this situation, questioning and resisting the terms of the contract. Here again, we see a linkage in identity between the traditional woman who simply accepts and a modern woman who questions.

In the second rhetorical deviation, the speaker changes from the "we" of stanzas 1 and 2 to the emphatic "you" in line 11. This shift reinforces the suspicion that the speaker sees herself as outside the boundaries implied by the traditional contract; its effect is to transfer the weight of the burden from "we" to "you," the *querido*. The irony is intensified when we read the poem's refrain for the third time in the context of these two shifts. The conflict between the two parties is heightened. We are reasonably certain that the woman is critical of the Chicano's position and that she hardly means, "we will marry, *querido* / we will marry." The speaker seemingly assures the *querido* that there is hope for future harmony between them, as long as certain conditions are fulfilled. She says "we will marry" six times, as though marriage could represent the fairy-tale ending to their present situation of misery. In reality, however, she is implying that she and the *querido* will never marry. Even if the poem continued for several more stanzas, each repeating the refrain, the less we would believe her.

The Chicano betrays his sexual contract with the woman by allowing an alien force to use her as his sexual possession. Hence the woman is doubly oppressed in a sexual way. The woman's point is that the Chicano only pretends to include the Chicana in his endeavors, a pretension implied by his desire to marry her, while he himself cooperates with dominant society, further intensifying her oppression.

Although the relationship among the three parties—woman, Chicano, and stranger—is conveyed in a sexual metaphor, the poem's implied message also has a racial context, for two reasons. First, the word "colony" in the first line denotes economic subordination of one group by another. The details of "charred huts" and "grey, wooden, one-room house" suggest economic impoverishment. Second, the threefold design of a Chicano, a Chicana, and "the stranger," especially when considered in relation to the implications of "colony," intimates that the stranger is probably a white male. The woman may say "stranger" to indicate his relationship to the ethnic community: "he is not one of us," in other words. The first two stanzas, in fact, echo the behavior of the white masters in the early American South when they not only exploited black men and women socially and economically, but further abused their power by sexually exploiting black women.[11] In Zamora's poem, even if the Chicano willingly allows the stranger to enter, his behavior implies that the stranger is his superior or his master and that the Chicano is the inferior or the subject.

The classic double standard permitting the man to engage in sexual relations without incurring negative social consequences is an active principle in Zamora's poetry, but in a sexual context it is not the emotional focus of either this poem or of "Notes." The separate characters of wife and mistress in "Notes" are conflated into the single character of the speaker in "When We Are Able." This fusion is once again a variation of Zamora's technique of establishing a connection with the traditional woman. The emotional focus of the poem is the speaker's awareness of the

Chicano's double standard in a racial context. Pretending to be her friend, her brother, he really exploits her. The contradiction is conveyed by the speaker's identification with the traditional woman whose first concern might be loyalty to *la raza*, regardless of the Chicano's behavior, and her own awareness of the Chicano's duplicitous conduct. This second feature of the poetic consciousness leads Zamora to assume the pose of the traditional *querida*, an object of male desire, in order to criticize and ironically to deflate the Chicano's claim to male superiority. In refusing to confront the stranger, the sign of the dominant society, the *querido* refuses to be strong.

Although both these poems are addressed to Chicano males, they are open to anyone who reads English, Chicanos as well as Anglos, because they are written almost entirely in English. Zamora's female identity is connected to the English-speaking dominant tradition. Her poetic voice occupies a liminal space in Mexican-Chicano culture, positioning itself both outside and inside this culture: outside because she writes in English; inside because she writes to the Chicano male. Her use of the word *querido* grounds the poem in a Chicano social context. "Notes from a Chicana 'COED'" presupposes a consciousness that is inside Chicano culture because it contains specialized words whose meanings and implications are understandable only to those familiar with Chicano culture and language. Words such as *gabacho, guisas, carnal, menudo* exclude both an English and a Spanish monolingual audience unfamiliar with the *caló* dialect of Chicano culture. While these audiences may overhear the conversation, they remain outside the communication situation. Words like *pájaros* and *mariposas*, however, include the general Spanish audience, and words like "gringo" and "barrio" are familiar to an Anglo audience. "When We Are Able" uses only one Spanish word, but it is an important one. The endearing tone of *querido* in Spanish serves to heighten and intensify the speaker's ironic tone. The themes and the rhetorical strategies of these poems, then, show that Zamora's poetic consciousness as a woman is both inside and outside, alienated from, as well as part of, a Mexican-Chicano tradition.

Zamora uses a similar reversal strategy to gain ironic effects in "Sonnet, Freely Adapted." The sexual relationship in "Sonnet" is male heterosexuality versus male homosexuality. The first two lines suggest a heterosexual male who inquires of the woman

speaker why she persists in keeping company with gay men. The
male may even have made a pass at her and been rebuffed. Irked,
he then inquires why she prefers gays to real machos, like himself.
The poem is a direct reply to the man's inquiry.

SONNET, FREELY ADAPTED
FOR J. R. S.

Do not ask, sir, why this weary woman
Wears well the compass of gay boys and men.
Masculinity is not manhood's realm
Which falters when ground passions overwhelm.
O, no! It is a gentle, dovelet's wing
That rides the storm and is never broken.
It is whispered, secret words that bring
To breath more hallowed sounds left unspoken.
Men, sir, are not bell hammers between rounds
Within the rings of bloody gloves and games.   10
Men, sir, aught not rend the mind round square's round,
Spent, rebuked, and trembling in fitted frames.
   So, I return, sir, worn, rebuked, and spent
   To gentle femininity content.

The woman speaker is "weary," either tired of defending
herself against the advances of heterosexual men or tired of being
asked by heterosexual men to justify her preference for gay men.
In turn, she replies that she is more comfortable in the presence
of gays: ("Wears well the compass" (ll. 1–2). She argues for an
unconventional masculinity which encompasses the opposing
qualities of gentleness and strength: "dovelet's wing / That rides
the storm" (ll. 5–6). This masculinity, she continues, brings "to
breath" or gives voice to sounds "more hallowed" than those
actually spoken by traditional men. The homosexual male is
closer to her ideal than the heterosexual male, who aims to fit
himself into typically masculine roles: "bell hammers between
rounds" (l. 9). The woman is implying that men like her addressee
think they are masculine only if they are violent, combative
machos. But because the "sir" does not share her view of life, she
withdraws to "gentle femininity content." Her resolution of the
sexual conflict is to retreat into relationships with male homosex-
uals or with women. She accepts her femininity, supposedly,
"content" with its gentleness.

Zamora gains critical ironic effects by attributing archaic
language and syntax to her speaker ("Do not ask, sir"; "manhood's

realm"; "gentle, dovelet's wing"). Throughout the first eight lines Zamora knowingly fails to fulfill the "maxim of manner"[12] which governs how a modern woman in a similar situation, and, with motives similar to those of Zamora's speaker, responds to a male making such an inquiry or wishing to flirt. Zamora intentionally flouts the maxim of manner by having her speaker assume an elevated vocabulary and tone, a strategy that creates ambiguity and achieves distancing effects between her speaker and the addressee.

The polite and emotionally subdued tone of the archaic language allows the speaker to say what she wants to say without saying it too directly. Too blunt an answer would only anger the male and prevent him from listening to her argument. Instead, she assumes a tone of mock submissiveness and polite deference. Although the speaker's archaic diction and syntax probably sound prissy and effeminate to her male addressee, a modern audience will catch the latent humor and sarcasm. The repeated use of "sir" is ironic for it does not mean to the female speaker what we assume it means to the male addressee—rank, respect, and manhood. The speaker adopts the pose of a woman who suffers a rebuke whereas she really intends her words to serve as a rebuke to him.

In lines 9–10—"Men, sir, are not bell hammers between rounds / Within the rings of bloody gloves and games"—the woman shifts from her archaic, formal language to a modern, colloquial, oral word usage. At a first-level meaning, these lines say that men are not agents of physical conquest. The second-level meaning is subliminal because "hammer," in colloquial speech, is a synecdoche for men, as it designates the male organ. These lines also say, then, that men are not agents of sexual conquest making the "rounds" among women. The woman shifts into an oral language that her modern macho addressee understands and uses. By employing his language ("hammer," "rounds") the speaker ironically establishes her own identification with male discourse, showing her addressee that she can use his language to undermine his masculine image. These lines are ironical because they capture an implicit contradiction between what the images connote—blood, violence, brutality—and the apparently innocent tone employed to express them. The audience observes the marked contrast between the male's image of himself and what the woman is demonstrating about him. These oral, popular references presuppose a modern audience that catches the wit of the puns, their humor and irony.

At the intertexual level "Sonnet, Freely Adapted" is Zamora's quarrel with the conventions of the traditional Elizabethan sonnet. As other women have done before her,[13] Zamora invades the sanctuary of the sonnet as a literary form used by males in the dominant tradition. The fact that she makes her interlocutor feminine and her addressee masculine in a poetic form traditionally employed to express a man's love for a woman is in itself a deviation from the reader's expectations. By so doing she challenges the basic feature of Renaissance love poetry: a man speaking to gain a woman's love. The reversal produces irony, for here a woman is addressing a man, not to idealize him, but to chide him. Tension and contradiction also emerge when Zamora puts unconventional content into a conventional frame. She argues against the rigidity of conventional roles for men and women, yet she casts her ideas within the tight and closed form of the sonnet ("fitted frames").

The syntax of Zamora's sonnet links it with Shakespeare's Sonnet 116 on love as a direct literary inspiration.[14]

SONNET 116

Let me not to the marriage of true minds
Admit impediments; Love is not love
Which alters when it alteration finds,
Or bends with the remover to remove.
O, no, it is an ever-fixed mark
That looks on tempests and is never shaken;
It is the star to every wandering bark,
Whose worth's unknown, although his height be taken.
Love's not Time's fool, though rosy lips and cheeks
Within his bending sickle's compass come;   *10*
Love alters not with his brief hours and weeks,
But bears it out even to the edge of doom.
   If this be error and upon me proved,
   I never writ, nor no man ever loved.

Lines 3–6 of Zamora's poem are strikingly similar to lines 2–5 of Shakespeare's. Shakespeare's sonnet states what love is not (ll. 2–4), and then follows with an exclamation and an emphatic statement about what love is (ll. 5–6). Zamora's rhetorical argument on masculinity follows the same pattern, except that she introduces her negation at the beginning of line 3 and ends it in line 4. She then gives the exclamation and follows it with a definition of what masculinity is.

Another deviation is the rhyme scheme. Although it has seven rhymes, the traditional number for a Shakespearean sonnet (aa, bb; cdcd; efef; gg), Zamora's poem begins with two pairs of rhyming couplets instead of a quatrain. The next eight lines adhere to the Shakespearean rhyme scheme (cdcd; efef) but deviate in stanzaic form since they are a series of four unrhymed distichs rather than two symmetrical quatrains. Zamora ends her sonnet with a rhymed couplet that summarizes her resolution.

Zamora's couplet does not have the tight relation to the thematic content of its preceding twelve lines which Shakespeare's couplet does to his. Certain elements, such as the "So," the repetition of "spent" and "rebuked," and the epigrammatic force resulting from the couplet's rhyme, convey a sense of closure, but the thought remains loosely connected to the logical argument presented in the preceding lines. The reader is left to supply the missing information: it is precisely because the speaker knows that her addressee will probably continue his macho behavior that she retreats—though not really "content"— to "gentle femininity." Because of these formal similarities between Zamora's and Shakespeare's sonnets, the "sir" may implicitly allude to Shakespeare. Zamora is really saying: "Women, sir, not only men, can use this form, and for the purpose not of praising men, but of rebuking them."

Zamora's sonnet thus contains enough similarity to and enough deviation from the Shakespearean model to suggest that she is freely adapting the form, as her title states. My earlier comment about the intrusion of the oral and popular language is also pertinent here. This intrusion, as I have suggested, may indicate the desire of Zamora's speaker to show her addressee that she can master his language. Similarly, I now propose that it may also indicate Zamora's desire to assert her power with respect to the literary tradition of the sonnet. Zamora is playing with the form, conforming to it but also deviating from it as she pleases. This shifting indicates a desire to gain power and a refusal to be dominated by the form.

Ironically, however, Zamora's shifting into the modern, oral language undermines her attempt to subvert the tradition. The discontinuity in language choice ruptures the dialectical tension in her intertextual argument with the sonnet form that she has thus far sustained. The technique that is her claim to power and autonomy is the very technique testifying to its loss. She gains her freedom at the expense of losing control of the form. One possible reason for this breakdown may be the sexual ambiguity surrounding the figure of Shakespeare, who is well known for taking the position of the opposite sex to create ironic tension in his address. A second reason may be that Shakespeare, the universal and sensual poet, is ultimately regional to Zamora. Whatever the reason, something in the tradition resists her attempts to subvert it. In section 4 of this chapter I show that Zamora has a richer response to her other main precursor poet, Robinson Jeffers.

In contrast with "Notes" and "When We Are Able," which are linked to an oral tradition, "Sonnet, Freely Adapted" is written in the dominant poetic language. Hence it presupposes a different audience from those of "Notes" and "When We Are Able." Whereas "Notes" and "When We Are Able" presuppose racially mixed audiences, the archaic, lexical language and the poetic mode of "Sonnet, Freely Adapted" suggest a literary and academic audience; its thematic content suggests a gay audience. "Notes" and "When We Are Able" contain elements that imply an oral tradition. The repetition of the slogan, the specific parallelisms— "in alleys, / in back seats . . . / in six-dollar motel rooms" (ll. 37–39); "that moon water / . . .that / penguin soup . . . / or that the Arctic Ocean" (ll. 67–70)—and the loose stanzaic structure of "Notes," for example, are all features suggesting an oral tradition. "Sonnet, Freely Adapted" implies a Chicano readership only insofar as Chicanos are represented as members of literary and gay groups and not as members of a specific racial community.

"Sonnet" and "When We Are Able" are both founded on logical arguments. "When We Are Able" is presented in the form of three three-line propositions, each stating a condition and each beginning with "When." Each proposition is followed by a two-line statement beginning with "we" and expressing the result when the preceding condition is satisfied. The syntactic sequence, "When . . . we," is comparable to "If . . . then," a form that implies a logical relationship between the two parts. The first part leads us to expect the second part.

Zamora's sonnet follows the conventional Elizabethan form: the first twelve lines state the argument and the last two lines present the conclusion. Whereas "Sonnet" is cast in a highly conventionalized form, "When We Are Able" is not. The length of "Sonnet" is predetermined, as the sonnet form cannot exceed fourteen lines. No prescribed rules limit the structure of "When We Are Able" to a set number of stanzas. As the refrain is a device common to ballads, folk songs, and nursery rhymes,[15] its repetition in "When We Are Able" is a stylistic feature connecting the poem to oral rather than to written literature. "When We Are Able" and "Notes from a Chicana 'COED,'" then, presuppose a relationship to oral sources, whereas "Sonnet" is definitely connected to literary and academic discourse.

Regardless of the tradition chosen, two distinct codes intersect in the poetry: an oral, popular code and a written, literate code. The rhetorical and linguistic resources Zamora relies upon to develop and expand her poetic universe come either from the dominant English-speaking cultural heritage or from the language of a social group that derives its poetic vitality from oral and popular culture.

3

The poems discussed in this section are based on the continuum of narrative, the other dominant poetic mode of "Gata Poem." In these poems Zamora is attempting, not to persuade a male addressee, but rather to express her relationship to her two main cultural and literary traditions. Like her poetic voice in the dialogue mode, her poetic voice in the narrative mode slips in and out of these two contexts. These poems represent different gradations of a poetic voice moving along a continuum of narrative which consists of different levels of concrete description and their intended effects on the reader or listener. These levels and their effects are all contained in the paradigm work, "Gata Poem."

One level of description informs through direct, objective statement. Its model is found in the first lines of "Gata Poem," which inform us of an event: "Desde la cima me llamó / . . . un chicano." A second level of description is intended to produce nostalgic or meditative effects and may arouse, though not necessarily, erotic sensations. A third level of description is explicitly sexual and is intended to arouse sensual, erotic effects. The third stanza of "Gata Poem," with its surreal, dreamy images, its meditative tone, and its erotic presentation of a male cat expiring on a female cat, is a good example of the second and third levels of description. A fourth kind of descriptive language, which parodies or denies sexual eroticism, is intended to produce effects of distance from and resistance to the sexual myth. The single line in English in "Gata Poem," interrupting the image of the naked and bronzelike Chicano, produces these effects. In summary, the two extremes of the continuum of narrative are concrete-objective statement and concrete-satiric statement. In between these two extremes are levels of narrative language which produce effects ranging from nostalgic-meditative to sensual-erotic. The various gradations of both continuums—of dialogue and narrative—may be regarded as the different pitches of the notes of a musical scale.

"Penitents" and "Andando" reveal speakers who desire to integrate themselves into a Mexican-Chicano culture which they perceive as masculine. Although the speaker of "Penitents" may be a woman,[16] a female identity is submerged in the image pattern of its final stanza and thus is only indirectly inferred. In the poems of the preceding section the feminine consciousness is directly and explicitly presented. Nothing, either directly or indirectly, indicates a feminine speaker in "Andando." Here the speaker responds in terms of a cultural identity. These poems suggest that Zamora, when she is not responding to a Chicano male figure, feels freer to express a desire to identify with her traditional culture. When she does so, she tends to subordinate her modern identity as a woman.

"Penitents" and "Andando" contain all the levels of description and their intended effects noted above, except that the critical, satiric effect is absent. Because it is, these poems have an overall nostalgic-meditative tone. "Notes" and "When We Are Able" express the ironic, satiric side of Zamora's feminine persona in a Chicano context; this element is present in a Mexican-Chicano context only when a male figure is directly implied as an addressee. In contrast, "Penitents" and "Andando," expressive of Zamora's poetic persona searching for its cultural roots, reveal a poet's fascination with traditional ritual and form.

The speakers of "El último baile," "Having Drowned," and "Bearded Lady" are explicitly defined as women. Although "El último baile" is written in Spanish, its speaker reveals no explicit consciousness of a Chicana identity. "Bearded Lady" and "Having

Drowned," like "Sonnet, Freely Adapted," are set in an English-American context. What distinguishes them from "Sonnet," however, is that they ostensibly respond to no specific anterior text. "El último baile" and "Bearded Lady" are spoken by women who are searching for their sexual roots. The persona's inability to resolve the problem of male and female sexuality leads her to a moment of fantasy in "Bearded Lady" in which she imagines a hermaphrodite figure who embodies both male and female characteristics. "Having Drowned" is probably Zamora's most enigmatic poem in an English-American context. I include it here because it shows the shifting position of the poetic consciousness. No sooner does the poem tease us into interpreting it along sexual lines than it leads us to negate that interpretation. The tone of "El último baile" and "Bearded Lady" is passionate and sensual; that of "Having Drowned" is mainly ironic, grotesque, and comic. These three poems contain all the different levels of narrative language and their intended effects. Together these five poems, written in the narrative mode, show that Zamora's feminine persona has ironic as well as mythical aspects, but that when searching for its cultural roots it is primarily romantic and nostalgic.

"Penitents," the first poem in *Restless Serpents*, is named after the Penitentes of New Mexico, a religious sect whose members have the same customs, languages, and faith. Historically closed to females, the group is noted for its severe penitential observances.[17] Its main ritual is reenactment of the Crucifixion, a drama that includes self-flagellation, the dragging of chains, and the carrying of crosses. The ceremony seems medieval in the modern urban world. In some ways it is testimony to a region's isolation, where customs, habits, and language of previous eras are continued into a modern world with relatively little or no change. The word *"edmanos"* in line 3, for example, is an ancient spelling for *hermanos* ("brothers") and may correspond to the pronunciation of that word in certain parts of New Mexico. The use of quotation marks calls attention to the fact that *edmanos* is not standard Spanish.

PENITENTS

Once each year *penitentes* in mailshirts
journey through arroyos Seco, Huerfano,
to join *"edmanos"* at the *morada*.

Brothers Carrasco, Ortiz, Abeyta
prepare the Cristo for an unnamed task.
Nails, planks and type O blood are set
upon wooden tables facing, it is decreed,
the sacred mountain range to the Southwest.

Within the dark *morada* average
chains rattle and clacking prayer wheels jolt   10
the hissing spine to uncoil wailing tongues
of Nahuatl converts who slowly wreath
rosary whips to flog one another.

From the mountains *alabados* are heard:
En una columna atado se
hallo el Rey de los Cielos,
herido y ensangrentado,
y arrastrado por los suelos.

The irresistible ceremony
beckoned me many times like crater lakes   20
and desecrated groves.
I wished to swim
arroyos and know their estuaries
where, for one week, all is sacred in the valley.

Personal, temporal, and spatial signs orient the reader to the
situation of the ceremony. Specific names of brothers (Carrasco,
Ortiz, Abeyta), identification of places ("arroyos Seco ["dry"],
Huerfano ["orphan"]"; "sacred mountain range to the Southwest"), and mention of times ("Once each year" [l. 1]; "one week"
[l. 24]) help to set the scene for the drama enacted by the
Penitentes. Readers familiar with the history and sacred ceremonies of this group will know that the "sacred mountain range"
is the Sangre de Cristo Mountains in northern New Mexico and
that the time is Holy Week. More important than the landscape
where the ceremony takes place, however, is the speaker's relationship to it.

The temporal and spatial sequence in the presentation of
events is linear. The first two stanzas which set the outdoor
scene, describe a series of actions in the order of occurrence. The
Penitentes "journey through" streams, meet other brothers at
their *morada* (an adobe or stone dwelling place), prepare the
chosen brother for his role as Christ in the "unnamed task," and
ready the accoutrements ("Nails, planks, and type O blood"
[l. 6]) for the ceremony. This sequence conveys a sense of tradi-

tional order and routine. The juxtaposition of the mysterious catalog of "Nails, planks, and type O blood" and the abstract "unnamed task" is intended to arouse curiosity about the events to follow. The task, of course, is the simulated crucifixion of the brother chosen to represent Christ. The phrase "it is decreed" shows that every detail of the ceremony is readied in accordance with ancient practice. There is no room here for change or innovation.

In stanza 3 the scene shifts from outside to inside the *morada*. Although the poetic consciousness continues to narrate in the impersonal third person, something quite other than detachment is suggested by the figurative language. Except for the first line ("Within the dark *morada* average"), the language describing the events in the interior is replete with images of objects whose shapes and sounds produce sadomasochistic effects. The instruments for self-scourging—chains, whips, and rosaries—make noises (rattling, hissing, wreathing, uncoiling) that conjure up the image of the serpent, a traditional phallic symbol. Beatings and floggings are the main activities suggested. The movement of chains and whips ("the hissing spine") is circular and winding, coiling and uncoiling. The prayer wheels go round and round, clacking and striking against the whip whose sting lets loose the wail of "converts" initiated into the brotherhood. The first two stanzas and the third, then, are marked not only by a different spatial order but also by the degree of intensity in the sensations evoked by the images.[18]

The mention of "Nahuatl converts" (l. 12), together with the hard, austere images and sounds, evokes the aggression of the Spanish conquest of the Amerindian peoples of Mexico. Nahuatl was the language spoken by the Aztecs in central Mexico. The nationalist bent of the movement in the 1960s identified the Aztecs as the mythical precursors of Chicanos. The mention of "Nahuatl converts" in a poem about the Penitentes of New Mexico, a cultural-religious phenomenon of Spanish origin,[19] reflects one of the central discontinuities in the Chicano consciousness of the 1960s. This consciousness nostalgically went back to a pre-Columbian era to revitalize a cultural identity with its supposed ancestors.

The first line of stanza 4 returns to the language of neutral description. Except for this first line, the stanza is an *alabado*, an ancient hymn originating in oral communities and dating back to the sixteenth and seventeenth centuries.[20] By quoting the *alabado* Zamora creates tension. The words are italicized because they are transposed from an oral context to a written one. They are not spoken, as they would be in their original context. So, to create authenticity, Zamora uses italics for words that in the context of the poem become all the more distanced. As four lines of stanza 4, then, already exist in the reservoir of a culture, the effect is to distance the speaker from the subject matter.

The hymn concludes the description of the ceremony, presenting a wounded, bloodied Christ who is dragged across the ground. The superimposition of the *alabado* on the poem's temporal sequence makes the reader see that what has been pronounced in the past is now occurring in the ceremony, creating the illusion of an eternal present. The *alabado* contains the poem's only rhymed lines. The rhyme of *Cielos* ["Heavens"] and *suelos* ["ground"] stresses the tension between high and low.

The final stanza of "Penitents" effects two shifts or "turns," each of which contributes to the poem's meditative, nostalgic tone. First, the narration shifts from third to first person, from a description of external events to a personal utterance. Second, it shifts from present to past tense. Both changes create the effect of a speaker reflecting on her personal life. The present tense in the preceding four stanzas gives the impression that the speaker is present and is observing every detail of the ceremony. In the final stanza, however, the reader realizes that the poet is reminiscing after the event to a receptive listening self.[21]

The second shift, from present to past tense, reverses the relationship between the narrating consciousness and the person addressed as the narrator becomes the addressee. The subject of the narration—the Penitente ceremony—becomes the agent of address. The cultural landscape silently gestures toward the speaker ("beckoned me"). The comparison in lines 20–21, "like crater lakes / and desecrated groves," implies a relationship of similarity between the two images. Crater lakes are formed on mountain peaks when a volcano erupts or on the earth's surface when a meteorite explodes. The volcanic explosion might be considered a desecration of a mountain and the meteorite explosion a desecration of the earth. In mythology groves are small, sacred woods where gods, goddesses, or other creatures, such as nymphs, live. Desecration of a grove would be an outrage that is forbidden by the deities. It shares with a volcanic eruption the quality of a desecration. Both produce awe and horror, ecstasy and fear, in the speaker. Crater lakes, though transparent and clear, are bottomless and limitless cavities. Their shape and depth (round and profound) and their connection with water suggest the female body, or a maternal womb. Groves also suggest a maternal womb because they are dark, protective, and nurturing. A sense of transgression and evil pervades the formation of a crater and the desecration of a grove. Hence the speaker sees crater lakes and desecrated groves as dangerous, threatening, and engulfing, yet their beauty seduces and attracts her. These phenomena enrapture her the way the ceremony does. Both are irresistible. The speaker feels a desire to merge with the larger matrix of her culture, represented here in the rituals of the Penitentes. As male rituals, they are dangerous and threatening, but their passion and sexuality seduce her. As she reflects on the ceremony, she reiterates in the present her wish of the past to "swim" the waters of the arroyos. Her desire to "swim arroyos" is a wish and not a statement that reports an actual event.

The landscape images that relate to the Penitentes are hard and austere. The Penitentes journey through dry and "orphaned" arroyos; in contrast, the narrator will swim arroyos. Since images of water, like those of earth and flowers, are traditional images of the female body,[22] the wish to swim arroyos suggests a female persona desiring to find a feminine route to her culture. The ceremony lures her just as crater lakes and desecrated groves do. The comparison implies a desire to desecrate the sacred norms of her culture, because she will invade its sanctuaries of male privilege. It is important to note that when the narrator does insert herself into the discourse, she does so primarily as a woman and not as a Chicana. Her female persona is implied indirectly by images and not directly through statement, as it is in the poems discussed in Section II. Zamora submerges the side of her poetic persona which overtly insists on its female identity in order to express the wish to relate to a male culture.[23]

The second poem, "Andando" ("Walking"), consists of the first two kinds of narrative language: description whose purpose is to set the scene, and description whose purpose is to evoke a contemplative, romantic mood. Its narrative lines set up an alternating sequence of two kinds of landscape: one external and physical, the other internal and psychological. Presented in the first person and bilingually, the poem gives us a stronger sense of a Chicano narrator than "Penitents." I assume that the persona is female, though the poem gives no clues, explicit or implicit, as to the correctness of my assumption.

ANDANDO

From tomb to tomb *voy andando,*
buscando un punto final
to an age *ya mero olvidado.*

Cuando en las ruinas del Xlak-pak
hallando un tesoro de oro
explorers are less puzzled

Than I am now on this mountain.
Con el alma del presente
yo sucumbo al pasado

And to the secrets rolling through tall weeds   10
of my *abuelos'* mountain. I listen to their
laughter among the field mice.

From tomb to tomb *voy andando,*
buscando un punto final
to an age *ya mero olvidado.*

This poem's orientation as to time and place is more ambiguous than in "Penitents" because the pilgrimage is primarily an internal one. The first-person pronoun, nonetheless, provides focus and direction for the series of images. As the speaking persona moves in and out between an external and an internal landscape, there are some hints about physical location. In the opening stanza the speaker is walking in a cemetery, from "tomb to tomb." This direct statement situates us in a place, though we do not know where the cemetery is. The next two lines are more metaphysical and abstract. Their function is to relate us to the emotional mood of the speaker, who is searching for the final point (*un punto final*) of an age almost forgotten (*ya mero olvidado*). In stanza 2 the speaker moves on to a different physical location, the ruins of *Xlak-pak,* and makes a comparison between ancient explorers and herself in order to define her feelings. Confronted with the treasures of her own culture, she is more puzzled in the high altitudes of "this mountain" (l. 7) than were explorers who found treasures of gold in the subterranean ruins of ancient cities. Whereas they are archaeologists of the earth, she is an

251

archaeologist of the soul, a soul searching to define itself. Here again we find a tension between low and high, between the subterranean and the celestial. The effect of the deictic *this* in line 7 is to create the illusion of a specific, concrete territory.

In lines 8 and 9 the speaker again slips into the spiritual realm, as her modern self yields to the spirit of a past culture. In contrast with "Penitents," wherein the speaker expresses a desire to succumb to the call of the Penitente ceremony, the speaker in this poem sees herself actually yielding. In stanza 4 her focus shifts outward to the specific location of her grandfathers' (*abuelos'*) mountain. As she could have used the feminine form, *abuelas'*, her choice of the masculine form indicates that she sees the culture as masculine. Finally, the unmodified repetition of stanza 1 in stanza 5 creates a temporal sequence that is circular. The circular pattern imitates the structure of the poet's meditation: from beginning to end and back once again to the beginning. The repetition of the stanza, the internal rhyme (*andando, hallando*), and the repetition of -*ado* in lines 3 and 9 (*olvidado, pasado*) give the poem a meditative-lyrical quality.

By returning to the situation at the beginning, the last stanza serves to announce the poem's conclusion because it lessens the reader's expectations of continuation. It also reasserts the speaker's commitment to her search for cultural roots. Because the poem ends by returning to its point of origin, it suggests an eternal repetition of the journey. One implication of this circular pattern is that the speaker will have to succumb again and again with no deviations. The pattern also emphasizes the idea that there is no place else to go except to the beginning. As in "Penitents," the only way that Zamora's female speakers can succumb to a traditional culture they perceive as male is to hold in check their modern consciousness as women.

Like "Gata Poem," both "Penitents" and "Andando" presuppose bilingual readers, but they do so in different ways. "Penitents" is obviously addressed to an English monolingual reader, who would, however, encounter frustration in several places. The words *morada, alabados*, and "*edmanos*," for example, are not translated, though *penitentes* is. Stanza 4, almost entirely in Spanish, represents the culmination of the three preceding English stanzas. Thus the English reader would be stopped by stanza 4. On the other hand, Spanish monolingual readers would be able to understand the core or central drama of the ceremony, but the poem's context would remain unclear to them. They would not be frustrated, however, as they would be unlikely to read the poem in the first place because it contains too much English. Only the bilingual reader would understand both core and context.

"Andando" contains enough Spanish and English to keep monolingual readers of both languages from understanding it. The bilingual, bicultural reader not only grasps the meaning of the poem but can also manage the internal, mental transformation required by the final line of stanzas 1 and 5: "to an age *ya mero olvidado.*" The Spanish phrase, *ya mero olvidado,* must qualify the substantive that immediately precedes it—the genderless "age"—instead of the masculine *un punto final* in the preceding line. The final *o* of *olvidado* requires that "age" be masculine. Either an English or a Spanish monolingual reader would find this combination comfortable. If the English reader knows that the *o* in Spanish is, in most cases, a masculine ending, he or she would relate *olvidado* to the genderless "age" in English. The Spanish monolingual reader probably assumes that "age" is masculine. Only the bilingual reader feels the clash in genders embedded in the line, for this reader, I assume, translates "age" into the feminine *epoca.* Tension results from the mental juxtaposition of *epoca* and *olvidado.* The bilingual person, in reading the poem, can merge feminine and masculine.

That "El último baile" is the only poem in *Restless Serpents* written entirely in Spanish makes it particularly important. Only "Gata Poem" and one other piece, "A tropezones en Stanford,"[24] each containing very few English words, rival it in this respect. As contrasted with these poems, then, no English words interrupt the flow of Spanish in "El último baile." Its language is passionate and lyrical, aiming to produce erotic effects and evoke a romantic mood.

EL ÚLTIMO BAILE

Ensangrentada me quedo
a medianoche bailando
en mis pensamientos
en la medianoche
muriendo fisicamente
sobre ondas de
aguas coloridas,
esperando la última luna

                    roja   mojada
            me quedo sola bailando   10
            bailando en mi medianoche
            bailando en la medianoche
            bailando rumbo a la mar
                    de la tranquilidad.

            THE FINAL DANCE

            Anguished I remain
            dancing at midnight
            in my thoughts
            at midnight
            dying physically
            over waves of
            colored waters
            waiting for the final moon
                    red   wet
            I am alone, dancing   10
            dancing in my midnight
            dancing at midnight
            dancing toward the sea
                    of tranquility.

Because "El último baile" is written in Spanish, we know that its lyric speaker is a woman. As she first describes a feeling, the adjective used is feminine: *Ensangrentada* (she is "anguished" but we do not know why). The poem's context is even more ambiguous and allusive than that of "Andando." Although it seems to refer to a specific circumstance or occasion, the details are beyond precise identification. The poem invites the Spanish reader to construct a circumstantial context that is appropriate to the speaker's reflections.

"El último baile" uses temporal and spatial indicators to create an imprecise landscape: it is midnight (*a medianoche*) and the speaker seems to be near water (*sobre ondas* ["over waves"]) looking at the moon (*la última luna* ["the final moon"]). The language evokes a primitive context with its setting of the natural elements: the moon, water, and blood. The central action of the poem is the dance, a form of ritual in traditional communities. Because it recreates a sinking into fantasy, sleep, or even death, the poem reflects not so much a specific situation as the inner life of the speaker.

The speaker's mind wanders from an outer to an inner landscape, from an impersonal to a personal plane. Dancing in her thoughts (*bailando / en mis pensamientos*), she sees herself in an objective midnight (*la medianoche*). The spiritual landscape suggested by the image of the speaker "dancing / in my thoughts" is transformed into a physical landscape by the image of *muriendo físicamente* ("dying physically"), so that spiritual anguish becomes inseparable from physical death. The extreme poles of high and low—*luna* ("moon") and *aguas* ("waters")—are also merged in the images. The word *Ensangrentada*, containing *sangre*, the word for "blood," suggests "passion," "fire," "death." The waters are transformed into color (*aguas coloridas*) by the red moon (*luna / roja*), and the moon's image, reflected in water, becomes a "wet" moon (*luna / . . . mojada*). The speaker is alone and withdrawn as she dances in her personal midnight (*en mi medianoche*) (l. 11). In line 12 her consciousness moves to the objective, impersonal midnight (*en la medianoche*). The mind's movement in and out, reinforced by the image of the dance, suggests the collection's title and its central image, the restless serpent.

The principles on which this poem is based are not logical (as is the particular syntactic form in "When We Are Able") but associative and iterative. The repetition of assonance (*a's, e's, o's*) and the gerunds (*bailando* and *esperando*) establish the dominant verbal pattern. The different gerund, *muriendo* (l. 5) keeps the pattern alive while providing variety, until the initial *bailando* is repeated three times toward the end of the poem. The word *ondas* ("waves") in line 6 is a variation on the dominant pattern of *-ando* because it reverses the position of the two vowels. The word for wave, *ola*, is buried in *sola*, so that when the poem is read aloud the sound of the first overlaps the sound of the second and lingers in the background. The *ul* in *última* turns up in reverse order in *luna*, a technique that gives line 8 a particular melodic quality. The *tr* beginning the final word, *tranquilidad*, requires a different formation of the lips from that required by the preceding labials *b* and *m*. The double dental in *dad* forces the reader to act out in a muscular way the stopping suggested by the line in its reference to death. The poem closes with *tranquilidad*, which means the opposite of *Ensangrentada* ("anguished," i.e., "restless"), its initial word.

Although written in Spanish, "El último baile" establishes connections with a bicultural rather than a Spanish monolingual reader in two places. In line 5, for example, the phrase *muriendo físicamente* ["dying physically"] is too abstract, too flat in the context of a poem that presupposes a process of reading based on the intuitively apprehended image. Rather than rely on the effects of a logically structured discourse, the poem invites its readers to supply associations and connections to images of the sea, the moon, the dance, waves, and water. But the indefinite *muriendo fisicamente* interrupts the flow of image association and puts the reader into an abstract realm. The phrase is a literal translation from the English. As such, it indirectly presupposes a Chicana poet whose usage of Spanish is influenced and affected by her knowledge of English. A fluent Spanish speaker might say *muriendo fisicamente* in some contexts, but not in the context of a lyrical, musical poem.

The second place where a bilingual audience is presupposed is in the title. The Spanish word *último* means "final" in the sense of "the last dance." To a reader who speaks both English and Spanish, *último* may suggest the English word "ultimate," or the acme of perfection. Here again there is tension between low and high, between sexual death as the termination point (*último*) and sexual death as the culmination of a process ("ultimate"). These contradictory associations enrich the poem by creating an ambiguous attitude toward the romance of dying by water. The poem attempts to represent a woman's surrender to the romance of a physical sexuality that offers her completion. Yet the reader who entertains both these associations at once must wonder whether the dying means ultimate fulfillment or ultimate loss.

The three words concluding the penultimate line—*a la mar*—pose another kind of intertextual conflict. This time the conflict concerns word usage in a literary and a popular context. In the Spanish language, the standard form for the sea is masculine—*el mar*—but the feminine form, *la mar*, is used as a literary convention in poetry for its alliterative qualities. It is also used in ordinary speech to refer to the sea by seafaring people or by people who live near bodies of water. In this poem Zamora must employ *a la mar* instead of the standard masculine form *el mar* both to maintain the octosyllabic line as well as to avoid the prosaic quality of the latter. In "El último baile," however, the phrase *a la mar* implies a connection with a literary, academic audience rather than with a popular audience because it is not part of the vocabulary Chicano communities use to refer to the sea. Historically, Chicano communities in the Southwest have been rurally based. Since World War II they have become increasingly urban. The expression, *a la mar / de la tranquilidad*, in the English sense of "the sea of tranquility" includes the place on the moon where the first American astronauts landed in 1969. The echo of this landing on a sea of tranquility also increases the tensions for the bilingual reader between the realms of fantasy and reality in this poem.

"El último baile" attributes qualities of ritualistic dance and sensual ecstasy to the experience of drowning. The poetic consciousness in the following poem, "Having Drowned," explores the theme of drowning, but here the metaphor of drowning is ambiguous and enigmatic. At best, drowning seems to be a metaphor for dying. Everyday life is like death except there is no finality to it. The poetic voice seems to argue that resurrecting the dead does not help matters. Life is a confused state where no one is allowed to die.

HAVING DROWNED

It is indecent by any standard
to drown and drown again
until the spirit drips assuredly,
absurdly dangling like a hag's rag
to be sopped and wrung and sopped again.

Having drowned, I cannot face the water
to lie flat among lily pads lodged in
frog ponds, nor to lie back awaiting
a caretaker's hook to divide
the drowning from the drowned.

Division is accursed provision.
Resurrecting the drowned is an ogre's task
diminishing to me and other seasoned dead
who reap no glee from the shrinking of the caretaker
in this momentary suspension.

"Having Drowned" is full of logical paradoxes. No one can drown more than once, yet the voice claims that drownings occur again and again. They are so frequent, in fact, that the speaker and others have become "seasoned dead" (l. 13), a comic, ironic image as one cannot improve upon the condition of the dead. The voice seems to want to make a distinction between two groups:

the "drowning" who are in the process of dying and the "drowned" who are already dead. Yet in the final stanza the speaker asserts that the resurrection of the drowned is possible. When the speaker uses the word "indecent" (l. 1) we expect her to apply it to a form of human behavior that relates to proper social manners. In lines 2 and 3, however, the voice mocks the substance of the first line, for the act of drowning has nothing to do with indecency. The serious tone of line 1 collapses into the comic tone of line 2. Line 2 frustrates a literal reading of "drowning," yet line 6 seems to ask for just that. The images of a spirit that "drips" and is "dangling" like a "hag's rag" tease us into thinking that the poem has a sexual code serving to mock the phallus, as if to say that the sexual act is neither romantic nor mythic. The word "spirit" is also difficult to place because we do not know if it is the woman's or the man's. It could refer to the male's since it drips and dangles, yet drowning might be a more fitting metaphor for women who "drown" in passion. The sexual code surfaces once again in line 9 with the mention of a "caretaker's hook," a synechdoche for the phallus, only to shift once again into the paradoxically absurd separation of "the drowning from the drowned." Then it appears once more in line 14, where "shrinking" suggests the physical contraction of the male genitals. That the speaker is a woman is clear, as to "face the water" means "awaiting / a caretaker's hook."

The images in "Having Drowned" do not follow a consistent code. On a general level the poem might be regarded as a commentary on the difficulty of the state of consciousness for Zamora. The consciousness wants to stay dead, so to speak, to find a comfortable perspective on its situation as a woman, but it cannot do so. It is always in a state of "momentary suspension." But this phrase undermines even this reading, because it probably refers to "caretaker," its closest referent. "Having Drowned" is an inexplicable poem.

"Bearded Lady," one of Zamora's most erotic poems, is a feminization of a religious ritual. Here soft images, such as "hair like linen," and the gentle action of stroking replace the harshness of "Penitentes" walking in "mailshirts" and flogging one another with whips. The search for sexual harmony is physically embodied in a lady with a beard, a creature who represents a mixture of the sexes and whose physical externals defy attempts to attribute to her a specific gender identity. The image of the beard functions on both a literal and a figurative level.

Figuratively, the poem is an allegory asserting the identity between female sexuality and female creativity. Each of its principal images, beard and treasure, functions as a metaphor for the female genitals. As such, they bring together two intimately connected experiences: eroticism and conception. The speaker wants to know about "love"; that is, she asks about creation, in both a physiological and an artistic context. The first stanza, consisting mainly of direct and abstract statement, culminates in the sensuous image of the "bearded lady," who, like a sphinx, imparts secret wisdom to the narrator.

> BEARDED LADY
>
> I wanted to know about love
> and was told to see the bearded lady.
>
> As she stroked her treasure, she
> told me of the melding wells of Julia,
>
> Of the kissing stones shaped
> like camels,
>
> Of the hair like linen
> found among the cloistered,
>
> And she stroked, and stroked, and stroked

The bearded lady is a generator of images. The image sequence that expresses her answer to the riddle is linked syntactically by the word *of*, a device suggesting that the three images are different ways of saying the same thing. The linguistic blend of "melt" and "weld" in the first image, "melding wells of Julia," suggests the drift of the poem's theme: to dissolve the division between male and female, between the hard and the soft, and to make them one. The female genitals are suggested by "wells" (roundness, depth, water, and darkness). These shape or meld the hard, or the male genitals, unto themselves. The "kissing stones" refer to the male genitals. The use of "camels" is not irrelevant, for they may suggest a male principle in a mythological context in which man's mastery of the camel brought with it the subordination of female goddesses.[25] In "Bearded Lady" the "kissing stones" are shaped like "camels," which, if indeed they refer to a male principle, refer to one presided over by a female power, or Julia. Implied is a desire to melt traditional male invulnerability and bring it under the control of a female force.[26]

The third image, "Of the hair like linen / found among the cloistered," titillates the imagination to discover its concrete equivalent. The image evokes the softness and refinement of hair, the purity of white linen, and the celibacy of cloistered nuns. The juxtaposition of the erotic ("hair") and the religious ("linen" and "cloistered") hints at a harmonious coexistence of the profane and the sacred, a recurrent motif in Zamora's poetry.[27]

The poem closes with the erotic gesture of stroking, a highly charged image in Zamora's poetic art. Within the context of the poem, stroking is the gentle, caressing motion of the lady's hand on her beard, in both a literal and a figurative sense. The triple repetition of the word "stroked" focuses the reader's attention on the gesture, which represents the ultimate pleasure in self-masturbation. Its intended effect is to mesmerize, to seduce the speaker—and, by extension, the female reader—into releasing the suppressed dimensions of her own female sexuality. The bearded lady's message to the speaker and her female audience concerns embracing their own sexuality. They must overcome the social taboos against touching and enjoying their bodies. These bearded ladies are similar to the freak in a circus sideshow because their desire to enjoy erotic pleasure without the male is an aberration of the normal social order.

The gesture of stroking in a sexual context is analogous to the creative strokes of the pen in writing poetry. Strokes, in Zamora's poetic universe, suggest the serpent's strike, and the serpent is the poet herself, striking and stroking with the craft of her art. The speaker in "When We Are Able," for example, pronounces words whose effect is to condemn the *querido*. With words, the speaker strokes the *querido*, pretending to offer him soothing comments but all the while condemning him with each new condition and each repetition of her refrain. "Bearded Lady" offers another variant of stroking. Her objective is to obtain sexual gratification by stroking, without the *querido*. In recreating her speaker's journey to rediscover the origins of her female sexuality, the poet is making a metacommunicative statement about her creativity, or her poetic craft. Dissatisfied with traditional forms of male-female sexuality, and unable to locate within an actual historical moment a harmony between man and woman to her satisfaction, the poetic consciousness of "Bearded Lady" resorts to a moment in fantasy when she can imagine the perfect androgynous figure. Zamora makes the cause of her alienation—the traditional male figure—the subject of her poetry. By writing poems, the poet, the "restless serpent," obtains vengeance, revenge even, on the male by expressing all that she, and other women like her, have never articulated to him. In the title poem ending the collection, the restless serpents are angry at their "master" for neglecting them. They bite the master in revenge, each time draining something from his blood. These serpents are the sign of the repressed that can explode at any moment, whether the repressed is a woman's sexual drive, a Chicana's longing to tell the history of her people, or the poet's impulse to express herself. Only the act of writing soothes the poetic consciousness. Through this act she confronts the anguish that causes her restlessness, a confrontation that soothes but does not resolve. The gesture of stroking connotes movement and the desire for mastery. It is lyrics, and "lyrics alone [which] soothe / restless serpents, strokes / more devastating / than devastation arrived."

4

In *Restless Serpents* Zamora repeatedly uses the work of other authors, usually male poets in the English-American literary tradition, to generate her own poetic texts. One influence, as noted earlier, is Shakespeare. Others are Edward Dahlberg, Herman Hesse, Virginia Woolf, Theodore Roethke, Guillevec, and Robinson Jeffers (1887–1962).[28] Of these, the most important by far is Jeffers. Whenever Zamora responds to Jeffers, her poetic strategy is to include the female voice which he excluded.[29] In her own poems she assumes the masks of Jeffers's female characters to express sentiments he never permitted them to express. In "Pico Blanco" she speaks as Jeffers's Cassandra in the poem with the same title.[30] By so doing, Zamora transforms his silent Cassandra who never speaks but is spoken to only by Jeffers. In "The Extraordinary Patience of Things" Zamora's speaker meditates on Jeffers's "Carmel Point," clearly identified by Zamora in her poem.[31] The most dramatic of the three poems influenced by Jeffers, in both content and form, is "California," which offers the clearest challenge to Jeffers as a male poet and blends Zamora's two main poetic modes, narrative and dialogue.

Like the narrative poems discussed in Section III of this chapter, "California" presupposes a woman speaker who makes a personal statement to no one in particular about some event whose primary significance is its relation to her own life. In this respect "California" is narrative-lyric: narrative because it reports events; lyric because it is a personal utterance. As it responds to neither a question nor a statement by any particular individual, it implies no direct auditor, as do the dialogue poems presented in Section II. If, however, we examine "California" against its precursor text, "The Roan Stallion" (1926) by Robinson Jeffers, Zamora's poem takes on the nature of an intertextual dialogue.[32] "California" is Zamora's attempt to rework and change the parent poem; in this respect it resembles "Sonnet, Freely Adapted." These two poems represent two divergent literary strands in the English-speaking cultural heritage: "Sonnet, Freely Adapted" is Zamora's attempt to transform a universal, sensual poet; "California" is her attempt to transform a minor, regional author. In this section I argue that Zamora transforms Jeffers more successfully than she does Shakespeare.

CALIFORNIA

"The night-wind veering, the smell of the spilt wine
  drifted down hill from the house."
Two gods lay at my feet; I have
  shot one, and that one killed the other.
Each in his turn, each in his fashion of late
  laid over me splitting hairs, splitting atoms.
The dog, dead too, leaped to his death.

Beasts they were, both of them beasts—one   8
  of the wind and rein, one of the night and wine
  and all of us pools in the moonlight.
My child stands witness to one aimed shot, three
  flamed and freeing ones, and one that plunged
  my wailing will to the center of this bloody corral.

The poem is named for the heroine of "The Roan Stallion." California, the daughter of a Scottish father and a Spanish-Indian mother, is married to Johnny, an Anglo gambler and drunkard

who uses her to satisfy his lust. Johnny brings home a roan
stallion, an animal representing sexual potency. California has a
mystical encounter with the stallion, which she perceives as a
transhuman power. One night she becomes the center of physical
warfare between Johnny and the horse. Johnny, lusting to do with
California what he has seen the stallion do with a buckskin mare,
wants to abuse California sexually, but as she has translated her
experience with the stallion into a mystically liberating one, she
repulses him and escapes to the corral. Johnny and his dog Bruno
pursue her. The dog leaps at the horse and Johnny dashes toward
California but falls under the stallion's forehooves. California,
armed with a rifle provided by her daughter, aims at and kills
Bruno. The stallion tramples Johnny. The poem ends as California
fires three bullets into the horse.

Read as an autonomous unit without reference to "The Roan
Stallion," "California" is written in a language of evocation and
suggestion rather than persuasion and precision. Although the
poem is indefinite as to place and time, it is imbued with a mood.
The nexus of wind, wine, blood, and night images, the splitting
of hairs and of atoms, and the spilling of wine mingle with images
of gods and beasts ("dog" in l. 7 and "corral" in l. 13, for instance)
to suggest physical and sexual energy, violence and conflict. The
first lines summon up a concrete image of a landscape (sound,
smell, color, movement), probably in California.

Without knowing the specific context of Jeffers's poem, we
assume that the "I" speaking is a woman and that the gods she
refers to are masculine. The central event is the killing of the
gods. "California," then, is an utterance by a woman with a child
who explains why she has shot two males. The relationship between the woman and the two gods is not explicitly defined, but
expressions such as "laid over me" and "splitting hairs, splitting
atoms" suggest conflict involving the release of sexual impulses
and energy. The poem's sequence—the subject of its first stanza
is two "gods"; that of the second, two "beasts"—invites us to
relate the two contrasting entities, for obviously some relationship between them is intended. The woman's utterance seems to
mock male powers, for gods are not supposed to die. She satirizes
the gods by reducing them to the level of beasts: "Beasts they
were, both of them beasts" (l. 8). The rhetorical emphasis on
"beasts" and "both" leaves no doubt that the woman regards
these male powers as beasts and not as gods. Although they share

the nature of beasts, they are, nevertheless, distinct from each other: "one / of the wind and rein, one of the night and wine." The pun on rein-rain is a clue that one of the gods-beasts is of the outdoors.

A second way to read the poem without reference to Jeffers is to put the associations it suggests into a historical frame. As the title is the name of the state of California, the poem has allegorical resonances. In the historical framework, the state is personified in the speaker, reflecting and presenting her view of the events. The two gods would refer to the conquerors of the land, Spanish and Anglo-American. The images evoke the blood struggle of the human and animal impulses that created the state, perhaps the havoc, frenzy, and lust of the gold rush. The merging of human and animal impulses is suggested in line 10: "and all of us pools in the moonlight." The child is a reference to future generations. The phrase "splitting atoms" refers to the liberation of energy in the conquest and the defense of the territory. More specifically, it suggests Berkeley and Livermore. In its colloquial and popular usage, "splitting hairs" conjures up an image of the state's condemnation of its conquerors for ignoring the important considerations of population and natural resources. Although the allegorical overtones are loose and sketchy, the historical struggle is probably the first interpretation the average reader would bring to the poem.

Even without regard to Jeffers, then, "California" has autonomy. The poet presumes a reader who will respond associatively to the images in the poem and will draw inferences from such associations, rather than a reader who will insist on clear statement and logical relationships. Some details, however, will remain unclear without the help of the parent poem. Why, for example, are the first two lines a quotation? Why did the woman kill only one god? How was the other god killed? And what is the meaning of *ones,* and *one* in lines 11 and 12?

Reading "California" with Jeffer's poem in mind slightly alters our perspective: instead of seeing the poem as narrative-lyric, we see it as a form of dialogue. By assuming the fictional mask of California, Zamora makes a direct response to Jeffers, who is clearly the implied addressee of "California." Considered with Jeffers's poem, Zamora's presupposes a reader who will see logical relationships between the two poems, searching in "The Roan Stallion" for the antecedents of the personal pronouns, the common nouns, and the events in "California." The two quoted lines that open Zamora's poem are the last two lines of "The Roan Stallion." This technique suggests that Zamora is criticizing Jeffers for ending the poem where he does. Attempting to complete the original narrative, Zamora retains its plot and characters, and even its terms, but gives them different meanings, as though Jeffers had not gone far enough. Zamora writes her own sequel to Jeffers in order to give woman the final word.

In "California" Zamora introduces four transformations of Jeffers's text. First, her attribution of a consciousness to the character of California is absent in Jeffers, whose California is a told consciousness. Jeffers never allows his protagonist to be critical of Johnny or, much less, of the stallion. Zamora's character, in contrast, is critical, even condemnatory, of her oppressors. She says what Jeffers's heroine might have said had she been given a voice in the matter. Thus Zamora's California enlarges and extends the original.

Second, Zamora lowers both man and animal to the level of beasts. As Jeffers presents Johnny metaphorically as a beast, Zamora's designation is nothing new. Her reference to him as a god is, however, a new dimension. It is a satiric reference, mocking Johnny for thinking himself a god and behaving as though he were one, whereas in actuality he is crude and vulgar. When Zamora's California insists that both gods are beasts (l. 8), she demolishes the aura of godliness surrounding the stallion in Jeffers. By demystifying her counterpart's perception of the stallion as a god, she reduces the stallion to Johnny's level. If the concepts of god and beast are in conflict in Jeffers with respect to the stallion, Zamora's are not: her transformation is to equate man and animal at the level of beast. God and beast are locked together from the speaker's female perspective. Zamora thus provides a critical female dimension absent in the original poem.[33]

The third transformation hinges on the interpretation of *one* in "one that plunged / my wailing will" (ll. 12–13). The identities of the referents of *one* in line 11 and of *ones* in line 12 are made clear in Jeffers. The "one aimed shot" is the bullet California uses to shoot Bruno; the "three / flamed and freeing ones" are the bullets that kill the horse, which in turn kills Johnny. The *one* in line 12 has no clear referent in Jeffers. Rather than referring to an actual bullet in Zamora's poem, it reflects the existence of a consciousness that knows that something—some unidentified presence or power—beyond the desire to escape the husband's lechery has driven her ("plunged / my wailing will") to the "center of this bloody corral."

Finally, Zamora removes all traces of ambiguity in the original California's motive for killing the stallion. In "Roan Stallion" Jeffers leads the reader to believe that California's motive for shooting the stallion is some obscure human fidelity to civilization. Caught between culture (Johnny) and nature (the stallion), California must opt for culture. Jeffers's reader, however, is left to wonder whether an instinct that the stallion, too, is her oppressor does not also prompt California's action. No such ambiguity exists in "California." We are certain that Zamora's protagonist shoots both man and beast because each has been her oppressor. Johnny's abuse of her was both physical and spiritual. The stallion represents a sexual energy that also prevents California from asserting her true nature.

This conflictual relationship between Zamora and her intertextual choice is, at deeper levels, a conflict between written, literary discourse and oral, popular discourse. If we are unaware that Jeffers is the literary source for this poem when first reading it, we are uncertain as to whether the quotation marks refer to written or spoken discourse. Only upon learning that they are the final lines of "Roan Stallion" are we certain that they are written discourse. The lines that follow are Zamora's rendition of California's own spoken words, left unspoken by Jeffers. California's fictional speech in Zamora's poem revises and corrects the written text of the dominant tradition.

The transformations made by Zamora's poem suggest a dialectical response to Jeffers. They imply a close identification between Zamora, the poet, and California, the fictional character. By assuming the persona of Jeffers's own creation, Zamora criticizes him, but her criticism also implies that his poem has had a significant impact on her. Zamora's involvement with Jeffers is more intense than her relationship with Shakespeare. She more successfully maintains a dialectical tension between herself and Jeffers, identifying but also criticizing. She challenges his story and constructs a new one that includes herself. The dynamic force behind the poem comes from a poetic voice that responds to Jeffers first as a woman and second as a Chicana. The dramatic artifice of the implied sexual allegory, the state presented as a woman raped by male powers, presupposes primarily a female audience. This frame of reference, however, does not exclude a Chicano audience. For one thing, it is possible to interpret the poem as a historical allegory; and second, Zamora has chosen to speak from the consciousness of a character who has a Latina name.[34] Zamora goes as far as she does with Jeffers because Jeffers, a modern American poet who writes about northern California, offers Zamora a congenial poetic mode. The northern California landscape, the dramatic persona of the native woman, and the theme of sexual domination of women by men are subjects that interest and provoke Zamora. Whereas Shakespeare may be remote from Zamora, Jeffers, the minor, local poet, is of major concern to her.

Ultimately, Zamora's poetic voice in "California" occupies a liminal space between her own voice and Jeffers's. Read as a narrative lyric, the poem has some autonomy but remains incomplete without reference to "The Roan Stallion." Read as an intertextual dialogue responding to Jeffers the poem makes its impact and can be fully explained, but it raises the question of independence of and autonomy from its literary source. The two poetic modes remain discontinuous with each other, suggesting a poetic consciousness that slips in and out between the two modes.

The poems of *Restless Serpents* present a dramatization of a shifting poetic consciousness. In the work of no other Chicana poet discussed in this book do we hear the same multiplicity of voices as we do in *Restless Serpents*. The many voices making up Zamora's two main poetic modes range from meditative, erotic, mythic, lyrical, and impassioned to discursive, ironic, comic, satiric, and analytical. In one sense, Zamora's poetry represents a hymn of all these literary voices, for no single voice predominates.

These voices evoke a multiplicity of divided selves: woman versus Chicana, woman versus man, female poet versus male poet, Chicana versus Chicano, and Chicana versus Anglo. The tensions between and among the different identities juggled by the poetic consciousness reveal pulls from different traditions and contexts: from poetic to nonpoetic, from English-American to Mexican-Chicano; from Aztec-mythological to Judeo-Christian. Zamora's poetic consciousness is a voice absorbing and resisting its literary and cultural influences, attempting to define itself in relation to intertextual choices from two distinct traditions.

If there is a fundamental loyalty marking Zamora's poetic consciousness, it is to her female voice, to her identity as a woman. Almost always tied to her female identity is her identity as a poet. Running third among her identities is her Chicana identity, because the poetic consciousness insists on proving its autonomy as a woman to the Chicano male as well as to the dominant culture. The only way it can prove its autonomy to the Chicano male is to engage in the struggle to transform him. Inherent in this belief is the assumption that one must master the male in order to criticize him. For this reason Zamora's poetry is silent with respect to the expression of her Chicana identity to the dominant culture.

Similarly, Zamora's obsession with correcting, modifying, supplementing, revising, and humanizing Anglo culture and its male poets also reveals a silence. Inherent in this objective is the belief that one must master the dominant culture in order to criticize it. Zamora's poetry thus helps to expose the circularity of one kind of cultural response available to ethnic groups in our society. By excluding Chicanos and Chicanas from participation in its mainstream, our society makes them desire it. The struggle of the consciousness is, therefore, always dependent upon the very object it desires to master.

AFTERWORD

My hypothesis in this study of four women poets is that Chicana poetry is a poetry of conflict and struggle. Each of these poets has adopted a different position with respect to the conflicting relationships implied in the triple identity as woman, Chicana, and poet. Alma Villanueva defines her identity as a woman in opposition to the dominant male society in the United States. The importance of her female identity supersedes her ethnic affiliation. She harmonizes and integrates her female and poetic identities. A Chicana consciousness forms a minor part of her poetic self, standing in a relationship of juxtaposition rather than of fusion with the other two identities. Lorna Dee Cervantes offers a different combination of the three identities. Whereas Villanueva seeks a universal community of womanhood not limited by ethnicity, Cervantes refuses to compromise her Chicana identity, holding firm to her ethnic roots and incorporating her female identity into this context. For Cervantes, the two identities of woman and Chicana are one. Consequently, she harmonizes rather than juxtaposes them.

Cervantes may be credited with the only lyrical moment presented in the poems by these four Chicanas. In "Beneath the Shadow of the Freeway" she succeeds in projecting a time in history when male and female conflicts will be reconciled. Such was never the case in the relationship defining her identity as a Chicana and her professed role as a poet. The interplay between these two identities makes up the central tension in Cervantes' poetry. Although she refuses to concede the particularities that define her social reality, she articulates other nonracial concerns worthy of expression but incompatible with her social voice. Unable to harmonize her identities as Chicana and poet, she fragments her poetic identity, speaking either in her social voice as a Chicana or in her lyrical voice as a poet. Despite their personal similarities in background, Villanueva and Cervantes make two different responses to the conflicts inherent in a Chicana poetics: Villanueva celebrates a universal female community and Cervantes memorializes the specificity of her cultural heritage.

For Lucha Corpi, as for Villanueva, an identity as woman is stronger than her identity as Chicana. In contrast with Villanueva, who defines her identity as a woman in a relationship of opposition to a male United States society, Corpi defines her female self in terms of an ambiguous relationship of identity and challenge with respect to a male Mexican society. A recent immigrant from a traditional Mexican culture, Corpi makes the strongest identification of all these poets with a form of womanhood defined by traditional male society. Her exposure to a social environment in the United States with fewer sexual restrictions on women has led her to seek freedom from the cultural constraints that prohibit women of her culture a choice in shaping their own sexual destinies. Because these constraints are always present in her struggle to realize her dream for sexual fulfillment, however, they restrict her search for a liberated womanhood. In a few instances, as in her short story and in the poem "Puente de Cristal," she reveals an awareness of a sociopolitical reality. Yet the personal need to clarify and define her identity as a woman takes precedence over her social identity as a Chicana.

Bernice Zamora is particularly problematic. She best exemplifies my hypothesis that Chicana poetry is concerned with conflict and struggle. Unlike Villanueva and Cervantes, who have chosen to favor one identity over another, Zamora presents a shifting poetic voice dramatizing a strong tension among her identities as a woman, a Chicana, and a poet, as well as among their implied counterparts of male, Chicano, and English-American and Mexican-Chicano literary traditions. As Zamora is the most conscious of the interrelationships among the three identities, her poetic voice articulates conflict and tension rather than synthesis and resolution. Like Villanueva, Zamora responds to the double dilemma by reenacting the history of woman's oppression without compromising her autonomy as a woman and a poet. But unlike Villanueva, who seeks an abstract community of women with no real basis in either Anglo or Chicano society, Zamora articulates a male-female conflict in the contexts of the Chicano male and of the English-American poet. Whereas Villanueva's female consciousness does not—perhaps cannot—contain the social specificity of a Chicana consciousness, Zamora's female consciousness enters into sharp conflict with a desire to assert her Chicana ethnic self. Her strong female consciousness leads her to distrust the traditional Chicano male. It is this distrust that differentiates her from a poet such as Lorna Cervantes. Whereas Cervantes envisions a moment of harmonious male-female relationships, Zamora's distrust keeps her from identifying with the Chicano male in a racial struggle against the dominant society, a struggle that includes herself as a member of the same community.

The existential choices these poets have made in defining their relationships to the three identities has resulted in the articulation of different kinds of poetic modes in Chicana poetry. Alma Villanueva's choice to transform her concrete social existence into a personal myth of womanhood and to integrate her poetic self into this vision is registered primarily in a mythic, cosmic mode. The expression of a Chicana identity is linked primarily to a documentary and narrative mode. These two modes ultimately imply two different audiences: a mythical community of women and a social community of women and Chicanos. These two communities are juxtaposed and separated rather than fused and integrated. Her decision to privilege a mythical audience of women communicates her alienation from both social groups as well as her desire to achieve their reconciliation.

The tensions in Lorna Dee Cervantes' dual vision of herself as a Chicana and a poet generate a narrative, discursive, "hard" mode to communicate the real, divisive world she knows as a Chicana, and a lyrical, imagistic, "soft" mode to evoke contemplative and meditative moods. The poems in this second mode are spoken by disembodied lyric speakers and imply an audience outside the social context of her ethnic group. In these poems Cervantes the Chicana is Cervantes the poet, free from her concerns as a Chicana with a strong commitment to *la raza*. The poems in the first mode are spoken by someone who is clearly identifiable as a Chicana, in both an ethnic and a gender sense, and therefore imply an audience interested in and willing to listen to the concerns of her specific community. As long as she speaks primarily as a Chicana or primarily as a poet, the two identities remain apart, and Cervantes is unable to achieve a lyrical transcending moment. In "Beneath the Shadow of the Freeway" she speaks as a woman within the limiting confines of her barrio. When addressing the question of male-female relationships in this Chicano context, she achieves her vision of a utopian moment grounded in concrete, historical time. She does so, ironically, in a strongly discursive and narrative poem.

Lucha Corpi attempts to find a language that will articulate a woman's consciousness and feelings, which have been ignored in the male literary tradition. She examines her own emotions and feelings and makes them the subject of her poems. At times she examines them directly, as when she assumes the identity of the lyric speaker. At other times Corpi projects her identity onto fictional women and only indirectly presents her own female consciousness. But whatever literary persona she adopts, her predominant mode of expression is lyrical and imagistic rather than rational and logical. In her specific context, this lyrical-metaphorical mode implies a readership of women. Although her poetry does not contain the clear markers of gender seen in the poetry of the other women, its subject matter, imagistic arguments, and lyrical metaphors delineate a woman's emotional consciousness that has been neglected in the male Mexican tradition.

Lucha Corpi is also aware of a dual audience with two different language systems. Her chosen form of bilingualism is translation, which enables her to communicate with her Spanish-speaking audience without excluding her English-speaking audience. By placing her Spanish poems and their English versions on facing pages, she juxtaposes rather than resolves the tensions between the two cultures. Like the other Chicana poets, Corpi experiences alienation from both societies.

From an analysis of "Gata Poem" I derive Bernice Zamora's two main poetic modes: narrative and dialogue. By discussing a few poems representing each mode, I show how her poetic consciousness responds either as a woman or as a Chicana, but seldom as both. In only one instance, that is, in "Gata Poem," does Zamora attempt to respond simultaneously to the Mexican-Chicano sociocultural context and the English-American literary context. Usually it is in the juxtaposition of several poems that we hear the multiple voices of the poetic consciousness, as it articulates in one poem a positive relationship to Mexican-Chicano culture and in another defines itself in critical opposition to the Chicano male. Zamora's poetic voice also reveals a shifting perspective toward the dominant literary tradition, now identifying with its poets as writers she admires, now criticizing them as males whose traditions have excluded women. The different gradations in her poetic modes, together with the contesting and disparate codes embedded in her texts, suggest division and fragmentation at the level of her implicit audience. The two main audiences presupposed in the totality of her poetry are an English-speaking one and a Spanish-speaking one. In contrast with Corpi's bilingualism, which suggests a juxtaposition of the conflict between two cultures, Zamora's bilingualism suggests a conflictual interaction of two cultures within a single poetic voice.

In responding to the conflicts implicit in their double dilemma as Chicanas and as women, these writers, then, have made choices that shape their poetic discourses. In so doing they have displaced other possible alternatives. For example, Alma Villanueva responds to the absence of a female consciousness in the Anglo-American literary tradition and thus affirms her relationship with other women in this context. In the end, her choice in favor of a universal female identity erases the genesis of the problem between woman and Chicana. My reading of *Mother, May I?* as a text in a determinate context, however, argues the juxtaposition of the two identities and raises the issue of the nonintegration of a particular Chicana experience with the quest for self-definition as a woman. Lorna Cervantes' decision to articulate the Chicana experience in her poetic discourse prevents her full incorporation into a mainstream poetic community. She unites woman and Chicana and achieves their momentary harmony in "Beneath the Shadow of the Freeway" within the limitations of her barrio environment. A strong Chicana identity impedes her from forming relationships with women of the larger society. Lucha Corpi's poetic discourse is shaped by her desire to articulate a female voice long absent in a Mexican lyrical tradition. She captures the notion of an alienation from two cultures along gender lines which prevents her from expressing alienation along racial-ethnic lines. Bernice Zamora's poetic discourse is conditioned by her response to the Chicano male's sexual oppression of the Chicana as well as to the dominant culture's sexual oppression of the woman. This response prevents her from dealing with the larger issue of the Chicana's social oppression in the United States. Zamora's insistence upon correcting, transforming, revising, and humanizing Chicano males and male poets of Anglo society implicitly communicates the desire to master the male oppressor. Her insistence on proving her autonomy as a woman in both cultural contexts produces a poetic discourse always dependent upon the very object it desires to master.

The unique contribution of these Chicana poets to American literature is to point out how difficult it is to resolve the issues of gender and ethnicity in two cultural contexts. Only these writers—as Chicanas, as women, and as poets having a relationship with a Chicano community in the United States—can understand this struggle in all its ramifications. By injecting into American poetry the consciousness of a Chicana ethnic community, long ignored by and excluded from American culture, they have helped to shape Chicano and American literature and to define and clarify the cultural forms that have kept them apart. In varying degrees, all these Chicanas have expressed a social voice in a struggle with a poetic voice. In so doing they have added a cultural and social dimension to Anglo poetry, whether written by men or by women. Although white women poets have injected a female voice into the new and different forms of consciousness represented in American poetry, only Chicana women can give that voice a Chicana dimension.

My discussion of this function implies certain social criteria that I think important to a Chicana aesthetics. For example, my analysis of Alma Villanueva and Lorna Dee Cervantes clearly shows the importance of a Chicana social consciousness and its value to the expressive whole of American and Mexican literature. Of and by itself, however, a Chicana ethnic identity is insufficient, for bonds common to women and men of other cultural groups must be forged. My reading of Villanueva's poetry makes clear that a universal and mythical womanhood must ultimately, in my opinion, remain a fiction. My discussion of Lucha Corpi's poetry implies that a social and cultural reevaluation of traditional Mexican norms for women is necessary if women such as Corpi are to gain freedom from cultural constraints prohibiting them from making their own choices. Finally, my analysis of Bernice Zamora suggests that to depend upon the source of oppression is to be trapped within the structures of that oppression.

Because Chicana poetry responds to different societal groups whose social and aesthetic interests vary widely, my investigative method has had to be eclectic and pluralistic. My critical approaches have been fashioned to accommodate the diverse styles and strategies employed by these poets. Although I have focused my analysis on their poetic texts, I have not considered them as autonomous creations. Rather, I have shown that they are grounded in the sociocultural experiences of these poets as Chicanas and as women. Part of Chicana poetry is rooted in and responds to the social community while another part has links to the academic community. Part of it deals with problems of real life while another part is conscious of itself as art. Because Chicana poetry responds to various social conflicts—academic versus social community, Anglo versus Chicano, women versus Chicanas, English speakers and Spanish speakers versus bilingual audiences—no one traditional theory of literary criticism is adequate to assess the social and poetic values of the works discussed in the foregoing chapters. In my analysis of these four Chicana poets I have had to shift from one critical model to another among the four I have used: the formal, the rhetorical, the sociological, and the cultural. I have also considered issues of language alternation and reader response. Given the fact that at a certain level all minority literatures challenge the dominant literary tradition, the critical models developed to deal with traditional literature are not entirely applicable to minority literatures. Ironically, they are at once useful and insufficient. What my analysis points to is the need to develop a comprehensive theory that can deal adequately with Chicano literature.

It has been my purpose to determine to what extent these Chicana poets have resolved the dilemmas that characterized Chicana writers and intellectuals during the 1970s. Yet I have been careful not to propose an ideal model by which to judge the success or failure of their poetic texts. Rather, the idea of synthesis between opposing tensions that have governed their responses has functioned in this book as a presence of something yet to be realized. In attempting to delineate these poets' responses to the dilemmas they face, I have argued that all the poems herein considered, except for Cervantes' "Beneath the Shadow of the Freeway," reveal their authors' inability to synthesize the existing tensions. Yet their inability to synthesize the three identities competing for their allegiance is not to be seen as a failure on their part. Indeed, when Lorna Dee Cervantes does achieve her vision of harmonious relationships between men and women, her success is confined to one brief moment—three o'clock in the morning beneath the shadow of the freeway that cut through her neighborhood. Rather than classifying these poems as failures because they do not resolve tensions, I see them as positive creations that demonstrate to their readers how difficult it is to be a Chicana poet. In the sense that their responses do not harmonize the diverse conflicts that face them, Alma Villanueva, Lorna Dee Cervantes, Lucha Corpi, and Bernice Zamora are Chicana poets representative of their historical times. The conditions surrounding a separate and fragmented society prevent them from realizing their visions of unity. In "Beneath the Shadow of the Freeway" Lorna Dee Cervantes has given us a model of what Chicana poetry can be. Like Cervantes, who envisions in this poem a moment when men and women will enjoy a close community, we can envision a moment when improvements in social conditions will make possible better communications between Anglos and Chicanos, Chicanas and white women, Chicanas and black women, English speakers and Spanish speakers. For the time being, however, Chicana poetry can only dramatize the struggle to achieve harmony and the impossibility of achieving it.

APPENDIX A

POEMS FROM *BLOODROOT*
BY ALMA VILLANUEVA

(WO)MAN

(wo)man
   Yes, Woman!
I celebrate our bodies,
our wombs,
intact and perfect even as
we're born
out of our mother's
    womb
I celebrate
because most   . . . If man is out
men have forgotten   of touch with
how to   the earth,
he is afraid   how can he
of us, he   touch woman)
denies us,
   —but in the process
   denies his own existence;
   when will he re/learn
   this ancient fact—

I rejoice in the slick/red walls of our
   wombs,
   the milk of our breasts

the ecstasy of our clitoris
and our need of man when we
open our legs and womb
to him
  the bloody circle thru our daughters
  and sons

I want to fly and sing
of our beauty and power.
to re/awaken this joy
in us all;
              our power lies in being Woman

I celebrate the absence of mystery of
the "eternal mystery of woman":
we are.

we are the trees of the earth
our roots stretching deep and strong.
the stone of the firmament,
sister to the stars
that gave birth to the soil.

let us never forget the dance
or lose the song
or cease to dream
or efface the mystery

zero in on life
myth
magic
mystery
revel in the extra ordinary
fill your
be
ing with it,

a bird is skimming the water
lands on a smooth surface,
the snow falls softly on a mountain
chilling the earths crust,

a sapling smiles at the wind,
a cloud gathers and spills its rain
on a hungry field,—

cock your head
and listen
it calls
    everyman
        not everyone
            hears

ZINZ

Jesus said
  we are all brothers
Buddha said
  we are one
Gandhi said
  the same
so did Martin Luther King
—do we inherently know
  and fear
    our connectedness?—

    an ancient
    African word:
    ZINZ
    man without race

long ago primal emergence
recorded in the One Mind
man belonged
  to the earth
    sky,
      water,
        minerals,
     plants,
         fungus,
    the magic day
    the mythical night
   the fertility
    and grandeur
     of all
  flowed through
    and through

  we fear the slip
  into the fertile slime—
  the embryonic ooze
  too fecund
  for the civilized nose

we were
collectively, together
born
out of
motherafricas
womb

I SING TO MYSELF

there is something
I carry deep
within me
like an over-ripe
fruit, one whose use is past and
won't rot and merge
and gags me
now and then;
      it is the fruit
of bitterness and distrust.
    oh yes, they planted the seed, but
I tend the soil . . .

I could weep and rage
against the man who never
stroked my child fine hair
who never felt the pride of
my femininity grow in his loins
      never desired me in a secret fathers
      way
the man who
   dropped his seed in my mother's
      womb, then called it quits.
her pain haunted me for years,
the way she looked when she
talked about him, the
desire and need that rose to her eyes—
      it repulsed and attracted me.

I could weep and rage
against all those who
looked into my hungry eyes
and shifted theirs so quickly;
all those who didn't see
my love and need mirrored
naked in my eyes.
my thin, boyish body always
10 degrees colder than everyone

elses, shivering even in the heat;
never finding a breast to rest
and warm myself
    except once or twice
for awhile and then somehow
they'd slip or be dragged away—

I could weep and rage
against the man I loved;
who loved me at his leisure and
neglected my deepest needs,   then
the final irony of his fear of
    (and final desertion)
my mounting self/love and strength

            (how were you to know I
            would only love you
             more, if only you'd
              been equal
            to the taking)
there are times this fruit
galls me and yet
this fruit is strange; the
skin is so very beautiful but
the flesh is putrid and bitter

    —no, you don't fool me any longer—

I will swallow you whole and
accept and transform you
till you melt
in my mouth.   (you/man only
           bit the apple:
             you must swallow
        death—
           I/woman give birth:
           and this time to
       myself)

I WAS A SKINNY TOMBOY KID

I was a skinny tomboy kid
who walked down the streets
with my fists clenched into
        tight balls.
I knew all the roofs
and back yard fences,
      I liked travelling that way
        sometimes
      not touching
        the sidewalks
      for blocks and blocks
        it made
          me feel

        victorious
         somehow
over the streets.
I liked to fly
    from roof
      to roof
        the gravel
            falling

                away
beneath my feet,
    I liked

              the edge
      of almost
not making it.
   and the freedom
      of riding
    my bike
        to the ocean
and smelling it
      long before
I could see it,
     and I travelled disguised
        as a boy
      (I thought)

in an old army jacket
carrying my
fishing tackle
to the piers, and
bumming bait
and a couple of cokes
and catching crabs
sometimes and
selling them
to some chinese guys
and i'd give
the fish away,
I didn't like fish
I just liked to fish—
and I vowed
to never
grow up
to be a woman
and be helpless
like my mother,
but then I didn't realize
the kind of guts
it often took
for her to just keep
standing
where she was.

I grew like a thin, stubborn weed
watering myself whatever way I could
believing in my own myth
transforming my reality
and creating a
legendary/self
every once in a while
late at night
in the deep
darkness of my sleep
I wake
with a tenseness
in my arms
and I follow

        it from my elbow to
          my wrist
and realize
    my fists are tightly clenched
and the streets come grinning
    and I forget who I'm protecting
and I coil up
    in a self/mothering fashion
      and tell myself
it's o.k.

YOU CANNOT LEAVE

you cannot leave
my aunt's house
without a
full stomach
    she would be
    offended;
she's small
and earth color,   her
face records
her mother's people
    the hills and desert of Sonora.
her eyes hold
an eclipse
    of clarity/pain:
        once,
            when I was small
      I remember
        her and I eating
          a cluster of grapes
            in a matter of minutes
            each one so delicious
              we couldn't wait
                for the next, and
                  when the last
                    grape was gone
                      we laughed because
                      the grape's skeleton
                      looked so funny—
before she was born
her father recognized
her mother and converted (he was a minister)
and married her; his indian
blood mixed with that
of the spanish
conqueror. I saw a
picture of his congregation
in Mexico, his wife's brother
holding their first born

who died before five,
and the majority of his
followers indian/eyes stared
out at me and I
recognized them,
    my aunt, not yet born
among them.

I grew up hearing
my aunt's visions and dreams,
she had no one but
a child to tell them to—
she saw the bombing
of Japan and the
back of God
    and a neighbor's son opened
the front door and called her
the day he was reported missing
in action, and she
dreamt my house and knew
where the trees stood before
she ever came—and she's
always apologetic for staying
"too long" and she's always
sorry you're leaving "too soon"—
    talking and telling in spanish
to english
in english for the skeleton
in spanish for the flesh,
we sit for hours
    she being older for awhile
    I being oldest in my turn
taking turns as we've
always done—
and she tells me
she tried going to
an anglo church, but their
faces were blank
and their
eyes
mute; they did not

recognize her—
and with the spontaneity of
a laugh held long
within her
    she smiles
as she tells me:
    —Mi gente son el color de la
        tierra.—
and the clarity overshadows
the pain.

    and she lapses and offers
me a cup of coffee and I
drink it or she
will be offended.

TO JESUS VILLANUEVA,
WITH LOVE.

my first vivid memory of you
mamacita,
we made tortillas together
yours, perfect and round
mine, irregular and fat
we laughed
and named them: oso, pajarito, gatito.
my last vivid memory of you
    (except for the very last
     sacred memory
     i won't share)
mamacita,
beautiful, thick, long, gray hair
the eyes gone sad
with flashes of fury
when they wouldn't let you
have your chilis, your onions, your peppers
    —what do these damned gringos
     know of MY stomach?—*
so when I came to comb
your beautiful, thick, long, gray hair
as we sat for hours
(it soothed you
 my hand
 on your hair)
I brought you your chilis, your onions,
   your peppers.
and they'd always catch you
because you'd forget
and leave it lying open.
they'd scold you like a child
and be embarrassed like a child
silent, repentant, angry
and secretly waiting for my visit, the new
   supplies
we laughed at our secret

we always laughed
            you and I
you never could understand
the rules
at clinics, welfare offices, schools
any of it.
I did.
you lie. you push. you get.
I learned to do all this by
the third clinic day of being persistent-
     ly
sent to the back of the line by 5 in the
     afternoon
and being so close to done by 8 in the
     morning
so my lungs grew larger
and my voice got louder
and a doctor consented
to see an old lady,
and the welfare would give you the money
and the landlady would remember to spray
     for cockroaches
and the store would charge the food till
     the check came
and the bank might cash the check if I got
     the nice man this time
and I'd order hot dogs and cokes for us
at the old "Ice Palace" on Market Street
and we'd sit on the steps
by the rear exit, laughing
            you and I

mamacita,
I remember you proudly at Christmas
time, church at midnight services:
you wear a plain black dress
your hair down, straight and silver
(you always wore it up
 tied in a handkerchief,
 knotted to the side)
your face shining, your eyes clear,

your vision intact.
you play Death.
you are Death
you quote long stanzas from a poem I've
    long forgotten;
even fitful babies hush
such is the power of your voice,
your presence
fills us all.
the special, pregnant
silence.
eyes and hands lifted up
imploringly and passionately
the vision and power
offered to us,—
eyes and hands cast down
it flows through you
to us,
a gift.

your daughter, my mother
told me a story I'd never
heard before:
        you were leaving Mexico
        with your husband and two
        older children, pregnant
        with my mother.
        the U.S. customs officer
        undid everything you so
        preciously packed, you
        took a sack, blew it up
        and when he asked about
        the contents of the sack,
        well, you popped it with
        your hand and shouted
        MEXICAN AIR!*

aiiiiiiiiii mamacita, Jesus,
I won't forget my visions and reality.
to lie, to push, to get

just isn't
enough.

*—translated from Spanish;
she refused (and pretended
to be unable) to speak
English.

THERE WERE TIMES

there were times
you and I
were hungry
in the middle of a city of
full bellies
    and we ate bread with
syrup on top and we joked
and said we ate dessert morning
noon & night, but
we were hungry—
so I took some bottles to the
store and got milk and
stold deviled ham because
it had a picture of the devil
on it and I didn't care—
    my favorite place
        to climb
        and sit was
            Devil's Rock,
        no one else
            would sit there, but
            it was the
                highest place
                around—
taking care
of each other,
an old lady and a child
being careful
not to need
more than can be given.
                    we sometimes went to the
place where the nuns lived and
on certain days they would
give us a bag of food, you
and the old Mexican nun talking,
you were always gracious;
and yet their smell of dead

flowers and the rustle of their robes
always made me feel
shame: I would rather
steal.
        and when you held my bleeding nose
for hours, when I'd become
afraid, you'd tell me
                —Todo se pasa.—

after you died I learned
to ride my bike to the ocean
    I remember the night
      we took the '5 McCallaster
          to the ocean and it was
              storming and frightening
                but we bought frozen chocolate
                bananas
                    on a stick and ate them
                        standing, just you and I
                            in the warm, wet night—
and sometimes I'd wonder why
things had to pass and I'd
have to run as fast as I could
till my breath wouldn't let me
or climb a building scaffold to the
end of its steel or
climb Rocky Mountain and
sit on Devil's Rock
and dare the devil
to show his face
or ride my bike till the
end of the streets hit
sand and became ocean
and I knew
the answer, mamacita, but
I wouldn't even say it to
myself.

grandmother to mother to
daughter to my daughter,

the only thing that truly
does not pass is
love—
and you
knew it.

APPENDIX B

POEMS FROM ALMA VILLANUEVA'S IRVINE COLLECTION

WITCHES' BLOOD

power of my blood, your secret
wrapped in ancient tongues
spoken by men who claimed themselves
gods and priests and oracles—they
made elaborate rituals
secret chants and extolled the cycles,
calling woman unclean.
men have killed
made war
for blood to flow, as naturally
as a woman's
once a month—
men have roamed the earth to find
the patience of pregnancy
the joy of birth—

the renewal of blood.
          (the awful, bloody secret: O woman
                    you dare birth
yourself)

call me witch
call me hag
call me sorceress
call me mad
call me woman.   do not
call me goddess.
I do not want the position.

I prefer to gaze in wonder, once
a month at my
witches' blood.

OF UTTERANCES

a woman is her own
(muse)
that's the main thing.
        —Anne Sexton

the "White Goddess"
to white men
to poets and men of genius
    "a source of inspiration;
    a guiding genius . ."
that beautiful Goddess
that legendary Angel,
                descending
    with her milky white limbs,
        full breasts, rosy at the
            tips with the milky
                stanzas and lyrics
                    to the touch of man:
the cunt all acceptance,   opening wide
                    to the mind of man   and
                giving birth to their children
        The Poem.   The Painting.   The Sculpture.

and I with my fetish for dark men.
and dislike (dis-taste) for sucking (this part's o.k.—
cocks and swallowing the salty sperm (this part's not—
of prose and rhymes.
we women just don't have any
dark and lovely,
                descending
"Black Gods"—   so being
a woman of resources
and imagination, I decided to become
my own source of inspiration;
my very own genius—
I grew my own wings, became my
own muse.

I decided to fly
and not
descend.

OF/TO MAN

you, man, are the snake in
my garden—
yeah,
a snake in the grass.
everyone since Eve & Adam's
been blaming ME
for The First Fuck—and it was
ME who got knocked up! well,
hell, I'm not sorry.
I can come over & over   (spiritual orgasms count, too)

and

you're limited to one
at a time: Is that the
main bitch?
well man, my man—
let's set herstory
straight. I come IN my cunt
IN my clit, you might say
my whole body is IN the
act: maybe you feel gypped and
someone dubbed me a
mystery.

some snakes are dark and fluid
and compelling— and for the life of me
I just can't resist them.

now, there's a mystery.

THE LAST WORDS

to Anne & Sylvia
& all those that burned before them
  in Salem & other places—

  Out of the ash
  I rise with my red hair
  And I eat men like air.
              —Sylvia Plath

if they knew my heart
they would

if they knew my heart
they would burn

if they knew my heart
they would burn me

if they knew my heart
they would burn me at the

if they knew my heart
they would burn me at the stake.

witches' blood must flow! dry and crackle—
sink into the mother, turn to ash—
red fire/blood release the utterance—
the last words
unheard by stupid mob—
the hysterical mob does not like to be
reminded of their true natures—
they would like to forget women like me.
they back away, cowering, from the heat of
my love
my words
my blood
calling me sentimental, bitter, minor, emotionally ill
                    [and ah, possessed].

they do not know I burn, self/imposed
in a fire of my

own making.
my witches' secret: the poem as
my witness.

this cannot be destroyed.
they burn in the heart, long after
the witch is dead.

APPENDIX C

MOTHER, MAY I ?
BY ALMA VILLANUEVA

October, 1978

PART I

1

I was always fascinated
with lights then,
with my hands
with my fingers
with my fingertips, because

if I squinted my eyes at them
lights sprayed off
burst off
and a joy burst inside me
and it felt good on my
eyes to see it, so

I squinted my eyes at
everything in this manner
and everything had joy
on it, in it. it was
my secret. only

my grandma knew. I knew
she knew by the way

she looked at things
long and slow and peaceful
and her face would shine, lights
all over, coming out of
her tiniest wrinkles;
she became a young girl.
there were things that could not
shine lights. we
avoided these. these things
took joy. these things
could make you old. I didn't
know it then, but

these things were death.

The Dead

The cement seems to go forever
but ends at the ocean. I've
seen it
and this is true. we sit
in big buildings, with
hard benches
and everyone is scared
and the lady talks
and her eyes don't see you. we
don't look at her too long. I
watch her mouth move,
move. she has a tongue. but

I know she's dead. I
can't feel her.

I like to play outside
with my panties off; the
air feels so good between
my legs. I
love to swing and spread them
wide. I
love to put my dolly's hand

there
and make her tickle me. we
make tents and hide
and sometimes the Tickle Man
gets me. but I
like him to. I
let him. when I
have to go to school I
go to the bathroom
and he finds me. he is
like my uncle but
he stops when
I say stop.
bathrooms are nice. no
one wants to look at
you then. later
they ask—what took
    you so long?—but
that's when you make things, I
think, like having babies; I
hear them talking sometimes:
—you have to push it out
hard.—I do that. I
like to look at what I
make. it even smells
good to me. sometimes
they're pretty, when you eat
too fast
and the corn comes right out.
it makes it yellow. one
time my aunt came in and I
peed and pooped and I
said—I just made a
    salad.—she didn't
look too happy. so I kept
it to myself. and I used
to swallow my tiny rubber
dolly and have a baby in my
poop. I loved to find it. my
grandma found me doing it. she
wasn't mad. she smiled

a little. she said
—it'll get stuck and grow as big
as you and you won't have any room
   left.—so
I stopped.
and she made me wear long pants
under my dresses so she
would know the wind
couldn't smell me.
and then I learned how
to hide.

2

my mother was beautiful.
she smelled good.
she put perfume on her panties
and her legs were smooth. they
sounded funny but they
felt slippery.
she had lots of boyfriends.
lots.
my mother was beautiful.
sometimes I slept in the kitchen
on chairs so
he could sleep with her.
sometimes I kissed her just like
he did.
she was always going away
with one of *them.*
she was always beautiful
for *them.*
and sometimes I cried for my
father but I didn't know who
he was.

playing

I am little and I sleep with you.
we pretend.
we pretend, I'm the mother
and you're the little girl

and you cry for me cause I
have to go to work and you
have to stay. I

laugh at you, big cry baby. I
go away and you pull me back
by my leg and we
laugh and laugh
till it's time to
get up.

3

my grandmother takes me to the first
day of school. everyone speaks
so fast. I can read and count
in spanish. I can say two poems
in spanish. you can't speak
spanish here. they don't like
it and the teacher is fat
and so white
and I don't like her. I run
home and my grandma says I can
stay. we
go to movies and chinatown and shopping.
she holds one side of the shopping bag, I
hold the other. we
pray and dunk *pan dulce* in coffee. we
make tortillas together. we
laugh and take the buses
everywhere. when we
go to the movies she cries and
she dances when she irons. I
comb her long hair and rub her
back with alcohol. one time
before we left the house, we
said our prayer and she was looking
for her hat and she was wearing
it and I
started to laugh and laugh and I
couldn't stop and she found
it on her head

and she spat—*grosera!*—and it
made me laugh harder and she gave
me the hand that meant a spanking
(and she never spanked me)
and she laughed too.
and when I flew she always
woke me gently—so the soul
    and the body will stay.—and I
loved to fly
and dream. I was
always the strongest and the fastest. we
always said our dreams. she said
she knew when her four babies
were dying because they always
pointed up with their fingers
and they'd die in the night.
and I think she dressed me too warmly
and woke me gently
to trick death
to let me stay.

Dreaming

the danger of flying
is coming back. you must
close your eyes. one
time I didn't and I saw me
laying there and I didn't like me
and I didn't want to come
back. I thought she
was disgusting. she
had to eat and everything. she
was stuck. I
wasn't. I came
back anyway and then she
stood up and looked in the mirror
and scared me
to life.

but I kept dreaming, no matter

how stubborn
she was.

4

I watch you put lipstick
on, red and beautiful, you
press your lips together
to make it stick
and I
grab you
and kiss you
on the lips with my
mouth open—is this
    how they do it,
mother?—
I ask
I wish
to be closer
to you
than lips or lipstick
or skin
I wish
to kiss

your womb.

playing

the pretend
place
is bed, we
lay together, you
tell me stories
about when you were
little and you were
bad, I
laugh and laugh
and we
are both 5
and no one's

the mother. we
hide from the
grown ups,

playing.

I think one time we
never switched
back and I stayed
your
mother and I stayed
bigger and I stayed
stronger, to take
care of you,
mother, we

forgot the world is bigger than
our bed.

5

the nun asked to look at
my hands. I thought she thought
they were beautiful, so I
put them out
and she hit them with
a ruler. it hurt it hurt
and she told me to
put them out
again and I wouldn't and she
tried to grab my hands so
I grabbed the ruler and hit
her and ran
home and my grandma let me
stay when she saw
my hands. there was
a beautiful young nun who
spoke spanish and english and she
sat in the dark on the other
side of the cage. the metal was black
and cold and beautiful. it had flowers

and I loved to put my face on it, it
felt so good and cold.
and when she came and sat and spoke
her voice was very warm. she
said she came from mexico. I
bet she didn't let them shave
her head. this boy who was
very bad sat behind me
and he put his fingers in my *nalgas*
when we prayed and when I turned
and stared at him, he'd
smell them and smile. he
whispered one time in the yard
   —they all have bald heads.—

6
I had a best friend who I loved
a lot. she was older
than me. she was bigger
but I was smarter
because I always
beat her in checkers. we were
playing in the park. we were
all alone and a man
came and said it was against
the law. we were
afraid and he said one of
us would have to go with him to
sign a book and Peggy said
   —she'll go.—and I thought, well
that's because I'm smarter than
her, so I went and Peggy ran
home. all of a sudden he picked
me up and he wouldn't put
me down and I told him
   —see this dress? my mother
bought it for me. she
has lots of money. she'll
   give you money
   if you let me
go. look! my dress is pretty

and new!—I'd been showing
off that day twirling in circles
pretending
I was kidnapped from a king
and queen
pretending
I was rich
because my dress was so beautiful.

he put me down.
he took off my dress.
he took off my t-shirt.
he took off my panties.
and then he said
   —do you want to suck something
     good?—
and I thought it must be bad.
it must be licorice because
I hate it because
he hates me and
he wants me to eat
something bad and maybe
if I eat something bad
he'll let me go. so I said
   —o.k.—
he put it in my mouth
and it didn't taste like anything.
it hurt my mouth but I
wouldn't cry and then
he made me lie down
and the stickers hurt
and I was getting all dirty
and I knew if I cried
he'd kill me. then
he put his fingers
there
and it hurt
and I almost screamed
but I didn't because I knew
he'd kill me. and
he touched me all over

and I lay there
and I didn't cry.
and I knew he could kill me if
he wanted to.
and I didn't care anymore.
he said
   —if I let you go, do you
     promise not to tell
     anyone? because
     if you do
I'll kill you.—
I didn't care.
I just said
   —I promise.—
And when he let me go I didn't run
I walked.
and when my aunt saw me she said
Peggy told her and the police were
finding me and I told her
   —I always have to do the dirty
work.—
and I didn't cry.

it was then I decided to become a boy.

7

I've found the rooftops.
I've found the fences.
I've found the highest rock
and I've sat on it.
I've found the secret places
in Golden Gate Park
and listened to voices.
I've found the ocean
and reached it, riding
my own bike.
I've found unmade buildings
and sat on the highest steel.
I bled there the first time
and knew it was special, but

I ignored it.
I fought the toughest boy
in school and
I made his nose bleed.
I play football and they pick me
first or second.
I climbed the statue on Dolores
street and sat on the horse
and couldn't get down
for hours. 2 people ask me
if I need help and
I say NO so
I jump and my feet burn but
I don't cry.
I saw my stepfather strangling
my mother, so
I broke the window
and hit him with an ashtray.
he fell.
I hated him. my mother had my brother.
I loved him.
I change his diapers.
I sing him to sleep.
I take him down to the park
and don't let anyone
touch him. we live
in projects. we live
in hotels. then she
gives me away

to strangers.

8

my grandma is too old
they say.
they say she can't
cook anymore or
sweep anymore or
iron anymore or
dance anymore. I know

they're wrong. can
she help it if
she sees death waiting
in the same car every night?
she looks out the window
and he looks up at her
and stares.
she isn't scared. she just knows
she's old.
she forgets and tells them
these things and
they put her in Laguna Honda.
they give her away
to strangers

too.

9

I visit her there and I hate it.
I walk down the hall where the
elevator lets you out
and old people sit on the
hard benches, on both
sides, staring,
staring. and they smell
like death cause they're
scared and
I hate it. grandma doesn't
smell, she's mad all
the time. she complains
too much, they say.
I bring her chilis and onions
and comb her hair
and rub her back
and she laughs, but her eyes
her eyes

10

grandma said—when a dog howls
   in the daytime someone

is dying.—they called
my aunt and said she
was dying, so we went
my aunt, my mother
and I. we went
but they said she

was dead already but
I didn't believe them so
I ran in and they were lying
again because
she sat up
and said
   —Alma, *no me quiero morir*—*
and then she died.
                AIIIIIIIII MAMACITA
mamacita
and then I cried.
and they all ran in
my aunt, my mother, the doctor
and they didn't believe me
and I couldn't stop crying so
they made me stop with some medicine
and I didn't cry again.
I didn't cry that night
or the next day.
or the funeral day.
what I did
was drop one rose
into the hole
and I felt it squish
and they thought I was selfish
and stubborn because
I dressed up in my new shoes
and a skirt and a red shirt
and I didn't cry.

they didn't know the rose
was me.

        *Alma, I don't want to die.

Part II

11

this family checks for lice.
this family says
    I don't appreciate a
    decent home.
this family makes me sleep separate
from
    their children.
this family says I steal.
    I don't.
this family has no mother or
father just
like me. a lady
gives out 1 frozen Twinkie
each
for lunches. we are
all orphans. I run

away to my aunt's
and she keeps me for
awhile. I get
mumps and I lay there
and cross my arms
and see lights spraying
off
my hands.
my feet. I eat

tortillas again. I am
happy. my aunt
and I talk and talk, in
spanish, in
english, we laugh, but
she doesn't dance. there

is a greyness on my eyes. it
goes away when I'm alone. my
aunt lives in the projects by
the bay. there is

a place by
the water where
rocks are. there are
voices there. I see
lights on
the water and
the rocks
and the lights
make the greyness go
away. there is
a place
inside
me they
cannot enter. that is
where

I'm hiding.

12 (about *13*)
I sleep all day.
I sleep all night.
I do not eat, much.
I do not talk, much.

my eyes are yellow.
my gums bleed.
I cannot roam
and play. they
found out.

I'm a girl. they
expose themselves. they
follow me. they
do not leave me
alone. they
stare
with their dead
eyes. they
speak
with their dead
mouths. there

is one who
is different. a
boy.—you
   will die
   if you
   don't start
eating—the
doctor says.
I eat.
we walk, the
boy and I.
we speak, the
boy and I.
we laugh, the
boy and I.
we kiss, the
boy and I.
approaching,
gently, dreaming, softly, child to child,
we love
on rooftops, doorways, parks, alleys
we love, the
boy and I. and

a child blooms
inside me.

13
I am alone again
—I can't marry you. they
   won't let me. they
   say,
she'll have 12 more
kids in 10 years, you
know those people.
                they
   say
   NO.—
we walk.
we cry. (the

boy cries)
I am alone again, but

a fullness starts.

14

I speak to you.
we sleep together.
your tiny foot
moves, one side to
the other, my mother
keeps me,
   —we women stick together.—she
tells
the clinic secretary
   —*she* didn't want to marry *him*.—
I prepare for you.
I buy tiny shirts (are
you really there?)
I buy a crib (are
you really there?)
I buy pink, pink, pink (a
daughter, a daughter?)
we lay together
at night (could I
keep you
inside
me forever?), little
comfort. tiny foot.

15

it starts. the
pain. my
mother and a friend, we
drink screwdrivers and we
walk to the hospital (2
blocks) a little drunk
and laughing. my friend and
I can't believe I'm
staying. my

mother does. the
nuns don't approve
of screwdrivers or
laughing. they
put me in a room
to wait for
pain. I

get up and walk. they
tell me to lie
down. they
leave and I
get up and walk and look
out the window. they
are angry
and give me a shot. I

wake up to
pain like
death. it is
morning and white and cold
and their knives and needles
hurt me. I

give birth dreaming.

16
another child. we
marry. we
sneak. (we
are still
too young) me
in black. he
in uniform. he
stays 2 nights
and then goes
for 2 years to
their armies, their guns, their prisons, their death—

again,
they pull my child from

me. numbed from
the waist down
the doctor watching
the clock (he is late for
something)
the water bursts
the head shoving (but they
pull him out
anyway)
the time
the time
but I trick them.
I give birth dreaming,

again.

17

he comes back, the
boy/man.
he does not cry
so easily.
he does not laugh
so easily.
he drinks too much
and
he hurts me sometimes.
he is angry about
something.
he wants to kill
something. but when
we make love
we are children
again.
he is my sun, I
turn and turn toward
him. I
give birth

to a son.

birthing

this is the way to trick
the dead. by
birthing, by
birthing.
this is the way to trick
the living. by
dreaming, by
dreaming.
watch out, Alma.
watch out, Alma. you
don't trick
yourself.

18

and then began the years
of silence, the years
my mouth would open
and no words would
speak,
my mouth locked tight.
and a loneliness grew

that I couldn't name.

19

I looked for it
in my husband's eyes.
I looked for it
in my children's eyes.
I looked for it
in supermarkets.
I looked for it
in the oven.
I looked for it
in the dustpan.
I looked for it
in the sink.

in the tv.
in the washing machine.
in the car.
in the streets.
in the cracks
on my linoleum. I polished
and cleaned and cared for everything
silently. I put on my masks, my
costumes and posed for each
occasion. I conducted myself
well, I think, but
an emptiness
grew
that no thing
could fill. I think

I hungered for myself.

20

the last diapers are thrown
away. (the baby is grown)
the husband is locked
away. (the husband is crazy)
will someone change
my diapers?
will someone lock
me in?
he sees things in the dark
at night. I turn
on the light and make it go
away. my children have
nightmares and cry for me. I tell them
I'm here. I lay
in the bed coiled up like a fetus, no thing
out
there can comfort me. I uncoil
and stand
and feed the children. no one
knows

I'm a liar.

21

we look for you, my
husband and I
we look for you till
I'm dizzy. are you
here, mamacita? are you
here? he says—here
it is.—he's found
you, a "13"
in the ground. they said
—Jesus Villanueva
is "13."—
I touch the
one, the
three.
I begin to cry
and no one stops
me. I didn't
know it but
a seed spilled out
and my mouth
ate it. I think

that's when the rose took root.

22

when she left this man she thought
she'd die.
but she didn't. she thought
the sun would go out
but it didn't.
and she heard a voice, distant
and small, but
she heard it.
and her mouth opened slightly
and a word spilled out. the word

was "I."

inside

I am here. (do
you hear me?) hear
me. hear me.
I am here. birthing
(yourself) is
no easy task.
I am here. (pleading)
I am here. (teasing)
I am here. (taunting)
I am here. (simply)
I am here.

PART III

23

it began
with the death of
her friend
and she took
her friend's husband
and she took
her friend's children
and her own
and they all
moved

to the country
to the trees
to the grass
to the hay
to the honeysuckle
to the daffodils
    in spring
to the naked ladies
    in fall
to the full creek
    in winter

to the tall corn

in summer
to the fresh lettuce
to the red tomato, apple
to the plump chickens
to their fresh eggs
to the turkey vulture
to the red-tailed hawk
to the great blue heron
    under the bridge
to the steer in the field (we
    ate him)
to the pigs in the pen (we
    ate them
too)
to the frogs in the creek
    that drown out
the night
to the wild turkey
    my son never
caught
to the plump quail
    we've never
tasted
to the frost on the bridge
    on the leaves
    on the trough
    on the spider's web
        with its millions
of stars
to the blossoming trees
    that scatter
like snow
to the dying leaves
    that warm
the ground
to the pruning of trees
to the plowing of earth
to the turn
to the turn

of the seasons.

24

and she went in, carefully.
she went in, cautiously.
she went in, trembling.
she went in,

alone.

Her myth (of creation)

it was dark, so dark
I was lost, so I
lay down flat
in my fear

and dark figures
with bleeding bodies
and staring eyes
with voiceless mouths

came to me
and I lay flat
with fear
till I realized they

were me. the dead.
and when I realized this,
a light burst through
the roof (I thought

I was on the highest
mountain on earth
looking, looking
with a shift
of my eyes) and the light
blinded me, so
I closed them. then I really
saw and

I was no longer afraid.
I did not weep.

I did not laugh.
I was not old.
I was not young.
"I am here."

I said.

25

it began
with the death of
a friend
and it ended
with the death of
another. this made
her angry
and she told the
man "I'm not going to die!"
and she told the
doctor (who wanted her
womb) "I'm not going to die!"
and I think they believed
her. she
was angry. so
the man, the doctor
and death
got scared

and left.

life cycle (up to 32)

some men carry birth
(my first husband went
    crazy with
it)
some men carry death
(my second sucks on it
    like a bone, like
a bone)
I carry both. I'm
a juggler.

I'm a juggler.

26

meanwhile,
the daughter had grown
and she loved her. (a
woman, a woman) they
endured the rebellions, the
jealousies of a mother, a
daughter, as
she had with
her mother. they mouthed
the same curses
she and her mother
mouthed "bitch, whore" the
unnameables, the
unutterables you say
to those you love, to
your mother, that bitch, to
your daughter, that whore
    of a girl

I love you.

the proof (about 33)

I've shrunk down
and kissed
my womb
and heard
my heart
and listened
to mothers
and daughters
everywhere.

I've grown back,
little mother,
with my child's heart
beating
with my woman's womb

birthing
mothers, daughters
everywhere. we
sit and stare. your
eye, a camera, my
eye, a camera,
the photograph
is love.

to mom

27

it is not easy to
end here.
it would be
a lie.
the sons are growing
too.
one is bigger and stronger
than me
and he loves me. (we
aren't passionate and furious, like
a mother, a daughter)
there are 3 little sons, my friend's
and my own. they look
at me with
tender eyes (sometimes) they are
boys who will be
men. and

I love them.

the thread (the amputation)

the thread is bloodstained. I
gave it to you, as my
mother to me, as her
mother to her
and it is thick with
blood, with life
and we are thick with

each other, my
daughter, my

daughter, my
girl; you
stand, staring
with your knife's
amputation: your
hands bloody: it
is your amputation—I
took it from my
mother: you
take it from
me—blood, my
daughter. love, my
daughter. life, my
daughter: life. now,

go and play.
become your
own mother
and spin your own lovely

thread.

28

she awoke
and liked it.
she breathes breath
with a capital B.
she eats food
with a capital F.
she feels life
with a capital L.
she wants a man
with a capital M.
she wants love
with a capital L.O.V.E.
she wants to play
with a capital P.
is that asking

Too Much?

29

he approaches, juggling
his words "would
   you
   like to
   dance?"
"sure." I
say.

mother, may I?

don't mistake my reassuring
words
for wisdom;
don't mistake my soothing
eyes
for peace;
we are
in such a large large
world
I've
learned the ropes
I've
cultivated my gardens
I've combed my shores
I've
played house
played god
created universes
in my kitchen
in my womb
and when I
hide I
play mother
to my own
little girl. I

was always
good at

make believe. all
I ask is
      may
I play?

epilogue

as in all
stories, there is a
story within a
story. there is the
story of my friend (the
one who walked
with me to the
hospital; she was why
I beat up the
toughest boy in school,
because he was going
to beat her up; she was my
best friend since 12; she still
is) who somehow
is always
there. her soft
eyes always
recognize
me.

(mom)

men come
and go. your friends

stay. women
stay. mom
said. perhaps

this is a story of
women raging against
women; of
women loving
women; of

women listening to
women, because
men don't have time
to because
men move
on, because
men haven't learned
how to
listen, to
speak as
women; so

the thread, the story
connects
between women;
grandmothers, mothers, daughters,
the women
the thread of this
story.

(mamacita)

when a man opens a woman, she
is like a rose, she
will never close
again.

ever.

(me)

pistils. stamens.
wavering in the sun.
a bloom on the bush.
a mixed bloom.
they wonder at it.
a bastard rose.
a wild rose.
colors gone mad.
a rupture of thorns.
you must not pluck it.

you must recognize
   a magic rose
              when

you see it.

(excerpted from my poem
Legacies and Bastard Roses)

NOTES

I: SETTING THE CONTEXT

1. Spanish-speaking writers before this period were primarily poets who were published in Spanish-language newspapers. Their poetry has not been researched in depth, but several studies appeared in the 1970s. One example concerning New Mexico, whose inhabitants have traditionally claimed Spanish rather than Mexican origins, is Doris Meyer, "Anonymous Poetry in Spanish-Language New Mexico Newspapers (1880–1990)," *Bilingual Review / La Revista Bilingüe* 1 (Sept.-Dec. 1975). 259–275. Meyer gives examples of poetry written by New Mexican Hispanos. Anselmo Arrellano introduces the poetry of a literate class in New Mexico in *Los pobladores nuevo mexicanos y su poesía, 1880–1950* (Albuquerque: Pajarito Publications, 1976). Tomás Rivera, foremost Chicano novelist of the 1960s, stresses the importance of Mexican-American newspapers as a vehicle for the literary contribution of writers of Mexican descent in the nineteenth century in "Into the Labyrinth: The Chicano in Literature," *New Voices in American Literature: The Mexican American. A Symposium* (Edinburg, Tex.: Pan American University, 1971). One difference between the poems presented by Meyer and Arrellano and those referred to by Rivera is that the former were composed to be read and the latter were composed to be heard; only later did they appear in print.
   Written literary works in various areas of the Southwest before World War II require further study and research before the historical and cultural relationships between the poetry of Spanish-speaking writers, regardless of their self-declared Hispanic identity, and the "new" literature that is the subject of this book can be explored.
2. Among the most important contributions to the genre of the novel are Tomás Rivera, . . . *y no se lo tragó la tierra / And the Earth Did*

Not Swallow Him, bilingual ed. (Berkeley: Quinto Sol Publications, 1971); Rolando Hinojosa, *Estampas del Valle y otras obras,* bilingual ed. (Berkeley: Quinto Sol Publications, 1973) and *Klail City y sus alrededores* (Havana: Casa de las Américas, 1976); Rudolfo Anaya's trilogy, *Bless Me, Ultima* (Berkeley: Quinto Sol Publications, 1972), *Heart of Aztlán* (Berkeley: Editorial Justa Publications, 1976), and *Tortuga* (Berkeley: Editorial Justa Publications, 1979); and Miguel Mendez, *Peregrinos de Aztlán* (Tucson: Editorial Peregrinos, 1974).

The playwright who best represents the dramatic output of Chicanos in this era is Luis Valdez, who organized El Teatro Campesino in 1965. His early presentations aroused in César Chávez' farm workers an awareness of the socioeconomic conditions that affected their lives. His theatrical production of *Zoot Suit* (1978) at the Mark Taper Forum was the first drama about the history and culture of Mexican-Americans to be produced in Los Angeles.

Alurista, the most prolific of male Chicano poets, published three collections of poems between 1971 and 1976: *Floricanto en Aztlán* (Los Angeles: Chicano Studies Center, University of California, 1971); *Nationchild Plumaroja* (San Diego: Toltecas en Aztlán Publications, 1972); and *Timespace Huracán* (Albuquerque: Pajarito Publications, 1976). Other important Chicano poets are José Montoya, *El sol y los de abajo and Other R.C.A.F. Poems* (San Francisco: Ediciones Pocho-Che, 1972); Tino Villanueva, *Hay otra voz Poems* (Staten Island: Editorial Mensaje, 1972); Raul Salinas, *Viaje / Trip* (Providence: Hellcoal Press, 1973); and Gary Soto, *The Elements of San Joaquin* (Pittsburgh: University of Pittsburgh Press, 1976), *The Tale of Sunlight* (Pittsburgh: University of Pittsburgh Press, 1978), and *Where Sparrows Work Hard* (Pittsburgh: University of Pittsburgh Press, 1981).

Elizabeth Portillo-Tramley wrote plays and short stories. Her best-known drama is "The Day of the Swallows," in *El Espejo–The Mirror* (Berkeley: Quinto Sol Publications, 1971), pp. 150–193; *Rain of Scorpions and Other Writings* (Berkeley: Tonatiuh International, 1975) is a collection of short stories. For reasons noted in the text of this chapter, no novels by Chicanas appeared in the period 1965–1975. Two novels published since then are Isabella Rios, *Victuum* (Ventura, Calif.: Diana Etna, 1976), and Gina Valdés, *There Are No Madmen Here Tonight* (San Diego: Maize Press, 1981).

3. The term "Chicano" designates the totality of experience of both men and women of Mexican extraction who live in the United States. As the Spanish language allows for gender specificity, Chicano may also refer to the male of this culture. Although my usage of the term includes both meanings, I frequently use it in its more limited sense, that is, to specify the male counterpart of Chicana. A Chicana is a woman of Mexican heritage who lives in the United States. To encompass the cultural and historical continuity between Mexico and certain geographical areas of the United States, I sometimes use the term "Mexican-Chicano."

4. Englewood Cliffs: Prentice-Hall, 1979. Joseph Sommers is the author of a landmark article in Chicano literary criticism, "From the Critical Premise to the Product: Critical Modes and Their Application to a Chicano Literary Text," *New Scholar* 6 (1977), 51–80.
5. Austin: University of Texas Press, 1982. Bernice Zamora is the only Chicana poet discussed by Bruce-Novoa.
6. Santa Barbara: Editorial La Causa, 1982.
7. Ypsilanti, Mich.: Bilingual Press, 1982.
8. Elizabeth Ordóñez, "Sexual Politics and the Theme of Sexuality in Chicana Poetry," in *Women in Hispanic Literature: Icons and Fallen Idols*, ed. Beth Miller (Berkeley, Los Angeles, London: University of California Press, 1983), pp. 316–339; Alejandro Morales, "Terra Mater and the Emergence of Myth in *Poems* by Alma Villanueva," *Bilingual Review* 7, 2 (1980), 123–142; Marta E. Sánchez, "Inter-Sexual and Intertextual Codes in the Poetry of Bernice Zamora," *MELUS* 7 (Fall 1980), 55–68.
9. Tomás Ybarra, "The Chicano Movement and the Emergence of a Chicano Poetic Consciousness," *New Scholar* 6 (1977), 83.
10. Sommers, "From the Critical Premise to the Product," 70.
11. *El Grito* 1 (Sept. 1973).
12. I am thinking here of Alurista's early poems in which he propounded the idea that northern Mexico and the American Southwest together formed a native Chicano homeland called Aztlán. He opposed Aztlán to the values of white America, presented as sterile and vacuous. Elements of the same dichotomous tendency appear in the novels of Rudolfo Anaya and Miguel Mendez.
13. Huerta, *Chicano Theater*, pp. 18–23, 195–199.
14. Sonia López, "The Role of the Chicana within the Student Movement," in *Essays on la mujer*, ed. Rosaura Sánchez and Rosa Martinez Cruz (Los Angeles: Chicano Studies Center, University of California, 1977), pp. 16–29. See also Adelaida R. del Castillo, "Mexican Women in Organization," in *Mexican Women in the United States: Struggles Past and Present*, ed. Magdalena Mora and Adelaida R. del Castillo (Los Angeles: Chicano Studies Center, University of California, 1980), pp. 7–16.
15. For a penetrating study of the writings of black women, see Barbara Christian, *Black Women Novelists: The Development of a Tradition* (Westport, Conn.: Greenwood Press, 1980). Clearly black women faced the same kinds of problems as Chicana poets during the same historical period. Some outstanding black American women poets are Sherley Anne Williams, Audre Lorde, June Jordan, Ai, Sonia Sanchez, and Colleen McElroy. Curiously, none of the Chicana poets I discuss are indebted to black women writers. Although Elizabeth Ordóñez claims ("Sexual Politics," p. 319) that the Chicana poet, Ana Castillo, empathizes with the processes and goals of black women's literature, there is little evidence that black women poets have influenced Chicana poets. The influence on Chicana poets, as on Alma Villanueva, for example, comes from white women writers.

16. Conflicts stemming from social class also arose, to some extent, when Chicanas interacted with white women's groups. Some Chicanas in the movement realized that they came from communities whose per capita income and educational level were significantly lower than in white communities. In emphasizing the categories of ethnicity and gender, I am not suggesting that the dynamic of social class was of no significance. I stress those categories because Chicana intellectuals and writers were more conscious of race and gender than of class as factors shaping their lives.

17. Alfredo Mirandé and Evangelina Enríquez give detailed accounts of nineteenth- and twentieth-century Mexican women active in the public sphere in *La Chicana* (Chicago: University of Chicago Press, 1979), pp. 68–95, 233–234. I would add two names for the contemporary period: Dolores Huerta, vice-president of the United Farm Workers Union, and Irma Castro, president of the San Diego Chicano Federation.

18. Mirandé and Enriquez give a helpful summary on the issue of Chicana feminism and list some primary sources in their bibliography (*La Chicana*, p. 234). Some women, such as Marta Cotera, Anna Nieto-Gómez, and Enriqueta Longauex y Vasquez, gave that issue a central position in their critical essays. Enriqueta Longauex y Vasquez, "The Mexican-American Woman," is reprinted in *Sisterhood Is Powerful: An Anthology of Writings from the Women's Liberation Movement*, ed. Robin Morgan (New York: Vintage Books, 1970), pp. 426–432. See also *Cotera, The Chicana Feminist* (Austin: International Systems Development, 1976), and *Profile of the Mexican-American Woman* (Austin: National Educational Laboratory Publishers, 1976).

19. Other important Chicana poets are Carmen Tafolla of Austin, Xelina, of Calexico, California, now living in Colorado Springs; Olivia Castellanos of Sacramento; Margarita Cota-Cárdenas of Tucson; and Gina Valdés of San Diego.

20. For discussion of the personal confessional mode of Sylvia Plath and Anne Sexton, see Karl Malkoff, *Crowell's Handbook of Contemporary American Poetry* (New York: T. Y. Crowell, 1973), p. 89.

21. Chicano interest in Octavio Paz resulted more from his essay on the pachuco (*El laberinto de la soledad* [Mexico City: Fondo de Cultura Económica, 1959]) than from his poetry. *Pachuco* is the generic name for the self-styled heroes of barrio culture in the 1940s who were identified by their dress, language, and behavior. See Octavio Paz, *Labyrinth of Solitude*, trans. Lysander Kemp (New York: Grove Press, 1961), pp. 13–18.

22. Boston: Beacon Press, 1972.

23. Bilingual ed. (London: Jonathan Cape, 1969).

24. For further information on *la llorona*, see Américo Paredes, ed., *Folktales of Mexico* (Chicago: University of Chicago Press, 1970), p. xvi.

25. Walter Ong, "Literacy and Orality in Our Times," in *Profession 79* (New York: Modern Language Association, 1979), p. 3.

26. I refer to that body of literary criticism which posits the notion of the text as plural. Among the many critics who have written on the idea of intertexuality, and whose presuppositions are reflected in my analyses, are Julia Kristeva, *La Révolution du langage poétique* (Paris: Seuil, 1974); Roland Barthes, *S/Z: An Essay*, trans. Richard Miller (New York: Hill and Wang, 1974); Jonathan Culler, *The Pursuit of Signs* (Ithaca: Cornell University Press, 1981); and Robert Scholes, *Semiotics and Interpretation* (New Haven: Yale University Press, 1982).
27. Boston: Houghton Mifflin, 1980.
28. Mexico City: Fondo de Cultura Económica, 1980. Villanueva's book includes a detailed introduction to Chicano poetry and historical and literary essays on Chicanos.
29. Ed. Toni Empringham (Santa Barbara: Capra Press, 1982).
30. Numerous Spanish-language radio stations flourished in the late 1920s and early 1930s in cities of the Southwest.
31. New York: Grove Press, 1960.
32. Malkoff, *Crowell's Handbook*, p. 252.
33. Allen, *New American Poetry*, p. xii.
34. For two different readings of Alurista's poetics, see Tomás Ybarra-Frausto, "Alurista's Poetics: The Oral, the Bilingual, the Pre-Columbian," in Sommers, ed., *Modern Chicano Writers*, pp. 117–132; Bruce-Novoa, "The Teachings of Alurista: A Chicano Way of Knowledge," in *Chicano Poetry*, pp. 69–95.
35. Part of Bernice Zamora's ambivalence as Chicana, poet, and woman comes from her identification with an Anglo-American tradition (see chap. 5). Whereas Eliot and Pound looked to classical literary expression because they found contemporary culture insufficient, Zamora reacts and responds to the English sonnet tradition and American writers such as Robinson Jeffers because they exclude a woman's voice.
36. For sources for my comments on the implied audience, see chap. 2, n. 39.
37. Bruce-Novoa, *Chicano Poetry*, esp. p. 226, n. 10.
38. Scholes, *Semiotics and Interpretation*, p. 16.
39. I am indebted to Elaine Showalter, "Feminist Criticism in the Wilderness," *Critical Inquiry* 8 (1981), 179–205, for the term "muted discourse." Showalter describes woman's writing as a "double-voiced discourse," or a combination of two alternative oscillating texts simultaneously at play with each other: an "orthodox" (or "dominant") and a "muted" story (see esp. p. 204).

II: THE BIRTHING OF THE POETIC "I"

1. Pittsburgh: Motheroot Publications, 1978. *Mother, May I?* is printed in its entirety in Appendix C, below.
2. Austin: Place of Herons Press, 1977.
3. In *Third Chicano Literary Prize* (Irvine, Calif., 1976–77), pp. 85–133.

4. James Cody, editor of Villanueva's *Bloodroot*, explains his fascination with her poems, but his reasons distort the issue of why Villanueva writes in the first place. In his introductory comments Cody says (p. i) he likes Villanueva's poetry because she writes like a man: ". . . her poems were of the universal quality, embracing all subjects and passions, that seemed . . . to come almost only from the writings of men. In addition, there was none of the self-pity that is in so much 'feminist' poetry." He continues: ". . . she does not ape men or brutalize her sexuality to escape the bonds that have existed traditionally for women. For her these bonds do not exist. Alma Villanueva is not a feminist, or a female poet, she is a poet."
5. Fernando Alegría, *Walt Whitman en Hispanoamerica* (Mexico City: Ediciones Studium, 1954), esp. pp. 314–331.
6. On May 24, 1983, Alma Villanueva told me she had not read Walt Whitman before writing *Bloodroot*. While confirming this in his introduction to *Bloodroot*, Cody insists that Villanueva's poems resemble Whitman's: "Though Alma had read almost no Whitman before our friendship began, I read her poems as if she were the female fulfillment of those words spoken so long ago [by Whitman ʼn "Poets to Come"]. Cody sees "a clarity of line, a forthrightness, a subconscious and assumed rhythm . . . that seemed to proceed from Whitman" and an "insouciant joy in the crude, the ordinary, the common, while elevating it, or accepting it equally with the rest of life" (p. ii). Had Villanueva read Whitman before writing *Bloodroot*, I imagine that the unconventionality of Whitman, who allowed practically everything to enter into his poems, employed free verse, used no rhyme, and believed in spontaneous natural song, would have appealed to Villanueva.
7. Alegría (*Walt Whitman*, pp. 320–331), in referring to *Song of Myself* and Neruda's "Ritual de mis piernas" ("Ritual of My Legs"), points to this difference in the way each poet speaks about his legs.
8. See "Cuerpo de mujer," the introductory poem in *Veinte poemas de amor y una canción desesperada* (p. 87), and Poems II, V, VI, and XIII (pp. 87–91, 95–96), in *Obras Completas*, 3d ed. (Buenos Aires: Editorial Losada, 1967), Vol. I. For an English version see *Twenty Love Poems and a Song of Despair*, trans. W. S. Merwin, bilingual ed. (London: Jonathan Cape, 1969).
9. For views on Plath's and Sexton's poetry and insights into their place in contemporary American poetry, see Gary Lane, *Sylvia Plath: New Views on the Poetry* (Baltimore: Johns Hopkins University Press, 1979); Charles Newman, *The Art of Sylvia Plath: A Symposium* (Bloomington: Indiana University Press, 1970); Mary Lynn Broe, *Protean Poetic* (Columbia: University of Missouri Press, 1980); Karl Malkoff, *Crowell's Handbook of Contemporary American Poetry* (New York: T. Y. Crowell, 1973).
10. Alicia Ostriker, "The Thieves of Language: Women Poets and Revisionist Mythmaking," *Signs* 8 (Autumn 1982), 68–90. Ostriker observes that childish language and bawdy are both variants of colloquial language. She notes that Rachel Blau DuPlessis uses "pun-

ning baby talk" in her poem "Medusa" to reveal "the power of sexual pain to thwart growth," whereas in Sexton it signals sexual trauma. Ostriker asserts that Erica Jong is one poet who uses bawdy to invade the linguistic preserves of male discourse (pp. 87–88).

11. Barbara Herrnstein Smith, *Poetic Closure: A Study of How Poems End* (Chicago: University of Chicago Press, 1968), p. 15.
12. *Bloodroot*, pp. 4–5; App. A, pp. 277–279.
13. Villanueva sometimes uses only a closing parenthesis.
14. *Bloodroot*, p. 1. The lines cited are the entire poem.
15. *Bloodroot*, pp. 2–3; App. A, pp. 280–281. The poems "(wo)man," "bloodroot," and "ZINZ" offer a feminine analogue to the myth of Aztlán in Chicano poetry in the late 1960s and early 1970s. According to this myth, Aztlán, reputedly in today's Southwest, was the legendary birthplace of the Aztec Indians. The Aztlán myth posited the existence of a collective unconscious for modern-day Chicanos whereby they retained continuity with their Indian heritage. For some Chicanos, Aztlán made possible a reintegration with their cultural roots. The Aztlán myth represents a unilateral rejection of United States culture.

Villanueva does something similar in a feminine context. Whereas Aztlán is a mythical utopia based on race, Villanueva's mythical matriarchy is based on gender. Like the poets of Aztlán (one example is the early Alurista of the *Floricanto* poems, 1971), Villanueva, too, criticizes Western culture: men have split the world into mind and body. Her revision is to affirm and celebrate the beauty of the feminine body, which is negated by Western civilization and is therefore the aspect of the human person to be elevated. Alejandro Morales discusses this feminine principle in terms of Mircea Eliade's Earth Mother in "Terra Mater and the Emergence of Myth in *Poems* by Alma Villanueva," *Bilingual Review* 7, 2 (1980), 123–142.
16. *Bloodroot*, pp. 20–21; App. A, pp. 282–283.
17. Roy Harvey Pearce, *Whitman* (Englewood Cliffs: Prentice-Hall, 1962), p. 6.
18. Villanueva does not use an apostrophe to indicate the possessive.
19. *Bloodroot*, p. 37. I cite the entire poem. This poem bears a thematic resemblance to Neruda's "Unidad," the fifth poem in *Residencia en la tierra I* (1925–1931). The concern for the poet's immediate sensory experience, the eternal repetition of natural events (the ebb and flow of the sea), and the subject's experience of time as "intuited pastness" are themes common to both poems. See Lane Kauffmann, "Neruda's Last Residence: Translations and Notes on Four Poems," *New Scholar* 5, 1 (1975), 122–124.
20. *Bloodroot*, pp. 49–51; App. A, pp. 284–286. The three poems I mention at the end of this paragraph appear on pp. 27, 29, and 47–48.
21. *Bloodroot*, pp. 57–59; App. A, pp. 287–289.
22. *Bloodroot*, pp. 52–54; App. A, pp. 290–293.
23. App. A, p. 293.
24. Indications of a witch-persona in Plath are mentioned by Lane, *Sylvia*

Plath, pp. 13, 144. Ostriker ("Thieves of Language," p. 86) observes that the framing element of Sexton's *Transformations* is the persona of the narrator-poet, "a middle-aged witch, me."

25. *Poems*, pp. 117–118; App. B, pp. 301–302.

26. "Of/To Man," *Poems*, p. 115; App. B, p. 300; "witches' blood," *Poems*, p. 105; App. B, p. 297; "Of Utterances," *Poems*, pp. 107–108; App. B, pp. 299–300. In *Poems*, "witches' blood" mistakenly appears as part of "The Hard Probing Plow." The poem begins with the words "witches' blood" (p. 105) and concludes with the same words (p. 106).

27. Robert Graves espouses this theory of poetry. In *The White Goddess* (New York: Vintage Books, 1960), originally published in 1948, he argues that a test of a poet's vision is the "accuracy of his portrayal of the White Goddess and of the island over which she rules," and that "a true poem is necessarily an invocation of the White Goddess, or Muse, the Mother of All Living" (p. 12). For Graves, poetry is a magical language that honored the moon-goddess in prepatriarchal times, survived in popular religious ceremonies and mystery cults, and was still taught during the times of the early Christian emperors "in the poetic colleges of Ireland and Wales, and in the witch-covens of Western Europe." He claims that one important difference between the classical and Romantic poet was his attitude to the "White Goddess." Whereas the classical poet claimed to be the goddess's master, the Romantic poet of the nineteenth century was a "true poet only in his fatalistic regard for the Goddess as the mistress who commanded his destiny" (pp. 12–13).

In my conversation with Villanueva on March 24, 1983, she said that in this poem she quoted, not Graves, but Sexton's quotation of Graves. As with Neruda and Whitman, Villanueva seems to come across a source in an indirect way, here Graves via Sexton, since she claims she had not read Graves when she wrote this poem.

28. *Bloodroot*, pp. 55–56; App. A, pp. 294–296.

29. Numbers in parentheses indicate the page or pages in Appendix C where the passage appears.

30. Norman Holland, *The Dynamics of Literary Response* (New York: Oxford University Press, 1968), pp. 38–39. Holland's explanation of the phases of child development in a psychoanalytical context is helpful for understanding the character's activities as a little girl (ibid., pp. 32–50).

31. Ibid., p. 39.

32. For comments on Plath's exaggerated hyperboles, see Richard Allen Blessing, "The Shape of the Psyche: Vision and Technique in the Late Poems of Sylvia Plath"; Marjorie Perloff, "Sylvia Plath's 'Sivvy' Poems: A Portrait of the Poet as Daughter," in Lane, *Sylvia Plath*, esp. pp. 66–67, 173.

33. Villanueva's male characters fall into categories of sexual deviants and innocent wimps. The rapist and the uncle who molest the child are examples of the former, and the Anglo schoolboy with whom the protagonist falls in love is an example of the latter. The only male character in the poem to whom the protagonist seems to

relate in a positive way is her second husband, but nothing is known about him. Men do not play a significant role in Villanueva's poetic universe because they do not participate in the creation of meaning. For example, the narrator dismisses sons with a passing reference before moving into her discussion of the mother-daughter bond.

Judith Kegan Gardiner, "On Female Identity and Writing by Women," *Critical Inquiry* (Winter 1981), p. 356, points out that Anglo women writers describe their male characters in terms of access to power: "they are wimps or brutes." Villanueva seems to share this tendency, for she depicts her male characters as one-dimensional. The tendency is, of course, in keeping with her primary objective of telling a woman's story. As Chicano male writers primarily portray women as either virgins or whores, Villanueva's portrayal of men is a neat reversal of the male tendency.

34. These terms are used by R. D. Laing, *The Divided Self* (Baltimore: Penguin Books, 1965), pp. 65–77.

35. Morales, "Terra Mater," following Mircea Eliade's discussion of myth, focuses on the grandmother as the contemporary incarnation of the Earth Mother in Villanueva's prize-winning anthology, *Poems.* Unlike Morales, I am not interested in validating the Eliade model of myth, but I do think that Villanueva consciously knows and uses archetypal conventions. She says in the study of her life and work by Elizabeth Ordóñez (*Chicano Literature: A Reader's Encyclopedia,* ed. Julio A. Martinez and Francisco A. Lomelí [Westport, Conn.: Greenwood Press, 1985]) that she has been influenced by Mary Esther Harding's *Woman's Mysteries: Ancient and Modern* (New York: G. P. Putnam's Sons, 1971). Harding was a disciple of Jung, who introduced her book, originally published in 1935. One of Harding's objectives in *Woman's Mysteries* is to expose and recover the "feminine principle" represented by Western culture via the presentation of feminine archetypes, such as the Demeter-Kore myth. The intention of making the grandmother in the grave scene a kind of Earth Mother is a buried presupposition of *Mother, May I?*

36. Sigmund Freud, "The Uncanny," trans. Alix Strachey, *Sigmund Freud on Creativity and the Unconscious* (New York: Harper Torchbooks, 1958), p. 148, defines the repressed in this way.

37. Ostriker, "Thieves of Language," esp. pp. 72–75.

38. Walter J. Ong, "Literate Orality of Popular Culture Today," in *Rhetoric, Romance, and Technology* (Ithaca and London: Cornell University Press, 1979), p. 289. Also appropriate on formulary devices and their relation to oral cultures are Ong's comments in "Transformations of the Word and Alienation," in *Interfaces of the Word* (Ithaca and London: Cornell University Press, 1977), pp. 17–22.

39. I cite only a few of the many critics who share my view of the literary text as a cultural product in a given situation of discourse. Robert Scholes, *Semiotics and Interpretation* (New Haven: Yale University Press, 1982), pp. 14–16, makes the useful distinction between a "work" and a "text": "the same set of words can be regarded as either a work or a text." A work is "a complete, self-sufficient object,

constructed of words on a page . . . seen as free of authorial intention, free of historical necessity, and free from the reader's projections of value and meaning." The major exponent of this method is the New Criticism school of thought. Scholes's preference is for semiotic analysis which takes the same set of words as a text: "open, incomplete, insufficient." He argues that "as a text . . . a piece of writing must be understood as the product of a person or persons, at a given point in human history, in a given form of discourse, taking its meanings from the interpretative gestures of individual readers using the grammatical, semantic, and cultural codes available to them."

Susan R. Suleiman and Inge Crosman, *The Reader in the Text: Essays on Audience and Interpretation* (Princeton: Princeton University Press, 1980), pp. 3–4; take as their central premise the notion that "all stories [texts] are implicitly or explicitly addressed to an audience." The audience is an entity inseparable from the notion of artistic texts. The authors present six varieties of reader-oriented criticism and compile an extensive bibliography on questions related to the reception of literary texts.

Peter J. Rabinowitz, "Assertion and Assumption: Fictional Patterns and the External World," *PMLA* 96 (May 1981), 408–419, says in a note (p. 418) that the "central disagreement in reader criticism is between critics who argue for the individual's freedom to 'create texts' and those who claim that the text imposes restrictions on response." My comments on *Mother, May I?* relate more to the second position, or to the way readers are reflected in texts.

40. Daniel Wilson, "Readers in Texts," *PMLA* 96, 5 (Oct. 1981), 848–863; Rabinowitz, "Assertion and Assumption."

41. *Bloodroot*, pp. 62–63.

42. Emile Benveniste, "Relations of Person in the Verb," "The Nature of Pronouns," and "Subjectivity in Language," in *Problems in General Linguistics*, trans. Mary Elizabeth Meek, Miami Linguistics Series, no. 8 (Coral Gables: University of Miami Press, 1971), pp. 195–204, 217–222, 224–230. Lucille Kerr, in notes to her article, "The Paradox of Power and Mystery: Carlos Fuentes' *Terra Nostra*," *PMLA* 95 (Jan. 1980), 91–102, comments on Benveniste's theories on the first-, second-, third-person pronouns and the difference among them (p. 108).

43. Nancy Chodorow, *The Reproduction of Mothering* (Berkeley, Los Angeles, London: University of California Press, 1978).

44. Robinson Jeffers, *Medea*, in *Medea: Myth and Dramatic Form*, ed. James L. Sanderson (Boston: Houghton Mifflin, 1957), p. 133.

III: THE CHICANA AS SCRIBE

1. This poem and all others mentioned or quoted in the text are from *Emplumada* (Pittsburgh: University of Pittsburgh Press, 1981).

2. I say "usually" because in "Lots: I" and "Lots: II" Cervantes, speaking as a woman, assigns no identifiable racial, cultural, or class

markers to her fictional speaker who responds to an experience of rape.

3. "Beneath the Shadow of the Freeway" and "Freeway 280" were originally printed in *Latin-American Literary Review* 5 (Spring-Summer 1977), 175–179. "Refugee Ship" appeared originally in *Revista Chicano-Riqueña* 3 (Winter 1975). "Beneath the Shadow" and "Refugee Ship" were reprinted in *The Third Woman: Minority Women Writers of the United States,* ed. Dexter Fisher (Boston: Houghton Mifflin, 1980). Except for some of Cervantes' other early pieces, such as "You Cramp My Style, Baby," "Trabajadores Culturales" (*Fuego de Aztlán* 1, 4 [1977], 39, 41), and "Para un revolucionario" (*Revista Chicano-Riqueña* 3 [Winter 1975]), surprisingly few of the poems in *Emplumada* are overtly expressive of a Chicana social consciousness.

4. Cervantes' spelling of Veracruz as two words reinforces her ambiguous relationship with Mexico.

5. See the special issue of *América Indigena* 38, 2 (1978), devoted to "La Mujer Campesina en la Sociedad Latinoamericana."

6. Set in an urban context, probably in California, "Cannery Town in August" (*Emplumada*, p. 6) focuses on a group of women going home one August evening after working all day in a cannery that processes spinach, tomatoes, and peaches. The speaker-witness describes the woman as "not speaking," "dumbed" by the cannery's "clamor." The metonymies of "bodyless / uniforms" and "spinach-specked shoes" stand for the women who "drift in monochrome" down the streets. They are like men because they "smell of whiskey" and have "peach fuzz" on their eyes and lips. Cervantes describes the hard, physical labor these women perform, "with no one / waiting in the shadows / to palm them back to living."

7. Vicente T. Mendoza, *El corrido mexicano* (Mexico City: Fondo de Cultura Económica, 1954).

8. Américo Paredes, *With His Pistol in His Hand* (Austin: University of Texas Press, 1958). According to Paredes, the "*corrido* of Gregorio Cortez" presents Cortez as a border hero surviving in a hostile Anglo community in southern Texas at the turn of the century. Cortez is one of several heroes of border *corridos* whom some official American newspapers of the time presented as bandits and outlaws capable only of murder and other crimes. For Paredes' discussion of both the thematic and the formal aspects of the *corrido,* see especially Part II, pp. 12 ff.

9. See Walter Ong's discussion ("The Writer's Audience Is Always a Fiction," in *Interfaces of the Word* [Ithaca and London: Cornell University Press, 1977], pp. 61–62) on the transition in Western culture from an oral to a literate society. Ong notes that the original transcribers of the *Iliad* and the *Odyssey* were not composing in writing but recording with minimal changes "what a singer was singing or was imagined to be singing."

10. Charles Altieri, *Enlarging the Temple* (Lewisburg: Bucknell University Press, 1979), esp. pp. 29–49. In his first chapter, "Modern and

Postmodern: Symbolist and Immanentist Modes of Poetic Thought,"
Altieri opposes an immanentist tradition to the symbolist tradition
in modern poetry, tracing the former to Wordsworth and the latter
to Coleridge. Symbolist poets (Eliot, Pound) affirm the creative mind
as the source of all value: "What matters is not what is there
in immediate experience but what the mind can make of it" (p. 36).
The poet of the immanentist tradition places value in the forces
at work in ordinary experience. The mind discovers and orders
meaning already present in nature. Experience is immanentist, not
transcendental.

    Accounting for their various differences, Altieri places post-
Modern poets (Robert Lowell, Robert Bly, Charles Olson, Frank
O'Hara, Denise Levertov) into the immanentist tradition. Given the
general parameters of his model, I would place Cervantes, as well as
all the other Chicana poets discussed in this book, within his immanentist poetics. In fact, the historical shift in the style of writing
poetry from symbolist to immanentist after World War II is, I think,
one factor encouraging Chicanas and Chicanos, and probably other
cultural minorities as well, to write. An immanentist style is far
better suited to their abilities and objectives than the high modernis-
tic and more "academic" style of Eliot and Pound.

11. In Robert Bly, *Leaping Poetry: An Idea with Poems and Translations*
(Boston: Beacon Press, 1975).

12. For examples of the decomposition of the poetic surface as it relates
to the poetry of William Carlos Williams, see Marjorie Perloff,
"'Lines Converging and Crossing': The 'French' Decade of William
Carlos Williams," in *The Poetics of Indeterminacy: Rimbaud to
Cage* (Princeton: Princeton University Press, 1981), pp. 123–132.
Using cubist painting as a comparative norm, Perloff argues that in
Spring and All Carlos Williams presents images that are difficult,
even impossible, to visualize. His poems begin with an image of a
concrete object only to end with another image that contradicts it.
In "The Red Paper Box," for example, the box turns out to be made,
not of paper, but of cloth or leather.

13. For more on the concept of "mother's brother," see Claude Lévi-
Strauss, *Structural Anthropology* (New York: Doubleday, 1967), pp.
39–43. For a more recent discussion of the phenomenon, see Sylvia
Junko Yanagisako, "Family and the Household: The Analysis of
Domestic Groups," *Annual Review of Anthropology* 8 (1979), 161–
205.

14. The changes were for the better, I think. Most of them eliminated
unnecessary repetition and helped to make the poem tighter and
more compact. A comparison of the poem as printed in *Emplumada*
(1981) with the one in *The Third Woman* (1980) yields three significant changes. Cervantes probably made these alterations for
Emplumada because the stanzas in which they appeared were still
the same in *The Third Woman* as in the original printing in *Latin-
American Literary Review* (1977).

In *The Third Woman* stanza 2 of section 5 reads:

inside
a grey kitten   a touchstone
purring beneath grandma's
hand-sewn quilts   the singing
of mockingbirds

The version in *Emplumada* is enriched because the grandmother sews quilts from the suits left by her husband; it also drops the unnecessary "hand-sewn."

The second change concerns stanza 2 of section 6, where Cervantes eliminates four complete lines that state too explicitly what the poem already suggests without them:

a mother's wisdom.
The lines on her face are beginning to show.
The bitter years are all so visible now
as she spends hours
washing down the bile.

The third change eliminates the future tense in the first two lines of the final stanza. In *The Third Woman* these lines read:

and in time, I will plant geraniums.
I will tie up my hair into loose braids.

The altered version in *Emplumada* gains the immediacy of the present tense, which in turn gives the phrase "in time" an aspect of ambiguity.

15. Ong, *Interfaces of the Word*, p. 103.
16. The idea of calling the girl-narrator's expression immanentist was suggested by Altieri, *Enlarging the Temple*.
17. Stephen Ross, " 'Voice' in Narrative Texts: The Example of *As I Lay Dying*," *PMLA* 94 (March 1979), 3–10, discusses a phenomenon in narrative similar to the dichotomy in literary voice which I discuss here.
18. For examples, see *Bloodroot*, p. 54; *Poems*, pp. 94, 106; and *Mother, May I?*, pp. 18–19.

IV: PROHIBITION AND SEXUALITY

1. The biographical information on Lucha Corpi is based on Barbara Brinson-Pineda, "Poets on Poetry: Dialogue with Lucha Corpi," *Prisma* (Mills College, Department of Ethnic Studies, 1979), pp. 4–9; Corpi's short autobiography in *Palabras de Mediodía / Noon Words;* and my interview with Lucha Corpi in June 1980. Corpi also gives autobiographical details in *Fireflight: Three Latin-American Poets* (Berkeley, Calif.: Oyez, 1976), pp. 43–44. Ten of Corpi's poems appear in *Fireflight;* most of them are reprinted in *Palabras de Mediodía.*
2. *Palabras de Mediodía / Noon Words*, trans. Catherine Rodríguez-Nieto (Berkeley: El Fuego de Aztlán Publications, 1980), contains an

eight-page introduction by the Mexican author, Juan José Arreola, also translated into English. Of the forty-eight poems in this collection, only two, "Time" and "Underground Mariachi," are in English, and they are translated into Spanish (pp. 74–75, 76–77). All the poems reproduced in this chapter are from this edition.

3. For examples in Mexican songs and lyrics, see *Cancionero Folklórico de México*, 5 vols., compiled and edited by researchers of the Centro de Estudios Linguisticos y Literarios de El Colegio de México, under the direction of Margit Frenk (1975–1984). For examples of men eating the fruit or cutting the flower, see the *Cancionero, Coplas del Amor Feliz* 1 (1975), 193–195. For a brief but helpful introduction to Mexican popular poetry and lyrics, see Jacobo Chencinsky, "El Mundo Metafórico de la Lírica Popular Mexicana," *Anuario de Letras* 1 (Mexico City, 1961), 113–148.

4. Printed in *La Cosecha*, a special issue of *De Colores* (Albuquerque: Pajarito Publications) 3, 3 (1977), 74–89. All translations from "Tres Mujeres" are mine.

5. This expression comes from the experience of people living in Mexico and other areas of Latin America. The phrase *una mujer muy sufrida* means a self-sacrificing woman.

6. According to Jacques Soustelle (*Daily Life of the Aztecs* [Stanford: Stanford University Press, 1961], p. 55), Iztaccíhuatl was a priestess in charge of the physical preparation for certain ceremonies, particularly the sweeping of holy places. The legend of Iztaccíhuatl as sleeping woman or princess is in the popular imagination of Mexican people, but it is not documented by sources on pre-Columbian civilization and culture. The name is frequently spelled with an *x* instead of a *z*. I follow the spelling given in Luis Cabrera, *Diccionario de aztequismos* (Mexico City: Ediciones Oasis, 1975), p. 84.

   Corpi's second reference to the princess in white, a little farther on, alludes to the "snowy peaks of two giants." Corpi is referring to the chain formed by Iztaccíhuatl and Popocatépetl, or the Sierra Nevada.

7. Iris Blanco, "Participación de las Mujeres en la Sociedad Prehispánica," in *Essays on la mujer*, ed. Rosaura Sánchez and Rosa Martinez Cruz (Los Angeles: Chicano Studies Center, University of California, 1977), pp. 48–80 (see esp. p. 56).

8. In a Mexican context, I am thinking of Octavio Paz's *El laberinto de la soledad* (Mexico City: Fondo de Cultura Económica, 1959), translated as *The Labyrinth of Solitude* by Lysander Kemp (New York: Grove Press, 1961); and novels by Carlos Fuentes, such as *La Región Más Transparente* (Mexico City: Fondo de Cultura Económica, 1958), translated as *Where the Air Is Clear* by Sam Hileman (New York: Obolensky, 1960), and *La Muerte de Artemio Cruz* (Mexico City: Fondo de Cultura Económica, 1961), translated as *The Death of Artemio Cruz* by Sam Hileman (New York: Farrar, Straus, 1965). These Mexican writers tend to represent the sociohistorical conquest as a rape by the Spaniards, thereby implying the virginity and purity of pre-Columbian civilization.

In a Chicano context, I include Corky Gonzalez, "I Am Joaquin," one of the first poems to appear in the Chicano movement; the early poems by Alurista; and even the novels *Peregrinos de Aztlán* (Tucson: Editorial Peregrinos, 1974), by Miguel Mendez, and *Bless Me, Ultima* (Berkeley: Quinto Sol Publications, 1972), by Rudolfo Anaya. Such poems and novels tend to simplify the process of colonization by romanticizing native American cultures as more natural and human than the corrupt and materialistic cultures, whether Spanish or Anglo-American, which overcame them.

9. See the play by Carlos Fuentes, *Todos los gatos son pardos* (Mexico City: Siglo Veintiuno Editores, 1970), for the variations on Marina's name: "Malintzin . . . Marina . . . Malinche. . . . Tres fueron tus nombres, mujer: el que te dieron tus padres, el que te dio tu amante y el que te dio tu pueblo. . . . Malintzin, dijeron tus padres: hechicera, diosa de la mala suerte y de la reyerta de sangre. . . . Marina dijo tu hombre, recordando el océano por donde vino hasta estas tierras. . . . Malinche, dijo tu pueblo: traidora, lengua y guía del hombre blanco."

For the English translation, see Rachel Phillips, "Marina / Malinche: Masks and Shadows," in *Women in Hispanic Literature: Icons and Fallen Idols*, ed. Beth Miller (Berkeley, Los Angeles, London: University of California Press, 1983), p. 112: "Malintzin . . . Marina . . . Malinche. . . . You had three names, woman: the one your parents gave you, the one your lover gave you, and the one your people gave you. . . . Malintzin, said your parents: enchantress, goddess of ill fortune and blood feud. . . . Marina, said your man, remembering the ocean he crossed to come to this land. . . . Malinche, said your people: traitress, white man's mouthpiece and guide."

10. Soustelle, *Daily Life of the Aztecs*, p. 2.

11. I am thinking here of the well-known comment made by José Martí during his stay in the United States: "He vivido en el monstruo y conozco sus entrañas, y mi honda es la honda de David" ("I have lived in the monster and know its very innards, and my sling is the sling of David"). José Martí was a poet, an intellectual, and a fighter for Cuban independence.

12. For examples, see "Quedarse Quieto" ("Keeping Still"), pp. 4–8; "Girasol" ("Sunflower"), pp. 72–73; "Time" ("Tiempo"), pp. 74–75; "La Casa de los Espejos" ("House of Mirrors"), pp. 102–107; and "Lento Liturgico," pp. 108–109. No title is given to the English translation of this poem.

13. See Brinson-Pineda, "Poets on Poetry," pp. 5–6.

14. Sandra M. Gilbert and Susan Gubar, *The Madwoman in the Attic* (New Haven: Yale University Press, 1979), p. 96.

15. Gilbert and Gubar (ibid., pp. 4–11) discuss the implications for women writers of the notion of "author" as male and the pen as a metaphorical penis.

16. Corpi defines *teponaztle* as a flute used by Indians to announce the celebration of festivities in honor of the gods (*Palabras de Mediodía*, p. xxvii), but I follow the definition given by Cabrera (*Diccionario*, p. 134): a percussion instrument sometimes used as a drum. Corpi

also identifies Francisco Gabilondo Soler, whom I mention at the end of the paragraph.

17. *Atole* is a Mexican drink made of cooked corn that is ground, dissolved, filtered, and boiled.
18. Corpi uses the words, "cultivadoras de indecibles" ("cultivators of the unsayable") to describe herself and her literary precursor in "Emily Dickinson," pp. 134–135.
19. Chencinsky, "El Mundo Metafórico," p. 145.
20. A more openly political poem is "Underground Mariachi" (see n. 2, above).
21. Oddly enough, terms that designate male genitalia are frequently feminine in Spanish, for example, *la verga* ("penis"), and terms that designate female genitalia are masculine, for example, *el coño* ("vagina").
22. Here I think Rodríguez-Nieto's English translations, though in general sensitive and accurate, impoverish the Spanish text. A few other examples occur in "Romance Negro"; for example, *arrancar* in line 18 is translated as "cut," a rendition that does not express the violence suggested by the Spanish word. For other examples, see nn. 35, 38, below.
23. Blanco, "Participación de las Mujeres," pp. 75–76.
24. Paz, *Labyrinth*, pp. 65–88; Fuentes, *Todos los gatos son pardos*, pp. 173–175. For a translation of the Fuentes passage on Marina as Chingada in *Todos los gatos*, see *Literatura Chicana: Texto y Contexto*, ed. Antonia Castañeda, Tomás Ybarra-Frausto, and Joseph Sommers (Englewood Cliffs: Prentice-Hall, 1972), pp. 305–306.
25. *Labyrinth*, p. 86.
26. Ibid., p. 80.
27. Two other Chicana poets have also reassessed Marina's image: Carmen Tafolla, "La Malinche," in *Encuentro Artístico Femenil* (Austin: Casa/Tejidos Publication, 1978), pp. 41–42, and Angela de Hoyos, "La Malinche a Cortez y viceversa," *La Palabra* 2 (Spring 1980), 69–70. Elizabeth Ordóñez, "Sexual Politics and the Theme of Sexuality in Chicana Poetry," in *Women in Hispanic Literature*, ed. Miller, gives examples, with commentary, of Chicanas who have attempted to reassess Marina in poetry (see esp. pp. 324–328). Also contributing to a reevaluation of Doña Marina's role as woman and cultural symbol in the conquest of Mexico are Adelaida R. del Castillo, "Malintzin Tenépal: A Preliminary Look into a New Perspective," in *Essays on la mujer*, ed. Sánchez and Martinez Cruz, pp. 124–149; Cordelia Candelaria, "La Malinche: Feminist Prototype," *Frontiers* 5 (Summer 1980), 1–6; and Phillips, "Marina / Malinche."
28. Both Phillips, "Marina / Malinche" (p. 114), and Candelaria, "La Malinche" (p. 3), speak of Marina's role as *la lengua de los dioses* ("the tongue of the gods," meaning the Spaniards).
29. Díaz del Castillo, *The Conquest of New Spain*, trans. J. M. Cohen (London: Penguin Books, 1963), p. 86.
30. Adelaida R. del Castillo, "Malintzin Tenépal," p. 143; Phillips, "Marina / Malinche," p. 111.

31. Bernal Díaz del Castillo, *Conquest,* pp. 85–87.
32. Paz, *Labyrinth,* p. 86.
33. Brinson-Pineda, "Poets on Poetry," p. 6. The next two quotations are also taken from this interview.
34. "Romance Liso" and "Romance de la Niña" appear on pp. 114–117.
35. Here again I disagree with the Rodríguez-Nieto English translation. The Spanish *fuego blanco* is "white fire" at its most basic level. I therefore use "rose of white fire" instead of "rose of pale fire," which more accurately refers to *rosa de fuego pálido.*
36. I borrow the terms "abstract" and "coda" from William Labov and David Fanshel, *Therapeutic Discourse* (New York: Academic Press, 1977), p. 109.
37. The metaphor connecting the color black with tragedy is part of a long tradition, and has, I think, racist implications.
38. By rendering *y al verla* as "at the sight," the translator suggests that the metaphor of the sexual experience is intended as a rape. The phrase *y al verla,* however, does not mean "at the sight"; more simply, it means "and upon seeing her."
39. The English translation mistakenly interchanges the first and third stanzas of the coda.
40. Brinson-Pineda, "Poets on Poetry," p. 7. I cite Corpi's anecdote: "Once while translating a poem she [Rodríguez-Nieto] said that it wasn't right. I had written a mixture of colors that I intended to pass for brown. She told me "That's dirty water." Then she thought the poem should end before it actually did. I told her, "No, I want my poem as it is." She said, "Then I won't translate it." 'So don't translate it,' I answered. That poem has never been completed."
41. Examples are "De mi casa" ("My House"), pp. 36–39; "Protocolo de Verduras" ("The Protocol of Vegetables"), pp. 48–49; "Carta a Arturo" ("Letter to Arturo"), pp. 60–61; and "Romance Liso" ("Smooth Romance"), pp. 114–115.

V: THE DRAMATIZATION OF A SHIFTING POETIC CONSCIOUSNESS

1. Since leaving Pueblo, Bernice Zamora has lived in Palo Alto, California, Albuquerque, New Mexico, and Houston, Texas. She presently lives in the San Francisco Bay area. Although she reads and writes Spanish, her primary language is English. She has taught English expository writing at the University of California, Berkeley, and creative writing in poetry for Chicanos at Stanford University. She is now in the final stages of a Ph.D. at Stanford in English and American literature. Her second collection of poems, *After the Salmon Leave,* will soon be ready for publication. For more biographical details and cultural information about Zamora, including statements about her poetry, see Juan Bruce-Novoa, *Inquiry by Interview* (Austin: University of Texas Press, 1980), pp. 203–218.

2. Joseph Sommers was the first to mention intertextuality in a Chicano literary context ("From the Critical Premise to the Product: Critical Modes and Their Application to a Chicano Literary Text," *New Scholar* 6 [1977], 59). For the most part, I follow the notion of intertextuality as argued by Jonathan Culler ("Presupposition and Intertextuality," *Modern Language Notes* 91 [Dec. 1976], 1380–1396). Although Culler does not define intertextuality as the investigation of sources and influences, I include this dimension of intertextuality, but I do not limit it to sources and influences. A revised version of Culler's article appears in his book, *The Pursuit of Signs* (Ithaca: Cornell University Press, 1981), pp. 100–118.

3. For examples of poems by Chicanas which protest the internal contradictions of the Chicano's sexual and political behavior in the movement, see Emy López, "Apartment 107" and "La Gringa," *El Fuego de Aztlán* 4 (Summer 1977), 32–33, 35; Lorna Dee Cervantes, "You Cramp My Style, Baby," ibid., p. 39; Lorna Dee Cervantes, "Para un revolucionario," *Revista Chicano-Requeña* 3 (Winter 1975), 21–22; Marcela Christine Lucero, "*Machismo* Is Part of Our Culture," in *The Third Woman: Minority Women Writers of the United States,* ed. Dexter Fisher (Boston: Houghton Mifflin, 1980), pp. 401–402; and Anna Montes, "Bus Stop Macho," *Comadre* 1 (Summer 1970), 24–25. For brief commentaries on some of these poems, see Elizabeth Ordóñez, "Sexual Politics and the Theme of Sexuality in Chicana Poetry," in *Women in Hispanic Literature: Icons and Fallen Idols,* ed. Beth Miller (Berkeley, Los Angeles, London: University of California Press, 1983), pp. 316–339. Tey Diana Rebolledo includes "You Cramp My Style, Baby," in her article of the use of humor by Chicanas, "Walking the Thin Line: Humor in Chicana Literature" in *Beyond Stereotypes: The Critical Analysis of Chicana Literature,* ed. María Herrera-Sobek (Binghamton, N.Y.: Bilingual Press, 1985).

4. Menlo Park, Calif.: Diseños Literarios, 1976. All the poems discussed, except for "Notes from a Chicana 'COED,'" are from this collection. "Sonnet, Freely Adapted" was first published in *Poetry,* a special edition of *La Onda* (Stanford University), 1 (April 1975).

5. The idea of tension and conflict rather than of synthesis and resolution is important for my reading of Zamora's poetry. This perspective distinguishes my interpretation from that of Juan Bruce-Novoa, "Rituals of Devastation and Resurrection," in *Chicano Poetry: A Response to Chaos* (Austin: University of Texas Press, 1982), pp. 160–184. Bruce-Novoa argues that Zamora's poetry moves toward resolution.

6. My decision to begin with "Gata Poem" rather than with "Penitents," the first poem in *Restless Serpents,* is another difference between my analysis and that of Bruce-Novoa. My order of presentation differs from his for three reasons. First, I want to discuss "Notes from a Chicana 'COED,'" an important poem for understanding Zamora's perspective which is excluded from *Restless Serpents.* Second, Bruce-Novoa's decision to begin with "Penitents" attributes an

importance to this poem which in my opinion it does not have. "Gata Poem" has a higher value for me because it reveals the contradictory relationship of the poetic consciousness as a woman and as a Chicana in both traditions. Third, as Zamora herself told me in a conversation on February 16, 1983, she did not intend the poems to be read as a narrative sequence. While I do not take an author's statements about his or her intentions in a work of art as dogma, I think it important to recognize them.

7. As the linguistic particularities of the poems I analyze relate to the definition of the poetic voice, I insist on noting whether the poems are written in Spanish or in English or in a mixture of the two. I also insist on discussing the implications of choosing one language over another. My attention to this aspect is another feature that distinguishes my discussion of Zamora from Bruce-Novoa's. Because he does not consider the language of a particular poem, he says that "Sonnet, Freely Adapted" is aimed at "Chicano machos" since "boxing is one of the macho rituals most admired among Chicanos" (*Chicano Poetry*, pp. 454–455). In addition to the fact that this assertion is unsustainable because the sport of boxing is also supported by Anglo and other ethnic groups, the possibility of a Chicano audience is practically eliminated by the poem's syntax and diction and by the literary conventions it presupposes, as I point out below.

8. Keith Whinnom explores the use of death as a euphemism for the sexual act in the context of sixteenth-century Spanish poetry ("Hacia una Interpretación y Apreciación de las Canciones del *Cancionero General* de 1511," *Filología* 13 (1968–69), 361–381, esp. 372–381.

9. This poem appeared in *Caracol* 3 (May 1977), 19. *Caracol*, published in San Antonio, Texas, for a few years, folded during the financial setback suffered by small presses in the late 1970s. To my knowledge, "Notes" has never been reprinted.

10. In "Pueblo, 1950" Zamora's ambiguous use of the pronoun "you" creates irony and humor because it refers to Fred Montoya in the first and second lines:

PUEBLO, 1950

I remember you, Fred Montoya.
You were the first *vato* to ever kiss me.
I was twelve years old.
My mother said shame on you,
my teacher said shame on you, and
I said shame on me, and nobody
    said a word to you

The irony depends upon the reader's also linking the "you" in lines 4 and 5 with Fred Montoya. When the final "you" makes clear that the referent of "you" is really the girl, the reader is confronted with the irony of the situation: the girl, not the boy, is made the object of shame. The confusion experienced in reading the poem humorously makes Zamora's point about the privileges that society gives the male. *Vato* is colloquial Spanish for "dude."

In another poem too long to quote here, entitled "Mirando

Aquellos desde los Campos" ("Looking at Them from the Fields"), Zamora also shifts perspectives, only this time the shift involves the two languages. The first half of the poem is in English, the second half, in Spanish. In the English part Zamora uses the Spanish third-person pronoun, *ésos* ("those"), as an adjective ("*esos* propagators") to speak about *aquellos* ("Anglos"). In the Spanish part she inserts a two-line phrase in English, using the second-person pronoun, *your*, to speak directly to Chicano males. Ironically, to establish a critical position of Anglo culture, Zamora must use Spanish, the language of the culture that gives dominance to the Chicano male. Also ironic is that she must shift into English, the language of the dominant culture, to establish a critical perspective of the Chicano male.

11. Frederick Douglass, *Narrative of the Life of Frederick Douglass, An American Slave, Written by Himself* (Boston: Anti-Slavery Office, 1845). Douglass tells the story of his Aunt Hester who was whipped by her owner because he had found her with a black man. Douglass's narrative makes clear there were many other cases similar to his aunt's (see pp. 3–8).

12. Mary Louise Pratt, *Toward a Speech Act Theory of Literary Discourse* (Bloomington: Indiana University Press, 1977). The "maxim of manner" is one of four sets of rules governing conversational behavior proposed by the British language philosopher, H. P. Grice, and discussed by Mary Pratt in her study on speech act theory. The maxim of manner states: "Avoid obscurity of expression. Avoid ambiguity." The language of Zamora's speaker violates this maxim. For Pratt's discussion on "flouting" see pp. 159–175.

13. For a discussion of Renaissance women who wrote sonnets in the Neoplatonic and Petrarchan traditions, revising and questioning the roles assigned to women in sonnets written by men, see Ann Rosalind Jones, "Assimilation with a Difference: Renaissance Women Poets and Literary Influence," *Yale French Studies*, no. 62 (1981), 135–153.

14. Bruce-Novoa, *Chicano Poetry*, pp. 172–173, discusses this Shakespearean sonnet as a direct literary source for Zamora's. I agree with his point that Zamora criticizes Shakespeare's magisterial position. Whereas Shakespeare can speak universally about love, the social conventions defining Zamora's milieu make it impossible for her to do so.

15. Barbara Herrnstein Smith, *Poetic Closure: A Study of How Poems End* (Chicago: University of Chicago Press, 1968), p. 30.

16. Zamora says that "the poem's persona is meant to be the spirit of females—mothers, wives, sisters, daughters of *penitentes*" (Bruce-Novoa, *Inquiry by Interview*, p. 206). Although I acknowledge her intention, I also think it important to stress that this poem implicitly defines the persona as female, in contrast with poems that explicitly do so.

17. Marta Weigle, *The Penitentes of the Southwest* (Santa Fe: Ancient City Press, 1970). Weigle's pamphlet and William Farrington's *Los*

penitentes: A Brief History (Santa Fe: Sunstone Press, 1975) both provide useful historical information.

18. Herrnstein Smith, *Poetic Closure*, p. 7.
19. For theories of origin, see Weigle, *Penitentes*, p. 5.
20. *Alabado* comes from the Spanish word, *alabar* ("to praise"). See ibid., pp. 18, 28.
21. Reuben Arthur Brower, *The Fields of Light* (New York: Oxford University Press, 1951), p. 21.
22. Alicia Ostriker, "The Thieves of Language: Women Poets and Revisionist Mythmaking," *Signs* 8 (Autumn 1982), 71. Ostriker makes insightful comments on the uses of myth in contemporary poetry by Anglo-American women. She defines the bent of their poetry as "revisionist mythmaking." That is, poets like H. D., Susan Griffin, and Anne Sexton, authors of book-length mythological poems, appropriate figures or tales from myth and use them for altered ends— "the old vessel filled with new wine." The poets "correct" the old stories so that they "can no longer stand as foundations of collective male fantasy." Their stories are "retrieved images of what women have collectively and historically suffered; in some cases they are instructions for survival" (pp. 72–73). My poets share common themes, interests, and approaches with those discussed by Ostriker, and they are also "revisionist" in bent, but as Chicanas they tread cultural terrain unavailable to Anglo-American women poets.
23. For another interpretation of this poem which sees the ritual in more positive terms than I do, see Bruce-Novoa, *Chicano Poetry*, pp. 162–166.
24. The title literally means "stumbling around at Stanford." One may either walk or talk *a tropezones*: jerkily, with fits and starts. The expression is mainly used in popular, familiar conversation. Its juxtaposition with "Stanford," a "gentlemen's" institution and a symbol of refinement and high culture, produces a comic effect because the phrase is contrary to one's expectations about Stanford: one should not "stumble" in style or speech at so high-toned a university as Stanford.

   "A tropezones en Stanford" is aimed at the Spanish speaker, though the effect of the word "Stanford" is to tease the English reader. The Spanish reader will transform "Stanford" into *estanford*, the typical linguistic adaptation made by Spanish speakers when pronouncing English words that begin with s. The title would then read "A tropezones en nestanford" instead of "A tropezones en Stanford." The Spanish pronunciation deflates the aura around Stanford because it undermines the correct English pronunciation. This effect is appreciated, however, only if the poem is read aloud.
25. Joseph Campbell, *The Masks of God: Occidental Mythology* (New York: Viking Press, 1964), III, 7. In a non-Western mythological context, Campbell implies a connection between warrior tribesmen's mastery of the camel and the horse and the fall of the cosmologies of the goddesses.

26. I would place "Bearded Lady" in a tradition of writing by contemporary women poets who attempt, in the words of Alicia Ostriker ("Thieves of Language," p. 75) "to retrieve, from the myth of the abstract father god who creates the universe *ab nihilo*, the figure on which he was originally based, the female creatrix." Ostriker refers to Sharon Barba's "A Cycle of Women," Rachel DuPlessis's "Eurdydice," and Adrienne Rich's "The Mirror in Which Two Are Seen as One."

27. I am thinking of poems like "From the Vestibule" and "As Viewed from the Terrace" (*Restless Serpents*, pp. 44, 48). "Gata Poem" also contains the opposition between the sacred and the profane. Its first line echoes the Virgin Mary's canticle, De Profundis: "Out of the depths have I cried unto thee, O Lord." In Zamora's version the male or Chicano god on the mountaintop calls out to the Chicana. The juxtaposition of the sacred and the profane in effect mocks the notion that a woman calls out to her lord. Zamora has the "lord" call out to the Chicana and then diminishes his aura of godliness by shifting into English in line 4.

28. Zamora begins "Mirando Aquellos desde los Campos" (*Restless Serpents*, p. 27) with a quotation from the prologue to Dahlberg's *The Sorrows of Priapus*, which she identifies in the text. Three other poets directly identified by Zamora as influences on her text are Herman Hesse (see "Without Bark," *Restless Serpents*, p. 34), Theodore Roethke (see "And All Flows Past," ibid., p. 68), and Guillevec (see "On Living in Aztlán," ibid., p. 17). A literary influence that Zamora does not identify in the text but one that she herself pointed out to me is Virginia Woolf (see "A Litany for Mad Masters," ibid., p. 73).

29. In "Living in Aztlán" Zamora does not criticize the nineteenth-century French writer Guillevec from the perspective of a woman. Instead she identifies with him as a poet. What they share in common is that both are minority poets who write outside the dominant culture.

30. Bruce-Novoa has identified this Jeffers source (*Chicano Poetry*, p. 176). For Jeffers's "Cassandra" see *The Double Axe and Other Poems* (New York: Random House, 1948), p. 117.

31. For "Carmel Point" see *Hungerfield* (New York: Random House, 1951), p. 97.

32. I was the first to explore the relationships between Jeffers's *Roan Stallion* and Zamora's "California" ("Inter-Sexual and Intertextual Codes in the Poetry of Bernice Zamora," *MELUS* 7 [Fall 1980], 55–68).

33. Bruce-Novoa (*Chicano Poetry*, p. 175), mentions important differences between Jeffers and Zamora. The critical element missing in Bruce-Novoa's perspective is the strong female dimension of Zamora's poetic persona when responding to Jeffers. He stresses "transhuman" (Jeffers) versus "human" (Zamora); I stress "man" versus "woman."

34. James D. Houston, editor of *West Coast Fiction: Modern Writing from California, Oregon and Washington* (New York: Bantam Books, 1979), claims that the discovery of California was foreshadowed in a sixteenth-century Spanish novel, *The Adventures of Esplandian*, by García Ordóñez de Montalvo. The novel, published thirty-two years before the Cabrillo expedition first sighted the West Coast and twenty-five years before Hernan Cortés named what is now the lower tip of California, influenced the expectations of the earliest Spanish adventurers. See Houston, "The Literary West: From Mark Twain to Joan Didion," *Los Angeles Times*, Jan. 6, 1980, p. 3.

BIBLIOGRAPHY

PRIMARY SOURCES

Cervantes, Lorna. *Emplumada*. Pittsburgh: University of Pittsburgh Press, 1981.

Corpi, Lucha. *Palabras de Mediodía / Noon Words*. Trans. Catherine Rodríguez-Nieto. Berkeley: El Fuego de Aztlán Publications, 1980.

———. "Tres Mujeres." *La Cosecha* 3, 3 (1977):74–89. Albuquerque: Pajarito Publications.

de Hoyos, Angela. "La Malinche a Cortez y viceversa." *La Palabra* 2, 2 (1980):69–70.

Tafolla, Carmen. "La Malinche." *Encuentro Artístico Femenil*. Austin: Casa/Tejidos Publications, 1978. Pp. 41–42.

Villanueva, Alma. *Bloodroot*. Austin: Place of Herons Press, 1977.

———. *Mother, May I?* Pittsburgh: Motheroot Publications, 1978.

———. *Poems: Third Chicano Literary Prize*. Department of Spanish and Portuguese. Irvine: University of California, 1977.

Zamora, Bernice. "Notes from a Chicana 'COED.'" *Caracol* 3 (1977):19.

———. *Restless Serpents*. Menlo Park: California: Diseños Literarios, 1976.

SECONDARY SOURCES

Alegría, Fernando. *Walt Whitman en hispanoamérica*. Mexico City: Ediciones Studium, 1954.

Allen, Donald. *The New American Poetry*. New York: Grove Press, 1960.

Altieri, Charles. *Enlarging the Temple*. Lewisburg: Bucknell University Press, 1979.

Arrellano, Anselmo, ed. *Los pobladores nuevo mexicanos y su poesía, 1899–1959*. Albuquerque: Pajarito Publications, 1976.

Barthes, Roland. *S/Z: An Essay*. Trans. Richard Miller. New York: Hill and Wang, 1974.

Benveniste, Emile. "Relations of Person in the Verb," "The Nature of Pronouns," and "Subjectivity in Language." In *Problems in General Linguistics*. Trans. Mary Elizabeth Meek. Miami Linguistics Series, 8. Florida: University of Miami Press, 1971.

Blanco, Iris. "Participación de las mujeres en las sociedad prehispánica." In *Essays on la mujer*. Ed. Rosaura Sánchez and Rosa Martinez Cruz. Los Angeles: Chicano Studies Center, University of California, 1977. Pp. 48–80.

Bly, Robert. *Leaping Poetry: An Idea with Poems and Translations*. Boston: Beacon Press, 1975.

Brinson-Pineda, Barbara. "Poets on Poetry: Dialogue with Lucha Corpi." In *Prisma*. Mills College, Department of Ethnic Studies, 1979. Pp. 4–9.

Broe, Mary Lynn. *Protean Poetic*. Columbia: University of Missouri Press, 1980.

Brower, Reuben Arthur. *The Fields of Light*. New York: Oxford University Press, 1951.

Bruce-Novoa, Juan. *Chicano Authors: Inquiry by Interview*. Austin: University of Texas Press, 1980.

———. *Chicano Poetry: A Response to Chaos*. Austin: University of Texas Press, 1982.

Cabrera, Luis. *Diccionario de aztequismos*. Mexico City: Ediciones Oasis, 1975.

Candelaria, Cordelia. "La Malinche Feminist Prototype." *Frontiers* 5 (1980):1–6.

Chencinsky, Jacobo. "El mundo metafórico de la lírica popular mexicana." Mexico City: Anuario de Letras, 1961.

Chodorow, Nancy. *The Reproduction of Mothering*. Berkeley, Los Angeles, London: University of California Press, 1978.

Christian, Barbara. *Black Women Novelists: The Development of A Tradition*. Westport, Conn.: Greenwood Press, 1980.

Cotera, Marta. *The Chicana Feminist*. Austin: International Systems Development, 1976.

Culler, Jonathan. "Presupposition and Intertextuality." *Modern Language Notes* 91 (December 1976):1380–1396.

———. *The Pursuit of Signs: Semiotics, Literature, Deconstruction*. London: Routledge and Kegan Paul, 1981.

Del Castillo, Adelaida R., and Magdalena Mora, eds. *Mexican Women in the United States: Struggles Past and Present*. Los Angeles: Chicano Studies Center, University of California, 1980.

———. "Malintzin Tenépal: A Preliminary Look into a New Perspective." In *Essays on la mujer*. Ed. Rosaura Sánchez and Rosa Martinez Cruz. Los Angeles: Chicano Studies Center, University of California, 1977. Pp. 124–149.

Díaz del Castillo, Bernal. *The Conquest of New Spain*. Trans. J. M. Cohen. London: Penguin Books, 1963.

Douglass, Frederick. *Narrative of the Life of Frederick Douglass: An American Slave, Written by Himself*. Boston: Published at the Anti-Slavery Office, 1845.

Farrington, William. *Los penitentes: A Brief History*. Santa Fe, N. Mex.: Sunstone Press, 1975.

Frenk, Margit. *Cancionero folklórico de México*. El Colegio de México, Centro de Estudios Linguisticos y Literarios, 1975–1984.

Freud, Sigmund. "The Uncanny." In *Sigmund Freud on Creativity and the Unconscious*. Trans. Alix Strachey. New York: Harper Torchbooks, 1958. Pp. 122–161.

Fuentes, Carlos. *Todos los gatos son pardos*. Mexico City: Siglo Veintiuno Editores, 1970.

Gardiner, Judith Kegan. "On Female Identity and Writing by Women." *Critical Inquiry* 8 (1981):347–361.

Gilbert, Sandra M., and Susan Gubar. *The Madwoman in the Attic*. New Haven: Yale University Press, 1979.

Graves, Robert. *The White Goddess*. New York: Vintage Books, 1960.

Harding, Mary Esther. *Woman's Mysteries: Ancient and Modern*.

New York: G. P. Putnam's Sons, 1971.

Herrnstein Smith, Barbara. *Poetic Closure: A Study of How Poems End.* Chicago: University of Chicago Press, 1968.

Holland, Norman. *The Dynamics of Literary Response.* New York: Oxford University Press, 1968.

Huerta, Jorge. *Chicano Theater.* Ypsilanti, Mich.: Bilingual Press, 1982.

Jeffers, Robinson. *The Double Axe and Other Poems.* New York: Random House, 1948.

———. *Hungerfield.* New York: Random House, 1951.

———. "Roan Stallion." In *American Tradition in Literature,* 2. Bradley, Beatty, Long, eds. New York: Norton & Company, 1956. Pp. 941–955.

Jones, Ann Rosalind. "Assimilation with a Difference: Renaissance Woman Poets and Literary Influence." *Yale French Studies* 62 (1981):135–153.

Kauffmann, Lane. "Neruda's Last Residence: Translations and Notes on Four Poems." *New Scholar* 5, 1 (1975):119–141.

Kerr, Lucille. "The Paradox of Power and Mystery: Carlos Fuentes' *Terra Nostra.*" *PMLA* 95 (1980):91–102.

Kristeva, Julia. *La Révolution du language Poétique.* Paris: Seuil, 1974.

Labov, William, and David Fanshel. *Therapeutic Discourse.* New York: Academic Press, 1977.

Lane, Gary. *Sylvia Plath: New Views on the Poetry.* Baltimore: Johns Hopkins University Press, 1979.

Malkoff, Karl. *Crowell's Handbook of Contemporary American Poetry.* New York: Tomas Y. Crowell, 1973.

Mendoza, Vicente T. *El corrido mexicano.* Mexico City: Fondo de Cultura Económica, 1954.

Meyer, Doris. "Anonymous Poetry in Spanish Language New Mexico Newspapers (1880–1900)." *Bilingual Review* 2 (1975):259–275.

Mirandé, Alfredo, and Evangelina Enríquez. *La Chicana.* Chicago: University of Chicago Press, 1979.

Morales, Alejandro. "Terra Mater and the Emergence of Myth in Poems by Alma Villanueva." *Bilingual Review* 7, 2 (1980):123–142.

Neruda, Pablo. *Veinte poemas de amor y una canción desesperada. Obras Completas.* Buenos Aires: Editorial Losada,

1967. *Twenty Love Poems and a Song of Despair*. Trans. W. S. Merwin. Bilingual ed. London: Jonathan Cape, 1969.

Newman, Charles. *The Art of Sylvia Plath: A Symposium*. Bloomington: Indiana University Press, 1970.

Ong, Walter. "Literacy and Orality in Our Times." In *Profession 79*. New York: Modern Language Association, 1979. Pp. 1–7. (Selected articles from the bulletins of the Association of Departments of English and the Association of Departments of Foreign Languages).

————. *Interfaces of the Word*. Ithaca: Cornell University Press, 1977.

————. *Rhetoric, Romance, and Technology*. Ithaca: Cornell University Press, 1979.

Ordóñez, Elizabeth. "Sexual Politics and the Theme of Sexuality in Chicana Poetry." In *Women in Hispanic Literature: Icons and Fallen Idols*. Berkeley, Los Angeles, London: University of California Press, 1983. Pp. 7–16.

————. "Alma Villanueva." In *Chicano Literature: A Reader's Encyclopedia*. Ed. Julio A. Martinez and Francisco A. Lomelí. Westport, Conn.: Greenwood Press, 1985.

Ostriker, Alicia. "The Thieves of Language: Women Poets and Revisionist Mythmaking." *Signs* 8, 1 (1982):68–90.

Paredes, Américo. *With His Pistol in His Hand*. Austin: University of Texas Press, 1958.

Paz, Octavio. *El laberinto de la soledad*. Mexico City: Fondo de Cultura Económica, 1959. Trans. Lysander Kemp. New York: Grove Press, 1961.

Pearce, Roy Harvey. *Whitman*. Englewood Cliffs: Prentice-Hall, 1962.

Perloff, Marjorie. *The Poetics of Indeterminacy: Rimbaud to Cage*. Princeton: Princeton University Press, 1981.

Phillips, Rachel. "Marina/Malinche: Masks and Shadows." *Women in Hispanic Literature: Icons and Fallen Idols*. Ed. Beth Miller. Berkeley, Los Angeles, London: University of California Press, 1983.

Pratt, Mary Louise. *Toward a Speech Act Theory of Literary Discourse*. Bloomington: Indiana University Press, 1977.

Rabinowitz, Peter J. "Assertion and Assumption: Fictional Patterns and the External World." *PMLA* 96 (1981):408–419.

Rivera, Tomás. "Into the Labyrinth: The Chicano in Literature."

In *New Voices in American Literature: The Mexican American. A Symposium.* Philip D. Ortego, Tomás Rivera, and José Reyna, eds. Edinburg, Tex.: Pan American University, 1971.

Ross, Stephen. "'Voice' in Narrative Texts: The Example of *As I Lay Dying.*" *PMLA* 94 (1979):3–10.

Sánchez, Marta E. "Inter-Sexual and Intertextual Codes in the Poetry of Bernice Zamora." *MELUS* 7, 3 (1980):55–68.

Showalter, Elaine. "Feminist Criticism in the Wilderness." *Critical Inquiry* 8 (1981):179–205.

Sommers, Joseph. "From the Critical Premise to the Product: Critical Modes and Their Application to a Chicano Literary Text." *New Scholar* 6 (1977):51–80.

Soustelle, Jacques. *Daily Life of the Aztecs.* Stanford: Stanford University Press, 1961.

Suleiman, Susan R., and Inge Crosman, eds. *The Reader in the Text: Essays on Audience and Interpretation.* Princeton: Princeton University Press, 1980.

Villanueva, Tino. *Chicanos: Antología histórica y literaria.* Mexico City: Fondo de Cultura Económica, 1980.

Weigle, Marta. *The Penitentes of the Southwest.* Santa Fe, N. Mex.: Ancient City Press, 1970.

Whinnom, Keith. "Hacia una Interpretación y Apreciación de las canciones del *Cancionero General* de 1511." *Filología 13 (1968–69):361–381.*

Wilson, Daniel. "Readers in Texts." *PMLA* 96 (1981):848–863.

Ybarra-Frausto, Tomás. Alurista's Poetics: The Oral, the Bilingual, the Pre-Columbian." In *Modern Chicano Writers.* Englewood Cliffs: Prentice-Hall, 1979. Pp. 117–132.

———. "The Chicano Movement and the Emergence of a Chicano Poetic Consciousness." *New Scholar* 6 (1977):81–109.

INDEX

Note: Poems are indexed in the language in which they were written. Translations are supplied when the author provided them.

367

Rabbit" of, 86, 113, 114–119, 124; uses English language, 21–22, 92–93, 97, 98, 137–138; uses parallels, 123–124; uses Spanish language, 97–98; "Visions of Mexico" of, 14, 88, 89, 94–97, 98, 99–103, 111, 113, 115, 116, 119, 124, 137; on women's role, 98, 99

La Chaneca, 157, 159, 160, 161

Chávez, César, 3

Chicana: defined, 338 n. 3; as identity (see Ethnic/cultural identity); in politics, 6; and racism, 5, 6; and sexual discrimination, 4, 5; social restrictions on, 5; and women's movement, 4–6, 340 n. 16. See also Chicana literature/poetry

Chicana literature/poetry, 2, 3, 4, 6–23; conflict and struggle in, 269, 270, 274, 275–276; and identity, 6, 7–9, 10–11, 23; implied audience for, 20–23; influences on, 2–6, 7, 13; language of, 20–21; modes of, 9–11, 271–273; as muted discourse, 23; roots of, 275; social consciousness in, 274. See also Cervantes, Lorna Dee; Corpi, Lucha; Villanueva, Alma; Zamora, Bernice

Chicano literature: access for, 15–17, 337 n. 1; anthologies of, 16; as bilingual, 16, 20–22; Mexico v. U.S. in, 3–4; oral and written, 11–15, 17; poetry as, 17–18; on social oppression, 3–4; studied, 1–2

Chicano movement, 2–3, 4, 5, 17, 216

Chicano press, 3, 16

Chicanos, 16, 139

Chicano theater, 2, 3, 4

Childbirth, 41, 43, 56, 77, 84

Chingada, 183–184, 190–191. See also Marina poems

"La Ciega," 168, 171–173

Civil Rights Act, 3

Cody, James, 342 nn. 4, 6

"Cofradía de Inservibles," 168, 169–170, 171

Corpi, Lucha, 2, 139–213, 274, 276; audience of, 22–23, 187–188, 190, 212–213, 272; as autobiographical, 142; bilingualism of, 21, 212, 272, 273; biographical information on, 12–13, 139–140; border-crossing images of, 143, 144, 152, 154; bridge images of, 143, 177, 178; Catholic images of, 156, 157, 165, 168, 187, 198; on La Chaneca, 157; "La Ciega" of, 168, 171–173; "Cofradía de Inservibles" of, 168, 169–170, 171; on desire, 141, 142, 152, 168, 170, 174–182, 194, 199, 200, 270; divided self in poetry of, 170–171, 172, 173; and English language, 212; ethnic/cultural identity of, 9, 140–143, 144, 145, 146–147, 148–149, 151–152, 153–154, 155–156, 195, 212, 270; and gender identity, 9, 149, 150, 154–155, 156, 174, 191, 213, 270, 272, 273; on grandmothers, 143, 144, 152–153, 163–164, 194; grotto images of, 147, 151, 153, 154, 155; hair images of, 163, 164; influences on, 13; Judeo-Christian images of, 157, 187, 191–192, 193; linguistic devices of, 162; on la llorona, 4, 194; "Lluvia/Rain" of, 158–159; lyric mode of, 10; Marina poems of, 182, 183–195, 205, 206, 207–208, 211, 213; on marriage, 205, 207, 208, 209, 210, 211; on Mexico v. U.S., 143–144, 147, 152, 153, 154, 155, 194; nature images of, 156–157, 159, 168, 187, 192–193, 194, 204, 205–206, 208; noon in poems of, 172; oppositions of, 204; orange images of, 204–205, 207, 210, 211; owl images of, 157, 189, 190; Palab-

La Lechuza, 157, 189, 190
"Legacies and Bastard Roses," 62, 63–65, 69–71
Levertov, Denise, 18
"Life Cycle," 329–330
Literature, 12. *See also* Chicana literature/poetry; Chicano literature
La Llorona, 14, 148–149, 161, 194
"Lluvia/Rain," 158–159
Lomelí, Francisco, 2
"Lots: II," 111

Maize, 16
Male-female relationships, 60–62, 92, 117, 118, 119, 128–129, 130, 131, 135, 217, 219, 225–227, 229–231, 233, 235–237, 246, 263–264, 271, 272, 276
Malinche. *See* Marina poems
Malintzin Tenépal, 150, 188, 189. *See also* Marina poems
Mango, 16, 87
Marimba, 159
Marina poems, 182, 183–195, 205, 206, 211, 213; death of Marina in, 193; Marina as Chingada in, 190–191; Marina defamed in, 190–191; and Marina legend, 157, 184; Marina as mediator in, 187; Marina as symbol of betrayal in, 150, 183–184; rape in, 189, 190, 192, 207–208
Marriage: in Mexico, 141, 152; as theme, 147, 152, 205, 207, 208, 209, 210, 211, 236–237
Men/males: Cervantes on, 114–119, 122, 123, 124–125, 126, 127, 128; in Mexican culture, 221; in past of poets, 38–39; sexual bias of, 216; Villanueva on, 32, 36–37, 41, 44–45, 49, 51, 344–345 n. 33; Zamora on, 11, 216, 217, 221, 222, 225, 229–230, 231, 233, 234, 235, 236, 237, 238, 239, 268, 271, 273, 274. *See also* Male-female relationships

Merwin, W. S., 13
Metamorphosis, 16
Mexico: marriage in, 141, 152; pre-Columbian traditions in, 97, 98, 103, 148, 149, 156, 157, 187; as theme in poetry, 94–97, 98, 101; v. U.S., 3–4, 143–144, 147, 152, 153, 154, 155, 194
Mexican-chicano. *See* Chicana; Chicano literature; Chicano movement
Migration, as theme, 96–97, 101
Mizquitli, 16
Moctezuma, 187
Mode, 15; dialogue (discursive), 10, 11, 88, 93, 103, 104, 105, 113, 117, 131, 132–133, 134, 135, 136, 218, 223, 224, 229, 230, 244, 245, 262, 272, 273; lyric, 10, 88, 103–113, 130–131, 132, 134–135, 136; mythic, 10, 26, 271; narrative, 10, 11, 26, 218, 222, 223, 224, 229, 244–245, 246, 247, 249, 250, 262, 272, 273
Montoya, José, 17, 21, 24
"Moonwalkers," 87
Mother, May I?, 7, 10, 22, 24–84, 137, 138, 216, 273, 303–336; as autobiographical, 27–28, 69; bad nun-good nun in, 60–62; death in, 48; divided self in, 50–51, 52–53, 55; earth mother in, 51; epilogue of, 28, 41, 62, 63–65, 66, 69, 71–72, 74, 77, 80, 82, 334–336; ethnic/cultural identity in, 57, 58, 60, 62–63, 67, 75–76, 82–83, 84; gender identity in, 25–26, 57, 63–65, 67, 72, 73, 74, 76, 77–78, 82, 83–84; grandmother in, 40–41, 44, 47, 48, 51, 53, 54, 57–60, 62, 65–66, 72–73, 75; hair as symbol in, 61, 62; implied audience of, 28, 67–84; linear sequence in, 24, 26; mother-daughter relationship in, 25, 40, 41, 47–48, 53, 62, 64–65, 76–78, 79–80, 81, 84; opposi-

tions in, 42–57; oral culture in, 59; personal pronouns in, 74–75, 76, 77, 78; poetic identity in, 28, 63, 66–67, 68–69, 73–74, 80–81, 82, 83, 84; pregnancy as theme in, 41, 43, 56, 62; rape as theme in, 41, 44–47, 50, 61–62; rose images in, 49, 64, 65, 66–67, 80; seed images in, 51, 52, 53–54; sexual conflict in, 60–62; social oppositions in, 57–67; Spanish language in, 58; summarized, 40–41; taking-in and giving-out in, 42–53; unknown father in, 25; woman's body in, 76
Mothers and daughters: Cervantes on, 122, 125, 126–127, 128, 129, 132; Villanueva on, 25, 41, 47–48, 53, 62, 64–65, 76–78, 79–80, 81, 84
Mujer sufrida, 145, 191

Nahuatl, 248
National Farm Workers Association, 3
Neruda, Pablo, 13, 26, 27
New Mexico, 337 n. 1
Newspapers, 17, 337 n. 1
"Notes from a Chicana 'COED'," 15, 230, 231–235, 237, 238, 243, 244, 245

"Oaxaca, 1974," 98
"Of/To Man," 37, 300
"Of Utterances," 37, 38, 54, 299
O'Hara, Frank, 18
Olson, Charles, 18–19
Ong, Walter, 15, 59
Ostriker, Alice, 56

Pajarito Publications, 16, 139
Palabras de Mediodía/Noon Words, 7, 21, 140, 141, 143, 156, 212
"Pasión sin Nombre/Passion without a Name," 174, 175, 179–182, 187, 198, 199

Paz, Octavio, 11, 13, 183–184, 191
Penitentes of New Mexico, 246, 248
"Penitents," 245, 246–250, 251, 252, 258
Philomena, 198
"Pico Blanco," 261
Plath, Sylvia, 10, 46; influences Villanueva, 13, 27, 28, 36, 37, 39, 40
"Playing," 79–80, 306–308, 309–310
"Poem for the Young White Man . . . ," 85, 86, 87, 88, 89–94, 97, 100, 113, 116, 119, 137
Poems, 7, 24, 26, 27, 31, 36–38, 40, 69, 82, 83, 138, 297–302
Poetic identity, 7; of Cervantes, 9, 10, 11, 86, 87, 137, 269, 270, 271, 273; of Corpi, 157, 212; search for, 161–162; of Villanueva, 8, 28, 32, 36, 40, 63, 66–67, 68–69, 73–74, 80–81, 82, 83, 84; of Zamora, 215, 216, 217, 218, 242, 245, 250, 260–261, 262, 267–268, 272–273

Poetry: Anglo, 18; black female, 339 n. 15; Chicana (*see* Chicana literature/poetry); Chicano, 17–18; as communication, 17–19; oral, 17, 18–19, 95, 103; personal, 24–25
Poets, male, 215, 217–218. *See also* Jeffers, Robinson
Popocatépetl, 148, 149
Portillo, Estela, 3
Portillo-Tramley, Elizabeth, 337–338 n. 2
Pound, Ezra, 19, 20
pre-Columbian images, 97, 98, 103, 148, 149, 156, 157, 187
Pregnancy, as theme, 29–30, 33, 41, 42, 43, 44, 56, 62
"The Proof," 330–331
"Puente de Cristal/Crystal Bridge," 174, 175–179, 182, 193, 270

Designer:	Linda M. Robertson
Compositor:	Prestige Typography
Printer:	Braun-Brumfield, Inc.
Binder:	Braun-Brumfield, Inc.
Text:	10/12 Trump Medieval
Display:	Hand-Lettered